A Season in Utopia

✈✈✈✈✈✈✈✈✈✈✈✈✈✈✈✈✤✈✈✈✈✈✈✈✈✈✈✈✈✈✈✈✈✈✈

BY EDITH ROELKER CURTIS

Anne Hutchinson, A Biography. 1930
Lady Sarah Lennox, An Irrepressible Stuart. 1946
Love's Random Dart, A Novel. 1960.

A

Season in Utopia

THE STORY OF BROOK FARM

>>>>>>>>>>>>>>>>>>>>>><<<<<<<<<<<<<<<<<<<<<<

BY

EDITH ROELKER CURTIS

THOMAS NELSON & SONS

Edinburgh   NEW YORK   *Toronto*

BOOK DESIGN BY FRANK KARPELES

Library of Congress Catalog Card No.: 61-8745

MANUFACTURED IN THE UNITED STATES OF AMERICA

TO PERRY MILLER
Who cleared away the mists surrounding
Transcendentalism, thereby strengthening the endeavor

Acknowledgment

IN 1939 THE LATE HARFORD POWEL SUGGESTED THAT I SHOULD WRITE A short, amusing account of Brook Farm. My brother, the late William Greene Roelker pronounced my first sketch superficial, thereby challenging me to more serious effort. I am grateful to them both for guiding me to an absorbing field of study which I have cultivated ever since.

The late Miss Clara Endicott Sears, Founder of the Fruitlands Museum, author of *Bronson Alcott's Fruitlands* and other historical studies, was an inspiration, and throughout a sustaining friend. Several unpublished papers from the Fruitlands Museum Archives contained in *A Season in Utopia* were loaned for publication to me by Cousin Clara—as I called Miss Sears. And William Henry Harrison, Curator of the Fruitlands Museum, has continued the practice, thoughtfully suggesting papers from the Museum's more recent acquisitions.

For other unpublished material I am indebted to the Reverend Vincent S. Holden, C.S.P., Custodian of the Archives of the Paulist Fathers; William Allen Hastings, for copies of letters from his grandfather, William Allen's Brook Farm correspondence; and Walter Muir Whitehill, who obtained for my study A. E. Bestor, Jr.'s *American Phalanxes*, a Ph.D. Dissertation, John Addison Porter Prize 1938, from the Yale University Library. My acknowledgment to Mr. Whitehill, Director of the Boston Athenaeum, would not be complete if I did not include his highly competent and helpful staff.

Slater Brown gave me editorial advice when the work was in progress; and, finally, Gorham Munson, recently of Thomas Nelson, welcomed *A Season in Utopia* with a cordial reception.

Contents

Contents

A Season in Utopia

⟫⟫⟫⟫⟫⟫⟫⟫⟫⟫⟫⟫⟫⟫⟫⟫⟫⟫⟫⟫⟫⟫⟩⟨⟨⟨⟨⟨⟨⟨⟨⟨⟨⟨⟨⟨⟨⟨⟨⟨⟨⟨⟨⟨⟨⟨

Mr. Hawthorne Arrives in an April Snowstorm

"THERE CAN HARDLY FLICKER UP AGAIN SO CHEERY A BLAZE UPON THE hearth as that which I remember at Blithedale," laments Coverdale, the narrator of Hawthorne's *Blithedale Romance*, recalling his arrival at the Utopian Community which bears such a striking resemblance to Brook Farm. "It was a woodfire in the parlor of an old farmhouse, on an April afternoon, but with fitful gusts of a wintry snowstorm roaring in the chimney."

One may safely assume that Coverdale's first impressions of Blithedale reflect his creator's on a similar occasion. For on the twelfth of April, 1841, Nathaniel Hawthorne set out from Boston and drove to West Roxbury to join "the company of socialists" which his friends, George and Sophia Ripley, just ten days before, had set up at Brook Farm. As may be seen from Hawthorne's letters, the real and the fictional journey are almost identical.

For Coverdale—as for Nathaniel Hawthorne ten years before—the weather proved treacherous that day. "When morning dawned upon me, in town, its temperature was mild enough to be pronounced even balmy, by a lodger, like myself, in one of the midmost houses of a brick block,—each house partaking of the warmth of all the rest, besides the sultriness of its individual furnace-heat. But towards noon there had come snow, driven along the street by a northeasterly blast, and whiten-

ing the roofs and sidewalks with a businesslike persistence that would
have done credit to our severest January tempest. It set about its task
apparently as much in earnest as if it had been guaranteed from a thaw
for months to come. The greater, surely, was my heroism, when, puff-
ing out a final whiff of cigar-smoke, I quitted my cozy pair of bachelor-
rooms,—with a good fire burning in the grate, and a closet right at hand,
where there was still a bottle or two in the champagne basket and a
residuum of claret in a box,—quitted, I say, these comfortable quarters,
and plunged into the heart of the pitiless snowstorm in quest of a better life."

On the long drive to Brook Farm, Hawthorne had but one companion,
Warren Burton, a graduate of the Harvard Divinity School who had
since turned reformer. Coverdale shares his conveyance with three fellow enthusiasts, bound for plain living, high thinking, and a communal
economy.

"So we all of us took courage," Coverdale goes on, "riding fleetly and
merrily along, by stone fences that were half buried in wave-like drifts;
and through patches of woodland, where the tree-trunks opposed a
snow-incrusted side towards the north-east; and within ken of deserted
villas, with no footprints in their avenues; and passed scattered dwell-
ings, whence puffed the smoke of country fires, strongly impregnated
with the pungent aroma of burning peat." Whenever they passed a
country man plodding through the snow they shouted a friendly greeting. Sometimes a wayfarer "would unmuffle his ears to the bluster and
snow spray," and respond. But these country people, for the most part,
"had no intelligence for our blithe tones of brotherhood." This lack of
faith in their cordial sympathy, on the part of the lowly and oppressed
laborers, depressed Coverdale and his fellow-travellers. It "was one
among the innumerable tokens how difficult a task we had in hand for
the reformation of the world."

As they ride on with still unflagging spirits, buoyed up by "air that
had not been breathed once and again!" Coverdale recalls his sense of
escape on getting out of town: "As we threaded the streets, I remember
how the buildings on either side seemed to press too closely upon us,
insomuch that our mighty hearts found barely room enough to throb
between them. The snowfall, too, looked inexpressibly dreary (I had
almost called it dingy), coming down through an atmosphere of city
smoke, and alighting on the sidewalk only to be moulded into the impress of somebody's patched boot or overshoe." With thoughts like
these, the travellers "made such good companionship with the storm"

that at their journey's end they professed themselves "almost loath to
bid the rude blusterer goodbye."

"But to own the truth," Coverdale confesses—his creator suffered a
similar malady shortly after arriving at Brook Farm—"I was little better
than an icicle and began to be suspicious that I had caught a fearful
cold."

One can readily imagine why the blazing hearth which welcomed
Hawthorne to Brook Farm, becomes in *The Blithedale Romance* a symbol of the better life which Coverdale and his friends hope to establish.
"The pleasant firelight!" the narrator exclaims. "I must still keep harp-
ing on it."

The new arrivals quickly shed their outdoor things. "And now we
were seated by the brisk fireside of the old farmhouse," Coverdale continues. "The same fire that glimmers so faintly among my reminiscences
at the beginning of this chapter. There we sat, with the snow melting
out of our hair and beards, and our faces all ablaze, what with the past
inclemency and present warmth. It was, indeed, a right good fire that
we found awaiting us, built up of great, rough logs, and knotty limbs,
and splintered fragments of an oak tree, such as farmers are wont to
keep for their own hearths,—since these crooked and unmanageable
boughs could never be measured into merchantable cords for the market. A family of the old Pilgrims might have swung their kettle over
precisely such a fire as this, only, no doubt, a bigger one; and, contrast-
ing it with my coal-grate, I felt so much the more that we had transported ourselves a world-wide distance from the system of society that
shackled us at breakfast time."

In 1852, when Hawthorne wrote *The Blithedale Romance*, more than
ten years had passed since his sojourn at Brook Farm; five since that
Community had become bankrupt. The bright torch of "Association"
which had burned so brightly in the eighteen-forties had flickered out,
as one Community after another failed. To lift the curtain of dust and
ashes which had buried the bright hopes of close friends was a ticklish
undertaking, fraught with possible misunderstanding. So Hawthorne
took the trouble to define his exact intention and design.

In his "Author's Preface" to *The Blithedale Romance*, Hawthorne
begs the reader to believe that his handling of the Community itself, is
no less fictitious than the imaginary characters which he has introduced
there. Foreseeing that many readers would detect in his Blithedale
Community "a faint and not very faithful shadowing of Brook Farm,"
the author "does not wish to deny that he had this Community in his

mind, and that (having had the good fortune, for a time, to be personally connected with it) he has occasionally availed himself of his actual reminiscences, in the hope of giving a more lifelike tint to the fancy sketch. . . ." Indeed, "His whole treatment of the affair is altogether incidental to the main purpose of the romance; nor does he put forward the slightest pretensions to illustrate a theory, or elicit a conclusion, favorable or otherwise, in respect to socialism. In short, his present concern with the socialist community is merely to establish a theatre, a little removed from the highway of ordinary travel, where the creatures of his brain may play their phantasmagorical antics, without exposing them to the actual events of real lives. . . ."

In other words, the analogy between Brook Farm and "Blithedale" should not be pushed too far, especially in an attempt to identify the members of the one with the characters of the other.

Despite the autobiographic form of the romance, Miles Coverdale, although Hawthorne frequently seizes his pen and dips it in the well of his own reminiscence, is not created in his creator's image. Although Coverdale eventually becomes skeptical in regard to "Association," he sets out for Blithedale in the expectation of establishing a new social order for mankind. Whereas Hawthorne joined the Community, investing $1,000 in the joint stock of the enterprise—hard-earned savings from his labor as measurer in the Boston Custom House—in the hope that membership in Brook Farm would enable him to marry Sophia Peabody to whom he had been engaged for the past two years. Hawthorne was not interested in reforming society. He wanted to find out if it really was possible to earn a living—and have sufficient leisure to write as he wished—in exchange for a half day of manual labor. The prospect of commanding a whole half day in which to hammer out a highly wrought page must have seemed to Nathaniel Hawthorne, exhausted by his recent slavery as a clerk, as if fate suddenly offered a daily ride on the winged horse.

More and more, as the characters in Blithedale go into action, the similarity between the real and the fictional diminishes. Although all social distinctions are abolished at Blithedale as at Brook Farm, the serving maids and farm hands are scarcely at their ease in the presence of the presiding lady, the glamorous Zenobia:

" 'Take your places, my dear friends all,' cried she; 'Seat yourselves without ceremony. . . .'

"We all sat down,—grizzly Silas Foster, his rotund helpmate, and the two bouncing handmaidens, included,—and looked at one another in a friendly but rather awkward way. It was the first practical trial of our theories of equal brotherhood and sisterhood; and we people of superior cultivation and refinement (for as such, I presume, we unhesitatingly reckoned ourselves) felt as if something were already accomplished towards the millennium of love. The truth is, however, that the laboring ear was with our unpolished companions; it being far easier to condescend than to accept of condescension. . . ."

If Zenobia is the very antithesis of Mrs. George Ripley's reserve and dignity, "grizzly Silas Foster" is a boorish caricature of young William Allen at Brook Farm; and if "good, comfortable Mrs. Foster," with her "back of generous breadth," bears any resemblance to an actual person, it is to some wife other than Allen's.

Inquiry of this sort so soon after the event could lead to injurious tittle-tattle. To use the current phrase, Hawthorne's "Author's Preface" is an attempt to convince the public that "all resemblance to persons living or dead is purely coincidental."

In one respect—purpose—the real and the fictional communities are identical. Both aimed to establish "the better life"; and the members of each, the real and the fictional, shared the same spiritual approach to the problem.

What was this "better life" that they had all "come out" of civilization to lead? Coverdale describes it, in a typically Hawthornian passage.

"The storm, in its evening aspect," he tells us, "was decidedly dreary. It seemed to have arisen for our especial behalf,—a symbol of the cold, desolate, distrustful phantoms that invariably haunt the mind, on the eve of adventurous enterprises, to warn us back within the boundaries of ordinary life.

"But our courage did not quail. We would not allow ourselves to be depressed by the snowdrift trailing past the window, any more than if it had been the sigh of a summer wind among rustling boughs. There have been few brighter seasons for us than that. If ever men might lawfully dream awake, and give utterance to their wildest visions without dread of laughter or scorn on the part of the audience,—yes, and speak of earthly happiness, for themselves and mankind, as an object to be hopefully striven for, and probably attained,—we who made that little semicircle round the blazing fire were those very men. We had left the rusty iron framework of society behind us; we had broken through many hindrances that are powerful enough to keep most people on the weary treadmill of the established system, even while they feel its irksomeness almost as intolerable as we did. We had stepped down from the pulpit; we had flung aside the pen; we had shut up the ledger; we had thrown off that sweet, bewitching, enervating indolence, which is better, after all, than most of the enjoyments within mortal grasp. It was our purpose—a generous one, certainly, and absurd, no doubt, in full proportion with its generosity—to give up whatever we had heretofore attained, for the sake of showing mankind the example of a life governed by other than the false and cruel principles on which human society has all along been based.

"And, first of all, we had divorced ourselves from pride, and were striving to supply its place with familiar love. We meant to lessen the laboring man's great burden of toil, by performing our due share of it at the cost of our own thews and sinews. We sought our profit by mutual aid, instead of wresting it by the strong hand from an enemy, or filching it craftily from those less shrewd than ourselves (if, indeed, there were any such in New England), or winning it by selfish competition with a neighbor; in one or another of which fashions every son of woman both perpetrates and suffers his share of the common evil, whether he chooses it or no. And, as the basis of our institution, we purposed to offer up the earnest toil of our bodies, as a prayer no less than an effort for the advancement of our race."

This passage, in which Coverdale makes it known that "Blithedale" is peopled with persons who have renounced worldly success to reform society, leads the reader to expect distinguished company, such as Hawthorne encountered at Brook Farm. "The creatures of his brain"— Zenobia, Priscilla, Old Moodie, Hollingsworth, and the rest—perform their phantasmagorical antics all too well. Apart from the author's reminiscence, the romance proves disappointing. Which is not surprising when one reflects that the story of Brook Farm would scarcely be worth telling if it had not been for the men and women who were associated with the Community. The impress on society, literature, education, and religion, which the Ripleys, Charles A. Dana, George William Curtis, Isaac Hecker, and Nathaniel Hawthorne (to name only the most outstanding "Farmers") made in their generation, has moulded the channels of thought in ours.

In the spring of 1841, the spiritual and intellectual force which this philosophy developed in the little group at Brook Farm amazed many. Such enthusiasm was extraordinary! Conventional people in the neighborhood of Boston began to ask one another about Transcendentalism. No one seemed to know exactly what it was. But it was evident that the new philosophy had a radical effect on conservative persons. Dr. and

Mrs. George Ripley, for instance. Could anyone explain why he suddenly had left his pulpit for a barnyard? It was rumored that Mrs. Ripley, renowned for her queenly manners, had become a slavey for her husband's followers. Heads shook sadly, and all agreed that Transcendentalism must be a heady sort of doctrine.

So it was; and the story of Brook Farm would be incomprehensible without previous inquiry into the philosophy which led to its founding. Who were the Transcendentalists? And how had they come by their unorthodox ideas?

↠↠↠↠↠↠↠↠↠↠↠↠↠↠↠↠↞↞↞↞↞↞↞↞↞↞↞↞↞↞↞↞↞

Eidolon, or The Sowing of New Ideas

ONE WINTER EVENING IN THE EIGHTEEN-THIRTIES, DR. WILLIAM ELLERY Channing, the acknowledged star of the Boston pulpit, set out from his mansion on Mount Vernon Street and repaired to the house of Dr. John Collins Warren on Chestnut Street, where Dr. Warren had gathered a well-chosen assembly to hear him hold forth.

Removing his blue camlet coat, shawl, and enormous hat in the narrow hall, Dr. Channing entered the parlor filled with large thoughts which he wished to open. A company of gentlemen, variously distinguished, awaited him. There was mutual greeting and introduction. Everyone chatted agreeably but too extensively on indifferent matters, so that, just as they were nearing their great expectation—to hear Dr. Channing set forth the one subject for which the gathering had been called together—a side door opened, and the whole company streamed in to an oyster supper crowned by some excellent wines. So ended—as Ralph Waldo Emerson recalled some forty years afterward—the first attempt to establish an aesthetic society in Boston.*

Scenes such as this, which Emerson records in accents curiously compounded of sympathy and satire, had been frequent in Boston since the early eighteen-thirties, when a great wave of humanity, of benevo-

* Emerson was very old when he wrote of this meeting. Whether he confused the occasion with some other or not, to my mind it gives the atmosphere of the pre-Brook Farm planning in a delightful and vivid manner.

lence, of desire for improvement—an all-embracing wave of social perception—had begun to pour itself among those who had the faculty of
large and disinterested thinking. Among these, Dr. Channing stood
pre-eminent.

When Dr. Channing addressed his congregation in the Federal
Street Church, the small frail figure took on the stateliness of a prophet.
No one who heard him preach ever forgot the solemn fire, the profound
earnestness. Ember-like eyes burning in the drawn, white face, Dr.
Channing took and held captive all minds to the end of his discourse—
the rich and prominent, with whom he was associated by inheritance,
the poor and downtrodden, whose champion he had become.

James Freeman Clarke in his Memoir of the great preacher tells us
that there was "nothing like his delivery, nothing even comparable to it
in any pulpit in America. It was not oratory, it was not rhetoric; it was
pure soul uttering itself in thoughts clear and strong as the current of a
mighty stream." And because Dr. Channing was as much concerned
about the evils of society in this world as in steering souls toward the
Hereafter, he was revered by the devout and the humanitarians alike.
Among those who were turning away from such gruesome Calvinistic
doctrines as Original Sin and Infant Damnation, he had become "The
Apostle of Unitarianism"; and the humanitarians, grateful for Dr. Channing's tireless zeal in promoting social reform, spoke of him affectionately as "The Great Awakener."

Though a frail little invalid, Dr. Channing throughout his life was
always the most accessible of men. He was as ready to talk with the
poor and obscure who found their way to 83 Mount Vernon Street, as
with the scholarly and prominent persons who came by appointment to
his study. Towards the end of his long ministry, he welcomed with particular warmth the younger divines who sought his counsel privately.
He looked to the younger men for the accomplishment of the great
ideas they had so often discussed. He urged upon them again the need
of a spiritual revolution in Christendom, of a new bond between man
and man, of a new sense of the relation between man and his Creator.
The present state of society was low and deplorable. Founded upon
wealth, how could it be sound? Were not all human beings part of a
great whole? It was obvious that if the mass of men continued to be
drained by the degradation of mind and heart in which they had been
sunk by the competitive system, the fortunate would be dragged down
by the underprivileged. Deep social changes were necessary to save
civilization. Only in Christianity, with its insistence on the powers and

principles of human nature—insistence on the dignity of each human being no matter how unfortunate or degraded—could the promise of a holier and happier society be fulfilled.

The earth seemed good to live in, to all who listened in their hearts to Dr. Channing. It was their privilege to live in this faith, and to share it with others; their duty to reform social institutions.

The younger divines came away challenged to new endeavor. How grand a thing it was to be a human being! Christianity was such a holy gift, and to serve it joy sufficient for this world.

It often came to pass that a word from Dr. Channing had launched a wide-spreading reform.

To one of these younger divines, George Ripley, Dr. Channing confided one of his "dearest ideas." Might it be possible, he wondered, to bring a group of thoughtful, cultivated people together, to make "a society" worthy of the name? He had long wished to see "Labor honored and united with the free development of the intellect and the heart."

"The Great Awakener's" dream of a society to reform society was like a hardy perennial with many varieties. To George Ripley he pictured the ideal community as one where labor and culture should be united. To another he wrote that he longed to see "an Association in which the members, instead of preying on one another, and seeking to put one another down, after the fashion of this world, should live together as brothers seeking one another's elevation and spiritual growth." From this little nucleus, as from Bethlehem, a legend would arise and take hold!

Dr. Channing soon opened his mind again to George Ripley. It was never "The Great Awakener's" way to urge anyone directly toward an undertaking. He merely suggested; then reminded. Yet it often happened that a word from him could change the course of a man's life. In this instance, Dr. Channing's conception concerning the "Union of Labor and Culture" became the cornerstone of "the noble experiment" soon to be undertaken by George Ripley and his followers at Brook Farm, West Roxbury, Massachusetts.

Young Dr. Ripley proved a likely proselyte. He often called himself "a child of Channing"; and he was beginning to be very restless in his pulpit.

Had he not worn the pastoral habit, a stranger might have taken the young divine for a doctor of philosophy. There was an air of suppressed vitality about him which suggested keen interest in the good life in this world. He had a Zeus-like massive brow capped with crisp dark curls, black eyes that peered at mankind in a friendly way from behind gold-rimmed spectacles, and, in that day when hirsute extravagances of all sorts were in fashion, George Ripley's firm and open countenance was clean-shaven and exposed.

When Dr. Channing cast this tempting fly—the ideal community—across the clouding pool of his existence, Dr. Ripley was about thirty-five, a Unitarian divine who had been the pastor of the Thirteenth Congregational Church on Purchase Street in Boston for more than ten years. A long time for a man not suited to the profession.

Upon graduating from Harvard, the first scholar in the class of 1823, Ripley had felt no urgent call to the ministry. He frankly had envied such scholarly classmates as were in a position to continue their studies in some foreign university. He could not forget, however, that his father, repeatedly elected Representative to the Massachusetts Legislature, had maintained a hardware store in Greenfield in order to provide the barest of livelihoods for his family of ten children.

His mother, descended collaterally from the same ancestors as Benjamin Franklin, imbued her ninth offspring with the precepts of "Poor Richard"; and George, who, even as a little boy, had dreamed of "some day making a dictionary," saw the facts in 1823, and acted accordingly. He had made the most of his opportunities at Harvard, and justified the sacrifices his parents had made to pay for his college education. He knew that the Unitarian Ministry offered brilliant graduates a secure living—and it also seemed to offer liberal expression to young men of scholarly, philosophical approach. He entered the Harvard Divinity School; and although he also taught mathematics to eke out expenses, he acquitted himself there with such credit, that upon his graduation in 1826 he was ordained pastor of a new Unitarian Society which had been gathered expressly for him.

The cornerstone had been laid on September seventh, 1825, by Henry Ware. Because of his "liberal" views Dr. Ware's appointment as Professor of Divinity at Harvard in 1805 had aroused opposition in the orthodox division of the Congregational Churches. This choice and the questions it brought into prominence had since then established Unitarianism as an independent sect and orthodox religion; and Ware was now an authoritative leader in the new and flourishing school for divines, whose good will was an added honor for Ripley, the young graduate. Today a speaker launching a young man on his career would more likely mention his qualifications than expatiate upon his future; but in the eighteen-twenties a speaker used lofty language, or he was not asked to speak at all. After laying the cornerstone of the church, at the corner of Purchase and Pearl Streets, Dr. Ware let his fancy soar. "From this place," he proclaimed, "shall forever go up, to the end of time, incense and a pure offering from multitudes of humble and believing hearts."

The multitudes never came. The preaching of the young pastor won him no renown; and the huge ugly structure adorned with a small belfry which had arisen on the corner of Purchase and Pearl Streets was never filled. When Dr. Ripley addressed his congregation he was lucid but lacking in feeling. His sermons were cogent and earnestly spoken, but they offered little inducement to walk past the Federal Street Church where the great Dr. Channing melted the heart with the true fire of eloquence. Why go on toward Griffin's Wharf through a neighborhood which had deteriorated sadly since the tea ships had lain there?

Though no orator, in a small room among friends Ripley was a good talker, especially when he discussed the New Learning of the European philosophers.

At college George Ripley had studied with Edward Everett, George Ticknor and other teachers who had traveled abroad and drunk in at the source the intuitive philosophy then coming into authority among liberal scholars in Europe; and soon after his ordination—in 1827—he had married Sophia Willard Dana, the daughter of Francis Dana of Cambridge, whose intelligence and intellectual curiosity were as keen as his own. Mrs. Ripley shared in his philosophical studies and encouraged him to import the works of Schleiermacher and Fichte from Germany, of Cousin and Constant from France, as well as those of Coleridge and Carlyle from England, so that they gradually had collected the finest library of foreign literature in Boston.

In *The Christian Register*, an organ of liberal theology which he edited for a short time, Ripley encouraged discussion of these and other philosophical treatises; and in 1830 he began to contribute to *The Christian Examiner*, the organ of Unitarian scholarship, articles which show clearly the increasingly liberal trend of his thought. *Degerando* (September 1830) upheld that writer's views concerning self-education as the means and art of moral progress; *Religion in France* (July 1831) pleaded for spiritual Christianity, without priest, dogma, or intellectual swaddling clothes; and an article on Pestalozzi (January 1832) discussed with enthusiasm the theories of the Swiss educational reformer —indicating that the experiment in "psychologizing education" at Neuhof may later have benefited the curriculum at Brook Farm. In the same issue Ripley made his first hesitant avowal that he shared the conviction of the European thinkers that man was a part of nature and a participant in a vibrant growth which could not be contained in any pattern. In reviewing the "Inaugural Discourse" of Charles Follen, a young German liberal recently appointed the first Professor of German at Harvard, Ripley seized the opportunity to defend German writers against "a confused idea, taken up with very little or no examination, that they are all given to mysticism, rhapsody, wild and tasteless inventions in poetry, and dark impenetrable reasonings in metaphysics."

Although the liberal tone of his articles increased year by year, Dr. Ripley took care that none of the new metaphysical lore should get into his sermons. Unlike his friend, Theodore Parker, he was no prophet burning to put new life into the Unitarian Church. A scholar and a humanist rather, who believed that everyone had a right to think out his own religion for himself. Circumstances had made him a pastor, and until he saw more clearly where the New Philosophy would lead him, he felt bound not to involve his congregation in any of the "odium which might attach to the heresies of their minister."

One of George Ripley's intimates, the forthright Orestes A. Brownson, may well have wondered at his guarded restraint in the pulpit. For Brownson had introduced the French philosophers, Constant and Cousin, to the readers of *The Christian Examiner*, as Ripley had the German. Knowing that it was largely due to their joint efforts in translation that the New Learning had reached New England, the two friends shared in a sense of discovery and leadership. Ripley must have seemed slow and cautious to Brownson, who cast off allegiance to an unsatisfactory sect as a boy discards an outgrown suit.

Orestes was the son of a poor farmer in Vermont; and as a boy he underwent a religious experience so profound that it left him restless and dissatisfied. Already he had been a Presbyterian, and a Universalist. Although ordained in the latter faith, he had preached as a free-lance minister in various pulpits in Vermont and upper New York State. Then, in the fall of 1829, Brownson joined Robert Dale Owen and Fanny Wright, leaders in Social Reform in New York City, and helped them to organize the Workingmen's Party. Brownson's intellect was powerful and his expression vehement, so that his pen and his word found readers and proscenium. With his usual abruptness, Brownson proclaimed himself a Unitarian in 1832. He did not have to wait for a congregation. A pulpit quickly was offered to him, in Walpole, New Hampshire.

The fever of philosophic inquiry was spreading rapidly among the younger divines. The New Philosophy, which released man's strong, inarticulate instincts—or, as they preferred to call them, man's natural emotions—held great fascination for the New England thinkers. They read Brownson's and Ripley's translations; and they envied Frederic Henry Hedge, minister in West Cambridge, "the one American, who really had read Kant in the original." The young liberals in the Unitarian Ministry—such men as Theodore Parker, William Henry Channing, a nephew of the great Dr. William Ellery Channing, John S. Dwight; and lesser lights amid a brilliant galaxy—Christopher Pearse Cranch, Cyrus Bartol, Caleb Stetson, and others—were asking themselves, just as George Ripley asked himself, where this fascinating "Newness" would lead them. They looked to James Freeman Clarke and Ralph Waldo Emerson to help them assimilate the ideas of Swedenborg, Cousin, Coleridge, Carlyle, and the great German writers.

With one exception, the young liberals felt a deep reluctance to breaking with their elders in the Unitarian Ministry, their early teachers. Emerson was the only one among them who shortly would admit that he had engaged in a profession for which he had no heart.

But Orestes Brownson, eager to be in the thick of the coming fight, removed from Walpole in New Hampshire to Canton, Massachusetts, to be near the liberals who were scattered in parishes around Boston. He contributed to the journals, visited various pulpits, expressing himself with his usual vehemence and force. Immediately, his influence was felt. It is significant that George Ripley began this same year to preach more boldly to his parishioners; and he laid the sermons in a place of safekeeping, to be published, in 1836, as *Discourses on the Philosophy of Religion*.

Already, in 1832, the slight crack in the solid structure of Unitarian Orthodoxy was widening ominously. (Those who delighted in the New Philosophy were called "Transcendentalists"; and their elders and teachers were referred to as "the Orthodox.")

In philosophical phrase, Transcendentalism is the doctrine that man can attain knowledge by intuitional processes which transcend the experience of the senses.

The Boston public thought the term delightfully apt. Did not the hazy holiness of the new sect transcend comprehension? To the "Vicars of Mammon on State Street"—Boston's businessmen—the term stood for a person with a hopelessly impractical mind.

2.

In the summer of 1832, Ralph Waldo Emerson had come to the conclusion that he could no longer administer the Lord's Supper unless the Bread and Wine were left out. This had led to a break with his congregation at the Second Church of Boston, and placed him at the head of the advance-guard among the liberals. For Emerson's sermons, distinguished by their sincerity and directness of language, had charmed the younger members of his congregation; and the success of his ministry clothed his resignation in an aura of sacrifice that won the respect even of those who did not agree with him; and those Unitarian ministers who were becoming more and more interested in the European Transcendental philosophers were behind him, to a man. Some of them felt that he had gone almost as their ambassador to Europe in the fall of 1832. Ripley and Brownson, and no doubt Parker, too, had eagerly awaited his return, so that they might hear from his own lips of the wonderful conversations with Carlyle, Coleridge, and Wordsworth, and the host of other scholars Mr. Emerson wrote he had met in his travels from Malta to Scotland.

After he came back and settled in Concord in 1833, although Mr. Emerson spoke out to his intimate circle and his lecture audiences, he was in no hurry to publish in book form an expression of the philosophy he had evolved since leaving the ministry. For three full years Emerson kept his followers waiting—until September ninth, 1836, when he at last published *Nature*.

In this brief pamphlet, Emerson proposed an inquiry—"To what end is Nature?" He then examined the various manifestations of Nature—the sublime, the useful, the beautiful, both visible and spiritual. Truth and goodness and beauty were almost synonymous in Emerson's metaphysic. Mere external beauty he did not regard as ultimate, of course; but rather as the herald of inner beauty, and only a part, not the last or highest expression of the final cause of Nature. "God and God only," said Emerson, "is the all fair." Man, he pointed out, is conscious of a Universal within or behind his individual consciousness. The "Over-Soul," as he called it, compels the spirit to manifest itself through the reason in various forms. The Over-Soul is God working "through His own instruments"—mankind. The Laws of Nature, Emerson pointed out, are a constant discipline to man. Therefore is Nature the ally of Religion; and prophet and priest have drawn deeply from her. To this one end of Discipline, all parts of Nature conspire. For Nature is always faithful to the cause of its origin; it always speaks of Spirit: "It is a great shadow cast always to the sun behind us." Indeed, the noblest ministry of Nature is to stand as the apparition of God.

From this highly debatable assertion concerning the universal benevolence of nature, it is evident that Emerson preferred glimpses of truth to digested systems. The scientist, he said, too often became so absorbed in classification that he ignored the wonderful congruity which subsists between man and the world. For man's power lies in Instinct, which is superior to his Will. Man cannot be a Naturalist—in the Transcendental interpretation—until he satisfies all the demands of the Spirit: love, perception, prayer. This son of generations of Christian ministers could break with the Church, but he still regarded prayer as "a sally of the soul into the unfound infinite . . . No man ever prayed heartily without learning something."

To pure Spirit, Nature is fluid, volatile, obedient. "Build, therefore, your own world . . . As fast as you conform your life to the pure idea in your mind, that will unfold its great proportions."

Whether welcomed or damned—and it got a mixed reception—*Nature* was recognized as the first clear blast on New England's transcendental horn. Ripley, Brownson, and the rest, although no one of them would agree on all the points in Emerson's discussion, welcomed it as a nobly conceived challenge to the Orthodox.

Emerson's lifelong friend, Henry Furness, now serving the first Unitarian Church in Philadelphia, already had prophesied, ". . . that the Unitarians must break into two schools—the old one, or English School, belonging to the sensual and empiric philosophy, and the new one, or the German School, . . . belonging to the spiritual philosophy." The break, led by Emerson from without the Church, and by Theodore Parker from within it, was now at hand. 1836 would mark the end of the formative period of Unitarianism in the United States, of which Dr. William Ellery Channing had been the distinguished exponent since 1803. Under his leadership, the Church had professed a semi-supernatural, imperfectly rationalistic dogma, while he labored to bring Christianity into accord with the progressive and philanthropic spirit of the time.

The second period of Unitarianism in the United States, which

Emerson and Parker were about to introduce, would be profoundly influenced by German Idealism, as Transcendentalism was called in
Europe; and its theology, although increasingly rationalistic, would be
heavily flavored with mysticism. In other words, it would reflect Emerson's absorption in Man's soul, Nature, and the Over-Soul.

So it was inevitable, when Harvard, the citadel of the Orthodox
Unitarians, celebrated its Bi-Centenary early in September—soon after
the publication of *Nature*—that Emerson, Ripley, and others who met
afterwards at Willard's Hotel, should agree that the views they had
heard expressed on that occasion seemed vapid and outworn.

They repaired at once to Ripley's house on Chauncy Street, to form
a society of those who felt drawn together by sympathy of studies and
aspiration, to exchange ideas. Convers Francis, James Freeman Clarke,
Orestes Brownson, and Bronson Alcott, when invited to become charter
members of the new society, all responded to the summons. Convers
Francis, pastor of the First Church in Watertown, Massachusetts, was
of an older generation, yet he "rejoiced to see the spiritualists taking the
field in force."

The first meeting was held at the Ripleys' on the nineteenth of September.* In this casual fashion the legendary "Transcendentalist Club"
was born. A second meeting soon was called. Invitations were sent to
those, who like the charter members, now regarded the Unitarian
Church—which had once seemed essentially liberal compared to the
Calvinism of their fathers—as binding and negative.

"Transcendentalist Club" is not the name the members used. They
called it "The Symposium," or simply, "The Club." Emerson always
referred to "Hedge's Club," because it was likely to meet when Hedge—
the only member who read Kant in the original—came down from
Bangor. Some member with a waggish wit dubbed it "The Club of the
Like-Minded"—because not one of these Apostles of the Newness
thought like another. Certainly it was a loosely knit society. There was
no chairman or president, no book of by-laws. The records were not kept
with care. Guests were welcome and many members attended irregu-
larly. It was simply "a meeting of Minds."

Abstractions were more popular topics for discussion than dogma;
and the members delighted in arguments concerning Truth, Individu-

---

* Rusk gives this date; but in R.W.E.'s *Journal* of Sept. 6, 1837 he mentions
a meeting of the Aesthetic Club at Mr. Clarke's in Newton. Present: Alcott, Clarke,
Dwight, Emerson, Francis, Hedge, Stetson, Miss Clarke, Miss Fuller, Miss
Peabody. . . .

ality, Law, the Personality of God. Such talks strengthened a sense of
companionship among New England thinkers, each having found his
way alone, to meet upon the common ground of further inquiry. The significance of the Transcendentalist Club arose from the circumstance
that it came into being just when the foreign ideas which Ripley,
Brownson, Emerson, and Hedge had been cultivating were burgeoning.

All at once Emerson's *Nature* created a furor—when the Orthodox
leader, Andrews Norton, formerly Dexter Professor of Sacred Literature
at the Harvard Divinity School, became indignant on reading the passage in which Emerson declared that the Idealist Philosopher is not at
all curious concerning the historical evidence for the Christian Miracles.
Professor Norton was disturbed because other Transcendentalists had
pointed out the inconsistency of the Orthodox position. Although the
Church had rejected the Calvinistic doctrines of Original Sin, Infant
Damnation, and the like, and was to this extent rationalistic, it still insisted on acceptance of the supernatural—the Christian Miracles.

To add to Norton's disquietude, George Ripley, in reviewing James
Martineau's *Rationale of Religious Enquiry* for the November issue of
The Christian Examiner, went out of his way to point out that both ends
of the Orthodox dogma broke against the middle—the spiritual dignity
of man. Ripley was willing to concede that the Miracles had happened;
but he pointed out that Jesus, far from requiring a faith in His Miracles
as the condition of receiving His Word, required a faith in His Word
as the condition of receiving His Miracles. The authenticity of the
Miracles was, therefore, irrelevant to an inquiry into man's relationship
to his Creator.

Ripley maintained that the Orthodox were annihilating the image of
God in the human spirit just as thoroughly as were their opposites the
Calvinists; and he called on them to go the whole way in their insistence
upon the supernatural, even to the point of accepting, as the only revelation known to Man, that of the Intuitional Faculties, "the Reason."

Although Norton had resigned his chair in 1830 to devote himself to
his *magnum opus* on the "Evidence" of Christianity, he was still regarded as the leader of the Orthodox; and when he took the unprece-
dented step of publishing a letter in the *Boston Daily Advertiser*, con-
demning Ripley's opinions as leaning toward infidelity, and rebuking
the presumption in so young a man for daring to present them, Ripley
was quick with a rejoinder. His letter, printed in the *Advertiser* the very
next day, put the case for Transcendentalism positively. He pointed out
that the distinction between the divine and the natural ceases to mean

anything at all when Nature is seen as a reflection of Divinity—or, as Emerson had written, "An Apparition of God."

After this skirmish the paper war was blown aside and forgotten for a time in the hurricane of an industrial depression—the first of such magnitude in the history of the nation.

As in 1929 the storm had gathered in the midst of an unparalleled boom. Railroads were expanding on a large scale. The cotton crop had surpassed expectations, and more bales than ever before were being shipped abroad. Real estate prices were going up and up. Foreign investors, eager to cash in on the rapidly mounting values, were pouring money into the United States—until early in 1836, when several Continental countries became involved in tides of liberal revolution.

Money began to tighten abroad. The flow diminished to a trickle; stopped. Hard pressed, the Europeans tapped the American reservoir; withdrew their capital.

On July eleventh, 1836—in order to keep coin in the country, and to check the lavish use of paper, especially in real estate transactions—the United States Treasury issued its since famous specie circular, which ordered government to take only cash payment and the notes of specie-paying banks for the sale of public lands.

Unable to meet the requirement, the Western banks collapsed. In the autumn, the three largest English houses engaged in the American trade failed. Export was ruined. Panic spread. In the spring of 1837, even the most powerful New York banks had to suspend specie payments.

New England, too, had entered into the mad and happy spree of speculation, and she came in for her full share of the general collapse. Suspension in Boston followed that in New York by forty-eight hours.

In his *Journal*, Emerson painted the picture in the impressionist manner: "April 22, 1837:—Cold April: hard times; men breaking who ought not to break; banks bullied into the bolstering of desperate speculators; all the newspapers a chorus of owls . . . Sixty thousand laborers, says rumor, to be presently thrown out of work and these make a comfortable mob to break the banks, and rob the rich, and brave the domestic government."

Public reaction to the crisis proved more subdued than rumor. No formidable mob arose. Reaction was much the same as in the nineteen-twenty-nine crisis. Confidence in the businessman was shaken. The

humanitarians—among them George Ripley—appalled at the waste of
competitive industry and the working man's lack of security, began to
study the social philosophy of Robert Dale Owen, Saint-Simon, and
Charles Fourier.

Emerson's next public challenge to the Conservatives—his address to
the Phi Beta Kappa Society of Harvard on August thirty-first, 1837—
proved more acceptable than had *Nature* to men whose fathers and
grandfathers had fought and died to throw off the political yoke imposed by England. When closely examined, however, this "Literary
Declaration of Independence" was quite as Transcendental as the
pamphlet had been. "The scholar," said young Mr. Emerson, "is man
thinking. His duty is first to know Nature whence all power and wisdom come, and then to make himself one with the mind of the past
through books, and at last to express himself in action— . . . He is the
world's eye; the world's heart." The scholar must remain, presumably in
spite of these responsibilities, "an aristocrat of the soul," and the "servant to good men." New England, still in the throes of the industrial
catastrophe, accepted young Mr. Emerson's theories as highly patriotic.
  Meanwhile George Ripley was editing a series of translations from
"The New Literature of Europe." This enterprise was a courageous one
in that it was undertaken without financial backing and at a time when
his assistants were otherwise occupied. The first two volumes, Philosophical Miscellanies from the French of Cousin, Jouffroy and Benjamin Constant, were published in Boston in 1838 under the resounding
title, *Specimens of Standard Foreign Literature*. "The scholar," said
Ripley, in a highly significant passage which shows clearly that his
thoughts were turning more and more to Social Reform, "should never
stand aloof from the concerns of the people, or set himself above them
as their 'condescending instructor.' Rather is he called upon to bring
his learning and philosophy to the aid of the common man, and to the
attention of the governors, so that all can work together to help the nation to comprehend its destiny and secure its accomplishment."
  Then, without warning, in July 1838, Ripley was suddenly distracted
from his social studies when that Unitarian renegade, Ralph Waldo
Emerson, on being invited by a committee of the seniors of the Harvard
Divinity School to deliver their Commencement Address at Divinity
Hall in Cambridge, accepted their invitation—before the authorities
could intervene.

What Emerson, age thirty-five, said on that occasion, fitted the aspirations of the liberal Unitarian ministers so well that "The Divinity School Address" instantly became their Credo. Today the address is still a classic expression of liberal religion in the United States. But in reviewing the address it is sometimes forgotten that Emerson was not content merely to proclaim the Over-Soul. He boldly denounced the Unitarian Church as dead and lifeless. Then, peering down into the startled faces of the graduating class, he challenged them as representatives of the Harvard Divinity School to consider what awakening they should undergo to fit themselves for ministry in the living world. Modern Christianity, proclaimed young prophet Emerson a hundred and more years ago, had ceased to do its proper work.

Emerson said only what Brownson, Ripley, and others had said before, but when he spoke he had the presence and authority of a prophet, and the gift of turning theory into poetry. Those who shared his views, on hearing their own words returned to them on wings, wondered at their own poverty of expression; the beatitudes they had not uttered.

Professor Andrews Norton, who, according to rumor, sat "fuming in his study, with shades and windows drawn to keep out the slightest infidelity," took up the challenge; and the long impending battle between the Transcendentalists and the Champions of Orthodoxy was joined.

With purposeful irony Dr. Norton waited almost a full year—until July nineteenth, 1839—so that he might denounce "The Latest Form of Infidelity" from the same rostrum on which Emerson had pronounced his "heresies," and so that he, too, might address the alumni and graduating class of the Divinity School.

It was his vigorous denunciation of the foreign learning which was "poisoning the pure stream of American Unitarianism" that disturbed the Liberals; for people were saying that that part of his address had scotched Transcendentalism for good. And, to the dismay of his followers, Emerson refused to defend his philosophy. Though the winged words he had spoken had turned like the boomerang to strike him, he would not be goaded out of his Olympian detachment. His friends, however, felt that a reply should be made. The two best qualified to make it were Orestes Brownson and George Ripley. Brownson was absorbed in socialistic reform, so the task fell to Ripley. He went to work with his customary conscientiousness.

However, when Ripley confided his argument refuting Norton's stand to Theodore Parker, minister of the Spring Street Church in West Roxbury, his friend was lukewarm in his praise. "Ripley is writing the reply to Dr. Norton," Parker wrote a mutual friend. "It will make a pamphlet of about one-hundred pages octavo; and is clean, and strong, and good."

The controversy waxed on arguments and rebuttals, the one following the other well into the new year. To a modern, both Norton's dogma and Ripley's refutation make dull reading. But 1840 was closer by over a hundred years to the era when doctrinal hairsplitting was as popular as discussion concerning forms of government is today, and the controversy aroused widespread interest. Ripley had actually translated some of the works Norton denounced, and he was at this time engaged in editing other translations made by close friends, so he was more interested in defending the European philosophers than in refuting a theology, which—as he firmly reminded the Orthodox—had not been revised since the days of Cranmer.

Ripley's arguments grew increasingly disappointing to his friend Parker, who, though equal to Ripley in scholarship, loved the Unitarian Church and labored to revivify it from within the fold. "There is a higher word to be said on this subject than Ripley is disposed to say just now," Parker wrote, meaning that he himself preferred to defend Christianity with moral truth rather than with scholarly digressions.

Since he had been elected to refute Andrews Norton, George Ripley kept on writing very dull pieces which were published late into the winter of 1839–40. That his conscience, not his heart, was embroiled in the controversy is plain, for honest George Ripley shrouded his rebuttals with a mist of anonymity—signing himself "An Alumnus."

Although his organ, *The Boston Quarterly*, was mainly concerned with social reform, Brownson's restless search for religious peace led him to examine the tenets of both contestants in the controversy, and even to expose the weakness inherent in the new philosophy. "So far as Transcendentalism is understood to be the recognition in man of the capacity of knowing truth intuitively, or of attaining to a scientific knowledge of an order of existence transcending the reach of the senses, and of which we can have no sensible experience, we are Transcendentalists," Brownson declared. "But when it is understood to mean that feeling is to be placed above reason, dreaming above reflection, and intuitive intimation above scientific exposition; in a word when it means the substitution of a lawless fancy for an enlightened understanding . . . we must disown it, and deny we are Transcendentalists."

Certainly Ripley, with his more disciplined nature, must have concurred. Indeed, he and Orestes were very close at this time. Together they had brought out "The Miscellanies"; and further translations of foreign philosophers were in progress.

Meanwhile, the need for a liberal journal had become pressing because the editors of *The Christian Examiner*, shocked by Emerson's "Divinity School Address," had withdrawn into the camp of the Orthodox. At a meeting of "The Club" held at that time, it was determined to found an "organ of spiritual philosophy." But nothing had been done about it since. Now, in the fall of 1839, steps were taken; and by December the project had acquired a staff. Margaret Fuller, reputed to be the most learned woman in America, had agreed to serve as editor; and steady George Ripley assumed "the business part." Bronson Alcott, who often bewildered his associates with his mystic images, gave the new organ a beautiful name—*The Dial*.

"And so with diligent hands and good intent"—and with Emerson's help, for it was he who sired the undertaking—the editors made plans to disseminate Transcendental opinions on art, literature, and social problems. The new periodical, Emerson noted in his *Journal*, would "ignore all the old, long constituted public or publics." This gallant independence rallied the younger poets and writers and gave them an organ; but the public, except for some three hundred subscribers, would return Mr. Emerson's compliment.

3.

"To talk himself out of his pulpit" was George Ripley's way of getting out of it. But he continued "to pray by the job" until May, 1840, when money to administer the parish fell short. This practical evidence of his failure as a pastor furnished an excuse to offer his resignation, one which Yankee parishioners would weigh carefully. Dr. Ripley wrote his "respected friends," the proprietors of the Purchase Street Church, suggesting that their interests might be better served by other hands. Then he and his wife left Boston to spend the summer on the farm of a wealthy friend, Charles Ellis, who perhaps did not as yet suspect that his property in West Roxbury would shortly be the setting for a noble experiment in community living.

The Ripleys had passed the two previous summers there in order to be near Theodore Parker, pastor of the Spring Street Church, whose parsonage was but a mile or two distant. Mrs. Ripley shared her husband's affectionate admiration for the great preacher, and her letters are warm in his praise. Parker was their "Savonarola," an excellent scholar in frank and affectionate communication with the best minds of his day. Yet he was also the tribune of the people and the stout reformer to urge and defend every cause of humanity with and for the humblest of mankind. In this and in an enthusiasm for book buying, the two men had much in common. But in temperament how different! As Sophia Ripley observed, Parker was "no artist . . . Highly refined persons might easily miss in him an element of beauty." Whereas her husband was a true scholar, contemplative, and, it must be admitted, at times a trifle over-cautious; the other was a man of impulse, bold, almost rash.

The two men enjoyed one another's company the more for these differences—so much that they could scarcely leave off talking once they had begun. When Theodore arose to take his leave, George would walk home with him; and when they reached the parsonage, if they had more to say, Theodore would return the courtesy.

After the long, confining winter passed in the deteriorating neighborhood of Griffin's Wharf, the Ripleys always found the peace of West Roxbury refreshing. This summer, the trees and fields and sky delighted them more than ever. An irrepressible buoyancy took possession of George Ripley when he walked through the wild little lanes with Theodore Parker, or mused beneath the grove with his wife. After the recent months of controversy and self-questioning, it was good to feel the soul expand in the contemplation of Nature. Was not Nature the reflection of the World Soul? The contemplation thereof a sacred rite of communion with the Deity?

Here, on the farm, it was practicable to give a trial to Dr. Channing's theory concerning the union of labor and culture. The dignified pastor of the Purchase Street Church was up at break of day, dressed in blue tunic and cowhide boots, milking a cow; and a long forenoon of work in the truck garden beneath the June sun set his mind in perfect tune for the task of editing. It needed to be! The first issue of *The Dial*, the herald of the spiritual revolution, would be published in July; and further *Specimens of Foreign Standard Literature*, by John S. Dwight, Margaret Fuller, William Henry Channing, nephew of the great preacher, and other members of the group, were in preparation. George Ripley was not always industrious, however, during this summer of indecision. Sometimes he lay "for hours on green banks, reading Burns and whistling to the birds."

Mrs. Ripley, too, had fallen in love with their retreat. In a letter to John S. Dwight—then a Unitarian minister in Northampton—Sophia wrote with pure delight of the "birds and trees, sloping green hills and hay fields as far as the eye can reach—and a brook clear running." The brook flowed by the foot of a green bank covered with shrubbery, below their window. It sang them to their rest "with its quiet tune," and "chanted its morning song to the rising sun." The little stream, surviving time and change, still winds its way past the spot where the Ellis farmhouse stood; and it gave the name by which the "noble experiment" in community living which the Ripleys were presently to found, is known to posterity—"Brook Farm."

Friends exclaimed at the loneliness and isolation of the Ripleys' retreat; and Sophia admitted that their refuge stood "two miles from any creature." They did not see so many persons in a month as they did in one morning in Boston. Yet they were not "entirely recluse." Margaret Fuller had lived the year before in Forest Hills; and "the brilliant sibyl of the plains" revisited friends in Jamaica, which was within walking distance of Brook Farm, to confer with her business manager of *The Dial*. And on Sundays the Ripleys could attend divine service in the Spring Street Church, West Roxbury, and hear one of Theodore Parker's heretical sermons. Mrs. Ripley reported that Parker was "creating a stiff breeze about him." With her usual brilliant analysis of religious and social theory, Sophia caught in Parker's sermons an echo and application of what her friends had been "silently dropping" for three years past. In her opinion this was one more proof that the Transcendental doctrine had already "sunk deep, taken root, and budded in the glowing hearts of the more fanatical men."

Would she have rejoiced if she could have ranked her George among the "glowing hearts"? Or did she already know that he was more scholar and reformer than pastor? Entering warmly into her husband's enthusiasm, Mrs. Ripley busied herself about the household, while Dr. Ripley served as an extra hand around the farm. Mrs. Ripley's moral fibre was such that she always graced any task, no matter how menial, with finished manners and a dignified presence. But the daughter of Francis Dana of Cambridge had enjoyed an unusually fine education for a female in those days. Before her marriage, she had taught school—in Fay House that was to become the office of Radcliffe College. A training which she would soon put to excellent use. But would Mrs. Ripley have been as eager to support Dr. Channing's ideal community, if she had foreseen that she would soon be ironing undergarments and night caps for ten or twelve hours a day?

It was the season when the hay is "in"; when the garden, planted in loving care beneath the pale damp hope of April, seems mere bait for woodchucks and insects. The green lushness of June had dimmed and shrivelled a little under the hot July sun and a paler sky. It was the season when nature in New England seems to delay the hopes of spring. Then the amateur farmer, forgetting the harvest, turns vacationist.

Strange stories had reached Theodore Parker's ears concerning the "Groton Convention." It was rumored that some very odd characters, "Come-outers" from Cape Cod, and "Millerites" from everywhere, had gathered in the little town of Groton, Massachusetts. So he persuaded his friend, George Ripley, to set out on foot with him to find out what the "Groton Convention" was about.

The two set out in high spirits. George enjoyed walking and talking with Theodore; and forty miles of both offered a pleasurable jaunt. On their way to Concord, where they planned to sleep that night, they picked up Christopher Pearse Cranch. This light-hearted young man, though a sincere Transcendentalist, drew the most amusing cartoons— caricatures of Emerson, the Prophet of the Over-Soul, and his arch enemy, Andrews Norton.

When they got to Concord, they went straight to the Manse to visit with eighty-nine-year-old Dr. Ezra Ripley, a relation of George's, and Emerson's step-grandfather. Built by William Emerson, whose widow Ezra Ripley had married, the Manse stands close "by the rude bridge that arched the flood . . ." His son, William E. Emerson, the father of Waldo, had snatched a long musket from the chimney piece in the Manse and hurried after his father to fight as a stripling in the battle that gave history a new turn. Such legends, which Hawthorne would soon relate in *Mosses from an Old Manse*, were perpetuated at this time by the brilliant company to be found there. Mrs. Samuel D. Ripley —Ezra's daughter-in-law, George P. Bradford's sister, whom George called "Cousin Sarah"—was one of the most admirably accomplished women in New England.

Ripley, Parker, and Cranch walked back to town and took tea with Mr. and Mrs. Emerson. Though he looked to Parker "as divine as usual," the latter afterward complained that Emerson could talk of nothing but *The Dial*, and to no one but Ripley, his co-editor.

News of the "Groton Convention" made Bronson Alcott prick up his ears, and he went along with them the next morning. Henry Steele Commager pictures the four on their way, "their transcendental banners fluttering in the breeze, their high talk drifting in the dust across the open fields."

They found the town of Groton swarming with reformers of all sorts. But it was the most backward-seeming fold, the "Come-Outers" from Cape Cod, who held ministers and churches, creeds and dogmas in disdain, who most impressed the visitors from West Roxbury. The Bible, they said, was just a good book—transcriptions of the Word, not the Word itself, for that was written in the living heart. The "Come-Outers" also rejected the Christian Sacraments. "All our meals," they said, "are the Lord's Supper, if we eat with a right heart." Ripley and Parker felt that these unlettered men and women had reached "Truths" which wise and learned men hesitated to proclaim.

Other professions made at the Groton Convention bewildered sincere inquirers. Some of those who attended were fanatical and bigoted; others, filled with sheer error. And some made the visitors from West Roxbury smile. Joseph Palmer attached an undue significance to his beard. He said God had given it to him, so it would be a sin to trim it, damnation to remove it. There was a young Mr. Dyer who insisted, "Truth is Christ, and Christ is Truth, and if we but knew all Truth this body would never die but be caught up and spiritualized." Queerest of all were the Millerites. They could prove by mathematical demonstrations that the Second Coming would take place in 1843; and they were zealous in warning their fellows of this stupendous event. As with the Atom Bomb, time could be running short.

Whatever their reflections on the long walk back to West Roxbury, the Groton Convention marked a milestone, for soon afterward both Parker and Ripley crossed the line where speculation ends, and action begins. Parker's sermons were no longer mildly heretical; he now frankly denounced the Unitarian Orthodoxy. The Church was narrow, said Mr. Parker; it was formal, polite; concerned with the letter and not with the spirit. The ministry was more anxious that their flocks should walk in the proper paths of dogma than that they should reach the goal of salvation. With the Come-Outers at Groton, Theodore Parker held that Christianity was not dependent upon dogma or ritual. Religion was rather a matter of right living and faith in the impulse that compelled a man to live nobly. Such faith came from God, the Over-Soul.

As Mrs Ripley had said, Theodore Parker was creating a stiff breeze about him. It soon would blow him out of the Spring Street Church in

West Roxbury, and into the old Melodeon on Washington Street in Boston. Unlike his scholarly friend George Ripley, and lacking Emerson's philosophic detachment, Theodore Parker loved the Unitarian Church, and to the end he labored to reform her from within.

For Ripley, also, the Groton Convention became a turning point; and as summer drew to fall his reluctance to return to his pulpit increased. In his experience the union of labor and culture had proved ideal. If only he might, as Dr. Channing had suggested, lead a group of people into the same happy way of life, surely he would have no reason to reproach himself for leaving the ministry?

When Dr. Ripley returned to his parish in Boston, his mind was made up.

4.

On receiving their pastor's resignation in May, 1840, the proprietors of the Purchase Street Church urged him to carry on. They feared that if Dr. Ripley left, many of his parishioners might follow him; and they foresaw that if this happened, the remainder of the society might be "too bereft" to support a pastor. Never one to shirk responsibility, Dr. Ripley agreed to stay, on the understanding that he should be released after a definite period even if inconvenient to the proprietors. It was a polite notice to the effect that the time had come to find someone to replace him.

During the summer Dr. Ripley's desire "for a reform in the philosophy of the day" had turned into determination to lead such a reform. On October first, soon after his return to Boston, he wrote a frank and open letter to his congregation, in which he said that unless a minister felt free to speak on all subjects uppermost in his mind without fear of incurring the charge of heresy or compromising the interests of his parishioners, he could never do "justice to himself, to his people, or the truth . . ." He then went on, without the slightest hesitation, to declare himself a Transcendentalist.

"What a brave thing Mr. Ripley has done," wrote Emerson to Margaret Fuller. "He stands now at the head of the Church militant and his step cannot be without an important sequel." As Perry Miller points out in *The Transcendentalists*, Ripley's resignation from the Purchase

Street Church took even more courage than Emerson's departure from the Second Church, because Ripley was an older man and took more of a risk for his own and his wife's future. Moreover, there was no real quarrel between Dr. Ripley and his congregation. It was rather that he could not believe their truest interests would be promoted by "being compelled to listen to one with whom you feel a diminished sympathy."

There is reason to suppose that he would not have tendered his resignation if he had not determined to found a community at Brook Farm; for soon after their return from West Roxbury, he and his wife set about promoting the plan. The times were in tune for it; as Emerson said, "We were all a little mad that winter. Not a man of us that did not have a plan for some new Utopia in his pocket." The madness took strange forms, and even Emerson with his enthusiasm for the "Newness" was appalled by the lack of restraint among those who foregathered in November at the Chardon Street Convention. "Madmen, madwomen, men with beards, Dunkers, Muggletonians, Come-Outers, Groaners, Agrarians, Seventh-Day Baptists, Quakers, Abolitionists, Calvinists, Unitarians, and Philosophers—all came successfully to the top, and seized their moment, if not their hour, where in to chide, or pray, or preach, or protest."

The philosophers were scattered, in or around Boston, so that meetings of "the Club" were difficult to arrange. Fortunately, Miss Elizabeth Peabody opened a foreign bookshop on West Street in August; and the Transcendentalists quickly fell into the habit of dropping in there to browse, and to discuss the dawn of the "New Day."

Elizabeth is the eldest of the subjects of Louise Hall Tharp's triple biography, *The Peabody Sisters of Salem,* and the most outstanding female of the three. She was the eldest of six children; and it appears that she had been deeply concerned about her mother's suffering in pregnancy and childbirth. The death of a baby sister whom Elizabeth tended when she herself was still in the impressionable age, made motherhood seem as grim to her as war to a maimed veteran. Blessed with vitality, a vigorous intellect, and masculine drive, as a brook leaps a dam in spring, Elizabeth found a natural outlet in teaching little children.

Education came first and last with Miss Peabody. By 1840 it was her conviction that it might be possible to promote the millennium by instructing the mature as well as the young. It followed that Dr. Ripley's plan—to found a noble community in West Roxbury—had a staunch supporter in Miss Peabody. The more so, because the great Dr. Channing had cherished the idea for half a dozen years.

Elizabeth, an unsought, unpaid secretary, content to cash rich spiritual dividends, had served Dr. William Ellery Channing. Was not the good life, Miss Peabody echoed, a process aiming at perfection? The perfection of civilization? Presently Miss Peabody saw Bronson Alcott dealing with a child; and recognized a genius who surpassed herself "in the general conception of this divinest of arts"—education of the very young. She brought Alcott and Dr. Channing together, and secured "The Great Awakener's" blessing on the school which she helped Alcott open in the Masonic Temple, on Tremont Street, in September 1834. Bronson Alcott, today a recognized pioneer in primary education, shocked the parents of his pupils, because he encouraged little children to talk too freely about themselves. The talks, which Mr. Alcott made very agreeable, were also "calculated to excite various moral emotions." The confidences he called forth from the uncalculating little innocents embarrassed their parents. So it is not to be wondered at, that parents soon withdrew Mr. Alcott's pupils.

Long after the expectation of a salary could have seemed likely, Elizabeth Peabody remained at Bronson Alcott's side; and she almost wore her eyes out copying notes of Mr. Alcott's conversations with the indiscreet tots. In the words of her biographer, "Records of a School brought recognition to Alcott. To Elizabeth Peabody it brought both recognition and misfortune." James Monroe published it in 1835, and when the book was receiving recognition, a warehouse burned. Elizabeth had to bear, personally, the financial loss.

Disaster and Miss Peabody—old bedfellows—again proved incompatible. Soon Boston people were telling one another that her new bookshop on West Street was the liveliest spot in town. In any case, it was a refuge for her friends. Hawthorne came often, to woo her youngest sister, and to dissuade Sophia from that fear of marriage in which wellmeaning Mrs. Peabody had ensnared Elizabeth. Horace Mann came less often, which did not displease Mary Peabody, the second sister. A trifle jealous of Mr. Mann's admiration for Lizzie, who shared his zeal for education, Mary preferred to assist the secretary of the newly created State Board of Education in his office. It seemed a more propitious spot for courtship. Mary could not forget that she had once discovered her elder sister stroking Mr. Mann's forehead; although Lizzie explained the poor man had a bad headache, Mary had found this strange behavior.

Although she thoroughly enjoyed the other notables who patronized the bookshop, her daughter's suitors—even if genius was written on their brows—did not please Mrs. Peabody. She much preferred the elderly shoppers. Sandy-haired, blue-eyed Mr. Alcott was so serene and kind! His "Orphic Sayings," recently published in the first issue of *The Dial*, echoed the noble gropings of a prophet, even if neither she nor anyone else quite knew what they meant. Sober-sided Dr. Ripley, who was continually buying foreign books, was a most valued customer. Mrs. Peabody surmised that he kept his friend, Theodore Parker, posted about the recent shipments from abroad. For whenever the shelves were freshly stocked, the pastor of the Spring Street Church in West Roxbury appeared, and added to his extensive foreign library. Most delightful of all, Dr. Channing came in every morning to read the newspaper. And the new prophet, Mr. Emerson, commuting from Concord, often stopped by. As some Transcendentalist wag said, even Mr. Emerson needed refreshment before engaging in another "Astral Errand."

The philosophers held Elizabeth in affectionate respect. Yet Miss Peabody sadly lacked the sophistication and style which are the traditional requisites of a mistress of a *salon*. Her appearance was not prepossessing. She was much too fat, and inclined to be careless in her dress. Then, her manners were often blunt, and she was often too outspoken. Miss Peabody interfered with people and tried to domineer over them.

More interested in education and reforms of various kinds than in promoting herself, Miss Peabody was completely generous and unselfseeking; and therein lay her charm. The Christian spirit—and Elizabeth Peabody was imbued with it—is ever most attractive.

The Sages found profit in conversing with the gifted ladies they encountered in the bookshop; a carefully selected group of Sibyls were included in the meetings of "the Club." Miss Peabody, of course, and her sister, Sophia, engaged to Hawthorne, or about to be. Mrs. Ripley; and for George's sake, his austere sister, Marianne. But Margaret Fuller was the brightest luminary in the female galaxy.

Miss Fuller's father, Timothy Fuller, a Republican lawyer, had crammed learning into her adolescent head as fast as goose is stuffed for *pâté de foie gras*. Ever after, in moments of fatigue, Miss Fuller fell prey to spinal affliction, nervous disorder, and severe headaches. One might add that she was at all times arrogant, and an intellectual snob. Yet she was a woman of generous impulses; and since her father's death in 1835 she had dedicated herself to the education of her brothers, and to the promotion of literature and the arts. Now—since the spring of 1840—Miss Fuller, assisted by Emerson, edited *The Dial*.

Emerson met Margaret Fuller in 1835, and in the *Memoir* which he, James Freeman Clarke, and William Henry Channing published after her death in 1852, he recalls his first impression: "She had a face and frame that would indicate fulness and tenacity of life. She was rather under the middle height; her complexion was fair with strong fair hair. She was then, as always carefully and becomingly dressed; and of lady-like self-possession. For the rest, her appearance had nothing prepossessing. Her extreme plainness, a trick of incessantly opening and shutting her eyelids, the nasal tones of her voice, all repelled; and I said to myself, we shall never get far." But they did—although perhaps not as far as Margaret hoped.

Meanwhile, Miss Peabody's "Reading Parties," received as a startling innovation in Salem, where she introduced this form of entertainment, soon found an audience among Boston's elite. Elizabeth Peabody, with her usual generosity, was quick to recognize a greater talent than her own in Miss Fuller's "Conversations," a form of lecturing briefly, which Bronson Alcott had imported from England. The audience was expected to participate by asking questions or offering germane remarks. Margaret mastered that manner of improving the mind to such purpose that Miss Fuller's "Conversations" were attracting wider interest that fall than those of Mr. Alcott. So Miss Peabody, though the recognized lady lecturer in New England—the first of outstanding talent, it was said, since Anne Hutchinson—insisted that Miss Fuller should hold her "Conversations" in the foreign bookshop on West Street. The place was convenient for the audience; and the arrangement proved beneficial for trade. Miss Fuller's remarks created a demand for foreign publications, and Miss Peabody satisfied it.

5.

Miss Peabody was to be a staunch supporter of Brook Farm in its Transcendental phase and the Ripleys received enthusiastic encouragement from her and her friends when they returned from West Roxbury in September, 1840. But it was to Ralph Waldo Emerson that George Ripley looked most fondly for guidance toward the fulfillment of his "high hope." Emerson, "the Mind" with the greatest sphere of influence; Emerson, the major prophet of the new sect. Were not all the tenets of Transcendentalism to be found in *Nature?* Had not Emerson rallied the scattered forces of reform with a clarion call—"The Divinity School Address"? George Ripley and his wife went to Concord, and propounded their plan.

A year and a half before Ripley approached him, Emerson had meditated upon the spiritual solace which a man gained from hard work on a farm, and how this might benefit society. In May 1839 he had written in his *Journal:* "I think we ought to have bodily labor, each man. Why else this rapid impoverishing which brings every man to the presence of the fact that bread is by the sweat of the face, and why this continual necessity in which we all stand of bodily labor, by walking, riding, fencing, pitching, shooting, or billiards, if not by plowing and mowing? . . . Labor makes solitude and makes society. It kills foppery, shattered nerves, and all kinds of emptiness. It makes life solid." These sentiments reflect the sense of physical well-being which many persons feel after a hard day's work outdoors in May. However, Mr. Emerson recovered from the urge to till the soil before the enthusiasm spread among his friends. Like the child who carries the measles to school, he looked about ruefully at the epidemic he had helped to spread. "Is it not pedantry to insist every man should be a farmer?" he asked himself in 1840. "Shall he cast away his skill and usefulness to go bungle with hoe and harrow?"

Mr. Emerson, always kind to his friends and hospitable to their ideas, invited the Ripleys, together with Margaret Fuller and Bronson Alcott, to meet at his house in Concord on October seventeenth.

Although he had his listeners at arm's length, George Ripley was not at his best that afternoon. Perhaps he was put off by the two doughty conversationalists, Miss Fuller and Mr. Alcott. But Mr. Emerson, as usual, was always a good listener.

Although he often appears cold and aloof in his letters and *Journal,* Emerson's personal magnetism was so intense that when he came into a room it was like the coming of a burst of sunlight. Yet he was both plain and awkward; his head was too small, he had a curious way of smiling with closed eyes. But even such mannerisms attracted. When aroused, his imagination took fire, and he spoke the wisdom of a philosopher in the tongue of a poet. At such moments Mr. Emerson seemed to young Julian Hawthorne, who saw him many years later, "the most beautiful of men," although Emerson's complexion was then "deeply seamed."

Picture him seated in a characteristic pose this October afternoon— with long legs crossed, and one flexible foot hitched behind the other ankle—bestowing encouragement on all present. But as his friend propounded his West Roxbury plan, Emerson's gracious response turned to disappointment and to ennui. He felt that although George Ripley spoke with the greatest simplicity and gravity, he preached "as to a congregation of Dr. Ripleys."

Miss Fuller generously refrained from throwing any cold water. She sincerely wished him "the aid of some equal and faithful friend." Privately she felt that Dr. Ripley was not the man for such an undertaking: "His mind though that of a captain, is not that of a conqueror."

Ripley must have dwelt too emphatically on the monetary aspects of his Social Plan, thereby lending it a sordid tinge in the eyes of the three leading "Minds." Alcott ever afterward referred to Brook Farm in terms of extreme condescension. The benign, dignified "Missionary of Culture" never was overly concerned with the practicalities of life. He never worried, for instance, about paying tradesmen.

Emerson was always above reproach in such matters; but he, also, disliked Ripley's tone. "I wished to be convinced, to be thawed, to be made nobly mad before the kindlings before my eye of a new dawn of human piety. But this scheme was arithmetic and comfort; this was a hint borrowed from the Tremont House and United States Hotel; a rage in our poverty to live rich and gentleman-like; an anchor to lee-ward against a change of weather; a prudent forecast on the probable issue of the great questions of Pauperism and Poverty. And not once could I be inflamed, but sat aloof and thoughtless; my voice faltered and fell. It was not the cave of persecution which is the place of spiritual power, but only a room in the Astor House hired for the Transcendentalists."

What a pity that George Ripley could not have seen this diatribe in Emerson's *Journal*. He would have been spared disillusionment in regard to his friend's intentions. As it was, he and Sophia serenely went on with their plans, ignorant of the chilliness of the leading "Mind." Weekly gatherings were held at their house to discuss their project; and when plans seemed nebulous, Mrs. Ripley sustained high expectations with hot baked potatoes and cold beer. All agreed that Mrs. Ripley's enthusiasm was magnificent. Her will for the enterprise strengthened many.

As always happens when money is scarce, the men in business, already in debt, lacked confidence and enterprise. Want followed hard on the heels of the working man. Hardship and unemployment had increased year by year since 1837. Conscientious men throughout the United States were deeply concerned. Competitive industry seemed to have failed; it had not provided security to capitalist or laborer. Some speculated about the advantages of a planned economy. Today, when the whole free world is still recovering from the impact of Hitler's "planned economy," and rallying strength against Soviet Russia's threat on similar terms, the effort of the social reformers in our country a century ago seems very small. They were not revolutionary; they entertained no hidden intention to overthrow the Constitution of the United States. The leaders, George Ripley, Adin Ballou, and the others, hoped to reform society by example on a small scale; and each community began with a small group of friends who all shared in the leader's faith and enthusiasm.

There were to be some thirty or forty such communities in the next decade, and the movement which inspired these experimental communities had a British tradition. In 1824, Robert Owen, founder of a successful Communism in New Lanark, Scotland, determined to establish a similar community in America. He bought Harmony on the Wabash River, a thirty-thousand-acre tract, part in Indiana and part in Illinois. The Rappites, the thrifty and industrious sect of German Christian Communists who owned Harmony, were anxious to move back to Pennsylvania. The New Harmony which Owen established was modelled on his communism in New Lanark. The natural thrift and industry of the Scot must have been a hidden asset, for although his first experiment proved successful and attracted wide attention, New Harmony fell slowly into bankruptcy. Owen's reputation as a businessman was held in such wide estimation, however, and he was so energetic in spreading his propaganda in America, that several communities were founded in the United States on his pattern.

The New Harmony experiment was a latter-day episode in the life of Robert Owen; and by the time the New England reformers turned to a planned economy New Harmony was a mere legend. Yet the experiment had established a precedent. Although the Shakers and Quakers antedated the New Harmonites, theirs was the first purely secular form of Communitarian experiment; and the gradual secularization of the Communitarian ideal was an accomplished fact in 1840, when the Ripleys were planning Brook Farm.

Boston people soon were talking about "the New Harmony to be established in West Roxbury." To recall such talk is misleading, because the Ripleys were not planning another imitation of Robert Owen's Harmony at New Lanark. They had conceived a purebred New England community in Brook Farm. When it came into being the only foreign influence was that of absentee and detached god-parents, the Transcendental Philosophers of Europe.

By one of those paradoxes which occur in life, a book was published in 1840 which would gradually transform Transcendental Brook Farm into a "Phalanx"—a citadel of the philosophy of the French social reformer, Francois Marie Charles Fourier. He was already dead, and already he was rated abroad as a somewhat erratic thinker. He might have remained unknown in America if it had not been for Albert Brisbane. This young man was imbued with a passion for social theory, and endowed with a talent for propaganda. After two years study under Fourier in Paris, he had returned to the United States to disseminate his teacher's doctrines. In 1840 he published *Association, or a Concise Exposition of the Practical Part of Fourier's Social Science*, more familiarly known as *The Social Destiny of Man*.

Undoubtedly the Ripleys read it, as they followed the trend in foreign social and literary thought. But the embryonic significance of the publication was not immediately recognized by them or their fellow reformers. The first notice of the book pertinent to the story of Brook Farm was that of Sophia Ripley in *The Dial*, a year or more after publication.

Although his motives were on the side of the common man, Brisbane was to prove himself almost as talented as Goebbels. But few realized his talent for propaganda when Brisbane first introduced the fantastic social philosophy of Charles Fourier in America; and the Ripleys would have been astonished indeed if they could have foreseen that they themselves would one day become "Fourierites."

In 1837, George Ripley had lamented that he "heard nothing from morning until night but the crash of misfortune and the ruin of hopes." In the fall of 1840 neither the lingering depression nor the Fourier-Brisbane publication interested him especially. He and Sophia had their own ideas of what the ideal community should be like; and they planned it on a small and delightfully personal scale. Already, they had persuaded their hosts of the past few summers, Charles and Maria Ellis, to allow the experiment to take place on their property—Brook Farm. From an agricultural point of view, it was not a happy choice. In his fondness for the place, George Ripley forgot that his beloved hillsides and fields were mainly composed of gravelly soil. The crops he had helped to raise had proved adequate for a household. He expected the lean acreage to enrich a community.

6.

It was generally assumed that Ralph Waldo Emerson was to be one of the subscribers to the Brook Farm Institute; whereas the leading "Mind" had decided that although community life might be a fine solution for other people, it was not for him.

George Ripley failed to gauge Emerson's temperamental antipathy to group activities; and Emerson, sensing that he had placed himself in a false position, grew increasingly concerned. On October eighteenth, 1840, the day after the Ripleys' visit to Concord, he thrashed the question in his *Journal:* "Shall I raise the siege of this hencoop, and march baffled away to Babylon? It seems to me that to do so were to dodge the problem I am set to solve, and to hide my impotency in the thick of the crowd. I can see, too, afar, that I should not find myself more than now —no, not so much in that select, but not by me selected fraternity. Moreover, to join this body would be to traverse all my trumpeted theory, and the instinct which spoke from it, that one man is counterpoise to a city, that a man is stronger than a city, that his solitude is more prevalent and beneficient than the concert of crowds."

It was indeed awkward. It could be said that Mr. Emerson had encouraged the project, and so should feel a certain responsibility. Yet at the mere thought of living in such a community. Emerson was on the defensive; "All my repulsions play, all my quills rise and sharpen."

Knowing nothing of Emerson's inner feelings, Ripley wrote him a long letter on November ninth. After setting forth the aims of the Association, and the arrangements in progress to house it, Ripley shyly reminded his friend that his own tastes and habits disinclined him to community life. He, too, shared the inclination "for being independent of the world, and of every man in it." Ripley pointed out that he was in a position to rent the Ellis farm for himself; in which case, he added, "I should have a City of God, on a small scale of my own; and please God, I should hope one day to drive my own cart to market and sell greens." Instead he stood ready to sacrifice this private dream of heaven "in the hope of a great social good." He was very eager to learn Mr. Emerson's intention. He had to wait five weeks.

In the meantime, Emerson wrote Margaret Fuller exactly how he felt: "I have not quite decided not to go. But I hate that the least weight would hang on my decision." By mid-December George Ripley's "coadjutors" had become numerous and Emerson realized, with deep relief, that his own defection would not halt the enterprise.

Emerson promptly decided not to subscribe to the Association. He had reached the decision "very slowly"; he might almost say "penitentially." With serene detachment he now congratulated his friend, Ripley, on a design which was both noble and humane. It proceeded, he saw plainly, "from a manly and expanding heart and mind that makes me and all men its friends and debtors."

The bestowal of his blessing did not satisfy Emerson's conscience, and he added with winning candor: "The ground of my decision is almost purely personal to myself. I have some remains of skepticism in regard to the general practicability of the plan, but these have not much weight with me. That which determines me is the conviction that the Community is not good for me. Whilst I see that it may hold many inducements for others, it has little to offer me, which, with resolution, I cannot procure for myself. It seems to me that it would not be worth my while to make the difficult exchange of my property in Concord for a share in the New Household." Or, as he had put it in a letter to his brother, he could get the same advantages at home without pulling down his own house.

Emerson had declared his belief in the virtue of manual labor in public and in private; and he did try to practice what he preached. But if it had not been for the helpful hoe of his young friend, Henry Thoreau, the vegetable garden which Mr. Emerson laid out so conscientiously each spring would have come to little. In this letter to Ripley, the subject had to come up, but when he came to it, Emerson's fluent thought stammered; "The principles in which I wish to amend my domestic life," he continued, "are in acquiring habits of regular manual labor, and in . . . ameliorating or abolishing in my house the condition of hired menial service."

Mr. Emerson's effort to ameliorate the lot of their domestics was sincere, but the results were not happy. Mr. and Mrs. Emerson invited their two maids to share their table, to address the master and mistress as Waldo and Lydian. But after the first highly uncomfortable meal, the two Irishwomen—an aunt and niece—always found some excuse not to sit down at table with their "betters."

Emerson could not end his long letter to Ripley without polishing the last grains of guilt from his star-bright conscience: "If the Community is not good for me, neither am I for it. I do not look on myself as a valuable member of any community which is not either very large or very small and select. I fear that yours would not find me as profitable and pleasant an associate as I should wish to be, and as so important a project seems imperatively to require in all its constituents."

The Ripleys were sadly disappointed. Their hope that Mr. Emerson might yet change his mind lingered on.

In other respects the Ripleys' Social Plan was progressing well. They had won the moral support of Theodore Parker, Orestes Brownson, and that of two possible participants, John S. Dwight and Adin Ballou. Gentle little Dwight dreamed of adding song and music to the daily round of some association, but he had not yet left his pulpit in Northampton. Ballou was a greatly beloved Universalist minister, and an enthusiastic supporter of Association. But he believed that success would be furthered by an avowal on the part of those uniting. "They should declare themselves abolitionists, anti-orthodox, opposed to war and intoxicating drinks . . ." Ballou, also a pioneer in the support of woman's equal rights, typified what Sophia Ripley referred to as "one of the more fanatical men." How different his platform from that of her George, who "wished to avoid the least appearance of coercion, and to depend altogether on the spirit of fraternity."

Dr. Ripley and his coadjutors were not against anything, even slavery. Although in their fashion they were as Abolitionist as William Lloyd Garrison, they regarded slavery as just one more manifestation of the evils of competition. Society must be reorganized before slavery could be abolished.

While plans were still in the making, a friendly separation took place between those who differed with Ripley. Adin Ballou established a company of "substantial reformers" at Hopedale. Another Society settled in Northampton. Massachusetts was breaking out all over with such hopeful spots!

On the last day of January, 1841, the proprietors of the Purchase Street Church, finally, but "most affectionately and regretfully," approved their pastor's retirement. Their sobersided minister had turned radical reformer, and they could not go along with him. Perhaps if glowing coals had fallen from his lips to ignite a reform within the

Church, differences might have been solved. But the "Child of Channing" was not a Channing—he was less of a priest and more of a man, to reverse his own phrase. Even his bewildered parishioners did not want to pick a quarrel with Dr. Ripley. His congregation was genuinely sorry to lose him. Their regret augured well for a mere "captain"—as Margaret Fuller had dubbed him—who aimed to found a Community for the benefit and education of mankind.

Dr. Ripley's farewell address, delivered on March twenty-eighth, was judged a model of dignified speech. It was so well liked that the Church had it printed. In summing up, Dr. Ripley explained that he had found it impossible to hold himself back from the forward trend in thought; and declared himself "a peace man, a temperance man, an abolitionist, a transcendentalist, a friend of radical reform in our social institutions." With his usual discretion George Ripley did not refer to the recent controversy or his part in it. In conclusion, he reminded the congregation that principles which he regarded as "the essence and reason of Christianity" had not proved acceptable to parishioners or proprietors of the Purchase Street Church. He then announced that his resignation, previously tendered, would that day be carried into effect.

Within the week—on April second or so—George Ripley, his wife and sister, and some fifteen others drove to the Ellis Farm in West Roxbury.

The short and highly wrought idyl of Brook Farm had begun.

A SEASON III IN UTOPIA

IN UTOPIA

↣↣↣↣↣↣↣↣↣↣↣↣↣↣↣↣↣↣↣↣↣≻≺↢↢↢↢↢↢↢↢↢↢↢↢↢↢↢↢↢↢↢↢↢

Transcendental Brook Farm

NO FORMAL DETAILS, NOT EVEN THE TERMS OF THE PURCHASE, HAD BEEN arranged when the Ripleys took possession of the Ellis farm. They just drove out to West Roxbury and moved in, together with the companions their enthusiasm had mustered. Plans and articles of association could be worked out later; but they would begin to practice their new creed.

In a letter to Emerson of November ninth—five months before—Ripley had forecast the spirit with which they now went to work. "Our objects, as you know, are to insure a more natural union between intellectual and manual labor than now exists; to combine the thinker and the worker as far as possible in the same individual; to guarantee the highest mental freedom by providing all with labor adapted to their tastes and talents, and securing to them the fruits of their industry; to do away with the necessity of menial services by opening the benefits of education and the profits of labor to all; and thus to prepare a society of liberal, intelligent, and cultivated persons, whose relations with each other would permit a more simple and wholesome life than can be led amidst the pressure of our more competitive institutions."

In the last paragraph of this over-long and repetitious epistle, he had summed up his immediate purpose in more concise terms. He aimed to found a Community where "thought would preside over the operations of labor, and labor would contribute to the expansion of thought." It was his hope to promote "industry without drudgery, and true equality without its vulgarity."

There was little time for such formulas, now that they had moved in. One and all had to roll up their sleeves and pitch in. Mr. Ripley looked to young William Brockway Allen for leadership in barnyard, pasture and field. That sturdy young man from New Hampshire lately had managed Theodore Parker's farm in West Roxbury. No doubt he had joined in the talk when the two divines lingered in the Spring Street barnyard to conclude an argument, and so learned of Mr. Ripley's Social Plan. In any case, Allen saw his chance, resigned his job, and went to work at Brook Farm. This proved a stroke of luck for the Ripleys; but how Mr. Parker felt on losing such a reliable helper is a matter for surmise. Mr. Parker, who had given his blessing to the Ripleys' enterprise, may have consoled himself for his loss with the reflection that his Transcendental friends had at least one experienced farmer among them.

The place was a dairy farm, with eight milch cows, pigs, and chickens to be cared for. Mr. and Mrs. Ellis, enthusiastic supporters of the enterprise, generously lent their property to the Ripleys without rent. But they left it in a mess. One Ellen Barker, a domestic, was sent ahead to clean the house; and foresighted William Allen neatened up the barn. Delighted with the transformation they had wrought, Mrs. Ripley reckoned that William and Ellen "had gone through the hardest and most disagreeable work that any of them would ever have to do."

Mrs. Minot Pratt and her three children arrived with the three Ripleys. Her husband, a printer and a foreman in the office of *The Christian Register*, would follow after severing his business connections. Pratt had set up George Ripley's early articles for *The Christian Register*, and he had since come to share his Transcendental views. Now he, too, had burned his bridges, and cast in his lot with the Ripleys at Brook Farm. In appearance he was a large, finely formed man, whose "serenity welled over in genial smiles." She was a plain, kind motherly woman. Faithful and fervent workers both, they soon inspired confidence and respect. Nathaniel Hawthorne pronounced the Minot Pratts "the very pattern of New England matrimony."

When Hawthorne joined the Community on April twelfth, he invested his savings in two shares of the joint stock of the enterprise at $500 a share, in the hope that membership in Brook Farm would provide the means of supporting a wife. He and Sophia had been engaged for more than two years, and there was still no adequate financial basis for marriage. "Think that I am gone before to prepare a home for my Dove, and will return for her, all in good time," he wrote her the day after his arrival; and again, a few days later, "There is a brook so near the house that we shall be able to hear its ripple in the summer evenings, and whenever we lie awake in the summer nights."

Sensing that Mr. Hawthorne was more interested in marrying Sophia Peabody and writing masterpieces than he was in abolishing the evils of competition or social reform, the Farmers were more enthusiastic about the talents of one Frank Farley than those of the great writer. According to Miss Peabody, who hovered over the tiny Community like a nervous mother hen, Farley was the very prototype of their ideal. Farley knew how to do "every species of work, from cooking and other kinds of domestic labor through all the process of farming and dealing with livestock." Such accomplishments were as rare as they were useful among these amateur harbingers; but what made Frank "the crown of all" in their eyes was the solace he found in the Fine Arts. In leisure hours, Frank drew; and he could also read aloud with "histrionic beauty."

After tea, the proud and happy Farmers insisted on taking Mr. Hawthorne to the barn to see the cows foddered. "There is a most vicious animal in the yard, a Transcendental heifer belonging to Margaret Fuller," he wrote in his *Journal* on April thirteenth. "She tries to rule every other animal, and a guard has to be placed over her while the other animals come in and out. (Whether the fact that the creature belonged to Miss Fuller, or that it was a Transcendental animal, caused it to be so undesirable a companion is not announced.)"

Though he mocked in private, Mr. Hawthorne was outwardly amenable to the union of culture and labor. Now that he was at Brook Farm he stood ready to convert himself "into a milkmaid." But he prayed to Heaven that Mr. Ripley might assign him the kindliest cows in the herd, else he would perform his duties with fear and trembling.

He was put to work at once. "After breakfast," Hawthorne recorded on April fourteenth, "Mr. Ripley put a four pronged instrument into my hands, which he gave me to understand is called a pitchfork; and he and Mr. Farley being armed with similar weapons, we all three commenced a gallant attack upon a heap of manure . . ."

Two days later Hawthorne boasted, "I have milked a cow." But within the week he was grumbling ominously: "I have read no newspaper, and hardly remember who is President and feel as if I had no

more concern with what other people trouble themselves about than if
I had lived on another planet."

William Brockway Allen, like Nathaniel Hawthorne, never would feel
wholly at ease among the Farmers. The New Hampshire farm-bred boy
and the great American novelist had one characteristic in common—
each had the professional approach. The idyllic atmosphere of Transcendental Brook Farm, though delightful, was not the right climate for
a young man of ambition. Though Hawthorne could laugh about it, his
notebook contains many testimonials of his increasing frustration. If
this was the Ideal Community, why was there no time, no place, for a
writer to write?

No such immediate and direct frustration perplexed Allen. Brook
Farm offered him a wider acreage to till than that of Mr. Parker on
Spring Street. To be treated with respect by such a scholarly person as
Mr. Ripley was highly flattering; although the talk at table was hard to
keep up with, and may well have bewildered better educated persons, it
inspired in Allen the desire to improve the mind.

Contentment and optimism ran high in William's breast that first
week in May; and on the third he began a long letter to his sweetheart,
Miss Sylvia Farrar of Westmoreland, New Hampshire. Apparently
their courtship had not yet reached the stage of endearment, for William addressed the woman of his choice with restraint:

Brook Farm, West Roxbury, Mass.
May 3, 1841

"My dear Friend:
I have thought of writing you a letter giving you a description of the
place & etc. for your amusement and improvement. I shall first give you
a description of the Farm and buildings. There are about two hundred
acres of land including mowing, pasturing, tillage, and wood land. It
is situated on the road to Newton about 1-½ miles from Spring Street.
It is beautifully diversified with hills and valleys there is a large meadow
on it which is partially surrounded with hills, some of which are covered with shrubs and trees, others are cultivated with various crops,
others are occupied as a pasture for the cows. We have not planted
much yet, the season is very backward, we have however planted ½
bushel of peas and ten bushel of potatoes; the peas are up, we intend to
plant some corn tomorrow, we shall plant ten or 12 acres this year in
all. The house is a large two-story one painted white with green blinds,
standing on the rising ground overlooking the meadow and babling

brook as it winds its way towards the River. There are four rooms on
the lower floor of the house, connected with the main house is a back
kitchen, workhouse, Chaise house etc. We have a very large barn with
a cellar to it opening on the south East side, this is occupied principly
as a stable for the Cows, Oxen, Horses, Pigs &c. We have at present
nine cows two oxen two Horses and four pigs."

The house Allen described is the Ellis farmhouse, the only dwelling
on the property at that time. It has since been pulled down. But the
Lutheran Orphanage which stands on the same spot today was built on
the same foundations; and although the Orphanage is lacking in the
warmth of an old farmhouse, there is still a broad hall with a door at
each end, that runs the length of the house. Perhaps it is not very different from the hall which the Farmers immediately lined with open
bookshelves—the place where Mr. Ripley, eager to share his rare English, French, and German books with everyone, spent his spare time
that spring, unpacking and arranging his library.

"Next comes our mode of life, I wish I could describe it to you as it
is," William continued, "but you are aware of the difficulty of giving a
perfect description of anything on paper (especially with us who are not
accustomed to writing) but I will give you as good a history of it as I
can. I will first state the members which compose the family, and give
you a short account of each.

"The present members of the family are Mr. and Mrs. Ripley, Rev.
Warren Burton, Mr. Nathaniel Haughthorn,"—spelling, punctuation,
and impulsive use of capitals, all are William's—"Mr. Graves, D. Farley,
Mr. Odion, Mr. Loid Fuller, Mr. Newcomb, Tuckerman, and Grace
Somebody, I don't know who, for I have not hear her called by any
other name yet, and whether she has any other or not is more than I
know, besides these there are two small boys one of which is a nephew
of Mrs. Ripley, the other is a son of Mrs. Barker the woman which I
spoke of in my former letter.

"Mr. Ripley is about thirty or thirty five years of age,"—actually, he
was over forty—"tall and well proportioned, very pleasant and agreeable
in all his ways. The same also may be said of Mrs. Ripley, she is really
angelic in her appearance and manners, they are a lovely pair. Mr. Burton is about forty years old, there is nothing very remarkable in his appearance, he is a literary man, he has written several books one of which
is called the District School as it was. Mr. Haughthorn is about 26 or 8
years of age, well proportioned fair features and pleasant manners. He
also is the author of several works one of which is called Grandfather's

Chair giving a description of it for several generations &c. These Gentlemen have been liberally educated that is they have been through College.

"Mr. Farley is about thirty, short and not very thick set rather dark with black hair and eyes, he is naturally active and wity, can suit himself to almost any sort of company and can entertain them with novel stories and wity sayings as well as one in ten or perhaps in ten times ten. Mr. Odion is a young man only 17–18 years old, he has been here but three days, so that I am not so well acquainted with him as with the others, for that reason I will not attempt to describe him. Mr. Fuller is a young lad about 14, very large of his age and as *awkward* as he is large. Mr. Tuckerman is about the age of Fuller quite small, bright, active and wity, he was sent here from Boston to improve his health, he is troubled with weak eyes. Fuller was sent here because nobody else could make anything of him.

"As to our manner of life, I will now try to describe it, I will first inform you how we spend a day in the first place. Mr. Farley and I rise about 4 o'clock and make two fires one in the kitchen and the other in the parlor, Farley then blows a horn at a quarter before 5, all hands then turn out to milk and take care of the cattle and Horses and pigs while the rest milk. All things being put in order at the barn we return to the Woodshed and pull off our boots frocks &c, and prepare for breakfast which is ready at half past 6 o'clock, after breakfast we talk a while and then prepare for the labours of the forenoon by putting on our coarse boots, blue frocks &c. We then proceed to carting manure or such work as is to be done. The way these literary characters appear in a barnyard shoveling is a perfect caution to all labouring men. We work till about ½ past 11 o'clock then all hands turn out put up the team feed the cows pigs &c. and prepare for dinner which is served up in fine stile at ½ past 12 o'clock. We eat and talk then talk and eat till we get enough, then we retire to the parlor or to our rooms as we please till 2 o'clock, then all hands are summoned to the fork, the shovel, hoe or spade as the case may be, the afternoon passes in all respects like the fore part of the day, we quit work in the field about 5 o'clock so as to get through with our work at the barn by sundown, the process of feeding Cows, milking &c. is the same at night as in the morning. Thus passes a day, or that is the way we spend a fair day, rainy days are somewhat different though the milking &c. goes on as usual, but after breakfast all go to their studies if they choose, sometimes I read and sometimes I go to work just as I happen to feel."

In the second and third parts of this long letter, dated May 7th and "Saturday evening," William rambled on about the late season, and his "dear Friend's" health, and then plunged into what must have seemed to her the heart of the matter; "Sylvia, I must say that I feel the most at home here of any place that I ever lived at. I enjoy very good health and feel very well contented considering my absence from you. I hope it will be so that you can come in the fall. I suppose you know that I spoke to your Father about it, though I think I did not tell you of it. He said that for his own part he was willing that his children should choose their own mates and live where they pleased." Since the parental consent was forthcoming, maybe Sylvia could overlook not being told of this important talk. Nevertheless, William must have been "uncommon uncommunicative," even for a New Englander.

Association with "these literary Characters" had inspired William to write Sylvia of the daily occurrences, and to write a little to her every day. Such a procedure, he remarked sagely, "assists a person very much. It not only helps them to write but it enables them to express their ideas much better."

But the Farm was closer to his heart, and the letter teems with vivid details about crops and barnyard. They had had "some snow here Monday but not enough to hurt peas though they were just coming up." They were getting along very well, considering all things. Though the weather continued lowering, they had a fine time planting sweet corn and beans one fine afternoon; and already had planted some two acres in all, and so got a good start despite the backward season. Mr. Ripley liked the horse Sylvia's father had sold him very much. "She lives like a Countess sure enough and that is the name which he has given her."

Apparently, Sylvia had her own reasons—as had Margaret Fuller—for doubting the advantages of "Community." She had not said No; but only her father has said Yes. So William wrote out a brief description of the principles of the Association for her consideration, promising a more definite account, sometime soon. "The first and great principle seems to be this, that people should labour for the good of others as well as for theirselves, that is they should live together like brothers, as no doubt it was the design of the Creator that they should. They have a constitution"—what they had was a tentative draft—"which prescribes the duty of the members. I have read the Articles but do not reckollect all of them. They are to raise a fund to build a house for the Institution and as many dwelling houses as are needed &c. All of the provisions are bought at wholesale by the Community and no charge will be made for the board of any individual belonging to the Society, a regular price is paid for every day's work that is done on the place by any person. One dollar is what they allow for every 10 hours work done by any person either man or woman but there shall be but 10 hours work paid for in one day. Each person is to choose his or her own employment as far as is practicable and all receive the same price for their labour. No charge shall be made for the board or schooling of any child under 12 years of age. These are some of the general ideas of this community but it is not established yet but they hope to get it organized this (Summer)."

In concluding, William confessed to his Sylvia that he had been to meeting, but the preacher, a Mr. Pierpont, had made him so very dull and sleepy that he had decided not to go to church "much more at present." He walked home with his brother, Abel, who, it seems, had taken over his former job. Abel and the rest of the folks at Spring Street restored William's spirits. "Write soon," he begged, "and ask your Father and Mother to write us, Wm. B. Allen."

From the first there was always more work than there were hands to do it. Yet the Directors of Brook Farm were so anxious to prove that labor was beneficial to the spirit if it suited the worker, that they allowed each person to choose his occupation. Mrs. Ripley chose to preside over the "Wash Room"—the laundry. Miss Ripley and Mrs. Pratt directed the housework. The ladies soon christened the farmhouse, "The Hive," because they were all as busy as bees.

Mr. Ripley went to work in the barnyard. He especially enjoyed milking. He said it was conducive to contemplation, "particularly when the cow's tail is looped up behind." All agreed that the dairy farm promised well; the yield increased day by day with regular feeding. Within a few weeks it had increased a third; and one of the young men drove to town every day to sell the surplus.

Mr. Ripley pitched in with Mr. Pratt; enthusiastic hands both, bossed by William Allen. Sophia boasted that her George did a harder day's work each day than the last and felt better than ever before. Probably William Allen was the only one who knew what he was about; and it is certain that Nathaniel Hawthorne preferred wielding a pen to digging with a pitchfork. Yet for a time he experienced moments of rare contentment.

"All the morning I have been at work under the blue sky on a hillside," Hawthorne recorded on May first. "Sometimes I have felt as if I were at work on the sky itself, though the material in which I wrought was ore from our gold mine. [The manure heap] . . . There is nothing so disagreeable or unseemly in this sort of toil as you think. It defiles the hands but not the soul. I do not believe I should be so patient here if I were not engaged in a righteous and heaven blessed way of life." But these tasks were not to his taste; and, as the days passed, his hope of leisure in which to write went glimmering. Some of the Farmers felt he had only himself to blame for his vexation. Mr. Hawthorne had refused to teach; in consequence he was allotted more than his share of Augean labor.

No sign of discontent marred his royal deportment, however. Mrs. Ripley found him "one to reverence, to admire with that deep admiration so refreshing to the soul." She called Hawthorne "Our prince— prince in everything—yet despising no labor and very athletic and able-bodied in the barnyard and field."

His own Sophia has recorded her first impressions of Nathaniel Hawthorne: "What a beautiful smile he has! He has a celestial expression." On another occasion, "He looked extremely handsome with sufficient sweetness in his face to supply the rest of the world and still leave the ordinary share to himself." And again: "He looked like the sun shining through a silver mist when he turned to say goodbye. It is a most wonderful face."

Admittedly, he looked with greater tenderness on his Dove than on mankind in general, but the portrait of Nathaniel Hawthorne in 1840 by Charles Osgood, in the Essex Institute in Salem, bears witness to the novelist's prince-like bearing and vivid presence.

At Brook Farm, the other Sophia, Mrs. Ripley, was bubbling over with enthusiasm for their new way of life. In an ecstatic letter to John S. Dwight, who was still tied to his pulpit in Northampton, and yearning to join his friends in West Roxbury, Mrs. Ripley declared, "More of laughing than of weeping we have had for the last few weeks, for a busy, merry household we are at Brook Farm."

According to Mrs. Ripley, the Farmers already felt established and perfectly at home in the country, and their relations to each other were "so natural and true" that they seemed to have "existed always." There was reason for encouragement. Thirteen now sat down to table in their large central kitchen; among them Lloyd Fuller, a younger brother of Margaret—the same 14-year-old "Mr. Fuller" mentioned by Allen in his letter to Sylvia. Lloyd had all the Fuller faults without their merits. Even Lloyd's overbearing manners seemed a virtue in disguise to Sophia

Ripley. She said "they serve to show how a refractory member can be kept in check by all the rest!"

More congenial spirits joined the community in the early summer, some young people, and two unusual men. The elder was George P. Bradford, kinsman and friend of Emerson. In the eyes of the world, Bradford's achievement was small, but the Farmers loved him because he united the charms of purity, fidelity, and manliness with scholarship. The younger, Charles King Newcomb, was such a frail and sensitive person that he had postponed his arrival, waiting "for the first pleasant day to come."

The Brook Farmers, proper Yankees every one, were tempted to look down their noses at Charles King Newcomb—at his large devout eyes and long black curls, and girl-like habit. This softly nurtured son of Rhode Island—a state which one Massachusetts divine in Roger Williams' era dubbed "Rid Island, or the Island of Errors," tried the Farmers' patience and provoked their laughter. The frail, overwrought young man was apt to break out in a chant—usually the solemn Litany—in the middle of the night. This habit was especially trying to his roommates in the "Hive."

In spite of the pressure of farm work, an educational program was drawn up. Already the primary school had opened in the little house on the Keith lot across the road. Everyone called it the "Nest." But the strict and formal manners of tall, straight, angular-featured Miss Marianne Ripley, the mistress, did not resemble those of a mother-bird. With that happy faculty the very young display for sizing up their elders, her pupils nicknamed this stiff, middle-aged New England spinster, "Her Perpendicular Majesty." Two sons of George Bancroft, the historian, were placed in her charge; and also Francis Barlow, destined—as a young soldier and older statesman—to shape history.

With so many new faces, there was an atmosphere of happy expansion at Brook Farm. Everyone gloried in the new life. Although it took two hours to drive eight miles on dirt roads to Boston, no one, except Mr. Hawthorne, complained of their isolation. "We don't hear from town oftener than once a week," Mrs. Ripley wrote John S. Dwight, "and have voted not to tell each other the news if we know any." Had they not, as "Come-Outers" should, come out of soul-destroying competition? Let the world come to them. They felt soothed to their very souls, and at peace.

Among their supporters, there was one who was not satisfied. Miss Peabody felt that the Farmers' ecstatic mood would not butter their parsnips. Mere bucolic enthusiasm would be chilled come Thanksgiving! From the first a staunch supporter of the Ripleys' undertaking, Elizabeth had every right to express her opinion. She also had an excuse to hover about the community, for she was collecting material for her essay, "A Glimpse of Christ's Idea of Society." Readers of *The Dial* would find in the October issue a glimpse into the Kingdom of Heaven as manifested in West Roxbury. "To form such a society," she would forewarn the reader, "is a great problem whose perfect solution will take all the ages of time; but let the spirit of God move freely over the great deep of social existence, and a creative light will come at His word, and after that long evening in which we are living, the morning of the first day shall dawn on a Christian Society." Though the evening of society in which Elizabeth Peabody lived seems enviably serene to children of the Atomic Age, those at Brook Farm shared both her fears and her high hopes for their undertaking. They did not intend merely to establish one more Utopia—a place where a few friends would live an ideal and novel existence. But Miss Peabody was more impatient than the Farmers themselves to see their little nucleus of the perfect society become an example to the nation.

Like Mrs. Ripley, Miss Peabody confided in John S. Dwight, who grew daily more interested in Brook Farm than in his Northampton pulpit. Whether Dwight was more affected by Sophia's ecstatic bubbling, or Lizzie's anxious pecking, is not known. But his enthusiasm for "the noble experiment" attracted both in liberal doses. "While they are so few," Elizabeth wrote him, "and the community plan is not in full operation, it is unavoidable that they must work very hard." On the other hand, if Mr. Ripley was content to play the milkman, Miss Peabody would remind him that there were other matters to be attended to.

In her kind, bustling, busybody way, she promptly organized a meeting to be held at her house on West Street on the eleventh of May. Though sadly lacking in monetary acumen where her own advantage was concerned, Miss Peabody became more practical when promoting a reform; and on this occasion she selected the company shrewdly. Each invitee "combined supposable interest in the plan with the solid cash in their purses or influence over the purses of others." With such a capable, high-principled, enthusiastic promoter, Brook Farm gained a firmer foundation. The meeting was successful, and in the weeks that followed the community grew. But the growth was too casual and the Association too informal to suit Miss Peabody.

In June she again confided her impatience to Dwight. She did not see how the community could "step out of its swaddling clothes" unless Mr. Ripley drew up articles for the Association. "He enjoys his work so much," she complained, "that he does not clearly see that his plan is not in the way of being demonstrated any farther than that it is being made evident that gentlemen, if they will work as many hours as boors, will succeed even better in cultivating a farm." Already, within the first few weeks, Miss Peabody had detected a weakness inherent in Ripley's leadership. He took a winning but ingenuous delight in his new way of life for its own sake. Since it was God-Chosen, the Lord would guide and provide.

Miss Peabody's attitude seems unduly severe when one considers that George Ripley had no choice but to postpone drawing up the articles of Association until the first crops had been harvested. In the meantime, he and Sophia had every reason to congratulate one another on the enthusiasm of their friends.

Almost before they were settled, Mrs. Almira C. Barlow sought a haven at Brook Farm for herself and her three young sons, Francis, Edward, and Richard. Her husband, David Hatch Barlow—another brilliant farm boy from Vermont—had graduated the first scholar in the Class of 1824, a year behind George Ripley's similar triumph at Harvard, and again following in his footsteps from the Divinity School in 1829. Everyone in the Ripleys' circle had smiled on the union of the beautiful daughter of Elisha Penniman of Brookline, and the Green Mountain scholar; pronounced them the handsomest couple in Boston. As was to be expected, the young minister had been given a good parish in Lynn.

When Mrs. Barlow sought refuge at Brook Farm it was common knowledge that she had taken her children back to her father's house in Brookline, and that her husband had disappeared. It had all happened rather suddenly, and no one knew why. The Ripleys extended a warm welcome, however; and Mrs. Barlow and her three little boys were ensconced in the Hive before the end of April. Almira soon gave them to understand that David had "gone to pieces"—a polite way of saying that he had become a drunkard. The ladies recalled that Almira had always been a flirt. Someone remembered that poor David was very fond of writing hymns, and that the one he had written to celebrate the church built in Concord for his friend, Waldo

Emerson, had been sung at the consecration. Perhaps the marriage might have held if David had composed odes to Almira instead of writing hymns?

But even the ladies conceded that Mrs. Barlow, with her lofty brow and long dark ringlets, had a very striking appearance; and the men became her slaves on sight. Hawthorne noticed her at once, and found her "a most comfortable woman to behold. She looks," he added, "as if her ample person was stuffed full of tenderness— indeed as if she were all one great kind heart."

In 1841, a great writer might have shied away from mentioning what we moderns bluntly call sex-appeal, but that was the quality in Mrs. Barlow that he referred to. Hawthorne was already deeply in love with Sophia Peabody, but he recognized a subject for a novel in Almira—the clash between a red-blooded beauty in distress, and a community of dreamy reformers. In creating Zenobia in his *Blithedale Romance*, perhaps Hawthorne compounded Almira Barlow's allure and warmth of heart with Margaret Fuller's intellect and arrogance. In spite of Hawthorne's "Author's Preface," imploring the public not to read "as if it had anything to do with Brook Farm—which essentially it has not—but merely for its own story and characters," this novel, published a decade later, stirred up much conjecture. The setting was unmistakable; and as regarded Zenobia, knowing readers persisted in embarrassing comparisons.

The Brook Farm ladies paid Mrs. Barlow scant tribute in their diaries and recollections. It appears that while they toiled over washtubs and sink, Mrs. Barlow sat in her parlor, a veritable Queen Bee among workers. And dear little Mr. Dwight was drawn into her thralldom, and became ever a more frequent visitor to Brook Farm. A day came when the poor man was detected slipping a note under Mrs. Barlow's supper plate. How sad if he had fallen in love! Georgiana Bruce, a young English girl who joined the Community in June, felt that although Mrs. Barlow's debonair disposition and sprightly ways made her an agreeable guest, it was regrettable that the lady "had not been baptized into the spirit of democracy."

But no one took seriously George William Curtis's attentions to the siren. Though it was an education in courtliness to watch him dance attendance upon her, everyone knew he was much too worldly-wise to be made a fool of.

George William Curtis and his elder brother, Burrill, came up from Providence to be prepared for college at the Brook Farm Institute

of Education. They proved a delightful addition to the "family."
Some ladies thought both the Curtis boys resembled "young Greek
gods." Others insisted that Burrill's countenance was more "Raphael-
esque" because his hair fell on his shoulders in graceful ringlets.
George, although very handsome, had not his brother's air of belonging in a Renaissance legend. But no one could deny that even
in his shirt sleeves, with his boots drawn over his trousers, George
had a peculiar elegance. The staid matrons often lined up in the
windows of the Hive to watch George escort the maidens across
the muddy barnyard. He did this with the grace of a courtier gliding
across a parquet at Versailles!

2.

By mid-summer the enterprise was well under way; and George
Ripley could boast, "We are now in full operation as a family of
workers, teachers, and students; and we feel the deepest convictions
that, for us, our mode of life is the true one, and no attraction would
tempt any one of us that we have quitted lately."

The day began with a "rising horn" and a rattle of pots and pans
from the kitchen. Anybody chancing to look out the window as he
dressed, could see those who were detailed to special early morning
tasks moving about the barnyard and truck garden. Mr. Ripley was
always among them. In tarpaulin straw hat, and a farmer's smock
of blue that hung down below the tops of his cowhide boots, he went
to and fro, fetching the brimming milkpails.

But he always appeared at the breakfast table in conventional
attire, and presided with an air that reflected his new contentment.
He was growing stouter. His face had lost its pallor and gained a
fresh healthy color—what could be seen of it. Affecting the "Come-
Outer" mode, Mr. Ripley now shaved only his upper lip, and had
grown a vigorous beard. Mrs. Ripley, tall, graceful, and slim, sat at his
right. Her light smooth hair was brushed back in the plain style
of the day, and she wore a fresh dress of "checked domestic." A
southern visitor, who had seen none but colored servants wear cotton
fabrics, was much astonished by the simplicity of her costume. But the

corrupt slaveholder gallantly conceded that the gingham looked "essentially royal" when worn by Mrs. Ripley.

Perpendicular Miss Ripley, the Founder's sister, sat at the opposite end of the table dispensing tea and coffee. The Group of Table Waiters, composed of half a dozen young men and boys, served. The fare was plain, but fresh from the farm; and the long, low dining room had a recently scrubbed look. White wooden benches served instead of chairs; all the tableware was white, and mugs took the place of cups and saucers; and all was set on white linen cloths. In this immaculate atmosphere, "a happy buzz" arose. For the Farmers considered conversation one of the arts; and on rising, like the lark, they greeted the day in high spirits.

Prayers were not held after breakfast, or at any other time. The Farmers had left all set religious creeds and forms behind them. Indeed, they felt so secure in their new philosophy that they refrained from regular, united avowal of man's reliance on superhuman aid. On Sundays, those who felt inclined walked over to West Roxbury to hear Theodore Parker expound his inspiring "heresies." Others "went to church nowhere." Some "communed with Nature." But every single one of them believed in Work; and immediately after breakfast they set about it.

By mid-summer they had organized the three Main Groups—The Field, The Mechanical, and The Domestic. Each Group was subdivided into units of three or more persons. Always a "harmonic" or uneven number, so a vote could be taken. "The Field," for instance, included Planting, Plowing, Hoeing, Weeding, Nursery; and they hoped to add a Greenhouse Unit within a year or so. The Mechanical was composed of a Carpenter, Printer, Shoemaker, and a chinaware unit, known as the "Britannia Group." "The Domestic" subdivided into Dormitory, Consistory, Kitchen, Washing, Ironing, and Mending units. The women attended to these tasks, of course; but they were assisted by a men's Household Brigade which lent willing hands wherever needed. If the young ladies took cold on washing day, the young gentlemen wrung and hung out the clothes for them. The boys performed the task punctually, although they got heartily laughed at, when, as sometimes happened, clothespins fell from their pockets.

Pupils were expected to work off their board and lodging by helping with the chores and household tasks, and so boys and girls were thrown together all day long at Brook Farm. This co-education was considered a daring innovation by some. Yet, as a rule, parents gladly entrusted their daughters' training to Mrs. Ripley, knowing her influence over her pupils was exactly what one might expect of a "woman of elegant manners and perfect self-control." Their confidence was justified. Two of the girls, Georgiana Bruce and Ora Gannett—later Mrs. Kirby and Mrs. Sedgwick—looked back on their sojourn at Brook Farm as the happiest influence of their youth. Tall, fair-haired, beautiful Ellen Slade became an example to all for the grace which she brought to the simplest task. All the girls thoroughly enjoyed their semi-emancipation from the strict conventions of the day, and, on the whole, neither they nor the young men abused their new freedom. Youth being what it is, occasional indiscretions must have occurred. But no whisper of scandal stands recorded. One young Farmer proposed to his bride over the pantry sink. As they plighted their troth the dish wipers sang, "If I Get There Before You Do"—but he could feel perfectly sure he was getting his girl before anybody else.

In addition to the formal Groups there was a Sacred Legion whose "noble duty" it was to perform the more odious tasks. The most brilliant men served the household, and even relished their duties. George William Curtis trimmed the lamps with a ceremony and faithfulness worthy of an acolyte; and Charles Anderson Dana organized four of the most elegant youths into a band of Griddle Cake Servitors. Though a most attentive waiter, Dana could often be seen reading a small Greek book between the courses. The young scholar's power of concentration was obviously intense, yet when firmly spoken to he replied with a genial smile.

Some of his contemporaries stood in awe of this tall young man in his early twenties. With his scholar's forehead, penetrating gaze, air of dignity and force, the future editor of the New York Sun seemed extraordinarily poised and sophisticated for his years. Indeed, his auburn beard gave him a professorial aspect. To Mr. Ripley's delight, Dana had brought a library of foreign books with him from Harvard. But the girls who set his room to rights complained that the bookcase was much too small to hold them. How could they sweep and dust properly when Mr. Dana's books not only cluttered the table but spilled off the chairs onto the floor? He was neither a prig nor a bibliomaniac, they discovered. On fine days Mr. Dana was invariably to be found in the orchard tending the fruit trees; and when they frolicked of an evening, it was very delightful to see how a young man of such innate dignity could play the fool in some trifling charade.

Though the pattern was set by the more fervent workers, almost everyone found satisfaction in performing the menial tasks. Which is not to be wondered at when one reflects that the Farmers' program offered what every person craves—varied occupation. George Ripley was not thinking in terms of individual happiness, however; he was building an example for what he hoped would prove a wide-spreading social reform. He often repeated Benjamin Franklin's saying: "If everyone worked bodily three hours a day, there would be no necessity for anyone's working more than three hours." But from the beginning, it was the individual who benefited from the "Social Plan." Ripley's followers at this time were drawn, for the most part, from the ranks of the delicately nurtured. Yet these gentlemen and ladies worked hard for long hours every day without tractors, or milking machine for the farm, without gas and electric equipment in the household, and almost everyone—except Hawthorne and Mrs. Barlow—felt that their new life offered a noble sweet simplicity. Indeed, many of those who were there in the Transcendental period, for the remainder of their lives, felt a vague nostalgia for Brook Farm.

Shortly before noon, hoe and broom were laid aside, and everyone prepared for an afternoon of study. When they met presently for a dish of Indian mush or brown-bread brewis, warm hearty food, "all were at rest and at their best." Courtesy was the rule; a cross word or a coarse expression was scarcely ever heard. Gentlemen and ladies stressed refinement in those days, and with the exception of one or two humble persons who were made welcome in the name of Universal Brotherhood, the Farmers were aristocrats.

Immediately after lunch the teachers in the Preparatory School held recitations. Now began the most serious business of the day. George Ripley had been quick to see that the Community's only immediate and likely source of income would be the Department of Education. By August, the Infant School in the Nest, opened in May under the direction of Miss Marianne Ripley, was so well established that it could be entrusted to the less experienced direction of Georgiana Bruce.

Born to wealth, but raised in poverty, this young English girl had endured a miserable upbringing at the hands of a spendthrift father and a self-pitying, sentimental mamma. The muddled parents could not quench their daughter's thirst for experience. Bound to get it,

Georgiana somehow had scraped up money for a passage to the United States; and with good luck she had found a post as nursery governess to the children of Dr. Ezra S. Gannett, in Boston. An attractive niece, Deborah Gannett, soon came to visit; and the two lively girls immediately became fast friends. "Ora" enjoyed visiting, and she had much to tell about a recent visit to Brook Farm. "Georgie" was fascinated. To a young woman bent on experience, life in that community appeared more promising than the post of nursery governess in the household of the kind Gannetts. Whether the two girls put their heads together, and put ideas into Dr. Gannett's, or whether the busy and competent minister took matters into his own hands, is pure surmise. In any case, he quickly secured a post for Miss Bruce in the Infant School in the Nest. Miss Abby Norton and Miss Ripley needed an assistant; and he could honestly recommend Miss Bruce. The young woman displayed upon occasion a disposition that was positively peppery, but she possessed sufficient discretion to control herself; and she offered vivacity of mind combined with a winning sentimentality. The terms were rigorous. To earn her keep and enjoy opportunities for greater education, the assistant teacher worked eight hours a day. No longer frustrated, Georgiana worked with such good will that she took over the direction of the Infant School with confidence.

Taking with her the Bancrofts, the Barlows, and Lloyd Fuller, Miss Ripley soon set up the Primary School in another part of the Nest. Two boys arrived shortly from Manila to augment her class. With Lucas and Jose Caralas, who spoke scarcely a word of English, and Lloyd, who littered the house with pages torn from a diary he kept "solely to denounce," Miss Ripley had her hands full. If Her Perpendicular Majesty ever lost her temper and her dignity, not a word is recorded on the subject.

Meanwhile, Harvard authorities became interested in the Preparatory School, for they knew that George Ripley, the first scholar in the class of 1823, would maintain a high standard of scholarship. Students were sent to Brook Farm from Cambridge, to be tutored for entrance into Harvard in the fall. Although absorbed in many other projects for the Community that summer, Mr. Ripley built up his Preparatory School rapidly. Young Mr. Dana—happily recovered from the eye affliction which had threatened further study in May—already held classes in Greek and German. He also gave instruction in tree grafting, an extracurricular activity for those who were interested. The Department of Belles Lettres was off to a splendid start under the direction of George P. Bradford, a great teacher, who aroused in his pupils a love of learning and a deep attachment to himself. George Ripley, whether minister or advocate of Transcendentalism, believed in intellectual training. Ripley, now the founder of a Utopia dedicated to social reform, although the task demanded hours of attention every day, yet somehow found the time to teach in mathematics and philosophy in the Brook Farm Institute of Education. He used his favorite authority, Cousin, as a text book for the nebulous subject, Transcendentalism. Meanwhile, the Brook Farm ladies who boasted of an education fitted into the staff of the Department of Education, finding their place as Miss Marianne Ripley and Georgiana Bruce had found theirs in the Infant and Primary Schools in the Nest. A niece of the Founder, Miss Hannah B. Ripley, taught drawing in all three schools. Miss Amelia B. Russell gave lessons in dancing; and the enthusiasm of the young people who flocked to her "hops" astonished the elder reformers. Dignified Mrs. Ripley taught history and modern languages in the Preparatory School, imbuing many young minds with a taste for both.

The Department of Education kept on expanding. John S. Dwight gradually was being forced out of his Northampton pulpit; and come November, he would take over the teaching of Music and Latin. And so it continued. The curriculum grew to include Italian, German, and French moral philosophy. The fame of the school gradually attracted students from remote places—Manila, Havana, Florida, and from distant states. Yet it never grew to be a large school according to modern standards. However small the enrollment—by the second year there were some thirty girls and boys—student life at Brook Farm was animated by pervasive enthusiasm; and it held to that high standard until the foreign and infectious notions of the French social philosopher Charles Fourier were introduced in 1844.

In that happy summer of high hope, 1841, educational policy at Brook Farm was based on perfect freedom of thought between students and teachers. There were no regular study hours. Each pupil studied where and when he would. This policy might not have worked well elsewhere, but at Brook Farm the moral preaching of the Faculty was matched by their intellectual vigor, and by zest for their new way of life. There was no need for disciplinary measures when they could arouse a sense of personal responsibility in regard to society, and communicate a passion for intellectual inquiry.

How well these teachers succeeded in their design is revealed in the records of those who taught and were taught at Brook Farm. Rarely have so few had such influence; for there can be little doubt that George Ripley and his followers helped to mould the modern American mind, as they helped to mould public opinion in their own time. The subsequent achievements of Ripley, Dana, and George William Curtis form a climactic epilogue to the story of Brook Farm. But the subsequent career of Mrs. Barlow's eldest son, a pupil in the school, is pertinent to this early period because it proves that the Farmers' Transcendentalism did not necessarily deprive their students of a practical approach.

Young Francis Channing Barlow served in the Union Army from the outbreak of the Civil War. He suffered wounds, covered himself with glory, and after the Wilderness Campaign was made a Major General, the youngest in the Union Army. After the war General Barlow entered politics and became Secretary of State of New York State; and finally wound up his long public service with the prosecution of the Tweed ring in New York City.

The effect that Transcendentalism had on Charles Newcomb was very different. This young man's claim to posterity is unique—Emerson praised him without qualification. "I recall one youth of the subtlest mind, I believe I may say the subtlest observer and diviner of character I ever met," he wrote years afterward. Though Emerson admitted that Newcomb was a man of no practical aims, a mere student and philosopher, he loved him for his mind which "overfed" on "whatever is exalted in genius, whether in Poetry or Art, in Drama or Music, or in social accomplishment and elegancy."

Ralph Waldo Emerson must have been aware of the faint aura of absurdity which surrounded his young friend, yet he loved Charles Newcomb. And it is pleasant to find a warm human attachment for a youth of small accomplishment, expressed by a great man seldom given to eulogy. Emerson felt that Newcomb had a genius for penetrating to the core of a subject, "so that a few words from him often impressed his hearers more than an hour's talk with one more healthily balanced." Clearly, Emerson sensed in Newcomb a strength not generally apparent and his intuition was partially sound. For although he afterwards became insane, the frail, overwrought Newcomb for a time overcame his extreme sensitivity, and served for three months as a private in the Union Army.

Newcomb, all his life, kept extremely busy writing—but with no desire for publication. Some people, he reasoned, write for their own time, others for posterity. His work, he modestly hoped, might prove "curious, if not valuable in coming times." Few writers have summed up their place in literature so accurately.

The Farmers thrust no household tasks on the frail Newcomb. He could devote his days and nights to "diarising," if he chose to do so. He gave them to understand that he had come to Brook Farm to escape from his dominant mother. He longed for a wife and family, dreamed of a life of action—and gave his full energies every day to long entries in his *Journal*. He spoke often of the "two-fold tyranny"— that of Mrs. Newcomb, and the impulsion to record his views on morals, politics, Shakespeare, and Nature.

The Farmers were rewarded for their patience and understanding. Charles Newcomb quickly gained a place in the annals of the School. He performed a most useful service in giving advice to parents. His aplomb in a family crisis was like that of a General. Emerson, fondly observing, dubbed Newcomb "The Abbe, or spiritual father."

That the ex-preachers and scholars would reap a richer harvest cultivating human brains than in working the gravelly New England soil was to be expected. But the speed with which George Ripley set up the Department of Education, and the high standard of tutoring maintained, paid dividends. The three schools were a success from the start, and for three years they stabilized the finances and enhanced the reputation of Brook Farm; and the interest which accrued in spiritual dividends for posterity is still accruing. For who is wise enough to compute the inestimable value of a noble example?

"The excitements of Boston have ever been few," Hawthorne observes in *The Blithedale Romance*, "and to see the regeneration of mankind going on under your own nose and eyes and with nothing to pay, proved an exhilarating and instructive experience." He was referring to the visitors who came to gape at the rustic antics of their relatives. For in this first bright summer almost everyone at Brook Farm belonged to "Boston's Best."

To this day, "Proper Bostonians" speak with mingled pride and amusement of some forebear who had the temerity to join Brook Farm; and in the summer of 1841, conservative Bostonians by the score drove out to West Roxbury to see what the Transcendentalists were up to. Heretofore, they had been more amused than alarmed by the professions of the new sect. But now that "those men" had set

up a Community which was designed to do away with the competitive
system, the movement took on the dark color of the Abolitionist
Party. In the eyes of State Street, both groups were conniving to
invalidate contracts. And the Ripleys had beguiled some of the most
sobersided of their young people! Brahmin visitors arrived with a
prejudice, and went away in carping mood.

Poor Mrs. Ripley! What impropriety! Fancy a cultivated lady
having to iron for hours on end each day! But Sophia went right
on pleating ruffles and nightcaps with the same conscientiousness
with which she taught the irregular French verbs. In her opinion,
it was far more rewarding to pleat the ruffle of a nightcap than to
pacify some conventional mamma who objected to the daring work
costume of the Brook Farm maidens. Conscious that their costume
was a symbol of Woman's Emancipation, the girls strutted about in
blimp-like bloomers, over which a short skirt was worn. The boldest let
their tresses fall about their shoulders—an added insult to current
fashion which then decreed that every modest female should wear her
hair bound up in a discreet "pug."

While the girls gloried in their sartorial emancipation, the men—
"every mother's son," according to Hawthorne—might have served
to set up as a scarecrow. For whatever the points of difference between
these philosophers, they were all agreed that the Community was the
place to wear out their old clothes. When Hawthorne rested on his
spade and contemplated his co-workers, he saw "a living epitome of
defunct fashions, and the very raggedest presentment of men who
had seen better days." Since "one downright stroke of the hoe was
sure to put a finish to these poor habiliments," it was easy to spot
each newcomer to the field, for he always resembled "gentility in
tatters." But as time went by, the newcomer, too, would have to lay
aside his old clothes and "take to honest homespun and linsey-
woolsey." The loose linen tunic worn over woolen trousers resembled
"a compromise between the blouse of a Paris workman and the
peignoir of a possible sister." Each man grew whiskers as a symbol
of emancipation. When the Farmers grasped the scythe, the razor
was thrown aside.

As the body-and-soul satisfying day drew to a close, the inner man
was strengthened with brewis; and then, when the last dish was sung
to the cupboard, the Farmers liked to gather for an evening of whole-

some fun. But the pursuit of entertainment gave the Transcendentalist little satisfaction unless it offered self-improvement of some sort. All were agreed that communion with Nature refreshed the spirit, and picnics were in order on fine summer evenings.

They had not far to go for a change of scene. Beyond the pleasantly rolling slopes of Brook Farm, wide meadows descended, circled by the sluggish Charles. On the way across the fields, Mr. Bradford, who knew the countryside as well as his friend and neighbor in Concord, Henry Thoreau, gathered flora to name at supper. On reaching the riverbank everyone clambered into a canoe or a flat-bottomed row-boat. The young people loved to paddle or row along the winding stream; and their elders found it delightful to recline against the stern seat and watch little capes and headlands arise as they rounded a bend, and the tiny islands that seemed to float in the tree-banked stream. One of these, which bore the disappointing name of Cow Island, was a favorite landing place. On moonlit nights twinkling showers of light trickled through the shade trees; and vapor rose like ghostly incense from the long sedges. On the way home across the fields, Mr. Bradford, who was always surrounded on a picnic, delighted to point out the constellations in the star-spangled canopy above, "quietly talking of all this beauty in a way to inspire love and reverence."

On Sunday, the favorite picnic spot was Pulpit Rock, a shattered granite boulder rising twenty to thirty feet from a heap of smaller rocks. Wild columbine, violets, mosses grew in the fissures. The canopy of a birch tree which had served as a sounding board when John Eliot, "The Holy Apostle to the Indians," addressed his savage congregation, still overshadowed the summit.

The rock still was used as a pulpit. On summer Sunday afternoons, Dr. William Henry Channing, nephew of Dr. William Ellery Channing, mounted it to speak to the Farmers. At this time the celebrated uncle was sinking slowly into death; but his nephew had lifted the torch from his hand to lead Reform, both as a Christian minister, and as "an Associationist from the Christian side." To put it in his own words, William Henry Channing believed that "associated life contained more of the spirit of Christ in it than any other form of society, ancient or modern." William Henry Channing, after undergoing a spiritual crisis in Cincinnati, a crisis so severe that he had left his ministry there and returned to his mother's house in Cambridge,

must have found fulfillment in addressing members of that Ideal
Community, which his uncle had been the first to conceive.*

These services at Pulpit Rock became a moving memory to those
who attended. By one of nature's happiest effects, the light fell on
Dr. Channing's slim, tall, stately figure as he mounted Pulpit Rock,
and blessed him when he bent his head in prayer.

In that brief instant of supplication, Dr. Channing's regular features
seemed as beautifully serene as a head on a Greek coin—until he bent
his piercing eyes on the congregation and began to speak. Then William
Channing's earnestness became almost painful. His delicate eyebrows
contracted in a dark scowl, and his lips curled to goad them on to
further reform in education, anti-slavery, good government, or any other
social project for the benefit of their fellowman.

The Farmers rejoiced in his preaching because William Henry
Channing refused to be bound by the ritual of the Unitarian Church.
(Indeed, of them all, guests or members, William Henry Channing
would be the spiritual leader of the Community—the one minister
who perfectly understood their endeavor.) In concluding the open
air services at Pulpit Rock, Dr. Channing looked heavenwards and
said, "Let us all join hands and make a circle, the symbol of Universal Unity, and of the at-one-ment of all men and women; and here
form the Church of Humanity that shall cover the men and women
of every nation and every clime." If the "Holy Apostle to the Indians"
watched these gatherings from the next world, surely John Eliot rejoiced to see his pulpit used to worthy purpose? **

On rainy Sundays, debating was a favorite pastime. One stormy afternoon, the Farmers gathered to inquire, "Is Labor in itself an ideal,
or being unattractive in character, do we in effect clothe it with the
spirit we bring to it?" This subject, still a lively topic, was a lively
subject indeed for Brook Farm ladies suffering from "dish-washing
hands," and the vis à vis gentlemen with palms calloused and blistered
from wielding the hoe. The discussion proved elevating, no doubt. The
Farmers were always "strengthening their endeavor" in this fashion.
But there was one among them who had made up his mind.

As early as June first, six weeks after his arrival, Nathaniel Hawthorne

* This is controversial. Ripley later told William Henry Channing that he
never would have founded Brook Farm without the encouragement of Dr.
William Ellery Channing; but it is certain that the latter disapproved of many
Brook Farm activities.

** Or would he, as a reader suggests, ". . . doubtless have dropped to his knees,
to pray for the Farmers' iconoclastic souls"?

confided to his *Note-book* that the Brook Farm way of life gave him
even more of an antipathy to pen and ink than that which he had
experienced in the Boston Custom House. After a hard day's work on
the farm, Hawthorne's spirit "refused to be burned out on paper."
It was his opinion that "a man's soul may be buried and perish under
a dung heap just as well as under a pile of money." In mid-August he
harped again on the thralldom and weariness. "Oh, labor is the curse
of the world," he lamented, "and nobody can meddle with it without
becoming proportionately brutified."

Many among them found the novelist strangely taciturn. He often
sat for hours on the sofa under the Hive staircase with a book in
his hands. His was a vivid presence; someone called Hawthorne a
statue of darkness; and it was evident that while pretending to read,
Mr. Hawthorne watched and listened to the life that flowed through
the hall.

Spying him there one evening, Ellen Slade was overcome by a
mischievous impulse to rout him from his lair. Seizing two of the
parlor cushions, she whispered to Ora Gannett, "Come on, let's throw
them all at Mr. Hawthorne—"

Quick as a flash he seized a broom that was hanging close by and
knocked the cushions back with a sure aim. He warded off the attack
and hit a girl every time. And they could only hit the broom. The
girls laughed aloud in glee, but not a sound escaped Mr. Hawthorne.
But his eyes, Ora noticed, "shone and twinkled like stars."

Another time, Ora found Mr. Hawthorne walking "with his hands
behind his back, head bent forward, the two little Bancrofts and other
children following him with pleased faces, stooping every now and
then with broad smiles, after which they would rise and run on again
behind him." Watching closely, Ora discovered, "Although he hardly
moved a muscle except to walk, yet from time to time he dropped
a penny, for which the children scrambled."

Ora Gannett admired the novelist very much; and to her delight
she became a favorite with him. One evening she coaxed Mr. Hawthorne to hear her recite the piece she was getting by heart for Mr.
Dana. After that he willingly coached her each week for the same
ordeal.

In spite of his serene demeanor, Hawthorne's misgivings concerning
his investment increased. On August twenty-second he wrote Sophia:
"It is extremely doubtful whether Mr. R. [Ripley] will succeed in
locating his Community on this farm. He can bring Mr. E. [Ellis]

to no terms, and the more they talk about the matter, the further they appear to be from a settlement. We must form other plans for ourselves, for I can see few signs that Providence proposes to give us a home here. I am weary, weary, thrice weary of waiting so many ages. Yet what can be done? Whatever thy husband's gifts he has not hitherto shown a single one that may avail to gather gold . . . But I am becoming more and more convinced that we must not lean on this community . . . I shall not remain here through the winter, unless with an absolute certainty that there will be a house ready for us in the spring. Otherwise, I shall return to Boston; still, however, considering myself an associate of the Community, so that we may take advantage of any more favorable aspect of affairs."

He continued to work in the fields and barnyard at Brook Farm until the first of September, when he went to Salem for a three-week holiday. Back again in the familiar town, and near his "Dove," the novelist felt as if twenty years had passed in the few months he had spent at Brook Farm. "The real me," he wrote, "was never an associate of the Community. There has been a spectral appearance there, sounding the horn at daybreak and milking the cows and hoeing the potatoes and raising the hay, toiling in the sun and doing me the honor to assume my name. But the spectre was not myself."

3.

When the frost was on the pumpkin, Miss Peabody at last had her wish. Mr. Ripley turned his mind to organization; and on September twenty-ninth the Articles of Association of the Subscribers to the Brook Farm Institute of Agriculture and Education were drawn up. George Ripley, Minot Pratt, and William Allen assumed charge of "General Direction." Although this meant that in future the heavy burden of responsibility would be divided, George and Sophia Ripley would continue to bear the greater part. Just as in the past, when others had merely talked of such a Community, the Ripleys had founded it; so, now, and in years to come, it would be the Ripleys who would toil the hardest to make a success of Brook Farm.

The cost of establishment proved very much less than they had anticipated. Ripley had written Emerson the previous November that

$50,000 would be needed. Now, after careful estimate, they found they could purchase the estate and buildings and retain sufficient surplus to carry on operations on the basis of ten families for one year for only $30,000.

According to the deed, dated October 11, 1841, the farm was bought from Charles and Maria Ellis for $10,500. It consisted of about one hundred and eighty-eight acres of land * in that part of the town of Roxbury which had lately been set off from Newton, situated on the westerly side of the road leading from Dedham to Watertown. There were also some twenty acres on the opposite side of the road. This parcel of land was called the Keith lot, and on it stood the Nest or Primary School.

On the same day the deed was signed—October eleventh—Ripley, Hawthorne, Dana, and Allen, acting as trustees, mortgaged the property to Daniel Wilder and Josiah Quincy, commissioners of the sinking fund of the West Railroad Corporation. The trustees agreed to secure the payment of $6,000, in three years and twenty-one days. They also made a second mortgage and promised to secure for George R. Russell, Henry P. Sturgis, and Francis Shaw, payment of $1,500 each; and to Lucy Cabot, $500. Though the Farmers were regarded as radicals and traitors to their clan, the names of those who invested in the enterprise proved that they still had friends on State Street.

Lindsay Swift, whose *Brook Farm* is the standard authority on the subject, points out, "If the consideration named in the deed from Ellis and his wife was the real consideration (and it probably was) it would seem that the trustees succeeded, at the start, in mortgaging their property for $500.00 more than it cost them."

In other preliminary financing the trustees showed shrewdness and foresight. All the required stock, at $500 a share, was subscribed before these papers were drawn. Each share entitled the holder to one vote on all matters relating to the funds of the Association. A shareholder drew five percent interest annually on the amount of his stock; and each could draw on the funds of the Association to an amount not otherwise appropriated or exceeding that of the interest credited to his favor. Although no shareholder was liable to an assessment, nor could be held responsible in his private property for debts incurred

---

* It has been suggested that the amount Ripley himself put into the venture should be stated. I have never heard this specified—except in a general way, that he put in all he had, and bore total loss.

by the Association, he, in turn, renounced all claim on any profits accruing to the Association for the use of his capital.

The Department of Education offered a tempting bonus to those subscribers who were also parents—each could receive free tuition for one pupil for every share he held, "to an amount not exceeding twenty percent of interest on his investment." As the School was highly recommended by Harvard,—which was fitting, considering the Ripleys' standing as scholars in Cambridge—this free tuition was regarded as a desirable privilege.

The four trustees were elected annually, and in them was vested the whole property of the Association. No share could be transferred without their consent; but a stockholder might withdraw his stock, with the interest due thereon, by giving twelve months' notice to the trustees. This proviso would soon irk Nathaniel Hawthorne, who had invested both enthusiasm and cash in the enterprise. He would find it easier to withdraw himself than to withdraw his investment, although committed to serve the year out as trustee, being elected to that office two days after his return to Brook Farm.

The provisos, generally speaking, were fair to all concerned, although there was a potential risk for subscriber and trustee alike—expansion. The capital stock of the Association, which now stood at $12,000, divided into shares of $500 each, could be increased at the pleasure of the Association. Therein lay the gamble, for the Directors frankly declared it was their intention "to purchase such estates as may be required for the establishment and continuance of an agricultural, literary, and scientific school or college, to provide such lands and houses, animals, libraries and apparatus, as may be found expedient to the main purpose."

Directors and Trustees were wary of admitting undesirables into their intimate circle, and it was agreed that every applicant for resident membership was to be received on a two-months' probation. At the end of that time the established members would decide on the applicant's compatibility, a two-thirds vote being required for admission.

Labor was an essential branch of their program, and the Articles encouraged it on a cooperative basis. A year's board was offered for a year's labor, with lesser amounts in the same proportion. Three hundred days was considered a year's labor, and entitled the associate to one share of the annual dividend. Sixty hours constituted a full week of labor from May through October; forty-eight hours from November through April. If the hours seem long and the return small, it should be remembered that these were hard times, and many were willing to work for their keep.

Some associates did not work. These were charged $4.00 board a week—which included fuel, light, and laundry. Children of associates, over ten years old, could board at half rate, but younger children cost their parents $3.50 per week, "exclusive of washing and separate fire." This stipulation and the limit on free schooling suggests that perhaps the childless Ripleys would have preferred the Planned Parenthood of our time to the unregulated breeding of their own.

These, in brief, were the more important articles understood and agreed on by the Direction, "for the safe, legal, and orderly holding and management of such property as shall further the purpose of The Brook Farm Institute of Agriculture and Education."

4.

After a long visit to Salem, Massachusetts, to see his family and his fiancée, Sophia Peabody, Hawthorne returned to Brook Farm late in September, 1841. He had stipulated that he would not return as a boarder, unless accepted with no obligations to work on the farm or teach. On the twenty-second he wrote Sophia that he hoped "to see these people and their enterprise under a new point of view, and perhaps to determine whether thou and I have any call to cast in our lot among them." He would devote his time to writing instead of plowing, and wait upon events.

At first all went well. He entertained "a friendlier disposition toward the Farm," now that he no longer was "obliged to toil in its friendly furrows." But during his absence the astute Directors—perhaps with an eye to detaining Hawthorne indefinitely—had elected him to high office: trustee of the estate, Chairman of the Committee on Finance. This no doubt accounted for his complaint—"I have not the sense of perfect seclusion which has always been essential to my power of producing anything. It is true nobody intrudes into my room; but still I can not be quiet. Nothing here is settled; everything is but beginning to arrange itself; and though I would seem to have little to do with aught but my own thoughts, still I cannot but partake of the ferment around me. My mind will not be obstructed. I must observe, think, and feel, and content myself with catching glimpses of things which may be wrought out hereafter."

Some of these glimpses would be wrought into *The Blithedale Romance* a decade later. In the meantime Hawthorne's notebooks were enriched because he could not settle down to write; and the entries made during the remainder of his stay are vivid reports of daily life at Brook Farm, set against the autumnal beauty of the surrounding countryside.

On September twenty-seventh, Hawthorne told of a ride in a wagon with William Allen to Brighton. They were carrying a calf to the weekly cattle fair. On this beautiful cool morning, the landscape looked greener than in mid-summer, with "occasional interminglings of the brilliant hues of autumn." They passed by "warm and comfortable farmhouses, ancient, with the sloping roof, the antique peak, the clustered chimneys of old times . . . There were villas, with terraces before them and dense shade, and wooden urns on pillars, and other tokens of gentility." Near Brighton, lanes and highways were thronged with country people, herding cattle to the fair.

When they got there, they found that village thronged with "cattle people and butchers who supply the Boston market, and dealers from far and near; and every man with a cow or a yoke of oxen whether to sell or buy, goes to Brighton on Monday." Between one and two thousand cattle jostled one another in the pens; and others, standing about the vehicles on the crowded streets jostled the pedestrians; ". . . this was a sort of festal day, as well as a day of business" and one saw "gentlemen farmers . . . in handsome surtouts, and pantaloons strapped under their boots . . . ; yeomen in black or blue Sunday suits, cut by country tailors and awkwardly worn." Others, like Mr. Hawthorne, himself, were garbed in the blue stuff frocks— "the most comfortable garment that ever man invented,"—especially for work around a farm. Country loafers, "poor, shabby out at elbows devils," and "dandies from the city, stayed and buckramed . . . All these . . . thronged the spacious bar room of the hotel, drinking, smoking, talking, bargaining," or "walked about the cattle pens looking with knowing eyes at the horned people."

William Allen was at the cattle fair to purchase four little pigs; which he, after careful deliberation, selected and paid for at five cents a pound. The little porkers—"all four of very piggish aspect and deportment"—were seized by their tails, and their legs tied. Thrown into the Brook Farm wagon, "they kept up a continual grunt and squeal till we got home."

Hawthorne enjoyed his visit to the fair in the bright sunshine. "I must see it again," he concluded, "for it ought to be studied."

Strolling into the woods after dinner with Mr. Bradford the next day—September twenty-eighth—Mr. Hawthorne met the apparition of an Indian chief, and almost at the same time a young gypsy maid—Ora Gannett. While Ora was telling his fortune, "the Goddess Diana (known on earth as Miss Ellen Slade) let fly an arrow" which hit him smartly on the wrist. Accompanying the girls—Mr. Hawthorne found them both "pretty enough to make fifteen enchanting"—they presently came "to a company of fantastic figures, arranged in a ring for a dance or a game." A Swiss girl, an Indian Squaw, a Jim Crow, some foresters, and children of all ages had gathered in the wood "in honor of Frank Dana's birthday, he being six years old."

Mr. Hawthorne, whose nature it was "to be a mere spectator," lay under the trees and looked on. Presently he was joined by Mr. Emerson and Miss Fuller—"here followed much talk." At last "the ceremonies of the day concluded with a cold collation of cakes and fruit."

Freed from obligation to labor on the farm, Hawthorne nevertheless gave a hand when he felt inclined. One morning he helped to gather apples; on the next he worked "a little" at digging potatoes. The most enjoyable aspect of farming, one suspects, was describing a process in his notebook in the afternoon. On his way home, Mr. Hawthorne "paused to inspect the squash field. The squashes lay in heaps, as they were gathered, presenting much variety of shape and hue—golden yellow lumps of gold, dark green, and the striped and variegated. Some were round, and some lay curling their long necks, nestling, as it were, and seeming as if they had life. Others, regularly scalloped, would make handsome patterns for dishes."

Among the livestock, pigs, grown and small, held a special fascination for Hawthorne. On October first, "a clear, bright, chrystal [sic] north-west windy cool morning," he went to look at their four black swine "in process of fattening." He found them nestling close together as deep in the clean rye straw in their stye as they could burrow—"the very symbols of slothful ease and sensual comfort." At his approach, the nearest pig uttered a low grunt and turned "an observant though dull and sluggish eye upon the visitor." At which they all did grunt among themselves "to express their swinish sympathy." Hawthorne supposed it was the knowledge that these four fat pigs were doomed to die within two weeks that gave them "a sort of awefulness" in his eyes. It made him "contrast their present gross substance with the nothingness speedily to come."

Hawthorne turned with relieved amusement to the four newly bought little pigs "running about the cow-yard, lean, active, shrewd." He threw them an apple; they scrambled for the prize; and the winner scampered away to eat it at leisure. Nothing within their reach, Hawthorne noted, was left unexamined; and they kept grunting all the time "with an infinite variety of expression." The more Mr. Hawthorne contemplated the swinish race the more intrigued he became. He fancied they possessed some especial significance, if one could find out. He was astonished at "their perfect independence of character. They care not for men," Hawthorne decided, "and will not adapt themselves to his motions, as other beasts do; but are true to themselves, and act out their hoggish nature."

On October second, Hawthorne left West Roxbury and visited both Boston and Salem—presumably to confer with friends, family, and his dear Sophia; and to make plans to extricate himself from any further obligation to Brook Farm. He returned on the seventh; and, it would seem, with his mind made up to leave as soon as he had obtained a substantial repayment on his investment of $1,000, and guarantee from the Directors to refund the balance plus interest. In the meantime, on every fine day, Hawthorne took a long walk in the morning, and painted a verbal picture of what he had seen in his notebook, in the afternoon.

"The woods," he recorded on October eighth, "present a very diversified appearance, just now, with perhaps more varieties of tint, though less marked ones, than they are destined to wear at a somewhat later period. There are some strong yellow hues, and some deep red; there are innumerable shades of green; some few having the depth of summer; others, partially changed towards yellow, look freshly verdant, the delicate tinge of early summer, or of May. Then there is the solemn and dark green of the pines. The effect is, that every tree in the wood, and every bush among the shrubbery, seems to have a separate existence, since, confusedly intermingled, each wears its peculiar hue, instead of being lost in the universal verdure of summer.

And yet there is a oneness of effect, likewise, when we choose to look at a whole sweep of woodland, or swamp shrubbery, instead of analyzing its component trees. Scattered over the pasture, which the late rains have kept tolerably green, there are spots, or islands, of a dusky red—a deep, substantial hue, very well fit to be close to the ground, while the yellow, and light fantastic shades of green, soar upward to the sky. These red spots are the blue-berry bushes." Of these blueberry bushes he was fondest of all in the display. He also loved the "sheltered hollows."

"Oh, the beauty of grassy slopes, and the hollow ways of the paths, winding between the hills, and the intervals between the road and the woodlot; and all such places, where Summer lingers and sits down, strewing dandelions of gold, and blue asters, as her parting gifts and memorials! I went to a grape vine, which I have already visited several times, and found some clusters of grapes still remaining, and now perfectly ripe."

In analytical vein he wrote "Sunlight is like the breath of life to this pomp of autumn . . . As I beheld it today . . . there were some trees that seemed really made of sunshine, and others of a sunny red, and the whole picture was painted with but little relief of darksome hues—only a few evergreens."

Recounting his long walks, Hawthorne made Thoreau-like studies of the wild life encountered. On October ninth, on a walk to Cow Island, "Coming within view of the river, I saw several wild ducks, under the shadow of the opposite shore, which was high, and covered with a grove of pines. I should not have discovered the ducks, had they not risen, and skimmed the surface of the glassy river, breaking its dark water with a bright streak, and sweeping round gradually, rose high enough to fly." On the same walk, he started a partridge; speculated about the small birds in flocks flitting about the fields; and studied little fish darting in shoals through the pools and depths of "brooks now replenished to their brims, and rushing towards the river with a swift, ember-colored current." Like Thoreau, Hawthorne was amused by the crows, whose cawing resounded at this season. Another afternoon, Hawthorne lay a long while in a hollow of the woods, watching a squirrel capering about among the trees over his head.

On these woodland strolls, human encounters were scarce. "In my whole walk," Hawthorne noted on October ninth, "I saw only one man, and him at a distance in the obscurity of the trees. He had a horse and wagon, and seemed to be getting a load of dry brushwood."

Another time he "came to where had once stood a farmhouse, which appeared to have been recently torn down." To meet as many people as "a grown girl, in company with a little boy, gathering barberries" in a secluded lane; "a portly gentleman, wrapped in a great coat, who asked the way to Mr. Joseph Goddard's"; and "a fish cart from the city, the driver of which sounded his horn along the lonesome way," was so exceptional as to be noteworthy.

The foliage reached its peak that year in the middle of October, for on the thirteenth, Hawthorne wrote, "No language can give an idea of the beauty and glory of the trees, just at this time. It would be easy, by a process of word-daubing, to set down a confused idea of gorgeous colors, like a bunch of tangled skeins of bright silk; but there is nothing in reality, of the glare which would thus be conveyed."

Within the week, the woods "assumed a soberer tint." "The bright yellow and rich scarlet" were "no more to be seen." Many of the shrubs had shed their leaves. Only Hawthorne's favorite, the clumps of blueberry, still glowed "like scarlet islands in the midst of withered pasture ground, or crowned the tops of barren hills." Their hue, "a lustrous scarlet," made "a beautiful fringe on Autumn's petticoat."

The mighty oaks, to be sure, had taken on "a russet brown tint"— in pleasant contrast to the evergreens. But scrub-oak leaves, withered at the edges, rustled a whispered warning of winter. No tree, even those in sheltered spots, dells which helped to retain leaves, would bear a close examination now. Each looked ragged, wilted, frostbitten.

By the twenty-second, Autumn "in a continual succession of unpleasant Novembry days made rapid progress in the work of decay." Yet in the sheltered spots one still came upon "a very peculiar sense of warmth." In one such place, Hawthorne saw a mosquito—"frost-pinched, and so wretched that I felt avenged for all the injuries which his tribe inflicted upon me last summer—and so did not molest this lone survivor."

Walnuts in their green rinds and chestnuts in their brown burrs were falling from the trees. A yellow maple leaf, bright scarlet at the tip, was a treasured reminder of the vanished glory. "A stone wall," Hawthorne observed in Novembry mood, "when shrubbery has grown around it, and trees have thrust their roots beneath it, becomes a very pleasant and meditative object; it does not belong too evidently to man, having been built so long ago; it seems part of nature."

The last entry Hawthorne was ever to make at Brook Farm, October twenty-seventh, 1841, records what would be a rare sight today. "Fringed gentians; found the last probably, that will be seen this year, growing on the margin of the brook."

Everyone at Brook Farm loved and respected Mr. Hawthorne. Though honored with high office—Treasurer of the Institute—now, suddenly, to Ripley and Dana's consternation, Mr. Hawthorne was leaving Brook Farm, for the winter anyway. It was some comfort that he would not try to withdraw his investment. At least, not immediately.

The Farmers could not understand why their program of Labor and Culture did not suit a novelist. Mr. Hawthorne's revolt against farming puzzled them—he was so fond of the animals. "He takes such pains," they said, "to put the two cows, Daisy and Dolly, in adjoining stalls at night because they are always together in the pasture." And everyone remembered how Mr. Hawthorne recoiled in horror from a platter of spare ribs cut from a pig he had tended, exclaiming, "I should as soon think of a sculptor eating a piece of one of his own statues!"

The truth of the matter was, Hawthorne had grown "sick to death of playing at philanthropy and progress." But the Ripleys' own enthusiasm for their new and improving way of life waxed high as the year 1841 drew to an end.

5.

Now that the formal organization had been set up, the household and schools firmly established and functioning smoothly, everyone felt full of confidence. It was less encouraging to find when the farm books were balanced that the harvest which had seemed so bountiful might be insufficient for their needs. Because of the increase in numbers they now used all the milk from the dairy farm, and had none to market. The hay, although plentiful, was of poor quality, mingled with sorrel and weeds. They sold it, but not at a top price. They were plowing up more land for produce this fall, but they knew they would have to fertilize it —another expense. And who would cultivate the new planting? There never seemed to be enough hands to go around! They could accomplish more, in less time, if the farming tools were not so crude and old-fashioned. Yet for economy's sake the old ones must serve until they wore to pieces.

In the midst of reckoning these handicaps, they ordered a great many expensive little trees for the nursery. Although he must have known very well that it would be years before the young fruit trees would bear, Charles Dana supervised the planting with buoyant optimism. Who could hold back from expansion when every mother's son had gained weight and a fine tan from the fresh air and exercise? When everyone, except the absent Mr. Hawthorne, vowed that practice with the scythe limbered up the soul?

Sobersided William Allen caught the contagion of confidence in their enterprise. Despite the meagre harvest he got married that fall and brought his bride to Brook Farm. The lady was the same Miss Sylvia Farrar of Keene, New Hampshire, whom he had addressed as "My Dear Friend" the previous May. His wife knew what to expect; and if William Allen then had entertained doubts as to whether "these literary characters" could make a farm pay, his own knowledge of farming had since made him one of the three Directors of the Institute.

In November, after months of hesitation, John S. Dwight finally joined the staff of the Brook Farm Department of Education. In a paper, "Music," published in the *Atlantic Monthly*, forty years later, Dwight attributed his initial success in improving the popular taste in music to the enthusiasm and support of the Farmers. "Then came the Brook Farm experience," wrote he who was called "the Music Director of Boston" in 1870, "and it is equally a curious fact that music, and of the best kind, the Beethoven Sonatas, the Masses of Mozart and Haydn, got at, indeed in a very humble, home-made, and imperfect way, was one of the chief interests and refreshments of those halcyon days. Nay, it was among the singing portion of those plain farmers, teachers, and (but for such cheer) drudges, that the first example sprang up of the so-called Mass Clubs—once so much in vogue among small knots of amateurs."

Dwight arrived at the Hive when all were having tea; and he was charmed by the gaiety with which everybody turned to and washed up. "All joined in—the Curtis brothers, Dana, and all. It was very enchanting, quite a lark as we say." Much of the industry was conducted in that fashion, "because it combined the freest sociability with the useful arts." Brook Farm, as Dwight later recalled it, had offered "a sort of pastoral life, rather romantic, although so much hard labor was involved in it."

Soon after his arrival, this bashful, slender, beaming little man surrounded himself with groups of singing children. The tiny tots sang by rote; the elder from the *Manual of the Academy of Music*. Dwight taught instrumental music as well, and he often came in from the fields to give a lesson. Sometimes the delicate little creature was so exhausted that he fell asleep on the sofa while listening to a pupil.

Dwight was too modest to admit that he was the sole instigator and unwearied worker in creating a taste for something better than the Swiss bell-ringers and the mangled psalmody, popular among the Farmers when he came. But Georgiana Bruce assures us that it was his genius alone which inspired them to attempt "Sometimes psalms, and sometimes songs, and sometimes the deep music of Beethoven."

The season was propitious for the arts. From Thanksgiving until Easter, Massachusetts people are compelled to rise above inclement weather; so, as the long winter closed in, the Farmers, following New England tradition, strove to implant a sense of finer values in youthful minds.

The good life as practiced at West Roxbury encouraged self-expression, and talent abounded at Brook Farm. The Amusement Group, headed by Miss Amelia Russell, frequently arranged an evening of entertainment at the Hive. Often they enticed the entire company into a game of "dramatic proverbs," or impromptu charades. On special occasions, those with histrionic talent presented *tableaux vivants*, or a scene from a play. On theatrical nights "scarlet shawls, old silken robes, ruffs, velvets, furs, all kinds of miscellaneous trumpery" converted Georgiana Bruce and her fellow enthusiasts into "the people of a pictorial world."

The scholarly preferred the evenings dedicated to the high education. On these occasions Mr. Ripley would elucidate Kant or Spinoza; or his wife might read Dante aloud in the original. Sometimes, splendid works of art were shown, "after engravings from old masters."

Dancing was a favorite recreation among the young people at the end of the day, and it was almost their only recreation which was not tinged with self-improvement or useful endeavor. Games of chance were considered a waste of precious time. Hunting was taboo. No one would have had the face to kill furry little animals for fun, and afterward sit down to supper with those members of the Community who were vegetarians. To chop wood or shovel snow offered a man a more rewarding exercise. Weather permitting, they skated on the Charles. What with thaws and snowfalls, the opportunities to skate were few. But they could always clear the floor in a jiffy for a reel or polka. Eager as the girls for the fun to begin, the men helped with the supper dishes; and as they washed and wiped, the rafters rang to the tune of "Oh Canaan, Bright Canaan," and similar melodies.

In the snowy season, visitors were few. A few faithful friends braved the slippery roads from time to time, and among these occasional visitors the pleasantest was Christopher Pearse Cranch, the same light-hearted young man who had accompanied George Ripley and Theodore Parker on their long hike to the "Groton Convention" in the summer of 1841. Cranch was the son of a Washington judge, and he had been educated for the Unitarian ministry, in itself an excellent introduction to Brook Farm. Unlike most of the other ex-divines, Cranch possessed ample means and a multitude of talents. He sang; played the flute, violin, piano and guitar. He could also act and draw, and in frivolous mood he was the cleverest mimic and caricaturist in New England. Cranch had "sunk the minister in the man"; and instead of turning reformer, this tall, graceful, prince-like creature—he had a striking head framed in a wealth of dark curls—turned landscape painter and poet.

Whenever the boys saw Kit Cranch alighting from the omnibus which plied to and fro from Boston, they rushed out to help him with his luggage; and as soon as the sweet piping of his flute proclaimed the good news of his arrival, young and old swarmed to the Hive to beg him for an "Hour of Diversion."

Kit always obliged. A ballad sung to his guitar quickly melted the more susceptible to tears; and after one and all were well worked upon, he would sit down at the piano and render that stirring lyric, *The Erl King*. When the last chords of the mysterious and awe-inspiring accompaniment had died away, Cranch, ranging with ease from the sublime to the motley, would casually produce his sketchbook and pass around his latest cartoons. These never failed to reduce them all to gales of helpless laughter. In a manner of speaking, Cranch sired the "funnies" of today; for his burlesque featured one, bewildered, whacky character —himself—in a succession of incongruous situations. He called his serial "The Pilgrimage of the Child Christopher Down East," parodying the Byronic lingo then in vogue.

To please the children, Cranch obligingly retired to the hall to produce his "menagerie." From behind the door, a cow would begin to low, and be answered by her calf. Presently a sow was heard grunting

beneath the high squeals of her litter; a cock crowed among the cluck-
ings of his harem. Sheep baa-ed. Then a house dog barked. A neighbor's
hound answered; and soon all the canines in a completely imaginary village were howling at the moon. Cranch could chug like a locomotive,
too. He would make it start at a nearby station and drag a train of rat-
tling cars far into the distance, tooting plaintively.

After this vivid reminder of the despised competitive world, the
gifted ventriloquist tactfully concluded his performance by taking the
Farmers right back to the spot they loved best—the bosom of Nature. It
was very weird, the way Kit Cranch could make himself into a chorus
of frogs, whistling turtles, and calling insects. He could simulate a
veritable symphony of summer night noises!

After all this, it was difficult to make the excited children go to bed.
Parents were firm; for everyone knew that Mr. Dwight loved to make
music with Kit Cranch. After supper there would be a concert by the
string quartet.

Not all visitors were as welcome. When Orestes Brownson stopped
by to hear how his son was getting along in school, he felt it his duty to
engage in religious discussion. The rustic giant from Vermont was
truculent in debate. Emerson, of prince-like courtesy himself, had long
complained that Orestes would never stop and listen to another:
"Neither in conversation, and what is more, not in solitude."

6.

Ever since the Ripleys' unhappy trip to Concord in October, 1840,
Emerson and Margaret Fuller had known that "Community" was not
for them. But Bronson Alcott, the third "Mind" present on that occasion, already dreamed of "Fruitlands"—which would be the most
impractical Utopia of them all. Though repelled by what Emerson stig-
matized as Ripley's "hotel" approach to reform, all three were keeping
a watchful eye on Brook Farm.

Miss Fuller was no longer a near neighbor. In November she had
removed her family from Jamaica Plain to Cambridge. Neither she nor
Bronson Alcott, who lived in Concord, braved the slippery roads to
West Roxbury.

Emerson did visit Brook Farm that first winter. Doubtless, he came "to lead the talk" and also to confer with George Ripley, who was still business manager and occasional contributor to *The Dial*.

Each visit further convinced Mr. Emerson that he had acted wisely in refusing to pull down his own house to join the Community. "Impulse," he wrote in retrospect, "was the rule in the society, without centripetal balance." Everyone who joined soon fell into "intellectual sans-culottism," in his opinion. He grudgingly conceded, "The Founders should have this praise, that they have made what all people try to make, an agreeable place to live in . . ." There was, he conceded, something about the freedom from household routine, variety of character and talent, variety of work, variety of means of thought and instruction, art, music, poetry, masquerade," and all the other facets of life at Brook Farm—that "did not permit sluggishness or despondency." It did not occur to Emerson that this cheerful activity might be the result of the tone set by honest, hearty George Ripley, and his poised, elegant-mannered wife, Sophia. He glossed over their happy influence with an unsympathetic comment: "In Brook Farm was this peculiarity, that there was no head. In every family is the father, in every factory the foreman, in every shop a master; but in this Farm no authority; each was master or mistress of his or her actions, happy, hapless anarchists." In summing up Mr. Emerson shrugged away the Noble Experiment his good friends the Ripleys had once undertaken. "It was a perpetual picnic," he recorded, "a French Revolution in small; an Age of Reason in a patty-pan."

At the time, Mr. Emerson was particularly disturbed by the Brook Farm custom which allowed every member to prescribe his own hours of work. In effect each person was controlled by his own conscience and the spirit of the Ideal Community. Among the fervent, the custom produced great industry—and it also produced exhausted workers. But there were newcomers, who, though professing themselves keenly alive to the advantages the Community offered for instruction, grew proportionately averse to labor as they "grew refined." In an Association which depended on the conscience of the individual members, it followed that the greater part of the drudgery should be done by the "religious workers." Inevitably, there were cranks among them. Mr. Ripley complained that one such, a distinguished friend of his and Sophia's, "Would hoe corn all Sunday—if I would let him. But all Massachusetts could not make him do it on Monday." This was gentle, little John S. Dwight, according to his biographer, G. W. Cooke.

Nor could Emerson, born and bred Yankee, endorse a co-related custom at Brook Farm—that time, not skill, or application to work, formed the basis of pay. "The country people naturally were surprised to observe that one man plowed all day, and one looked out the window all day, and perhaps drew his own picture; and both received the same wages."

No one can deny that this system was impractical. But the Farmers had not gone to Brook Farm to make money. The wages were for all alike—ten cents an hour, and a chance to do what you wanted to do.

However critical at heart, Emerson must have kept his opinions to himself when he visited Brook Farm. For on December seventeenth, 1841, Ripley again wrote, urging Emerson to join the Community. The farming, Ripley claimed, had realized ten per cent of the value of the estate. The Direction had "adjudged their enterprise successful to date." They felt called upon to expand, however, and could do so only by persuading friends to invest in their stock. This was offered at $500 a share, and a five per cent interest was guaranteed.

Emerson again declined, in much the same terms as the year before. This year he appended some observations made by his friend, Mr. Edmund Hosmer of Concord, "a very intelligent farmer, and a very upright man."

After reading Mr. Ripley's letter to Mr. Emerson, Hosmer, it appeared, admired the spirit of the Brook Farmers, but doubted whether their theories were practical. Hosmer did not approve of "cooperation in labor" except when it was needed. If, for example, a farmer had to get in a load of hay in a hurry before a shower, he admitted that it could best be done by hiring three men to help and a promise to pay based on the proceeds of the crop. But Hosmer warned Mr. Emerson against placing financial confidence in gentlemen farmers. "No large property," he observed, "can ever be made by honest farming." Unless the gentlemen at Brook Farm were willing to put their farm in the hands of a shrewd foreman who would "sell the produce without any scrupulous inquiry on the part of the employer as to his methods," in Hosmer's opinion, the return would prove small. Such procedure, Hosmer opined, would not be approved by "Mr. Ripley and his coadjutors."

Hosmer added that it was unjust to pay all laborers alike. One man, he pointed out, brought capital to the enterprise and received interest on it. In his experience, a capitalist was usually an unskilled laborer; and the skilled farmer without capital could often do twice as much work in a day as he. "A worker's skill," Hosmer said, "is his capital. It would be unjust to pay him no interest on that." This shrewd Concord farmer was not convinced that workers would do extra work for the benefit of their own community unless they received extra pay. He said he had to give his boys a cent a basket for the potatoes they brought in, although they knew that the whole produce of the farm was for them. If he did not give this bonus, the yield declined.

Summing it up, Hosmer spoke out boldly; and Emerson did not scruple to report him. It was Hosmer's opinion that if he had run his farm the way Brook Farm was run, it would have put him and his family in the poorhouse long ago.

From this sound, earthy advice, George Ripley turned away. That it was transcribed and sent on by Waldo Emerson must have hurt him deeply, for he sent his friend and leader no further invitations to join Brook Farm.

7.

"A Glimpse of Christ's Idea of Society" concluded in *The Dial's* January issue heralded Miss Peabody's high hopes for the Brook Farmers in 1842. In the October issue, she had observed, "those, who have not the faith that the principles of Christ's kingdom are applicable to real life in the world will smile at it"—at Brook Farm—"as a visionary attempt. But even they must acknowledge it can do no harm in any event. If it realizes the hope of its founders it will immediately become a manifold blessing. Its moral aura must be salutary. As long as it lasts it will be an example of the beauty of brotherly love."

With her teacher, Dr. Channing, Miss Peabody believed: "The problem of the present age is human society, not as a rubric of abstract science, but as a practical matter and universal interest; an actual reconciliation of outward organization with the life of the individual souls who associate; and by virtue of whose immortality each of them transcends all arrangements. Transcendentalism," she reminds the reader, "belongs to no sect of religion, and no social party. It is the common ground to which all sects may rise and be purified of their narrowness for it consists in seeking the spiritual ground of all manifestations." Long before the birth of Jesus, man had organized society on a basis of competition. But the Christ, she pointed out, had desired to reorganize society, and "went to a depth of principle and a magnificence of plan for this end which has never been appreciated except here and there by an individual, still less been carried out." Miss Peabody believed implicitly in the incomparable delight "of working in a community banded by some sufficient idea to animate the will of the laborers." If such communities had not been successful in the past she was sure it was "for love of wealth, and because they sacrificed family and individual." Miss Peabody regarded all the various forms of Socialism in Europe as inadequate. The Europeans did not sufficiently stress the value of the Individual Soul. "This world may be a Kingdom of God," she asserted firmly, "to all who apprehend God and Nature truly."

There was plenty of time in the long winter evenings between New Year's and Valentine's Day to contemplate these inspiring notions; and also to debate the Articles of Association which had been drawn up in October. At last, each little detail was settled to the satisfaction of the leaders, for on February seventeenth, the Articles were signed and twelve directors appointed:—three apiece for Industry, Education, Finance and General Direction. The six appointed to the two last-named committees constituted the Board of Trustees.

When the snowy isolation of late winter abated, those who ventured over the muddy roads in Jonas Gerrish's stage which plied from the Hive to Scollay Square—in Boston—and back every day, brought news of an exciting new development in the Association Movement. It was rumored that Albert Brisbane, disciple of the French social philosopher, Charles Fourier, was raising money to buy a column in Horace Greeley's *New York Tribune*. Speculation concerning the Brisbane-Greeley agreement to promote Fourierism was keen at Brook Farm. Suddenly, everyone was talking about Brisbane's extraordinary talent for publicity, but few had heard of Charlies Fourier as yet. When questioned, Mr. Ripley recommended *The Social Destiny of Man*, Brisbane's exposition of Fourier's Social Science; or he referred inquirers to Mrs. Ripley's review of the book, which he, then editor of "Record of the Months," had published in the October, 1840, issue of *The Dial*.

"This work," Sophia had written, "is designed to give a condensed view of the system of M. Fourier for the improvement and elevation of productive industry. It will be read with deep interest by a large class of our population. The name of Fourier may be placed at the head of modern thinkers, whose attention has been given to the practical evils of society and the means of their removal. His general principles should be cautiously separated from the details which accompany their exposition, many of which are so exclusively adapted to the French character as to prejudice their reception with persons of opposite habits and associations. The great question which he brings up for discussion concerns the union of labor and capital in the same individuals, by a system of combined and organized industry. This question, it is more than probable, will not be set aside at once, whenever its importance is fully perceived, and those who are interested in its decision will find materials of no small value in the writings of M. Fourier. They may be regarded, in some sense, as the scientific analysis of the co-operative principle, which has, within a few years past, engaged the public attention in England, and, in certain cases, received a successful practical application."

It is evident from this review, which, without doubt, reflected her husband's views as well as her own, that the Ripleys were no more interested in Fourierism than they were in other social plans, or communities such as Hopedale.* Indeed, Sophia distinctly informed her readers that certain aspects of Fourierism were decidedly too French for the chaste New Englanders.

There is no indication that the Ripleys had changed their attitude in the late winter of 1842. It is more probable that they shared the reservations of Miss Peabody, who had commented on Fourierism in *The Dial* two months before Brisbane launched his campaign in the *Tribune*. "Brisbane has made a plan worthy of study in some of its features, but erring in the same manner," she declared. "Fourier does not go down into a sufficient spiritual depth to lay foundations which may support his superstructure. Our imagination before we reflect, no less than our reason after reflection, rebels against this attempt to circumvent moral freedom and imprison it in his Phalanx"—Fourier's term for his rigidly determined social unit. "Yet we would speak with no scorn of a work which seems to have sprung from a true benevolence, and has in it such valuable thought. It is in his chapters on the education and uses of children that we especially feel his inadequacy to his work. But he forestalls harsh criticism by throwing out what he says as a feeler after something better. As such it has worth."

Soon Brisbane persuaded Greeley to grant him space whether he could pay for it or not. Accordingly, on Saturday, March the fifth, 1842, the *New York Weekly Tribune* ran three articles which had run separately in the daily. The weekly was a convenient digest of doings in the great world intended for the out-of-town reader; and the impact of Brisbane's opening blast was undoubtedly threefold at Brook Farm. The first article, by Hugh Doherty, editor of the London *Phalanx*, gave a

* The Adin Ballou Christian Communist Settlement (1841–1857).

résumé of Fourier's life, emphasizing those episodes which had convinced him that society in his day was unorganized and irrational, and the individual the prey of caprice, force, and fraud.

From Doherty, *Tribune* readers learned that François Marie Charles Fourier was born in 1772 at Besançon of middle-class parents. On leaving school he traveled for various firms throughout Belgium, Holland, and Germany. His father, a prosperous linen merchant, died in 1793, leaving his son $20,000—in francs, of course. Fourier invested his entire fortune in a colonial produce concern in Lyons, and lost it all within a year. The warehouse in which he had stored the raw materials and spices he had imported was sacked by some revolutionaries; and the outgoing vessel laden with goods in exchange, shipwrecked. His confidence in the existing social order was further disturbed by his experiences in the Army. Serving as a dragoon 1793–95, on the Moselle and Rhine, he revolted against the wastage and futility of war; and on his return to Marseilles he witnessed the dumping of grains by a wholesale house. To maintain a high price by such means, when the poor were starving, horrified Fourier; and from that day he studied the possibility of founding a new social order based on pure reason.

In 1799 he discovered the cornerstone of his social science, "The Laws of Attraction, and The Destiny of Man." This was composed of "The Three Axioms." First, all the Harmonies of the Universe are distributed in Progressive Series, or, The Series distributes all Harmonies. Second, the Creator being one Infinite Harmonious Being, everything in Nature must be an imitation of His own attributes, and therefore, there exists a Universal Analogy in every order of Creation. Third, the Permanent Attractions and Repulsions of every Being in the Creation are exactly in Proportion to their respective Functions and Real Destines in the Universe—"Universal Analogy."

If the reader is confused by this jargon, it is likely that the *Tribune* readers were, too. The wonder is that Brisbane succeeded in popularizing Fourierism with just this sort of material; or that Fourier succeeded in acquiring any disciples. Indeed, he had had a hard time finding any. He had to wait until 1816 before he found his first, Just Murion. In the meantime Fourier had returned to Lyons and become "Courtier Marron," an unlicensed commercial agent. This provided a livelihood, kept him in touch with practical affairs, and afforded leisure for study.

The first fruit of his cerebration, *Treatise on Domestic and Agricultural Association*, was published at Besançon in 1822. Both Fourier's dissertations and his book were totally ignored. Undeterred, he set to work once more, and published his *Elementary Treatise* in 1829. This attracted some attention and at last gained him support among the Saint-Simonians. In the next few years Fourier and his followers among the Saint-Simonians founded *La Reformé Industrielle*, with Councils of Industry, Internal Arrangements; Tribunal of Justice, Commercial Council, etc. The alliance was natural, for though differing in many respects, the social system of Fourier had this in common with that of Saint-Simon—both clung to property, both were devotees of inequality. As Sir Alexander Gray observes in *The Socialist Tradition*, "These two fathers of Socialism are not in essence particularly Socialistic; they are disfigured by strangely conservative features which do not appear in the child."

Having tasted success, Fourier wrote a number of extraordinary books in which he said the same things over and over again. He died in 1837, at the age of sixty-five.

The Farmers were not in the least interested in the last years of Fourier, but they were thrilled by his "Theory of Attractive Industry" as presented in the second article by Albert Brisbane. With his instinct for choosing an illustration so vivid that even the dullest person could understand, Brisbane pointed out that it is good for us to work at what we like, just as it aids digestion to eat what we like. Indeed, if we live in harmony with the laws of our individual nature the benefits to ourselves and others prove incalculable. For the providence of God extends to the social world; and to bring about the millennium man has only to follow his "Passionate Attractions."

An Association planned on the model of a Fourier Phalanx, would offer—Brisbane promised—individual liberty, and it would also provide the most favorable conditions for enjoying the new rights. Industry would prove delightful as well as rewarding; and children, too, would enjoy school, because their education would be conducted according to their attractions. Since the petty tyranny of a malevolent person could be worse than that of the political tyrant, labor directors would be elected to keep the ill-intentioned in their place.

The third article described the growth of Fourierism in America, and the steps Brisbane and his followers were planning further to promote the cause.

As the weeks went by, Brisbane's style became increasingly emphatic and his matter repetitious. Yet the immediate response was sensational. Groups of Fourierites—quickly dubbed "The Fury-ites" because of their fanatic zeal—sprang up all over the country. By March twenty-sixth,

1842, Brisbane happily advised his followers: "We are now writing a series of articles for *The Democratic Review, The Boston Quarterly Review* (The first article in the latter will appear in April), and the *Evening Post* is taking notice of our efforts . . ."

Much of Fourier's doctrine would point out that political liberty is only one liberty; and that if man is restricted in the work he would do, he is a slave. Brisbane admitted that Americans enjoyed more political liberty than Europeans, but he pointed out that the Social System was the same in both continents, and it was that which he wished to change.

Aware that years might elapse before it would be possible to establish a phalanx composed of sixteen hundred and twenty people, or build a phalanstery to house them and secure five thousand acres to sustain them, Brisbane planned on a more modest scale. It was his immediate hope to persuade four hundred people to invest $1,000 apiece to found a small phalanstery. He insisted that the capital would be safer in such an Association than in a business enterprise. Such capital would be guaranteed by the ardor, intelligence and personal interest of all the members, qualities which would also insure abundant production. Noninvesting members would be guaranteed freedom of action and control of the full reward of their labor by the possession of its fruits.

Fagged by the long winter—in New England the cold winds blow through March and early April—the Farmers read Brisbane's column with ever-increasing interest. The elaborate joint-stock organization of a Fourier Phalanx, avowedly designed to safeguard every type of vested property interest, made a strong appeal to men who had established their own community in such a way that it, also, aimed to protect the property rights of each subscriber. The Brook Farm ladies, though cheerful drudges, marveled at the comfort and ease Brisbane promised, for in the model phalanstery everyone would live in a luxury unknown in America in 1840. Fourier's housing-unit, situated in the middle of five thousand acres in a fertile and beautiful countryside, was to be like a huge apartment hotel, with private suites and sumptuous halls for private parties or public gatherings. It would be adorned with conservatories filled with rare tropical plants and patios for sunbathing.

Brisbane took care never to advise his public that such an "ideal township" had not as yet been established anywhere; that the luxurious phalanstery was nothing but a figment of the imagination conjured up by Charles Fourier, who had died in 1837 without sufficient backing to put his social science to a test. Indeed, no one in Europe had paid the slightest attention to Fourier's ideas until he managed to gather a group of disciples in 1815. One, Victor Considerant, had talent and ability. Considerant lately had established phalanxes at Conde-sur-Vesgnes, France. He was writing voluminously at this time, to gather support, and also to found a phalanx in Texas. For, oddly enough, the essentially Gallic Social Science of Charles Fourier obtained a readier hearing and more extensive investment in the United States than ever it had in France. The genius of Albert Brisbane in the hitherto undeveloped art of propaganda was beginning to turn many a sober head.

8.

The Directors of Brook Farm, who were still wondering why all their hard work of the summer before had yielded returns that fell far below expectation, continued to be much interested in Brisbane's propaganda. Then, suddenly—it was spring again! The warm sunshine brought a rush of outdoor work and scores of curious visitors, and, also, sympathizers, who were only waiting for a promise of the Community's success to join. The year before, Hawthorne had found it "absolutely funny . . . to observe what a glory was shed about our life and labors in the imagination of these longing proselytes." Often some enthusiast would snatch up a hoe and set to work on a cabbage patch, but always the "new enthusiasm grew as flimsy and flaccid as the proselyte's moistened shirt collar after a quarter of an hour's labor under the July sun."

Hawthorne's enthusiasm for community life had "sensibly exhaled" when he wrote *The Blithedale Romance*. But he seems to have been almost the only person, among those who were at Brook Farm during the first two years, who afterward viewed the experience through jaundiced eyes. In any case, there were many proselytes this second spring who were not so easily discouraged. By May, the Hive and the Nest were filled to overflowing; and every day brought a few applicants. Happily the Directors had foreseen the housing shortage and plans for another dwelling were drawn up. As soon as the crops were planted, all the men set to work—and with such a will that the new building was ready for occupation within a few weeks.

The new house stood on a long ledge of pudding stone overlooking the entire property. With their usual aptitude for hitting upon picturesque nomenclature, the Farmers christened it the Eyrie. No trace remains; but according to the descriptions in letters and reminiscences, it was a long, narrow, wooden structure, painted gray, with high French windows opening onto a series of terraces descending toward the brook. The long, high parlor had excellent acoustics for concerts and recitations; and it was here that George William Curtis and Christopher P. Cranch sang to John S. Dwight's accompaniment. There were smaller rooms, in the back, for recreation and study. The third floor afforded more privacy than Attica at the Hive—it is inconceivable there could be less!—and such young intellectuals as the Curtis boys, Dana and Newcomb, moved up there at once. The second floor was reserved for the Ripleys, and their precious library of foreign books. Perhaps George Ripley had discovered that a few of his followers were persons who did not appreciate his generous offer to share his treasures. If that was why he moved his library into his own private apartment in the Eyrie, it is the first indication that the halcyon days already were waning.

9

One cold, rainy morning in May, 1842, a delegation of young people waited upon their elders to ask permission to stage a woodland festival in blossom-time. They pointed out that the expense would be trifling. Amelia Russell, Mistress of the Wardrobe, had plenty of odds and ends on hand for the masquerade; and the players themselves would supply the refreshments.

The elders bestowed their blessing, on condition that the party would not take place until after the truck garden got off to a good start. The date was then set for Friday, the fourth of June—a time in New England when the full leaf presents a color scale in lush and varied tones of green, woven against the darker tapestry of pine, cedar, and hemlock. Sometimes the tender green is fringed by an occasional cluster of larches, flaunting lace and feathers.

As the day drew near, everyone prayed for good weather. "Old Man East Wind" might suddenly sweep in, bringing clouds and drenching rain; or a late frost might nip the buds of the flowering dogwood. Last year the wax-like petals had had a brown edge, like gardenias after a ball. This year, though the season again was late, the winds were kind.

Ankle deep in June, the long awaited weekend dawned calm and bright, in tune with heaven. Crowning miracle of all—the dogwood blossoms unfolded petals of purest white.

After the festivities, Sarah Allen, a cousin of William Brockway Allen, sat down and wrote a long letter to his wife, Sylvia. For William, worn out with hard work and worry at Brook Farm, had taken his Sylvia back to Keene, New Hampshire. He knew he had it in him to earn a fair livelihood at farming; but it had become painfully clear that the Ripleys were more interested in cultivating people than cabbages. Although William had left them at the height of the planting season, everyone at Brook Farm hoped the Allens would come back when William recovered his health and spirits. In the meantime, it would do no harm to remind the Allens that holidays at Brook Farm were fun.

The festivities had begun, Sarah reported, on Saturday afternoon with a sail on the Charles River—in a boat large enough to hold herself, "Caddy Allen, Charles Newcomb, G. Wells, Manuel and Odionne"— the two Spanish boys from Manila. After "a beautiful sail" they got back about eight o'clock and marvelled at all those who had remained behind—because each and every one had "decorated their heads with dogwood blossoms, some very splendid blossoms that William Bliss had gathered in the woods."

To help William Allen's sisters, Delaney and Mary, wash up the tea things, Sarah stayed at the Hive; and then the girls all went up to the Eyrie to hear a German gentleman sing. The long music room there, decked with dogwood boughs, "looked beautifully," and was packed to overflowing. There were so many visitors come for the festival that the young people overflowed all over the floor.

Mr. Edwin Morton, a newcomer among the visitors, had come at the suggestion of his brother, Ichabod, to inspect Brook Farm. Sarah found him a very pleasant man who looked "almost exactly like his brother." She added that he seemed "very much pleased." Presumably Edwin was charmed by the Community; for he and Ichabod soon built a large double house on the top of the hill. Because the brothers came from Plymouth, and as there were ample accommodations for transients in their twenty-room building, it would promptly be christened "Pilgrim House."

Sunday dawned bright and fair for the "Picnic Party" which Sarah Allen and Abby Morton had undertaken to manage, together with George William Curtis and Manuel. All four spent a busy morning. The boys set up the big, long, trestle-table and a throne at one end of it for Mrs. Ripley—who, according to rumor, would appear dressed as Queen Elizabeth.

The girls fried doughnuts and made ham sandwiches in the Hive kitchen—amid the quantities of frosted cakes and the dozens of little apple-tarts which faithful Mrs. Pratt had prepared. Those who could not bake as well as she gave "little cakes got in Boston."

When all was ready, the girls found "a sweet pretty place . . . just over the fence in Mr. Estes' woods," for "the washtub, full almost of lemonade, which McNeil and Russell made in the morning with great blue ties tied on their waists." Approving the shady spot which the boys had picked for the Directors' and Distinguished Visitors' table, the girls laid it; and then spread another table cloth on the ground for the younger and less formal group. It looked very nice, Sarah Allen reported; "Trimmed with ground pine, and wreaths of willow all around the cake."

Just before noon, all four went home to change into the costumes which Eleanor, the little seamstress, had come from Boston several days before to sew.

When they assembled in the glade, everyone, almost, was in fancy dress. There were quantities of Scotch boys, Flower Girls, Turks, and ever so many Foresters; and more than one Greek Maiden and Gypsy Fortune Teller. Among the more original, Sarah noted, Ida Russell as a Black Nun; Charles Dana, a Tyrolese Peasant; and Abby Morton as an Indian Princess "looked beautifully."

More and more guests kept arriving in the afternoon, among them a Mrs. Leach dressed as an old loafer. As such, Mrs. Leach told a pitiful story "about having a large family dependent upon her, and her having seen better days . . ." The Farmers must have been a quick audience, because everyone, apparently, spotted Mrs. Leach as a fake, and thought her a scream.

The big hit of the afternoon was George William Curtis, dressed as Fanny Elssler, the famous dancer. Sarah Allen reported, "He looked capitally . . ." And Georgie Bruce, who filled in the page of Sarah's letter which had been left blank for her, "Laughed till the tears came into her eyes at the capers George cut." She added, "The belle of the day without dispute was Ora. Ellen [Slade] was not half so beautiful."

Come evening, all went up to Eyrie, and held a Fancy Dress Dance.

They all felt tired, Sarah confessed, on this Monday after the "Picnic Party," but not as exhausted as they had expected. What a relief,

though—speeding the parting guests! Five had left right after breakfast
in the omnibus; and all but one or two had gone by the end of the day.

There was little else for Georgie to communicate to Sylvia Allen on
this blank page that Sarah had so thoughtfully provided, except to say
that Mrs. Barlow was returning from New York, where she had been
staying for a week or so. The siren was expected back that very day.
Georgie, tongue in cheek, took it "as a great compliment" to her "ma-
tronly care," that young Edward had not "missed his mother since she
left."

Through both Sarah's long letter and Georgie's postscript shines a
tableau vivant—Mrs. Ripley, in queenly robe, presiding over the Farmers' Early Summer Festival, from a throne in the woods.

As time passed by, the Farmers would love to remember her en-
throned—because, as Queen Elizabeth, Mrs. Ripley had seemed so entirely at ease; and if the hands she presented to her courtiers had rough-
ened in the past year, her bearing was regal that day. Poor Sophia, a
Cinderella story in reverse, would spend more and more hours each day
among the cinders.

10.

"Dolon," an obscure allegory of Greek Pantheism versus Transcendental Nature Religion, by Charles Newcomb, appeared in the July 1842
issue of *The Dial*. The boy, Dolon, "had always been in Nature, un-
specially and really, as if in his proper place." Although he preferred to
roam the woods and drink at the fountain whose waters soothed his
extreme sensitivity, to please his parents, Dolon had become an honor
student in school.

One day when Dolon sat brooding on his favorite boulder, he spied
a man in a red tunic and white dress in the Greek style, peering down
at him from a tree. The two stared at each other intently—Dolon in admiration, the stranger in excitement, as if he had found someone he had
been searching for. Silently, the pagan-like creature climbed down from
his perch and disappeared into a cave.

When he told them of his encounter, Dolon's parents forbade him
to return to the spot. They warned him that he must have seen the
escaped madman who believed he was a High Priest in a Greek temple.

But they neither informed the authorities, who, presumably, were searching for the madman; nor did they restrain Dolon.

Like one enthralled, the boy went back to the wood to meet his doom. The New England pagan murdered him with a knife, and dragged his body into the cave to be sacrificed to Pan.

This fustian allegory is of some interest because it was published at Emerson's particular request, and so represents "a sign of the times." In June, Emerson had written Margaret Fuller, "I wish you to know that I have *Dolon* in black and white; and that I account Charles N. a true genius; his writing fills me with joy, so simple, so subtle, so strong it is. There are sentences in *Dolon* worth the printing of *The Dial* that they may go forth."

Despite Emerson's high praise, Newcomb never again consented to publish. In time, when it appeared that his young friend never would "seek an audience," even Emerson came to doubt Newcomb's genius.

In the same issue, Mr. Emerson excoriated the "Reformers" with a vehemence the Ripleys may well have resented: "They miss the fire of the moral sentiment with personal and party heats, with measureless exaggerations and the blindness that prefers some darling measure to justice and truth. Those who are urging with the most ardor what are called the greatest benefits of mankind, are narrow, self-pleasing, conceited men, and affect us as the insane do. They bite us and we run mad also . . . It is a buzz in the ear." Though he could mock at Utopian dreamers, in the next breath he voiced the general perplexity of his generation, which he called, "Our torment in unbelief; the Uncertainty as to what we ought to do; the distrust of the value of what we do, and the distrust that the necessity (which we all at last believe in) is fair and beneficent."

Brisbane's genius for propaganda made him highly aware that certain aspects of Fourierism would shock many Americans, and so he was careful never to bring up the Frenchman's advanced ideas on "Familism," or his weird notions about the Cosmos. The column he wrote for the *New York Tribune*—which was gaining in public attention week by week—stressed over and over again Fourier's Theory of Attractive Industry, and the practical advantages of living in a phalanx.

The very name, *Attractive* Industry, had universal appeal for the worker, whether household drudge or factory slave; and Brisbane with sure instinct, harped away, week in, month out, on the delights of working in "Groups and Series." Instead of monotonous repetition, the Harmonian would have "Parcelled Exercise,"—short hours in any one occupation. This would ensure a variety of tasks. Instead of being a cog in a vast machine, the worker in "Groups and Series" would enjoy friendly rivalry, in a half dozen diversified jobs. But Brisbane never clearly explained how this glamorous program was to be arranged.

His other theme was the Phalanx. Brisbane never wearied of expatiating on the advantages of all living together under one roof—in the vast housing unit or "Unitary Building." "Forty or fifty women could do the ironing for three hundred families in a few mornings' work." Indeed, all household tasks would be similarly reduced. Conflagrations—Brisbane referred again and again to the fire hazards as if it were a frequent occurrence for a family to be burned out—certainly would be reduced to almost nothing, because of the precautions taken in the construction of the edifices. For Association would have its own special architecture, in which Unity and Harmony would be combined. But Fourier knew that man naturally dislikes uniformity, and he graciously had planned the phalanstery so that each family would find an apartment to suit each individual purse and taste.

Though a disappointed businessman, Fourier held vested interest in respect. "The world does not want an equal division of the present scanty amount of wealth," his American Apostle informed readers of his column, "it wants an immense increase of production, and then an equal division of the same, according to, as each has aided in creating it." But the good will of all the workers as well as that of the investors was essential if there was to be unity of individual and collective interest. Interest on the Association stock would, therefore, be paid from the total production—the earnings of capital and labor. Members of Direction—the Directors—would be drawn from both groups.

Mr. Brisbane, lately in Boston, while there had pressed one of his articles on Mr. Emerson for publication in *The Dial*. "He pushes his doctrine with all the force of memory, talent, honest faith, and importunacy," Emerson observed waspishly in his own piece, "Fourierism and the Socialists," also printed in the July issue. But it was the Fourieristic System itself which raised Emerson's quills and inspired a flow of images. "The force of arrangement could no further go . . . It was not daunted by distance, or magnitude, or remoteness of any sort, but strode about nature with a giant's step, and skipped no fact, but wove its large

Ptolemaic web of cycle and epicycle, of phalanx and phalanstery, with laudable assiduity. Mechanics were pushed so far as fairly to meet spiritualism. One could not but be struck with the strange coincidences between Fourier and Swedenborg."

From so much, it is clear that Emerson had by-passed Brisbane, and was thinking now, of Fourier's doctrine in the complete, unexpurgated edition. Where and how he got it is uncertain. Brisbane's tract, *The Social Destiny of Man*, was in print, but the works of Fourier had not been translated as yet. Emerson, of course, had European correspondents, who kept him informed of the movement abroad, and one of these may have sent him Fourier in the French. In this same article, Emerson reported that Hugh Doherty, editor of the London *Phalanx*, had become very much alarmed by the invention and manufacture of a machine by which four men could cultivate four thousand acres with ease. If that should come to pass, Doherty warned, it was high time for laborers to band together to avoid starvation.

"Association and Colonization" was the motto of Doherty's London *Phalanx*; and it already had inspired Fourierites to found a Colony at the Abbaye of Citeau in France; and it was promoting another—a hundred intrepid souls would shortly set sail for Santa Catarina, fifty miles from Rio de Janeiro. In the meantime, it gave Doherty great satisfaction to report that festivals had been held the previous April on Fourier's birthday, in London, Paris, and New York.

Emerson, himself, recognized in Fourier a fellow crusader in the cause of the individual against class and circumstances: "Genius . . . must now set itself to raise the social condition of man, and to redress the disorders of the planet he inhabits . . . Society, concert, cooperation, is the secret of the coming Paradise."

Emerson mulled over the ideas of his time, that isolation makes drudgery of work; that "concert"—each doing what he likes in a congenial group, makes a happy society. Not for him, of course; but, possibly for humanity.

Then, in his shrewd Yankee way, he went on to analyze the theory of Attractive Industry. According to Fourier, his theory would "speedily subdue, by adventurous, scientific, and persistent tillage, the pestilental tracts; would equalize temperature, give health to the globe, and cause the earth to yield 'healthy imponderable fluids' to the solar system, as now it yields noxious fluids."

"The Hyena, the jackel, the gnat, the bug, the flea, were all beneficent parts of the system; the good Fourier knew what those creatures should have been, had not the mould slipped, through the bad state of the atmosphere, caused, no doubt, by these same vicious imponderable fluids. All these shall be redressed by human culture; and the useful goat, and dog, and innocent poetic moth, or the wood tick to consume decomposing wood, shall take their place. It takes sixteen hundred and eight men to make one man, complete in all the faculties; that is to be sure that you have got a good joiner, a good cook, a barber, a poet, a judge, an umbrella-maker, a mayor and alderman and so on."

Emerson enjoyed "illustrating" the flights of Fourier's disordered imagination: "Now fancy the earth planted with fifties and hundreds of these phalanxes, side by side—what tillage, what architecture, what refectories, what dormitories, what reading rooms, what concerts, what lectures, what gardens, what baths! What is not in one will be in another, and many will be within easy distance.

"Then, know you all that Constantinople is the natural capitol of the globe. There, in the Golden Horn will be the Arch Phalanx established; there will the Omniarch reside. Aladdin and his magician, or the beautiful Scheherezade, can alone in these prosaic times, before the sight, describe the material splendors collected there. Poverty shall be abolished; deformity, stupidity, and crime shall be no more. Genius, Grace, Art, shall abound; and it is not to be doubted that in the reign of "At-Ind.' all men will speak in blank verse."

After this rare outburst of pleasantry, Emerson summed up his serious reactions to the Fourier doctrine: "Our feeling was that Fourier had skipped no fact but one, namely, Life. He treats man as a plastic thing; something that may be put up or down, ripened or moulded, polished, made into solid, or fluid, or gas, at the will of the leader; or, perhaps as a vegetable, from which, though now a poor crab, a very good peach can by manure and exposure be in time produced; but skips the faculty of life, which spawns and scorns system and system-makers, which eludes all conditions, which makes or supplants a thousand phalanxes and New Harmonies with each pulsation. There is an order in which in a sound mind the faculties always appear, and which according to the strength of the individual they seek to realize in the surrounding world. The value of Fourier's system is that it is a statement of such an order, externized, or carried outward into its correspondence with facts. The mistake is that this particular order and series is to be imposed by force of preaching and votes on all men, and carried into rigid execution. Whereas, the true and good springs from within each man.

"Let us be lovers and servants of that which is just, and straightway, every man becomes a center of a holy and beneficent republic."

Brisbane's article, *Means of Effecting a Final Reconciliation between Religion and Science,* after Emerson's richness of image and insight, reads like a prize essay in a preparatory school. The prophet of Brisbane's piece, "The Genius to do it," is, of course, Charles Fourier. For he was the one who opened "The Book of Beauties" to introduce "Universal Unity in Five Cardinal Branches." Furthermore, Fourier had proved immortality scientifically; and totted up the necessary conditions for the reconciliation of religion and science—a good social order to provide richness for all, a high moral tone among mankind, and the right genius to propagate these ideas. Brisbane let it be clearly understood that he was that genius and well-qualified for the task. He felt perfectly sure that his propaganda exalted faith and satisfied reason. In each phalanx that sprang up, men and women would unite and harmonize freely!

If Mr. Emerson had had the good luck to get a look at Fourier's scientific conclusions—and obviously he had—he could make fun of some of the absurdities in the System. But those who had no access to Fourier in the original, had to depend on the tempting tidbits Brisbane fed the public in his column. The effects of the depression of 1837 lingered on; and discouraged persons read about the benefits to be found "in Association" with mounting excitement.

Meanwhile the Farmers, generally speaking—like the public—learned only as much of Fourierism as Brisbane chose to publicize. His selective faculty was shrewd, indeed; and he based his distribution on the classic American pattern—the town meeting. In July, 1842, when the Fourier Association of the City of New York announced a series of lectures to be held in its hall twice a week, at a cost of six cents per seat, it was made known that the real purpose of these gatherings was the formation of small, local Fourier Societies throughout the land. Aware that "nothing succeeds like success"—he had no misgivings about the cliché—Brisbane constantly reminded his public that Fourierism was gaining in spots as remote from one another as Spain and Jefferson City, Missouri.

The demand for Fourieristic pamphlets had increased so rapidly the publisher was always in arrears in meeting it, according to Brisbane.

11

A wave of optimism overtook the Farmers as interest in the Association Movement gained momentum through the press. On August eighth, 1842, "Extract from a private letter of a member of the West Roxbury Community," appeared in the *New York Tribune*. The writer, who without a doubt was George Ripley, reflected the fever and haste of expansion at Brook Farm. "We number now about seventy souls, of whom some fifteen are Associates, the remainder pupils, boarders, and persons whose labor we are obliged to hire. We own two finished houses, hire another, and are building two more. As soon as these are done we shall have not less than one hundred persons . . . A shoemaker, a blacksmith, and a carpenter would serve us greatly, and keep within ourselves large sums which we now have to pay out. We congratulate ourselves especially that our organization is not fixed and finished but constantly tending toward something better."

In addition to Pilgrim House, the Carpenter Group, one of their most competent units, hurriedly knocked up a six-room dwelling in the shape of a Maltese Cross for a Mrs. Alvord, a rich widow in very poor health. These two, and the "Eyrie," all three were built between the nineteenth of April and Labor Day.

On August thirteenth, another letter, presumably from Ripley, appeared in the *Tribune*. Taking up from where he left off—that their Association was not fixed but tending toward improvement—he continued: "I am convinced that our Association could not exist long if it were not so. And here I fear that an Association on Fourier's system might well suffer. That system seems to leave little to be done by circumstances, but starts with definite rules for every possible case. Still I desire to speak with great diffidence on this point, especially as my own experience shows me, more and more, the immense practical wisdom embodied in Fourier's plan." This is especially interesting testimony as it represents the halfway mark between disbelief and conversion to Fourierism.

O. B. Frothingham, Ripley's biographer, in his *Transcendentalism in New England*, states categorically that at the period when Ripley founded Brook Farm he was wholly unacquainted with the systems of socialism current in Paris, and that "The name of Charles Fourier was unfamiliar to him." It seems very unlikely that Ripley had not read Fourier in the original before Brisbane published; or, at least learned of the new Social Science as early as 1838, when Brisbane returned from France. Ripley may even have conversed with Brisbane two years before he founded Brook Farm. In any case, the theory of "Attractive Industry" was not far removed from the Union of Labor and Culture; and the words "Unity and Harmony" were as sacred at Brook Farm as ever they should be at a phalanstery! Yet for some reason the two standard authorities on Brook Farm chose to ignore Ripley's growing interest in Fourierism. Perhaps the memory of a distinguished Transcendentalist gentleman—a former Unitarian Divine—debasing himself and his followers with the notions of an unsound French philosopher was utterly distasteful to both writers.* Neither fully explored this experimental venture of George Ripley's.

Mrs. Alvord died before Thanksgiving. She had complained that her new house was hot in August and cold when the early frosts began. On the same principle as that upon which they had named the unruly heifer, the Farmers christened it "The Margaret Fuller Cottage." Even newcomers understood what was meant. The arrogant sibyl had condescended to pay Brook Farm a visit at husking time. It was Miss Fuller's first prolonged stay, and it had not gone off too well.

As often happened, Miss Fuller made a disagreeable impression on many. Even Emerson, who later became her close friend, on first acquaintance had found Margaret's personality antagonistic. Emerson felt that her manner expressed "an overweening sense of power, and slight esteem of others." Horace Greeley, though he recognized her genius in an age when everyone was prejudiced against a female who aspired to a career, confessed that at first he had felt uneasy in her company in a drawing room. This would not deter him from persuading her to leave *The Dial* to join *The Tribune*, in 1844. "The men thought she carried too many guns," he wrote in his autobiography, "and the women did not like one who despised them." But if Margaret Fuller ever had condescended to appear behind the footlights, the astute journalist reflected confidently she would "soon have been recognized as the first actress of the nineteenth century."

* Lindsay Swift, author of *Brook Farm*, and O. B. Frothingham, Ripley's biographer.

In the eyes of Horace Greeley—as in the eyes of other admirers—
Margaret Fuller lacked beauty. "Yet the high, arched dome of her head,
the changeful expressiveness of every feature, and her whole air of
mingled dignity and impulse gave her a commanding charm." Miss
Fuller's odd physical mannerisms were pronounced "expressive," in the
critical jargon of the time. She could contract her pupils almost to a
point—"and then, a sudden dilation, till the iris seemed to emit flashes.
A singular pliancy of the vertebrae and muscles of the neck enabled her,
by a mere movement to denote each varying emotion . . . In moments
of tenderness, or pensive feeling, its curves were swanlike in grace; but
when she was scornful or indignant, it contracted and made swift turns
like that of a bird of prey . . . In the animation yet abandon, of Margaret's attitude and look, were rarely blended the fiery courses of north-
ern, and the soft languor of southern races."

Her friends called her neck a "swan's"; her enemies said it reminded
them of a "snake." So it is not surprising that Miss Fuller got a mixed
reception at Brook Farm, where all made it their creed to speak and act
their mind.

"The first day here is desolate," Margaret confided to her diary. "You
seem to belong to nobody—to have a right to speak to nobody."

But she was never one to let herself be ignored for long. She knew her
"own," as she called those whom she instinctively recognized as potential satellites; and when Margaret chose she could draw such persons to
her with compelling magnetism.

Georgiana Bruce was such a one; and in the aura of the English girl's
devotion, Miss Fuller took heart. "The freedom of this place is delightful," she wrote a few days later. She found it "glorious to roam the
woods at will."

Miss Fuller's first "Conversation" at Brook Farm had proved a trying ordeal. The topic, "What We Can Do For Ourselves And Others,
In Its Largest Sense," failed to arouse the usual discussion. None but a
few elders had responded, despite Mr. Ripley's hearty approbation of
her choice of theme. He said she had introduced the very thing the
Brook Farmers were about.

The young people, who had thrown themselves on the floor because
there were never enough chairs to go round, commenced to sprawl, and
yawn. Quite a number went out when they had had enough. "The people," Miss Fuller recorded, "showed a good deal of *sans culottism* in
their manners."

It was most upsetting. It never occurred to Miss Fuller that she was a bore. Such rudeness, she fumed, and to one accustomed to deference! No respect for the boldness and animation her part required! One of the young women had actually treated her with impudence. What evils sprang from "want of conventional refinement!" This young woman, Miss Fuller determined, "will see that she ought not to have done it."

After this disappointing reception, it was a comfort to lie in bed long after the rising horn, and toy with a late breakfast brought to her bedside by Georgiana Bruce. This considerate young person, anxious to spare Miss Fuller's sensitive lips from contact with the coarse Britannia ware, had gathered together "some remnants of ancient china." When appropriately thanked, the dear child stammered that it was her dearest wish to save Miss Fuller some little fatigue during her stay; it was a privilege "to wait on one so worthy of all service."

But it grew tiring for Miss Fuller to have to explain to everyone, every day, why she had not joined the Community. As often as she could, "the Sibyl" fled to "the perfume of the woods."

One afternoon Sophia Ripley arrested her flight, and held her for "a good talk." Margaret could not plead fatigue or headache. Sophia had been her first promoter. In the fall of 1839 Margaret had appealed to Sophia to help her start her first class, her first series of "Conversations." "The advantages of a weekly meeting, for conversation," she had written, "might be great enough to repay the trouble of the attendance, if they consisted only in supplying a point of union to well-educated and thinking women, in a city with great pretensions to moral refinement." She sketched briefly her ambition: "To pass in review the departments of thought and knowledge and endeavor; to place them in due relation to one another in our minds. To systematize thought, and give precision and clearness in which our sex are so deficient, chiefly, I think, because they have so few inducements to test and classify what they receive. To ascertain what pursuits are best suited to us, in our time and state of society, and how we may make best use of our means for building up the life of thought upon the life of action."

In response to this appeal, Sophia Ripley and Elizabeth Peabody had put their heads together; and together they assembled a group of aspiring ladies in Miss Peabody's bookshop on West Street. That occasion, November sixth, 1839, had launched Miss Fuller's since famous "Conversations."

So what could Margaret say now when pressed to join Brook Farm? She owed Sophia loyalty, but surely she did not owe her life to Community? After listening politely to Sophia's promotion talk, Margaret admitted that Association *might* prove the salvation of mankind. But it was as yet, she reminded Sophia, only an experiment. Until Association proved successful, she for one did not think it worthwhile to lay such stress on it. She had not discouraged others from joining, had she? That, Margaret thought privately, might be impossible in future. It was extremely awkward to speak her mind when all three Ripleys were "acting out in their own persons what they intend."

Margaret reminded Sophia of her frail health. "My position would be too uncertain here," she pointed out, "as I could not work."

"They would all like to work for a person of genius," Sophia countered. "They would not like to have this service claimed from them, but would like to tender it of their own accord."

"Perhaps," Margaret replied, "but where would be my repose when they were always to be judging whether I was worth it or not?"

Margaret Fuller refused to be caught. Each time anyone tried to persuade her to join Brook Farm, assuming patience she let the person talk. There might be dignity in labor—for others. But it should be clearly understood that Miss Fuller would never feel the urge to peel potatoes.

One evening during Miss Fuller's stay, a husking bee was held in the barn, "Men, women, and children all engaged." There was not quite light enough to bring it out, but it was nevertheless a most picturesque scene. Within half an hour, the literary luminary stole away to hear another confidence beneath the stars. After her chilly reception, such tributes were especially gratifying. A few days passed in which faltering persons pressed Miss Fuller so hard for advice that she felt like a squeezed orange. "Too much absorbed by others," she grew "almost sick." Yet she "drank in" such outpourings, "as a wine-bibber drinks a rare wine, warming to the heart." These quaffs of conversation with the bewildered young made Margaret Fuller feel superhuman, sibyl-like, almost divine.

"Certainly there should be some great design in my life," she confided to her *Journal,* "its attractions are so invariable."

As her visit drew to a close, Margaret Fuller reflected. Although each day had seemed interminable, at least she knew more about Association than she had when she came to Brook Farm. Then, with that detachment which made her a superior woman, she admitted to herself that one could not judge such an experiment fairly unless one joined in it.

But how wise she and Waldo were to resist pressure! Sensitive natures, persons with genius, could not stand daily and close contact with a whole Community of lesser mortals. She preferred to prepare a tasty little dish of intellectual fare for the Boston ladies; and Waldo, of course, had "hitched his wagon to a star." She would always be careful not to bind herself to a central or any doctrine. Had not she and Waldo agreed that man or woman stood "Much nobler . . . unpledged and unbound?"

12.

In October, 1842, two links with Brook Farm's brief past were broken.

On the seventeenth of the month, Nathaniel Hawthorne, who had married Sophia Peabody of Salem on the ninth of July, wrote Charles A. Dana, Secretary and Treasurer: "I ought, sometime ago, to have tendered my resignation as an Associate of the Brook Farm Institute, but I have been unwilling to feel myself utterly disconnected with you. As I can see but little prospect, however, of returning to you, it becomes proper for me now to take the final step. But no longer a brother of your band, I shall always take the warmest interest in your progress, and I shall heartily rejoice at your success—of which I can see no reasonable doubt."

The Ripleys had persuaded Hawthorne to delay his resignation the year before, in the hope that the finances of the Community might improve so rapidly that he might shortly withdraw his investment of $1,000, without embarrassing the Directors; and so now Hawthorne's letter must have cast a disturbing shadow. Especially since the Directors somehow or other had scraped up $475.95 of the capital plus interest Mr. Hawthorne had invested in the Brook Farm Institute of Agriculture and Education in the spring of 1841.

In a docket, labelled "New Entries 4–198, March 1846" in the Middlesex Court of Common Pleas, Cambridgeport, Massachusetts, there is an I.O.U. signed by Ripley and Dana, dated November seventh, 1842, promising to pay Hawthorne, on demand plus interest, the balance of the debt, $524.05. The tiny scrap of paper on which the three illustrious autographs appear looks as if it had been hurriedly torn from a lined-paper school notebook; and this informal, highly casual appearing document has survived to go on, bearing witness to the measures the "First American Novelist" ultimately took to recover his investment in Brook Farm.

Messrs. Ripley and Dana made no general announcement of this transaction; and perhaps this was justifiable. Ripley must have feared panic as he feared nothing else. And Hawthorne already had his following. When one considers what the effect of Hawthorne's withdrawal might have led to, it seems wise on the part of Ripley and Dana to have kept the figures to themselves.

Six days after Dana received Hawthorne's letter—October twenty-third—Dr. William Ellery Channing died in Bennington, Vermont. Increasing infirmity had compelled the great preacher to resign from his pulpit two years before; and he and George Ripley had long since reached a parting of minds.

In the heat of the religious controversy aroused by Emerson's "Divinity School Address," followed by Ripley's debate with Professor Andrew Norton, the "Great Awakener" had withdrawn his approval of Ripley, dismayed by the sudden and highly disconcerting independence of thought and action—the very qualities Dr. Channing had encouraged in the younger divines. His feeling toward them remained kind. He had summed it up in a letter to a British friend, one Miss Aiken, on July eighteenth, 1840:

"We have some signs among us of a 'Transcendental' school, as it is called, i.e., we have some noble-minded men, chiefly young, who are dissatisfied with the present, have thrown off all tradition, and talk of deriving truth from their own souls. They have some great truths at bottom, but of course wanting the modification which always comes from looking over the whole ground and seeing what is due to other truths. One discussion has risen out of this movement respecting the place which the Miracles hold in Christianity. This school rests the religion wholly on internal evidence. A great question will be: What was the inspiration of Christ? Whether it was different in kind or only in degree from the inspiration granted to all? This begins to be agitated. In all these things, I see aspiration after something better, not always wise —how can it be?—but a presage of good whether near or distant."

To learn that the prophet of his youth had seen a presage of good in his endeavor would have heartened George Ripley; but it is unlikely that the ailing old gentleman, Dr. William Ellery Channing, sent him a message to that effect. But Ripley, the one-time "Child of Channing," was not the sort of man to forget the great spiritual leader who had blazed so many trails in social reform. In those days communications were slow, and it may not have been until early November that the Ripleys received the news of Dr. Channing's death. Perhaps George and Sophia looked at one another for a long instant, then looked away across grey November fields, and drew a deep breath.

For they were aware that their knowledge of sociology was greater than Dr. Channing's had been. The "Great Awakener" had appealed to every man, whether State Street banker, or degraded miner, to practice the word of Christ. Each man who aimed to do this would save his own soul and light a bright candle for those in darkness; and gradually the contagion of such internal personal reforms would spread throughout mankind to bring about the Kingdom of Heaven on Earth.

George Ripley and the other Associationists had a more modern and realistic approach. They were aware that a man's behavior might depend on his environment. They felt keenly the injustice of one man attending a machine another man owned; and to see the American working man, hitherto a paragon of self-reliance and initiative, doing the same little task every hour every day seemed a threat to the nation's liberty; as if the Machine had trapped free men into a new form of slavery. For even in good times the hours were long and the pay low; and in bad times a man lost his job and was left without land, trade, or other means of livelihood. George Ripley and his friends honestly believed that they had established a practical alternative: that it was only in an Association that a sound man could count on a permanent home and job. They correctly identified the snag in the new Machine Age economy—unregulated competition. But their corrective was at once mediaeval and modern—"A Guild"—an order in which buying would be carefully regulated to some theory of the "just price." The question has not yet been settled.

Such questions were bewildering to the students of economy and the leaders of social reform in 1842. Which of them could foresee the new bounty the machines would produce? Lacking the gift of prophecy they underestimated the tremendous impetus of the new technology. All that they did see had proved disheartening for the worker; and it seemed inevitable that the control of the new Machinery would remain in the hands of those enterprising persons who would continue to exploit the want of enterprise in others.

13.

After the brilliant foliage of October, the warm and golden days tipped at dawn and sunset by hint of winter, the gray sedges left by heavy frost, the bare trees and wind-tossed clouds of November seemed unusually dour and threatening to the Farmers. Even on the days when the season seemed to linger in its course, days when the sun glowed kindly, and the moon rose full and golden in a lavender twilight, they could not forget that another lean winter was upon them.

The second harvest yielded a lesser return than their first. Though the crops had increased, there were now more mouths to feed. To refit the farm implements they had hoped to replace seemed a discouraging task. Last fall, William Brockway Allen had shown them how to sharpen worn blades, hew wooden handles, patch old harness. How cheerfully William had directed farm business! With what patience Sylvia had transformed green girls, Georgie, Ora, and the rest, into competent cooks and scullery maids! The Allens' enthusiasm for "Community" had seemed to the Ripleys as enduring as their own. They were still at a loss to account for their young friends' sudden withdrawal; and they were distressed that neither William nor Sylvia had written since returning to New Hampshire in the spring.

Apparently, it had done William good to be at home again where no one had heard of The Union of Labor and Culture, and farmers were far too busy in the short, hard-rushed summer for philosophical discussion. But come December, he began to miss the good company at Brook Farm, and half-regretting his hasty departure, he wrote Mrs. Ripley a heart-warming letter, as may be seen from her affectionate reply:

Brook Farm Weds. eve'g. Dec. 22 (1842)

Dear William,
    I can hardly tell you how much pleasure your letter of last week has given me, & all yr friends here. To find that with returning health your old feelings of love & kindness returned, is a most pleasant thing to us. I never gave you up entirely, as having taken a life-long leave of us, for I always felt that there was something in you & something in us that drew us together, & that this was the home of your affections after all. Where you had done a great deal & enjoyed

a great deal as well as suffered; which we all must do every where. We are having a very good time this winter, & wish Sylvia & you were here to enjoy & labour with us. Things are going on in every department better than ever before; more order prevails, & the wheels turn smoothly. We have hands enough except one to do sewing— & a good deal of that has been turned off here the last six weeks. Shoemaking is carried on at a great rate, & no one considers himself fit to walk abroad without a pair of Mr. Rykman's boots. Mr. and Mrs. Harlow have come, with their son (a very capable lad of sixteen) & a little daughter. Mr. Bradford is back again. Miss Russell is a host, interested and efficient in all kinds of work & all kinds of play. She irons, does housework, does up muslins—teaches French, keeps a sewing school & dancing school! You will be surprised to hear that Abby Morton has taken Sarah's place in the chamber work, & Sarah and I have taken the sole charge of affairs in the wash-room. Things were growing worse and worse there for want of a head. We knew how we thought it ought to be done & were willing to do it, so asked leave to take & make ourselves responsible for it. So far we have got along very well. Today (Weds) at noon we had finished off the washing entirely—the room was thoroughly cleaned & a good fire burning for the ironers, who had already done two forenoon's works. Two-thirds of the clothes were dried and folded & the rest entirely hung out. So we find that it was want of plan and not want of hands that prevented it from going on well before.

The wash room held no challenge for Mrs. Ripley, for she had run it before. But what slavery laundry work was in those days! A more vivid contrast to the bounty bestowed on modern housewives by the Machine Age could not be found. Indeed, throughout the letter Sophia's cheerfulness sounds somewhat forced, for in one breath she says everything is running better than ever before, and the next that this was not the case until she straightened matters out herself.

After all this, one is relieved to learn of more festive occupations: "We are making preparations for a Christmas celebration next Monday eve'g & a New Year's Fancy Ball the Monday after, so all are very merry & very busy." A pity Mrs. Ripley did not postpone replying to William until after the holidays, for it would be interesting to know how they celebrated Christmas at Brook Farm. Probably they did not make much of it; for it is perhaps significant that Mrs. Ripley concluded her letter on December twenty-second, with love or regards to various members of his family, but never a "Merry Christmas!"*

George Ripley added the following to his wife's letter:

* Typical of 19th century New Englanders not to make much of Christmas— an inheritance from Puritanism.

My dear William,

   I assure you I was very glad to hear from you again, and to find the kindly interest with which you still looked on your old home at Brook Farm. It will give me great pleasure, and I do not doubt that all here would share in it, to have you working at our side again, although except for the moral and social ideas which we are attempting to carry into effect there is scarce any inducement for you or others to join us. It is in vain to think of making the farm very profitable so long as we are paying this heavy interest; and we must be content to work hard for a long time to come, with small pecuniary reward.

This explains the nature of the differences between them clearly, and sounds almost like a warning to William, that although they would like to have him with them again, he is not to expect a quick fortune. William took the warning; he did not return to Brook Farm. He stayed in New Hampshire until 1855; and then took his family to Minnesota and later Kansas, where the land was richer and the farms larger than in his fondest dream.*

George Ripley's postscript concludes on a sombre financial note: "Money is still very short. I enclose $100. $70 is for you from Bartlett's note & $30 for Mr. Clarke from Stephenson's. I have given you credit for about $2.00 for use of wagon to Bartlett & Int. I have tried my best to get the balance of Reuben Stephenson's note, but in vain; & Bugbee thinks there is but little hope for his doing anything at present." It was probably to ease the tension that his friend, Mr. Parker, had just invested $1,000 for which they would have to give a mortgage on the place. He also reminded Allen that their annual meeting for the choice of a trustee was coming up, and that after the meeting he would receive papers to sign, retiring himself. A gentle hint, perhaps, that he would not be nominated for that high office again. "We mean," he concluded, "to arrange our affairs for next year so that the responsibility will be very much divided; we are acting on this system now; and it works well. All we need is a perfect method, great energy, and cheerful courage, and our success is sure."

An equal and more disturbing disaffection, more personally painful to Ripley, was already hatching between himself and Brownson, which could no longer be ignored. It must have seemed incredible to George Ripley that he and Orestes, the close friend who had shared with him the discovery and spreading of Transcendentalism, now abruptly dis-

* His love of the land has descended to his grandson, Mr. William Allen Wheeler, until recently Director of Agricultural Research at The Field Seed Institute of North America, Washington, D.C., who owns this unpublished letter of the Ripleys and kindly permits its use.

agreed. To be sure, Orestes in years past had been relentless about discarding a sect which failed to satisfy his logical mind. But disavowal was pardonable in an earnest seeker after truth, as George Ripley had reason to know. Their friendship had flourished during their pilgrimage. It was disintegrating now.

Looking back over the years—how much they had shared! Both had begun the quest as "pupils of Channing"; then together they had outgrown "The Great Enlightener's" guileless reliance on individual inner reform. The Dean of New England Reform, Dr. William Ellery Channing, had been so confident in this sanguine expectation, that he had once told a group of English miners, "Your true strength lies in growing intelligence, uprightness, self-respect, trust in God, trust in one another. These can not fail to secure for you your just share of social privileges."

At first Brownson had been more advanced than Ripley in social reform. Already in 1836, Brownson's impatience with the conservatism of the non-ritualistic Protestant ministries had led him to found, in Boston, his own church, "The Society of Christian Unity and Progress" —by which he hoped to rally aid for the underprivileged, fulfill the Gospel, and found the Kingdom of God on Earth. Brownson was also the more political-minded of the two. In the election year of 1836, George Bancroft, the future historian, had written to Brownson as a leading Democrat, to get his support for Van Buren, pointing out that their principles accorded on many points, and that "The day for the multitude has now dawned." Brownson, who feared "the absolute control of associated wealth" had given his support to Van Buren—and he had been duly, if not promptly, rewarded two years later with the stewardship of the United States Marine Hospital in Chelsea.

By that time the depression of 1837 had convinced Brownson that if the people wanted liberty, praying was not enough. To further the cause of reform Brownson began to lecture in New York City where the Loco-Focos—since 1835 the party of Radical Democrats bitterly hostile to the privileged classes in control of Tammany—were finding new encouragement in Van Buren's campaign policy.

Not satisfied with these activities, Brownson founded *The Boston Quarterly Review*, in which he proclaimed that "the people's sovereignty" was "limited only by justice as embodied in state-rights." In Brownson's view, the injuries of capitalism far exceeded the injuries of slavery; and he admonished the Abolitionists to leave the care of the slaves to their owners, who, after all, had every reason to keep their hands in good condition, and to direct their energies instead to the cleaning up of the slums in the industrial sections in the north. As Arthur M. Schlesinger, Jr., in *Orestes A. Brownson, A Pilgrim's Progress* points out, "Seeing in minority rights the one safeguard against the rule of consolidated capital, Brownson was forced to hold the state-rights doctrine sacred." One might add, at the cost of condoning slavery.

In 1840, just before the election, Brownson had published an extremely radical article, "The Laboring Classes," in which he argued that the Government must strictly limit its own power; demolish the banking system and credit; root out monopoly and privilege; and abolish inherited wealth. These radical opinions dismayed the Van Buren administration then in the throes of the presidential campaign; and when the Whigs reprinted the article, giving it wide circulation as evidence of the socialistic leanings of the Democratic High Command, the latter repudiated Brownson. Indeed he was attacked on all sides as a dangerous revolutionary—from such unexpected quarters as fellow Democrats and old friends in Massachusetts.

Brownson always loved an argument; and he was not one whit dismayed by the attacks. Indeed he counter-attacked with a second installment of "The Laboring Classes," more insistent than the first that "property should be held subordinate to man, and not man to property."

Such was Brownson's faith in the virtue and destiny of the people that he would not admit even the possibility of a Whig victory until the results of the election were known. When defeat could no longer be denied—Harrison won 234 electoral votes, Van Buren 60—Brownson's shock was great. It was no longer possible for him to ascribe the defects of society to the fact that the democratic principle had been obstructed. These defects were inherent in democracy itself. More disturbing still, the gullibility of the people which showed itself so flagrantly in 1840 might well show itself next time in a more dangerous aspect.

At first Brownson had tried to rally his party to its principles of strict construction and state-rights. But gradually "the failure of the people to support their own party",—he never forgot or forgave them—changed Brownson's philosophy. Faith in the people had meant to him what faith in God means to most men. "Properly so," observes Schlesinger, "because he regarded people as visible manifestations of the spirit of God." But, after the disillusionment of the election, Brownson felt as if the people could not be "basically virtuous." They must be, therefore, "basically corrupt."

As long as Brownson had dedicated his faith to a definite vision of democracy, his religion had been of secondary importance. But the disruption of his faith in human nature had since driven him toward the search for a religious faith that might satisfy him. The deepening of Brownson's religious sense did not happen suddenly, as in the vision of the mystic. It happened gradually, as if he were painfully adjusting his beliefs to emotions that had changed more than he knew himself. Such old friends as George Ripley were astounded to hear Orestes Brownson, "long the prophet of reason and master of logic," turning with scorn on intellect, the guide he had followed so long. "Alas!" declared Brownson, "we have seen enough of mere individual reason. It is impotent when it has not, for its guide and support, the reason of God, speaking not only to the heart, but through revelation and the traditions of the race."

In November 1842, Brownson published an article about Brook Farm in *The Democratic Review* in which he said the Community was good because it was simple and unpretending. It did not aspire to reform the world. It intended no harm to the State, the Church, the family or private property.

The article pleased neither himself nor Ripley. Brownson remarked to a friend that he hoped the Farmers would merit half the praise he had bestowed on them—for although he delighted in the people at the Community, and had sent his son to school there, he no longer in his heart approved of their way of life.

On the eighteenth of December, 1842, Ripley wrote Brownson, thanking him for the notice. But it is evident that Ripley considered his Community damned with faint praise, for he continued in sorrowful vein: "If I had never known you, I should never have engaged in this enterprise. I consider it as the incarnation of those Transcendental truths which we have held in common, and which you have done so much to make me love . . . With the vivid feeling that the great revolution in my life plan was the inevitable fruit of the ideas for which you most valued me, I will own to something of disappointment that you should give us so little sympathy or recognition when a friendly word would have been cheering. . . ."

The year of 1842 continued to close in an atmosphere of old friends drifting away. But both George and Sophia Ripley would keep on whistling up faith in their enterprise; and they were still determined to maintain the Community according to their own original pattern.

➤➤➤➤➤➤➤➤➤➤➤➤➤➤➤➤➤➤➤➤➤✕◀◀◀◀◀◀◀◀◀◀◀◀◀◀◀◀◀◀◀◀◀◀◀

Change in the Wind

THE THIRD WEEK IN JANUARY, 1843, BROUGHT A NEW AND VITAL personality to Brook Farm—Isaac Thomas Hecker, the future founder of the Paulist Fathers. After his arrival, anyone who chanced to drop into the smokey old Hive kitchen was likely to see a tall young man in a baker's regulation white cap, making bread by the oven. His skin was pockmarked and his features plain, yet there was something in the expression of this tall, shy-mannered newcomer, which attracted interest and aroused curiosity.

Hecker, then in his twenty-fourth year, had left his brother's bakery shop in New York to stay at Brook Farm, at the suggestion of Orestes Brownson. For the previous six months, Isaac had undergone a religious conflict so intense that his health became affected. During these months of bewilderment and suffering, Brownson, alone among Isaac's intimate circle, understood his need to work out his problem in an environment remote from family ties; and Brownson now hoped that the life in the West Roxbury Community might help his young friend to regain peace of mind.

Their friendship had begun when Hecker had heard Brownson speak on "The Democracy of Christ," at the Stuyvesant Institute in New York, on March fourth, 1841. Brownson spoke again, the following day, at Clinton Hall, on "The Reform Spirit of the Age"; but it was the first

lecture which turned Hecker "once again to the person of Christ, not as
the vicarious mediator of Methodism,"—the faith of Hecker's mother—
"but as a teacher of social theories." Father Vincent F. Holden, archi-
vist of the Paulist Fathers, in *The Early Years of Isaac Thomas Hecker*,
anticipating the influence of this new friendship, writes that this approach to Christianity on its social side gradually would lead Hecker,
whose attitude in 1841 was one of mild scepticism, "much deeper into
the divine nature of Christ and His Life," and would slowly turn him
"toward the problem of his own religious life which soon absorbed all
his attention."

Hecker's quick response to Brownson's views drew them rapidly together. Each knew instinctively he needed the other. Brownson, disil-
lusioned in regard to bringing about the Kingdom of God on earth, was
turning his logical mind toward salvation; and the latent mysticism in
Hecker was beginning to make him feel dissatisfied with mere social
reform.

By the fall of 1841 the two were intimate friends; and Isaac, with the
help of his brother, John, arranged for Brownson to deliver four lectures
on "Civilization and Human Progress" in New York in January 1842,
and invited him to stay at his house in Rutgers Street during the entire
three weeks necessary to complete the course. Brownson would soon be
asked by John L. Sullivan of *The Democratic Review* if he would merge
his *Boston Quarterly* with the New York organ and serve as contribut-
ing editor. Brownson was then at the height of his career as speaker and
writer; and almost everyone who knew him was afraid to engage him in
an argument. As Hecker himself said, "No one loves to break a lance
with him, because he cuts such ungentlemanly gashes." That young
Isaac Hecker dared to stand up to this warrior is an indication of his
own calibre.

Young Isaac did not mind when Orestes banged his fists on the
table or shouted at him in argument. The logician and the mystic
complemented one another; and so, although during Brownson's stay
at Rutgers Street, much time was spent "in the discussion of social and
political questions," when Hecker had Brownson to himself more time
undoubtedly was spent in the discussion of philosophic and religious
themes.

Arthur M. Schlesinger, Jr. (in his biography with the apt subtitle,
A Pilgrim's Progress) describes Brownson's state of mind, in January,
1842. Brownson, he says, ". . . was sparring for time until his emotions could transform his belief in the Church from an idea into a

fact . . . Young Hecker was a great comfort to the lonely Brownson in these anguished days."

Hecker, himself, when they first became friends, was still absorbed in natural ties. He had no unusual spiritual experiences until June 1842, when a new, intensive and religious influence suddenly took over the direction of his life, awakening his spiritual nature, putting him in conflict with his family and friends, and causing him to fear that he might become too engrossed in the bakery business.

The influence made itself felt in dreams. Each dream had for him "a practical good," bearing on his life. They were "impressive instructors." The substance of the dreams presented "Real pictures of the future, as actual, nay, more so than my present activity." He could not deny these instructors, they were "so patently of divine origin." By the late summer and early fall these dreams had begun seriously to trouble him.

One preternatural experience, in particular, exercised a profound influence, and forever eliminated for Hecker the possibility of marriage. He describes it in detail in *The Diary*, entry of May eighteenth, 1843. "About ten months ago, or perhaps seven or eight, I saw (I cannot say I dreamt for it was quite different from dreaming as I thought I was seated on the side of my bed) a beautiful, angelic, pure being, and myself standing along-side of her, feeling a most heavenly pure joy. And it was [as] if it were that our bodies were luminous and they gave a moonlike light which I felt sprung from the joy that we experienced. We were . . . unconscious of anything but pure love and joy, and I felt as if we had always lived together, and our motions, actions, feelings and thoughts came from one centre. And when I looked towards her I saw no bold outline of form, but an angelic something I cannot describe, but in angelic shape and image. It was this picture [which] has left such an indelible impression upon my mind; and for sometime afterward I continued to feel the same influence, and do now at times, [so] that the actual around me has lost its hold on me. In my state previous to this vision I should have been married ere this . . . (for there are those I have since seen who would have met the demands of my mind). But now this vision continuously hovers over me, and prevents me by its beauty from accepting any [one] else. For I am charmed by its influence, and I am conscious that if I should accept anything else, I should lose the life which would be the only existence wherein I could say I live."

Before the close of 1842, Hecker had had several more such preternatural experiences; each issuing another command to renounce his home, family, friends, and work—everything he still held dear—and to contain his soul in patience. His "instructors" did not vouchsafe as yet what was expected of him.

In her standard work on the subject, *The Mystic Way*, Evelyn Underhill presents what she calls a "somewhat arbitrary classification . . . of the mystical life." She discusses the first phase—the awakening of the Self to the consciousness of the Absolute. It would appear that Hecker had reached this stage in his encounter with the "Heavenly Being." This "Vision" as he called it, abrupt and accompanied by intense feelings of joy and exaltation, is typical of the first phase of "The Mystic Way." Now he was entering the second phase, "Purgation," in which the Self, awakened to Divine Beauty, realizes by contrast its own finiteness and imperfection, and attempts to eliminate by discipline and mortification all that stands in the way of its progress toward union with God. For Hecker, this was a period of bewilderment. All he knew—all he would know during his stay at Brook Farm—was that he was being "called with a stronger voice than that of the average conscience," but he was not sure where it might lead.

Unable to face the implications of such a sweeping renunciation alone, Isaac confided his troubles to his mother and brothers. Each tried to be kind and helpful, but none of them really understood his suffering. When Isaac first fell sick from this inner conflict, the doctor had recommended marriage—a cure which the apparition of the Divine Being made forever impossible. In his extremity, Isaac went to Chelsea, Massachusetts, to seek counsel of his friend, Orestes; Brownson continued to reside there in spite of losing his appointment as Steward of the Chelsea U.S. Naval Hospital. The older man, himself in a state of spiritual dissatisfaction, understood Isaac's need to get away by himself; and overcame the Heckers' objections to Isaac's withdrawing for a time to Brook Farm.

Hecker had left home "stripped of all his former attachments." Not because he wanted to be stripped of them, but because of "the Spirit that controls." He must be faithful to the bidding of his guiding Spirit, for only then could he be satisfied and at peace. He took what comfort he could in ". . . the firm hope that time would disclose . . . the meaning of all that was strangely mysterious . . ."

George William Curtis afterward wrote that Hecker had come to Brook Farm to study, but that he was too restless to take hold of any subject, and merely dropped in on various language and philosophy classes. This is hardly to be wondered at when one considers the severity of the religious crisis he was passing through. Fortunately, the very nature of the task that was allotted to him, placed Isaac on the Community hearthstone, where his vital nature quickly became known.

"The bread-baking has fallen into my hands," he wrote his family on January nineteenth. "I take whole charge of the bread for the Community, in which there are ninety persons, consuming about fifty to sixty lbs. of bread a day, which I bake in one batch once a day. They have had very poor bread. I commenced last week with some baker's yeast which I made, and have had very good luck. The bread has pleased them very much. The room that I now have is in the same house with the oven, which my former room was not. There is a stove in it, and all things comfortable. When I am not at the bread I sit in my room; that is in the daytime."

The cultural impact of the place stimulated him, for Hecker continued, "In the evenings there is always something taking place. I have this evening been to a Singing School of which there are two; the first has been these four months; the second commenced last week for new beginners. The first was held this evening, the second tomorrow. Taught by Mr. Dwight of the Community—a lecture of his will be in the next *Democratic Review* for February, on Handel's Messiah; he translated De Wette's *Theodore*. Last evening, Mr. Alcott and Mr. Lane—some of the 'newness-ites'—were here, and there was a 'Conversation' held in the parlor of the house called the Eyrie . . . Every evening is occupied with a meeting and sometimes two. . . ."

The "Conversation" Hecker attended that evening in all likelihood was about Alcott House, Surrey, England. In the spring of 1842, Emerson had made it financially possible for Bronson Alcott to go to England and visit the school which a group of British educators recently had founded in his name. Alcott was received by his British disciples with all the reverence due an apostle; and one of them, Charles Lane, accompanied by his son, William, had returned to America with Alcott in the late summer.

This opportunity to hear the pioneer of modern primary education expound the practice and application of his ideas in far away Ham, was eagerly attended by the Brook Farm pedagogues. In their opinion the recognition of Mr. Alcott's theories was long overdue. Now, at last, the obloquy which the wise, child-loving, gentle man had endured when the Temple School closed, was effaced by the honor paid him as a progressive American educator, by his British colleagues. This was cause for rejoicing among his friends, who did not foresee that their prophet would remain without honor in his own country for years to come. When Mr. Alcott led the talk concerning "the blossoming of tender minds," Mr. and Mrs. Ripley, Georgiana Bruce, Dana, and Bradford listened with delight; while Miss Marianne Ripley became so carried away with enthusiasm that her notes as recording secretary were written in a scrawl very unlike her usual neat script.

Mr. Alcott was not satisfied with the laurels bestowed on him by the British educators. He planned to found Fruitlands—another community. Mr. Lane had come to America to join him in the enterprise. In spite of their respect and affection for Mr. Alcott, the Ripleys listened with disquietude to their visitors' conception of "True Harmonic Association." Such necessities as food, clothing, heat, did not figure from a practical standpoint, in their calculations. Mr. Alcott talked as if his "consociates" would be clothed, and also nurtured, like "the lilies of the field." Mr. Lane preached "Ceasing from Doing."

Mr. Emerson, as was his custom, had made a study of this latest importation of European philosophy. Though he deplored the growth of the socialist movement in the United States, "which had drawn many of the best minds in this country also to accuse the idealism which contents itself with the history of the private mind, and to demand of every thinker the warmest devotion to the race," he interpreted Lane's philosophy with sympathy and insight—and in words more easily understood. "Man must cease from self-activity ere the spirit can fill him with truth in mind or body."

This, to be sure, was in the tradition of the mystics. But George Ripley had reason to know that such doctrines did not help to get the crops in. Mr. Ripley still spoke confidently of the day when Brook Farm would sustain itself; but he knew that starvation and failure were just around the corner. To him, the fate of those who might for love of Mr. Alcott fall foul of Mr. Lane's doctrine certainly brooked no encouragement.

Young Isaac Hecker, on the contrary, was attracted to Lane's philosophy by instinct. He continued to be troubled by dreams and to experience visions which seemed to transmute every day happenings into symbols and images. Because Charles Lane's theories about social reform were somewhat mystical in character, Hecker would turn to him in the months ahead—hoping for a guidance he would not find.

Hecker's closest friend would still be Brownson, however. Both men already were drawn toward a more ritualistic religion. But Hecker was concerned as to which was the better means to salvation: should he serve humanity through socialism? or join a religious organization?

Isaac made trips to Chelsea, where the two friends debated such questions by the fire in Brownson's study; and the older man came to West Roxbury to see his son, whom he had placed in the Brook Farm School, and to talk with young Hecker. As the days grew longer Brownson's visits became more frequent. On sunny afternoons in February, Isaac and Orestes would stroll for hours in the orchard. Sometimes they lingered, ignoring the supper bell, through the creeping damp of a February twilight.

Georgiana Bruce knew they must be discussing philosophy as well as social problems. She also felt that Mr. Brownson overrated his influence on Isaac. It seemed to her that the younger man's spiritual growth was the better rooted.

The English girl was very much interested in Hecker. They often walked together along the banks of the ice-floe'd Charles. Their relationship was strictly platonic; their talks philosophical. Georgiana questioned Isaac about his views on "associative principles"; he probed her about salvation.

2.

With customary good will, George Ripley still welcomed his old and close friend, Orestes Brownson, to Brook Farm. But Orestes was fonder than ever of an argument, and his manners had not improved with the years. By mutual consent their talks were infrequent; when they did enter into a discussion, the tension increased almost to the breaking point. Ripley simply could not understand this strange Brownson, who was doing his best to deny the ideals they had cherished together for the past eight years; and Brownson would not allow Ripley to ignore "the flaw" in Transcendentalism, which eventually would lead several of the Farmers, including Sophia Ripley, and her niece, Sarah Stearns, to Catholicism. "The flaw" was Nature Worship, which added up, logically, to Pantheism.

As Perry Miller, Professor of American Literature at Harvard University, has explained: at first, "Communion with Nature" seemed to offer a delightful escape from outworn dogma. For who could doubt the manifestation of God in sky, landscape, or ocean? The Transcendental-ists did not perceive the danger in pushing the reciprocity between man and nature to a point where the landscape is not only a state of the soul, but the soul is a state of the landscape. Who could tell on reading Shelley's *Ode to the West Wind*, for example, whether the poet is rid-ing the gale, or the wind blowing him hither and thither? This sort of looseness soon got Margaret Fuller so confused that she could not de-cide whether the ocean's mood reflected the state of her soul, or vice versa!

In the first year of "high hope" Mr. and Mrs. Ripley had imbued their followers with such a sense of security in the new way of life, that no one at Brook Farm felt the need for religious ritual of any sort. Now, outspoken denunciations of the Nature Philosophy and sectarian dis-pute alike were frequent.

What had happened to mar the idyllic serenity of the "halcyon days"? In this winter of 1843, restlessness and dissatisfaction polluted the pure air of Brook Farm. Some among them sought ritualistic reli-gion; others demanded a more specific and practical economic program. Meanwhile, Albert Brisbane reiterated the refrain—it is impossible for a Fourieristic phalanx to fail!

3.

In the space of one short year, Brisbane's propaganda had attained spectacular results; and his column in the *New York Tribune* exulted over the manifold activities of the "Fury-ites," as his converts were called by the irreverent. Readers of the *Tribune* learned in January, that a President, a Vice President, and six Directors had been drafted from among members of the Fourier Association of New York to draw up a constitution to be used as a standard in setting up a phalanx. In February, the document, together with plans and sketches of a magnifi-cent phalanstery, were proudly presented. Though designed for the benefit of "the friends of Association" the editor had the instruction of the public also in mind. For in these days enthusiasm for Association was spreading like a prairie fire in a high wind, igniting groups all over the country, especially in northwestern New York. The publishers of Brisbane's pamphlet, *Association; or, A Concise Exposition of the*

Practical Part of Fourier's Social Science could hardly keep up with the demand. To reassure the public, Messrs. Greeley and McElrath announced that a second edition was in the press. The Speakers Bureau also had more requests than their lecturers were able to fill—which was unfortunate—because this was the time to sow the seed far and wide.

Yet Brisbane already foresaw that it might endanger the cause to father communities which did not conform to Fourier's specific plan; and readers of the *Tribune* presently were informed that the "F. A. of N. Y." had firmly declined an invitation to endorse the Sylvania Association about to be established in Pennsylvania. Since the members would be drawn from only one class of society, labor, Sylvania could not possibly offer an opportunity to demonstrate "Harmony," and other advantages of Fourier's system. Now that Fourierism had caught the popular imagination, Mr. Brisbane announced his opinions with the confidence of a dictator, and his dictums were regarded as absolute by the faithful.

Many thoughtful men throughout the land shared Brisbane's confidence in Association. From faraway Ohio, Mr. James Handasyd Perkins, formerly of Boston, now a leading spirit in Cincinnati, and his colleague in reform, Mr. J. P. Stuart from Zanesville—a less known and less fortunately named city in the new West—anticipated a rich Fourieristic future. Settlers in remote districts were especially responsive to Association. As one backwoodsman put it, "phalanstery" was just a fancy name for a blockhouse. By whatever name, the pioneers knew the value of collective enterprise in a lonely land where an occasional Indian still prowled.

Mr. Brisbane, as perhaps was natural in a First Apostle, was inclined to look down upon the works of the disciples. Parke Godwin's magazine, *The Pathfinder*, was criticized or damned with faint praise. But any variation from Brisbane's flat-footed style was so welcome to Associationists that Godwin triumphed over the Apostle's disdain; and when Isaac Hecker brought a copy of the new magazine to Brook Farm, he afterward reported to his family, "It pleased many, especially Mr. Ripley who feels an intense interest in it . . . He asked me about Godwin, wanted to know if he is sincere."

By April, 1843, many Associations had sprung up in the neighborhood of Rochester, New York. A speaker at the Society for Universal Inquiry and Reform proclaimed, "That the Paradise of Eden is to be regained at some period or other there are but few who doubt, though by what peculiar means this heavenly boon is to be secured, is yet alto-

gether problematical." To this, Brisbane had a ready answer—that
Fourier had discovered and clearly demonstrated the means. "The
boon,—the Paradise itself will be the Moral Harmony of the Passions
in Associative Unity, the Kingdom of Heaven which comes to this ter-
restrial world."

4.

George Ripley's growing interest in Fourierism dismayed the Conservative; and soon some of the most attractive members of the Brook
Farm Institute made plans to leave. One of them had enjoyed her sojourn at Brook Farm "without consideration or effort for the general
good." It was common knowledge that Mrs. Barlow had trifled with the
heart of one of their foremost leaders, John S. Dwight.

However at fault in the beginning of the affair, Almira since had
tried to withdraw with tact and delicacy. In a letter of January sixth,
she warned her talented, junior admirer, that he was "getting too much
attached . . . You seem to wish to absorb me quite; demand too much
of my time, my sympathy, my tender expression." She valued him as a
friend, but "how to keep the friend, and reject the lover," puzzled her.
But she would be very sorry to break with him entirely. "There's much
in our congeniality of tastes and similarity of opinions to bring us together in various pleasant interchange," she pointed out. Just because
they could not have "intimate communion," Almira did not see why
they should give up what they "could get of genial trustful friendship."

Though Mrs. Barlow's intentions toward the gifted little gentleman
sound highly commendable, her conduct was never quite above sus-
picion. There were some who noticed that Mrs. Barlow soon began to
cast her eye in another direction.

The Farmers promptly warned young Isaac Hecker against the lady.
Actually, he was too absorbed in gaining his family's consent to his remaining at Brook Farm, at least until the summer, to give much
thought to Mrs. Barlow. Isaac had written them for permission to stay,
again and again, but he had received no satisfactory reply. Towards the
end of March he went home to Rutgers Street to discuss the question
face to face. In the middle of April he returned to Brook Farm with
the permission he had sought.

On one of her return visits to the Community, a "bright, vivacious, dark-skinned, rich complexioned damsel"—as Hawthorne called Ora Gannett—went out to the kitchen to see some of her friends. Ora "there beheld, on one side of the chimney, a strange young man with the regulation baker's cap on his head." Everyone at Brook Farm knew Isaac Hecker by this time, and no one was surprised when Ora proclaimed that in spite of his plainness young Mr. Hecker was extremely attractive. Ora found Isaac's expression ". . . earnest, highminded, and truthful."

A warm, tender, and loving friendship was born between Ora Gannett and young Isaac Hecker. Indeed, Isaac had a talent for friendship with women, as well as men. Already he was regarded with sisterly affection by Ida Russell, the half sister of Amelia, head of the Amusement Group; and Georgie Bruce, the peppery young English socialist-intellectual, felt in Isaac a tower of spiritual strength.

On Saturday, April fifteenth—almost the day after Isaac returned from visiting his family in New York—Almira Barlow took him out for a walk. "My time was spent very pleasantly," Isaac wrote in his newly begun diary. "The scenery was beautiful; the Gothic formed woods were very striking, the beautiful green pine trees and the mass of tints covering the ground; the heavens with the clouds, the sun bursting through them at intervals; the silence and shady mystery of the woods; above all, a soul susceptible of love and beauty, gave to all, such an enchantment and my heart so filled with love that I felt guilty of enjoyment."

That the fascinating Almira was decidedly taken with Isaac Hecker is apparent from Hecker's entry in *The Diary* on April eighteenth. "If this book is not a-going to be the revelation of my thoughts, what is it good for?" Having declared this rash intention, Hecker proceeded to put it into effect with breathtaking candor:—"The afternoon of yesterday a [lady, Mrs. . . .] came into my room and we entered into a conversation—a communion. Before, I have had intimate conversation with [her] and from the reports I have heard of [her], I was influenced to keep myself at a certain distance, so that instead of being [the motive], it is vice-versa. Instead of [I] dissait aller to [her] she put forth her—what—love openly to me."

At this point Hecker changed his mind about recording all: "No, I will not write down this interview. I will scratch out the names I have written above."

Father Holden observes, "If this were the only entry on the subject it would be hazardous to conclude that the person in his thoughts was Almira Barlow . . . But it is significant that the only name he attempted to scratch out in his *Diary*, where, in spite of his efforts, it is discernible, was Almira." Moreover, Father Elliott, who wrote a full biography of Isaac Hecker, although he does not mention Mrs. Barlow's name in the *Life*, did recognize it and permit it to be used in the typewritten copies of *The Diary* that were made under his supervision.

Out of context, these entries concerning Hecker's relationship with Mrs. Barlow give a false impression of his interest in her; but to anyone who has read *The Diary*—the original is one of the treasures in the archives of the Paulist Fathers—it is clear from the many more entries concerned with spiritual matters that Hecker was almost totally absorbed in his religious conflict. On April twenty-fourth, he wrote of a dream, "a warning embodiment of a false activity and its consequence, which will preserve me under God's assistance, from falling." On May eighth, he wrote, "On Friday night I saw a red, fiery, glaring-eyed, copper-skinned, singularly dressed fiend. In stretching to grapple with it I awoke, sitting up in my bed with my arms extended." These dreams were far more vivid to him than reality.

Mrs. Barlow, however, may have persisted in her attentions, for on May sixteenth, Hecker analyzed his motives for remaining celibate. "I suppose the reason why I do not now in my present state feel disposed to connect myself with any person, and rather avoid a person whom I felt I might or could love, is that I feel my life is in a rapid progress, and that my choice would not now be a permanent one. For when I reflect upon what choice I would have made some time back (if there had not been something deeply secret in my being which prevented me) would be to me now I am afraid very unsatisfactory, I feel conscious there could not have been a change of growth mutually, equally; because the natures of some are not capable of much growth; I mistrust whether there would not have been, as often happens, an inequality—hence a disharmony, an unhappiness."

Hecker would continue to be a fond friend of Almira Barlow's for months to come—perhaps because she, too, was restless and at a loss, although for very different reasons. But she never had been popular among the Brook Farm ladies—it was said she had but one friend among them, Ida Russell. The discreet disapproved of Almira's goings on, for, although the exchange of pleasantries between the sexes was a popular pastime at Brook Farm, and found expression among the unattached in a frequent exchange of notes, when a bachelor slipped a note under

Almira's plate, and received one of her "perfumed replies" at tea, more than one observing eye had reason to know that an innocent walk in the moonlight—such as George William Curtis often proposed to Caroline Sturgis—was not in question.

On April twenty-seventh the Direction voted: ". . . the parlor in the Hive should be converted into a dining room, and the parlor occupied by Mrs. Barlow to public use." Though the room was sorely needed—for more useful purposes than those to which it lately had been put—the Directors probably would not have assumed such a peremptory tone, if the lady had been more discreet.

The enchantress did not take the rebuke to heart. This was May—the lovers' month. And Mrs. Barlow had many admirers. As the petals of spring blossoms fell, the Directors reluctantly made up their minds about Almira Barlow. On May twenty-seventh, Mrs. Barlow was ordered to vacate her rooms by the first of June.

Meanwhile, Hecker's religious conflict was increasing in intensity. Father Holden writes of Hecker at this time, ". . . nothing seemed to take hold of him but study. But even with that he experienced a difficulty. At times he could not apply himself to his books because of his upset state of mind."

In the eyes of the very young, Hecker in distraught mood could be quite terrifying. One bright May morning, little Annie Page and John Van Der Zee Sears were hunting for arbutus on the far side of the Piney Woods when they "came upon Mr. Hecker walking rapidly up and down in the secluded little dell that served him as a retreat. He was wringing his hands and sobbing so violently that we two scared children stole away, awed and terrified." Probably the unhappy young man had just suffered one of the strange and compelling dreams that commanded him to renounce the world.

As a rule, there was nothing terrifying about Isaac Hecker. To George William Curtis, Hecker at Brook Farm "was the dove, floating in the air not yet finding the spot on which his foot might rest." Hecker's gentleness and spiritual strength drew many people to him. His friends became close friends; and each was different from the other. The poetic Burrill Curtis, the scholarly Dana, the didactic Brownson, all were devoted to him.

5.

Mr. Alcott and Mr. Lane put a notice in the June issue of *The Dial* to announce the founding of "Fruitlands," their new community at Harvard, Massachusetts. Theirs was a highly Transcendental manifesto—a declaration to the effect that noble souls could bloom without animal nourishment. Even manure was taboo, on the ground that it would "contaminate" the thin, gravelly, New England soil of this "New Eden":

"Beginning with small pecuniary means this enterprise must be rooted in a reliance on the succors of an ever bounteous Providence whose vital affinities being secured by this union with uncorrupted fields and unworldly persons, the cares and injuries of a life of care are avoided. The inner nature of every member of the Family is at no time neglected. A constant leaning on the living spirit within the soul should consecrate every talent to holy uses cherishing the widest charities . . . Our plan contemplates all such disciplines, cultures, and habits as evidently conduce to the purifying and edifying of the inmates. Pledged to the spirit alone, the founders can anticipate no hasty or numerous accession to their numbers. The kingdom of peace is entered only through the gates of self-denial and abandonment; and felicity is the test and the reward of obedience to the unswerving law of love."

Emerson commented on this notice in the October issue of *The Dial* in one pithy sentence: "We are not yet ripe to be birds."

At the end of June, 1843, Mr. Alcott and Mr. Lane left the "uncorrupted" fields of Fruitlands to visit Brook Farm. Alcott had founded his new, "ascetic" Community some three weeks before with the help of his friend, Lane. It did not trouble them a whit to leave Mrs. Alcott three months before Beth was born, in the weeding season, to hoe the garden with such help as she could muster from her three little daughters.

Both philosophers were Grahamites, who adhered to the vegetarian diet of Sylvester Graham. They even denied themselves tea and coffee, subsisting mainly on cold water and unbolted flour. The visitors knew that their diet would be available, for Mr. Alcott had often presided over the Grahamite Table in the Hive. But he had forgotten, perhaps, that all the Farmers were not of his persuasion—that the cow was almost sacred at Brook Farm.

Miss Peabody had waxed quite poetical about cows in her *Plan of the West Roxbury Community*. "A true life," she wrote, "although it aims beyond the highest star, is redolent of the healthy earth. The perfume of clover lingers about it. The lowing of cattle is the natural bass to the melody of human voices."

George Ripley, who shared these sentiments, innocently showed Lane about his farmyard. He pointed with pride to sixteen cows, two teams of oxen, and another of draft horses, all grazing in the meadow; and then he escorted his British visitor to the pig pen, where a litter of pigs wallowing in mud tugged at the teats of a great sow.

Lane was unspeakably revolted, and he was rude enough to betray his feelings. At that moment a coolness arose between the two men. Ripley felt that if the mere sight and smell of cattle proved so profoundly shocking to Lane, he was carrying Graham's theory too far.

Thereafter the Englishman held Ripley responsible for the deplorable tendency of the Brook Farmers to serve "as cook and chambermaid to cows." The Farmers, in turn, pronounced Mr. Lane altogether too austere and sadly lacking in his companion's seer-like charm. As always happened when Mr. Alcott visited them, "The Grahamite Table" where the strictly vegetarian diet and unbolted flour recommended by the dietician, Sylvester Graham, were served, suddenly became popular.

The young people delighted in Mr. Alcott's benign presence and Transcendental expressions. "Sir," a maiden might whisper to her *vis à vis*, "Sir, is the pie within the sphere of your influence?" And he, as he passed her the dish, would retort slyly, "Pray slice from the center to the periphery!" Such jokes were the better because Mr. Alcott never noticed that he inspired them, or if he did, the mimicry did not disturb his serenity in the least.

But no one would have dared to poke fun at Mr. Lane, who, it was suspected, had come to Brook Farm in the hope of persuading Hecker to join Fruitlands. The subject certainly was discussed between them, for on June twenty-fourth, Hecker pondered the question in his diary; "I have some thoughts of leaving Brook Farm for Fruitlands. Here is everything delightful, fine, beautiful, cultivated people, some of whom I love much; the situation is pleasant, exceedingly so, and I am loved in return by many; which makes it all desirable and happy for him that lives in the spirit of these things. But their life is not deep, holy, self-denying for perhaps me; at Fruitlands there is not one that I am acquainted with; only four persons; none of the amusements such as they have here, which are a great deal to me, such as music, etc. There, is all inward; here, is more outward in comparison with them, but not with the world. This place is a step between the World and Fruitlands . . . They live upon simple, very simple diet, without tea, coffee, milk, butter fats, any kind of flesh or animal food, or what is produced by animals. They work as their conscience dictates; no one is master, no one servant. Their life is one of self-denial and a constant striving after a deeper and more holy life in all directions. There are no external advantages to gain there, so no one will go there from such motives."

Shortly after returning to Fruitlands, Lane wrote his friend Oldham, in England, that although young Isaac had resided several months in West Roxbury, the youth by no means was satisfied with "their schoolboy dilettante spiritualism." Lane kept on urging Hecker to come to Fruitlands.

Isaac blew hot and cold. On July seventh, he confessed to his diary: "I can hardly prevent myself from speaking how much I will miss the company of those whom I love and associate with here . . . Here all refining amusements, cultivated persons, and one whom I have not spoken of; one who to me is too much to speak of, one who would give up all for me. Alas! Her, I must leave to go!"

Father Holden, who made a close examination of this passage concludes, "At one time the diary contained the name of this person. Later, however, Hecker tried to obliterate all traces of identity by drawing numerous lines through the name with his pen." Almira Barlow had obtained a reprieve in the order of banishment; it was her name Isaac tried to scratch out.

By the eleventh of July, Hecker had made up his mind to go to Fruitlands on the following Tuesday. Mr. Ripley promptly presented his bill, $75.62. Explaining that he would ask his family to supply the balance, Hecker paid $25.62 on account.

6.

Although the Directors had relaxed their stern edict to evict Mrs. Barlow and her three little boys on four days' notice, they had not altered their views concerning her unfitness for Association. In mid-July they made it painfully clear that it was high time for her to pack up and move on.

In February 1843, Almira had toyed with the idea of joining Mr. Alcott's Fruitlands, when and if it should be founded. There is a letter from Mr. Alcott to her among the Hecker Papers, in which the matter is discussed with candor. Although Mr. Alcott addressed Mrs. Barlow with the courtesy due a charming lady of his own world, he also made it quite clear that if she became a member of the Fruitlands Community she would have to adopt the ascetic discipline which he and Mr. Lane had established there.

Nothing came of this exchange, of course. Almira was not interested, really, in the salvation of mankind. She preferred to devote her attentions to certain individuals among the species.

Poor Almira! These must indeed have proved trying days for her. Isaac—her favorite young man—had gone off to this "Eden" of Mr. Alcott's, where they ate nothing but vegetables, and had but few of those to eat. Meanwhile, the Directors of Brook Farm, egged on by their women-folk, were making it increasingly clear that she had out-worn her welcome.

At this critical juncture, Mrs. Barlow was saved, as it were, by her own weakness. For it was that very "fondness for the company of men," which suddenly paid her a heartwarming dividend.

Bored by the long arguments on Fourierism, gentle Mr. Bradford recently had removed himself and his two star pupils, the Curtis brothers, to his native Concord. He had found lodging for the boys with one Captain Garrett, an elderly farmer recommended by Emerson. It was a continuation of "The Union of Labor and Culture." The boys went haymaking with Captain Garrett, and continued their tutoring with Mr. Bradford, the Dean of Brook Farm. Their life seemed almost as idyllic in Concord as it had been in West Roxbury.

Yet something, some indescribable element, was lacking in this newly refreshing, unprejudiced atmosphere of Concord. The element of femininity which Almira Barlow radiated so abundantly, perhaps? Yes—that was what one missed among these Philosophers and their clever, well-bred, but highly restrained women folk.

It was the incomparable George William Curtis, of course, who gallantly undertook to find living accommodations for Mrs. Barlow and her three young boys in Concord.

One can imagine the sigh of relief with which the beautiful Almira received the good news that a lodging, at last, had been found. Licensed imagination permits a further glimpse. For surely it is in character for George William to meet the lady at stage or railroad coach, and convey her, her luggage, and her three boys to the lodging?

7.

The desertion of three of their most attractive men was a grave loss to the Farmers. George Bradford's departure, in particular, distressed the Ripleys. He was an outstanding teacher, and it saddened them to recall how enthusiastic he had been about their new way of life, but two short summers ago. Could it be that their closest, noblest friends were beginning to lack faith in their enterprise? Or did it signify merely that the more gently nurtured among them lacked the physical stamina necessary for the Union of Labor and Culture?

Even Minot Pratt, who had been with them since the beginning, was growing restless. One hot July evening he sat down and wrote his old friend, George Ripley, that he and Mrs. Pratt had decided to withdraw from the Community as soon as seemed practicable. Pratt explained that both he and his wife found it difficult to impose a proper discipline because their young boys were under a two-fold influence—that of the parent and that of the Association. Clearly, the Pratt boys, reputed to be lively youngsters, were quick to play the one against the other to escape punishment.

Although he may have been tempted to remind his friend, who had been with him from the beginning, that this dual authority which Pratt complained about was inherent in Association, George Ripley—in a long and hitherto unpublished letter of July twenty-third, 1843*—preferred to discuss the case of the Pratt boys on a strictly pedagogical basis. Assuredly, it was painful to their teachers as well as their parents, to see the Pratt boys "growing up with such an apparent aversion to useful industry, whether of mind or body, and voluntarily declining advantages for which others are glad to pay a high price." With his usual fair-mindedness, George Ripley admitted, if the boys "were wholly under the control of the Association, or wholly free from its influence, perhaps there might be more in their endeavors, more improvement in their

* In the Library of the Fruitlands Museums.

characters." As pedagogues still are apt to do, he attributed the problem to some parental lack. The Pratt boys suffered from "a peculiar temperament that time and patience alone might improve."

Headmaster Ripley would brook no conclusions concerning the young Pratts which might reflect criticism of the Brook Farm Schools. In regard to the pupils preparing for college, Mr. Ripley almost boasted—never had he taught a group which displayed so many attractive traits. And he was sure the pupils all were receiving much better influences than were enjoyed at any other place of education he was ever acquainted with, because most of the parents gave him such "warm, earnest, and uncalled for expressions of approval and gratitude." His conscience, he declared, was "easy and happy on that score altogether."

Having delivered his mind and championed his schooling system, George Ripley climbed down from the pedagogical rostrum to discuss, man to man, in friendly fashion, what he knew was the underlying cause of Pratt's restlessness—the suddenly crowded living conditions at Brook Farm. He, himself, was not at all satisfied with their housing. Indeed one detects in this letter a note of embarrassment, because he and Mrs. Ripley were enjoying a suite in the Eyrie, whose only other occupants were scholarly bachelors. From there, he looked with daily admiration on the patient toil and perpetual sacrifice which some Associonists were enduring faithfully in the common cause; and he especially deplored the inconveniences the Pratts had to put up with in their "crowded central position in the Hive, the most unfavorable probably, for a family of children that could be chosen on the place." Ripley advised his friend to avail himself at the earliest opportunity "of a more retired situation."

"Restricted accommodations, the confusions and disorder"—from which they all alike suffered—were, Ripley reminded Pratt, incidental to their limited resources, among the evils they had expected to grapple with, for the sake of establishing social reform. With unconscious irony he went on to say that although he had been sorely perplexed for the past week with pecuniary cares, he had not yet lost faith in the abolition of competition and other ideals which had inspired their enterprise. In conclusion he shrank from trying to influence the friend who had been at his side since the beginning, but he could not help adding that if the Pratts left Brook Farm their "place could hardly be made good."

To a twentieth century eye, this glimpse of George Ripley clambering down from the Eyrie, lantern in hand, to slip a disturbing letter

under Minot Pratt's door, occasions incredulity and surprise. But in the
eighteen forties, long, high-flown epistles were in fashion. A way of let-
ting off pent-up feelings, perhaps as easing to the spirit as the phone-
call of today.

In New England, July is the season of droughts, heat waves, and
thunderstorms. Although the July mugginess is reflected in his reply to
his close associate, Ripley understood why crowded living conditions
suddenly exasperated his staunch and patient friend so much that
neither he nor his wife could bear the thought of spending another hot
summer in the Hive.

Probably "Old Man East Wind" came up—Boston newspapers always call the East Wind "Our Summer Life-Saver," because the cool-
ing sea breeze cools tempers as well as temperatures. On this occasion
the complaints of the Pratts blew over, and they stayed on at Brook
Farm for almost two more years.

8.

Visitors were more numerous than ever in the summer of 1843.
Sometimes Amelia Russell, "Mistress of the Wardrobes," was sorely put
to it to find enough beds. For two years the guests had been entertained
without charge, but now that the guest book showed a record of thousands of names within a year, the Directors felt compelled to ask a
small amount for board—especially since many came out of idle curiosity and others proved misfits seeking a refuge. As public interest in
Association gained throughout the United States, the numbers of visitors steadily increased.

Leaders in the movement made it their business to visit the various
Communities and report on their progress—as a result, less prosperous
Communities sought to amalgamate with the more successful. In fact,
the Reverend Adin Ballou of Hopedale, Massachusetts, and Mr. Collins of Skaneateles, New York, were approaching Mr. Ripley with this
intention at this time. But the Hopedale creed had too much coercion
in it to please Ripley; and the leaders at Skaneateles aimed to abolish
private property—so that nothing came of these tentative advances.

Brook Farm itself was being eyed by Horace Greeley, the young
founder and editor of the *New York Tribune*, and Albert Brisbane, the

First American Apostle of Fourierism. Both men were birds of a national, almost international feather, with reputations far showier than those of the New England hue, and their flying visits created a flutter at Brook Farm because everyone felt honored by their interest.

Greeley, "Compassionate to weakness, generous to a fault," had both suffered himself and been wracked by the general misery he witnessed during the depression of 1837. Why must want exist in a world of plenty? Was there no remedy?

Most opportunely, a messenger bearing good tidings had arrived in 1838 from Paris. This herald announced with the utmost confidence—human misery need not exist, if man could be persuaded to adopt the social plan of Charles Fourier.

The messenger, of course, was none other than Mr. Greeley's fellow traveller from New York; and Mr. Brisbane never let anyone forget that he had imbibed the doctrines that were to save mankind from Fourier, himself. Indeed, he had considered it such a privilege that he had renounced "the grand tour" so that he might remain in Paris to sit at the feet of "The Master."

Mr. Greeley felt it truly providential that this revelation had been vouchsafed to a young man of liberal education, one who knew how difficult it would be to realize Fourier's captivating theories in "slow, conservative Europe." A young man, furthermore, of wealth, which would enable him to promote the doctrine in these "progressive and unshackled" United States.

Though Greeley's journalistic sense had warned him to proceed cautiously until public sentiment had been sounded, privately he made no secret of his conversion to Fourierism. In the first two years, however, Brisbane made but few converts. The few proved enough to encourage the firm of Greeley and McElrath to publish Brisbane's summary of Fourier's doctrines, *The Social Destiny of Man*. The second partner's contribution to the enterprise, like his name, has a faraway echo and slightly ghostly resonance, because—with the exception of the column in the *Tribune* which a number of converts had purchased on a promise to pay basis—every bit of the propaganda published by Albert Brisbane was financed by Horace Greeley.

Since March 1842, Brisbane's interpretation of Fourierism in the *New York Tribune* had formed the basis of a schism between the Directors of Brook Farm. Sober George Ripley—fascinated, perhaps, by Brisbane's fabulous promises, repeated again and again—gradually had become converted to Fourierism. This, in spite of the objections of

Charles Anderson Dana, whose judgment he had reason to respect. Dana pointed out the absurdity of reconstructing Brook Farm in terms of a comparatively gigantic phalanx. Yet even Dana could not deny that their present status was doomed. In 1841 and 1842 they had failed to support themselves on the land; and in this midsummer of 1843 it had become apparent that in spite of all their hard work, the harvest would again be lean.

Some of the Farmers—notably the late comers and younger element —were as fascinated by Brisbane's promises as Mr. Ripley. And Mr. Brisbane was delighted to let them hear the new doctrine from his own lips. Indeed, ever since his first visit of inspection in May, he had been determined to turn Brook Farm into a phalanx. The expectation of a lean harvest was propitious to his design.

Brook Farm, founded on Transcendentalist principles—the visitors conceded politely—, constituted a noble but imperfectly worked out social plan. Whereas Fourier's conception, Composite Association, or Harmony, with its community kitchens, common living quarters, co-operative buying, and the like, was far more economical. The two spreaders of the word—Messrs. Brisbane and Greeley—believed so earnestly in their doctrine that their conviction lent them an air of infallibility difficult to resist.

Greeley was too busy to visit them often. He came and went like an apparition—to the astonishment of Miss Amelia Russell, "Mistress of the Revels." She declared that she almost mistook him for a ghost: "His hair was so light that it was almost white; he wore a white hat; his face was entirely colorless, even the eyes do not add much to save it from its ghastly hue." Greeley's light drab coat and nether garments increased his ghostliness in her eyes.

Though Mr. Brisbane did not regard Brook Farm as a suitable setting for a phalanx, he was determined to make it serve; and he came more and more frequently and stayed longer each visit. During the hot weather he brought several volumes of Fourier with him and settled down to translate them. After hours spent digesting the Master's theories—these could be bewildering, such as Fourier's conviction that the sea was slowly turning into lemonade—Brisbane invariably began to spout propaganda. To the regret of some, the readings of Dante or rendering of Beethoven were often renounced because Mr. Brisbane insisted on propounding the doctrine that was destined to bring peace and plenty to mankind.

The idyllic element of life faded from Brook Farm in the torrent of

Brisbane's argument. In his presence the young people felt it a sin to be gay; and the elders wondered why he could see nothing good in their manner of life. There were moments when young and old rebelled—to little avail.

One sweet summer night, wearied of his preaching, the Farmers coaxed Mr. Brisbane out to bask in the moonlight by the brook. Perched on a boulder he went right on preaching Fourierism.

Seeking to distract him, a pretty maiden cried, "What a beautiful moon! What a beautiful world!"

Mr. Brisbane gazed at her severely. "What a wistful moon! What a dismal world!" he corrected—and continued his discourse.

9.

If, in after years, Brook Farm would seem "a green isle in a nostalgic haze"—to borrow William Henry Harrison's beautiful image—those who left the Community in July 1843 did not easily cast off the ties of affection that bound them to their former home. Like grown children making their way in the world they came back to the Ripleys' for approbation and encouragement.

Hecker's first venture had proved unsatisfying. "This morning I depart from Fruitlands," he wrote in *The Diary* on July twenty-sixth. "I have learnt much since I have been in contact with some of the most prominent men of this school, the spiritual mystics. I feel I could not get much more from them if I should stay longer. They did not appear to me to be mystical nor so highly spiritual."

He planned to pick up belongings he had left at Brook Farm before returning to New York, but he may have stopped to visit Brownson on the way. A fortnight later, on August 13th, at Brook Farm Hecker wrote in *The Diary*, "Here I sit with pen in hand, the book lying on the table by which I am sitting in a light tunic and drab velvet skull cap, made by the hands of one who has become nearer to my heart than any other human being that I have ever become acquainted with, and whose nearness I will feel most when I have left this place." It would seem that Hecker was thinking of Almira Barlow. If he was, it was but a passing regret. Other entries in *The Diary* show that Isaac was far more concerned about his spiritual state and his relations with his friends.

However she was in his thoughts to some extent, for two days after he reached home Hecker wrote to her to Concord, where she had now settled with her family. This was the beginning of a correspondence between them, which Hecker would sustain from New York for about a year. For although she soon complained of "the impersonal tone" of his letters, it is certain from the entries in *The Diary*, that he received quite a few letters from her. Their content is unknown because not one of Mrs. Barlow's letters is to be found among his papers, although he saved a number of others from his Brook Farm friends.

Among the most interesting of these—to be found in the Hecker Papers, preserved in the archives of the Paulist Fathers in New York—are seven hitherto unpublished letters from Charles Anderson Dana. Though undated, from the content the following must have been written in late August 1843, soon after Hecker's return to New York:

Dear Isaac,
   I snatch a moment to write you a word—not a letter—I live in hope of some blessed region, in some of my future transmigrations where there shall be time enough to do all I wish to—but in this present condition that is not to be thought of.
   Since your departure Brook Farm goes quietly on. Nothing of any note has happened. Miss Ostinelli is spending a few weeks with us, and we have her exquisite singing pretty often. George Bradford has not yet returned. Burrill [Curtis] would have been back ere this but for a lameness in his foot. Mr. Ripley had a very pleasant visit in New York and Albany, but nothing more. No cash gains. Brisbane is in Boston and has produced quite a stir there; some four hundred people attend his lectures; they held a meeting yesterday to form a Fourier Society at which Mr. Ripley presided. Brisbane is delighted with Brook Farm, says we have a nucleus here he knows of nowhere else.
   Of all else that is worth hearing I presume you are not without information. Ida and Rose Russell have been here a day or two. We had a very fine exhibition of tableaux the other evening at Morton House [the official name was Pilgrim House].
   For myself, I follow my path, and keep something like an equilibrium. Who knows what the Fates bring? Wait, oh unquiet soul; life has peace for thee also!
   You do not forget us; we do not forget you. Shall not some good day bring you to us again?—Write me.
   John Dwight and Jane Sturgis send their love.
                                                  Affectionately yours,
                                                  Charles A. Dana
                                                  Brook Farm, Sunday.

These were anxious and depressing days for Dana. He had not yet been converted to Fourierism, but he had withstood the temptation to leave Brook Farm when his friends had left. And now, hardly more than a month later, what they had foreseen was coming to pass. It seemed inevitable to him now that Brook Farm would be converted into a phalanx. His letters to Hecker reflect a much needed glimpse into the discussion which preceded the change to Fourierism—unfortunately the nineteenth century authorities on Brook Farm, Lindsay Swift and O. B. Frothingham, present but a brief summary of these critical months.

The *Brook Farm Records* of this period also are tantalizing. The entry of August fifth, 1843, for example, states merely that J. Burrill Curtis had withdrawn from the Association, but there is no indication that he would return to wind up his affairs and visit with friends as of yore. On that same day Mr. Ripley was appointed to draw up bylaws, but of what nature is not revealed. But after reading Dana's letter it is obvious that the bylaws would reflect the Fourieristic trend. Indeed it is possible that the resolution to rewrite them may have been inspired by the exciting news from France, reported in the *Tribune* two days before.

Ever since the "February Revolution" which had taken place in the Chamber of Deputies in Paris, earlier in this same year of 1843, exciting bulletins from *La Phalange*—the Fourieristic journal published in France—had appeared in the *Tribune*.

On the fourth of March, *La Phalange* had proclaimed, "There are in the Chamber of Deputies, happily, men who sympathize with our ideas; who, in conversation are not afraid to confess" that they regard "association of the interests and classes of the peoples, the true triumph of democracy . . . But these men will not declare themselves publicly, or teach these principles to France." And on April twenty-fifth, *La Phalange* quoted a speech by Monsieur Mauguin, a deputy from the vineyard country, who believed that the question of the division of great estates into small vineyards—*Le Vinicole*, this policy was called—was at the bottom of all industrial and economic problems.

"Public spirit is roused," *La Phalange* announced triumphantly. "The way is being prepared for profound discussions, and the members of both chambers, can, from now on, scale the true height of these questions . . . —which they occupy themselves freely with in private conversations—but which, until now, they have not brought to the Chamber except in a more or less vague or timid form."

Yet another, and far more eloquent voice had spoken—the voice of the poet, orator, statesman, Alphonse Marie Louis Lamartine. "Political questions which were in my eyes first, are now secondary to economic problems," he had declared. "No longer is it the forms of government—there are graver questions to be considered now. These are the social problems. I pledge in advance my support to any ministry which will actively occupy itself with these problems."

Scion of an ancient house, landlord of immense properties near Mâcon, in La Haute Savoie, the handsome, elegant, and above all eloquent poet, Count Alphonse de Lamartine, for the past two years had been playing a devious political hand. But his prestige was still unblemished; and on the strength of his espousal of the cause of the Common Man, *La Phalange,* hitherto a weekly, soon acquired sufficient backing to be published daily.

Such items as the above, duly publicized by Brisbane in the *New York Tribune,* led his American followers to believe that interest in Fourier's System was well established in the French Chamber, and spreading throughout France. What many of these Americans did not know about was Lamartine's method in the political forum—his habit of playing both ends against the middle.

At this time he advocated a "Moderate Revolution" and championed elections based on property and far removed from universal suffrage. Unfortunately for Lamartine's political aspirations, his program pleased neither Left nor Right, and he soon became quite isolated in the Chamber. Meanwhile, his popularity with the people was growing tremendously.

His biographers agree that Lamartine was never genuinely interested in the Common Man. But he did dread the possibility of another tremendous proletarian upheaval; and so it is safe to assume that in 1843 when he endorsed Mauguin's speech in favor of Le Vinicole, Lamartine was merely up to his old trick of trying to placate the extreme revolutionaries.

In those days a packet boat—even in summer—took three or more weeks to cross the Atlantic, and Lamartine's motives were not easily detected by readers of the *New York Tribune.* His fellow deputies long since had appraised Lamartine's endorsement of *Le Vinicole* as a play for popular support; but to Brisbane's followers in the United States, Lamartine's flirtation with the Socialists seemed a turning of the tide—a tide that might "sweep the whole world."

10.

If any "Mammons from State Street" attended the Fourier meetings in Boston, in August 1843, they must have marvelled to find
George Ripley playing such a prominent part. A leaf in the sketch book
of Christopher Cranch, whose drawings reflect the reaction of one old
friend to Mr. Ripley's conversion, depicts that dignified gentleman,
armed with a butterfly net, skipping cautiously in pursuit of a gorgeous
butterfly, above a caption which explains that he is chasing Fourier's
"Butterfly Passion"—man's natural craving for change.

If to posterity—as well as to his contemporaries—there is something
incongruous in a former minister of the Unitarian Church lending himself to Fourier's dubious doctrines, for Ripley himself these were confident days. His little Community—there were only some seventy persons living there at this time—had suddenly become the vanguard in a
national movement. Had not Brisbane singled out Brook Farm at the
recent meeting in Albany where Greeley and W. H. Channing also had
spoken, to praise its "beneficial operation"? To be sure, Mr. Brisbane
had observed that the Association in West Roxbury was both small and
imperfectly organized, but under all its disadvantages he had seen
blessed results flowing from it. "There," he had declared, "all the members dwell in content and harmony, free from the vexations, cares, and
oppressions which bear down so many thousands of the suffering poor
in all parts of our land . . ."

The appearance of his old friend, William Henry Channing, on the
same platform with Brisbane, must have seemed to George Ripley another indication of the strong Fourieristic tide that was sweeping all
mankind into one vast brotherhood. The two friends had not met frequently since 1842, when Channing's dislike of ritual had led him to
resign from his ministry in Cincinnati and retire to his mother's house
in Cambridge.

Channing lately had begun to preach again in Brooklyn, New York,
at meetings held in a schoolhouse on Sunday afternoons. At first he addressed a small company of persons who, like himself, disapproved of
fixed religious ritual. His biographer, O. B. Frothingham, writes, "The
preacher's faith in the Fatherhood of God and the brotherhood of man

was so sublime, he worked so hard and prayed so devoutly for the coming of the Kingdom of Heaven upon earth, that he was a bond of unity, keeping the divergent elements in peace." Channing's congregation multiplied rapidly, and within a few months he removed the ministry to the Stuyvesant Institute on Broadway. There so many flocked to hear him preach—among them Horace Greeley, Henry James the Elder, Christopher Cranch and his wife, the Curtis brothers—that a larger hall soon had to be rented in Crosby Street. When William Henry Channing preached, like his uncle, Dr. William Ellery Channing before him, "He was a flame, a breath of mountain air, a pure breeze from the north. He lifted up drooping hearts. Daily life became richer for his elevated teaching. His words were full of immortality. Cheerfulness and peace went with him, with the thought of him. He was a power of love, a radiant presence."

On the ninth of the previous April, Channing had submitted the "Principles of Christian Union" to the congregation. As the name implies, the first principle was belief in Jesus Christ, the Saviour and Anointed of God; the second, faith in the living inspiration of the human soul. From this it is evident that Channing's "Christian Socialism" had little in common with Brisbane's Fourierism except a mutual concern for the improvement of social conditions. To put the case of the underprivileged before the public, and to define his own position, Channing planned to found a new magazine to be called *The Present*. As the date of publication drew near, everyone wondered—"would Channing hold out his hand to Brisbane?"

The first issue appeared on September fifteenth. "The call of *The Present* is for the union and growth of Religion, Science, and Society," the editor announced. "A confession of Faith" followed—faith in the progressive conquest of good over evil. Dr. Channing looked to the gracious and good people, "the ministering servants of Providence," to further "this grand work of salvation" in which man would reform government, trade, distribution of wealth, education, rank, pleasures, home, and their own characters, "after the models of divine righteousness."

Amid the trumpeting of the angels, W. H. Channing sounded a note prophetic of our own day—that the United States manifestly had been created to prove human brotherhood, and that it is the destiny of our great country to unite the interests of all the nations on earth. It was in the hope that he had expressed the Universal Faith of the present, Dr. Channing explained, that he gave that name to his organ.

His uncle, Dr. William Ellery Channing, believed that reform worked from within. Fourier held it worked from environment. William Henry Channing believed in both.

Concerning Fourier's Social System, though the editor of *The Present* found the French philosopher "wanting in love," and sometimes contemptuous and arrogant, he planned to introduce his readers to "Passional Harmonies" and to "Attractive Industry." His attitude toward Brisbane himself was more friendly. It was due to the efforts of Mr. Brisbane more than any other, Channing wrote, that "every day brings tidings of some new Association."

In concluding his introduction to *The Present*, Channing urged all who labored for Social Reform to write for his organ. The views of all would be welcome. For were they not all working together upon the principle of United Interests—the watchword of Humanity? Social Reform, the editor felt sure, was already "sweeping Christendom and civilization."

The new wave of popular interest did not prevent George Ripley from experiencing fits of doubt and despondency. "Oh, for men who feel this idea to advance humanity by Association burning into their bones," he wrote Isaac Hecker on September eighteenth. "When shall we see them? And without them what will be phalanxes, groups and series, attractive industry, and all the sublime words of modern reform . . . ?"

George Ripley, half distraught by the financial straits of his Association, continued, "Just look at our case, with property amounting to $30,000 the want of $2,000 or $3,000 fetters us and may kill us. That sum would free us from pecuniary embarrassments, and for want of that we work daily with fetters on our limbs. Are there not five men in New York city who would dare to venture $200 each in the cause of social reform without being assured of a phalanx for themselves and their children forever? Alas, I know not. We are willing to traverse the wilderness for forty years; we ask no grapes of Eschol for ourselves; we do not claim a fair abode in the Promised Land, but what can we do with neither quail nor manna, with raiment waxing old and shoes bursting on our feet."

In this letter—which is among the unpublished Hecker Papers—Ripley somewhat naïvely urges Hecker to come back to Brook Farm not as "a self perfectioner" but as "a true worker." One feels certain that Ripley would not have written so frankly had he seen the recent letter from Brownson in Hecker's portfolio commending Isaac's decision to depart from Fruitlands. Brownson added, "I am glad that you are at home. I believe upon the whole you will find it better for you. These Communities after all are humbugs. We must rehabilitate the Church and work under its direction." In Brownson's view Brisbane's lectures in Boston had *not* produced a sensation. "Fourierism will not take us," he concluded crisply, "and Brisbane will not recommend it."

When Brownson referred to the Church, he meant, of course, the Church of Rome, to which he was admitted within the year; and on the third of October he wrote Hecker that he was resuming publication of *The Quarterly*. "I shall come out boldly for the Church," he explained, "on the principles you and I have so often discussed."

Hecker, himself, had not yet made up his mind. He was still torn between the Episcopal Church and Roman Catholicism. That Transcendentalism was not for him was the only decision he had reached since leaving home the previous January. Few of his Brook Farm friends —either those who remained at the Community, or those who had left— could comprehend Hecker's craving for a ritualistic religion. Yet, as many Transcendentalists later discovered, the transition was not so incongruous as one might suppose. To the majority, however, questions of religious philosophy were entwined with social reform. George William Curtis, for example, shared William Henry Channing's dislike of religious ritual; and with Brownson and Hecker he rejected Fourierism as too materialistic.

Curtis summed up his views in a letter of September sixteenth—to Hecker, who would certainly not share them: "So Unitarianism protests against the misunderstood doctrine of the Trinity, and is so far good. Presently it becomes a sect and its life is no more full and flowing, but a dead formula existing by its claim to superior spirituality; which claim is valid till this perpetually flowing wave that appeared in Christianity—in the Reformation, in the endless reforms of our reformations, at last appears also in Transcendentalism and leads the deeper, truer souls to New Truths for more universal beauty. It must have new forms still and the wise man lends himself to no organization. A World Traveler, he can pitch his tent nowhere . . . On this side and that he passes groups who have reached the limit of their discretion and turned their backs upon the East. (Dawn of Each New Day.) He overtakes a studious Fourier who dies wondering how to live, and sees his hearty disciple"—Brisbane—"improving the circumstances while the soul asks no new clothes but what it has."

George, and perhaps his brother, Burrill, were staying at Brook Farm for a few weeks, on the way from Concord to New York. Their father and stepmother had removed from the fair but small city, Providence, and established themselves in the metropolis. Some said the brothers had joined Brook Farm to protest their father's remarriage. If so, they had learned to accept it now; and George William—for worldlier motives than his friend, Isaac—was already beginning to outgrow Brook Farm. He even was able, in a letter of October eighth to Isaac, to propound shrewdly about the Founder of Brook Farm. "I feel daily," he wrote, "that while our friend, Mr. Ripley, mourns over the social evils, his own life is postponed and his ability to remedy the evils weakened and deferred."

11.

In the October issue of *The Present*, Channing announced "A Call," signed by J. A. Collins, N. H. Whiting, John Orvis, and J. O. Wattles. The summons was to a meeting at the community in Skaneateles, New York on October fourteenth and fifteenth, 1843. The group led by Collins at the community in Skaneateles, New York, labored for "a reorganization of the social system by a community of property and interest throughout the country." They were communists of an ineffectual nature.

True to his pledge—that he would grant all social reformers a rostrum —W. H. Channing said, "Though dissenting from this view, and believing confidently that Property in a system of 'United Interests' will be found a source and a means of kindliness and not of selfishness, and that it is an indispensable condition for the preservation of individuality, I yet sincerely wish the originators of this humane enterprise success, and assure them of the respect and sympathy of those who differ from them. Let the social reformers of our day, of the extreme right, extreme left, and centre, march in one unbroken line; though each wing may have a different banner, the central oriflamme is love."

Dana was about to join the Brisbane wing under the Fourier banner, but he was still content to let Mr. Ripley and Lewis K. Rickman—who was so much more experienced in "Industry" than they that the Ripleys revered him as "The Omniarch"—do the honors for Brook Farm at Skaneateles. In their absence Dana wrote Hecker for the last time on an intimate, untroubled note. Their spiritual paths already had diverged. But neither of them seems to have been aware of that as yet; and that is what makes this letter* of greater interest than its content:

> *Mein liebster Isaac,*
> Your letter, short enough to have been written by me, came by Herr Ryckman, and did me no little good; nor was I sorry that it was not written from your under but from your upper current. I was glad to have it, at any rate. I saw a day or two ago, your letter to G. Ripley, which has cheered the two or three who have read it not a little. It is much to be assured that one's own best endeavors are shared by true hearts, and that earnest souls are not insensible to the faith on which we rest. Courage, *mein theurste Bruder,—Die Wahrheit wird siegen* within us and without us.
> Of our welfare and ill-fare though the latter is not apparent— George Ripley will tell you. We toil on and sow our seed which doubtless shall not perish. Eleanor is married and gone for a little visit. Probably we may have another event of the same sort among us; though it is so doubtful that nobody is told of it. I think of venturing in that mystical estate within three or four months. I wait to see if I can arrange some business affairs first. Do not tell anybody yet.
> What a fine article this no. of *The Present* has.
>
> Mit treuer Liebe
> Karl

The article Dana mentioned referred to the new Fourieristic organ, which the *Tribune* had announced on October twenty-third. Formerly planned as a semi-monthly, such was the effectiveness of Brisbane's plea for five hundred subscribers in New York City that within a few days *The North American Phalanx* appeared as a weekly under the heading, "Our evils are social, not political, and a social reform only can eradicate them." Above to the left, "Social, Political, and Religious Unity, Social Progress, Social Reform upon Conservative Principles"; and to the right, "Social and Political Liberty and Equality. Association, Attractive Industry, Unity of Interests." This illustrates Brisbane's faith in the power of repetition.

W. H. Channing extended a hearty welcome to this "long wished for and timely publication," and then proceeded to make reservations in regard to Fourierism. ". . . However high our estimate of Fourier it is still very plain that he must in many things have been fallible. A science of 'Universal Unity' is not for this generation. While granting some principles and admitting some conclusions, it will of course be found that others require modification or even rejection. And it is

---

* Hecker Papers.

highly probable that examination and experience will disclose many deficiencies to be supplied. Meanwhile let us ponder the important test of *The Phalanx*."

In the spirit of gathering all sects of social philosophy under his "central oriflamme of Love," W. H. Channing could encourage Brisbane in one breath and praise Brownson in the next for "the consistency of progress" in his articles in the *Democratic Review*. Perhaps Channing might not have felt so favorably disposed had he known how Brownson felt about Christian Socialism. On November eighth, Brownson wrote Hecker: "I look at Channing's movement in New York. His theory of Christian union is beautiful, nay true; but he will fail. For to succeed he must institute a New Church, and to do that he must be a New Christ, and even greater than Christ. He starts outside of the Church and says: 'Go to now, let us all be one Church.' The principle of union, he says, is love. Nothing more true. Therefore if you love you will all be one. Nothing again more true. But the precise difficulty is men do not love, and it is because they do not love that they are alienated and divided."

12.

Getting back to the farm has ever been a delight to New Englanders, after a stimulating trip to New York such as George Ripley enjoyed that October. Even in November the landscape affords refreshment to native sons and daughters. Though frosts and gales strip trees and hedged lanes, staunch trunks and outstretched branches of elm, oak, maple and chestnut offer a pattern of infinite variety against sky or evergreen. Some days dawn blue and soft as a May morning to gather dark clouds come noon. A light carpet of snow can vanish in a suddenly rising temperature, which, at dusk, bares the Hunter's golden moon rising in a lilac tinted after-glow. Heaven seems close at such moments in New England, as the poet-ambassador, James Russell Lowell, sang about a day in June.

Wearied by the long jolting ride on the railroad, and the jogging drive to Brook Farm in Jonah Gerrish's stage, George Ripley would change to smock and boots, and hurry out to the barnyard to help with the chores as usual. As he settled down to the familiar rhythm of the

milking pail, he may well have meditated upon the financial status of
Brook Farm, and the benefits derived from his trip.

It would be possible, for the first time in two years, to remit $32 to
Nathaniel Hawthorne in the near future—the plaintiff duly acknowledged the remittance on the back of George Ripley's and Charles A.
Dana's personal note on November seventh, 1843. There was a certain
satisfaction in reducing the total debt—$524—by even that little. And
as for the recent trip, although he never could abide Collins' communistic views, his stay at Skaneateles had brought a half promise from
young John Orvis, recent convert to Fourierism, and an experienced
lecturer, that had made it worthwhile to attend the convention there.
Orvis had agreed to visit Brook Farm come spring, and if it pleased him,
he would desert Skaneateles and join the Association in West Roxbury.

George Ripley found another source of encouragement emanating
from the *Phalanx's* office in New York. An extraordinary number of people, it appeared, were making inquiries about Association. Sustained by
a flow of letters from north, west, and south—as well as from the eastern
seaboard—Brisbane's propaganda headquarters fairly seethed with bustle
and activity.

Horace Greeley had been pounding away against the "cant of ex-
clusiveness" at Brook Farm, ever since 1842. "My fear for your system,"
he had written Dana on August twenty-second of that year, "is that it
is adapted only to angelic natures and that the entrance of one serpent
would be as fatal as in the Eden of old." Fourier's system avoided this
danger, in Greeley's opinion, "by having a rampart of equal people in
every phalanstery." Naturally, the editor now congratulated young Dana
on his recent conversion.

Though one of Brisbane's first converts to Fourierism, Greeley had
refused steadily to take everything "on Fourier's authority, though on
many points he commands my concurrence." Actually, Greeley's brand
of Fourierism amounted to nothing but a firm belief in the practicality
of Association. In March 1843, when asked by Noah Webster for an
authoritative interpretation, Greeley presented a brief summary that did
not touch on the heart of Fourier's system at all. The journalist's superficial interpretation is shocking when one reflects that he was trying to
force a philosophy on the public which he had not taken the trouble to
understand thoroughly.

To George Ripley, Greeley declared himself completely satisfied—nay,
enthusiastic!—in regard to Brisbane's propaganda. In an age of causes,
no other reform had ever spread so quickly! Greeley did not doubt that

all the recently established Associations in Vermont, Pennsylvania, Indiana, Illinois, and especially those in western New York, would become self-sustaining in the course of the present year. Did not Brisbane predict that with the aid of his expanding Speakers' Bureau, the movement would continue to gain influence rapidly in the press?

Ripley shared Greeley's and Brisbane's enthusiasm, yet he still hung back from converting Brook Farm into a phalanx—for the ultimate responsibility was his alone. Yet, he was increasingly fascinated by Brisbane's glamorous descriptions of the elaborate joint-stock organizations of the Fourieristic phalanxes, avowedly designed to safeguard every type of vested property interest. These had, for Ripley, a sound appeal. As he saw it, property, whether inherited or earned, represented the material reward of some person's endeavor. To ask the property owner to share this reward with those who perhaps had not exerted themselves sufficiently or made the most of their opportunities was, therefore, merely to offer a premium on idleness and wasting.

During Ripley's visit to the *Phalanx's* office, he must have learned what friends of Association throughout the United States would read in the *Tribune* on November fifth, that "Books for the subscription of the Capitol Stock of an Association to be located in the vicinity of the city of New York were to be opened in a few weeks. Land twenty-five miles from New York at $35.00 per acre." That Brisbane had persuaded a group of successful businessmen to invest in a phalanx, must have counted heavily in Ripley's ultimate decision—together with Brisbane's constant insistence that the reason Brook Farm was in the red was because it was organized on too small a scale. Unfortunately, George Ripley did not foresee that the North American Phalanx, soon to be established at Red Bank, New Jersey, would inevitably seem of more importance to Albert Brisbane than the experiment he was inducing his West Roxbury friends to undertake; or that the man who would convert Brook Farm into a phalanx, might abandon it when most needed. To George Ripley, on the contrary, the founding of a large phalanx on the Eastern seaboard, seemed one more indication that the tide of Fourierism was sweeping the land.

It was poverty rather than conviction which was pushing the harder heads among them—such as young Dana—toward Fourierism at this time. Dana summed up why he went along with Mr. Ripley years afterward in an address delivered at the University of Michigan on January 21, 1895. The Farmers, he said, had more applications than they could house, and no capital with which to build. Since Fourierism was gain-

ing adherents all over the country, they thought they, too, would make
a greater impression if they adopted his system—and so advance universal social reform, their heart's duty and desire.

In a letter of November eleventh from New York, George William
Curtis twitted little John S. Dwight about the effect the approaching
change at Brook Farm might have on his personal standing. Curtis predicted that a fog would befog Dwight's fair name as "a dweller at that
place, unknown to perfumed respectability and condemned of prejudice
and error." Fourier's theories were anathema to perfumed respectability—and one suspects that they made little Mr. Dwight extremely uncomfortable. Yet he knew he would stay on, regardless. For how could
he abandon so many enthusiastic pupils? "With ears attuned to so
much warbling," they thought nothing of walking seven long miles to
Boston to drink in the symphonies. Mrs. Harrington's cake shop offered
sustaining refreshment after the concert, and then back they would
tramp to Brook Farm, "elated and unconscious of fatigue, carrying
home with them a new good genius, beautiful and strong, to help them
through the next day's labors."

All were not so rugged, of course; and some preferred a Lyceum Lecture or an anti-slavery meeting at Fanueil Hall. But every single female
among them these days was distressed by the shabbiness of her attire.
With the Association in financial straits, the "religious" would not re-
plenish their wardrobes and the vain had not the face to do so. In all
the Hive, Georgiana Bruce found only two bonnets "fit for city eyes."
Fortunately, the happy possessors forced these on whoever was going to
town. The men were no better off. Without a decent looking coat
among them, "the gentlemen found it desirable to adopt a tunic." Their
shabby raiment could not dim their bright spirits, however, and there
was laughter and gaiety when they piled into the big farm wagon for
the long, slow trip to town.

Always a sociable man and fond of cultural activities Mr. Ripley
shared in these outings as often as he could. Indeed, he may well have
been singing his way home on that evening, early in December, when
Mrs. Ripley poured out her heart in a letter to Margaret Fuller.* "The
money does not come," Sophia wrote. "We have meetings every week
at which the men out of the Association are present. They are called
upon to help us and are full of spirit and good sense in their suggestions. They are very united, and are attempting to make an arrange-

* The letter is in Harvard University's Houghton Library.

ment by which our mechanical departments may be increased and the support of the establishment thrown in a great measure upon them. Our faith increases even when hope is faint, and love abounds." (This remark on the part of Sophia Ripley indicates that Channing's Christian Socialism was more sympathetic to her than Brisbane's Fourierism; and that she, like Brownson, entertained doubts if the latter would prove a solution to their economic problem.)

Poor Sophia was sadly disturbed about her husband at this time. "I suffer very much from George's perplexities (*entre nous*) because I cannot aid him in them," she confessed sadly, "and one does not feel that right to rise above the trials of others into a clearer and serener atmosphere where our own trials of every kind can often lift us."

George Ripley made up his mind within the week; for he heartily endorsed "The Call" which appeared in *The Present* on December fifteenth. Mr. Ripley let it be known that he expected great things of this convention. "We the undersigned, induced by the earnest solicitations of others, as well as by the pressing wants of the times and our own wishes, do hereby call a Convention of the Friends of Social Reform in New England and elsewhere, to be holden in Boston, December twenty-sixth and twenty-seventh, 1843—the last Tuesday and Wednesday of the month." The objects of the Convention were clearly set forth:

> To counsel and to aid the great cause of Social Reorganization.
> To contemplate progress, at home and abroad, of Fourierism.
> To build an Association that will be a home where all who love truth
>   and would live in it can find refuge and consolation.

This document was signed by L. W. Ryckman of Brook Farm; and two "of Roxbury" but soon to become Farmers—F. S. Cabot and J. Allen.

Elsewhere in *The Present*, Channing blandly informed the public, "Our whole history has prepared us for such an effort"—Association—"to actualize the idea of union. This nation was born, it may be said, in our system of townships. It has grown into a systematic whole of counties and States, bound in one by a Central Constitution. We have but to apply the true principle of organization to our towns, and the United States may at once place itself in the Combined Order." His other leading thought for the month is less quill-raising. "Attractive Industry," said Channing, "suits a people of working men—Americans."

As the year drew to a close, Brisbane patted himself firmly on the back. "The name of Fourier is now heard from the Atlantic to the

Mississippi; from the remotest parts of Wisconsin and Louisiana responsive echoes reach us, heralding the speed of the great principles of Association; and this important work has been accomplished in a few years, mainly within two years . . . What," he asked confidently, "will the next bring forth?"

◄◄

The Change to Fourierism

PUBLIC RESPONSE TO "THE CALL" TO CONVENE IN BOSTON EXCEEDED THE leaders' fondest hopes. "This Convention," W. H. Channing announced in the January issue of *The Present*, "marked an era in the history of New England." Many were there from a distance, and a most varied multitude from the immediate neighborhood and from the city. "Come-outers" of all shades of ultraism were side by side with Conservatives of most varying degrees of consistency; mechanics and ministers, farmers and brokers, scholars and merchants, men and women of most dissimilar walks of life, listening and speaking of what they felt was a common duty and a common want for themselves and for all. Public interest and attendance increased to such a degree that the Convention, which had expected to adjourn on Wednesday December twenty-seventh, continued through Thursday and Friday.

W. H. Channing interpreted the enthusiasm as "a public movement toward Social Reform according to the Order of Love. Association," he prophesied, "will accomplish all other reforms—abolitionist, pacifist, temperance, woman's rights, health—by perfect obedience to the Creator's laws."

Hopedale, Brook Farm, and North Hampton were well represented. The New England delegates, and also those from elsewhere, showed, on the whole, a true spirit of harmony throughout the proceedings. The only discordant note was sounded by Dr. John A. Collins of Skaneateles, New York, who raised the issue of "Communitism," an offshoot of "Owenism," which held for common ownership of property, including wives. Channing deplored Collins' introduction of such dubious doctrines, and his militant attitude in maintaining them. The New Englander, however, was determined to be true to his conviction that all social reformers, whatever their differences, were animated by the same noble aim, and so he conceded that the "Communitists" were entitled to a satisfactory test of their ideas, which he, for one, would observe in the pious hope that their love would prove strong enough "to triumph over the errors of their creed."

Despite Channing's lofty tone, it was the crying need for "a proper organization of industry" which had gathered this multitude. The majority of those who came wished to be convinced that the evils of the competitive system could be dissolved under some form of Association.

The Fourierites alone among these Utopian Reformers had such a plan drawn up and ready to present—Fourier's "Laws of Moral and Industrial Attraction." In consequence they controlled the Convention; and their leaders got quickly down to the real business of the day (the promotion of Fourierism). It was resolved to promote the formation of Fourier Societies in New England cities and towns, and to spread the doctrine by lectures, tracts, and conventions. Such a program would fall flat unless the leaders could point to an existing Association organized on Fourier's principles—some place where a thorough test was in process. A resolution was passed to that effect—and Brook Farm's fate was sealed.

A final resolution before adjournment commended the *Phalanx* and *The Present* for their editorial support. If Brisbane was responsible for coupling Channing's journal with the Fourieristic organ, the New Englander did not allow his hand to be forced. "Quite far am I from saying that as now enlightened I adopt all Fourier's opinions," Channing wrote in concluding his report of the Convention. "On the contrary, there are some I reject; but it is a pleasure to express gratitude to Charles Fourier for having opened a whole new world of study, hope, and action. (It does seem to me that he has given us the clue out of our scientific labyrinth, and revealed the means of living the Law of Love.) Years of application and trial, however, would alone qualify one to pronounce fair judgment upon the System of Universal Unity."

Miss Peabody, watching with trepidation the mounting Fourieristic tide engulfing her Brook Farm friends, wrote a guarded review of the

Convention for *The Dial*. "We still have a certain question about Fourierism, considered as a Catholicon for evil. But our absurd horrors were
dissipated, and a feeling of genuine respect for the movement insured as
we heard the exposition of the doctrine by Mr. Channing and others."

2.

The basis upon which the Brook Farmers presently began to reorganize their Association was limited to the Theory of Attractive Industry,
as practiced in the Unitary Dwelling or Phalanstery. Ripley was undoubtedly informed in all aspects of Fourierism, but as far as Brook
Farm was concerned, he wished only to change the Industrial order of
the Association.

Until increased prosperity should enable them to build a phalanstery,
the Farmers would content themselves with their four scattered dwell-
ings—the Hive, Eyrie, Pilgrim House, and Margaret Fuller Cottage.
However, they were confident that when Fourier's principle of Attractive Industry was established, prosperity would rise like a river and bear
them to success.

The Directors began at once to set up classes to instruct the Farmers
in the religious significance which Fourier had attached to his "Discovery." For Fourier had regarded himself as the Newton of the spiritual
world; and as such he unhesitatingly proclaimed that God governed the
universe by Attraction—by pleasure, not by constraint. Surely it would
be inconsistent for a good God to have made Man with evil impulses
with which he must constantly contend?

Instead of trying to correct God, Man should try to learn how God
planned for us to use our natural impulses. Fourier attempted to show
how Man, if he summoned the courage to abolish artificial Man-made
restrictions—the so-called Moral Code—would straightway overcome
all the trickery, deceits, hypocrisy, and parasitism of civilization. The
immediate establishment of "Harmony" would follow.

All this, of course, was at odds with Christian teaching; and George
Ripley, former Unitarian Divine, by no means admitted that Morality
turned the world inside out and upside down. However, if it was possible to make Brook Farm's unprofitable industry pay by reorganizing
their various departments according to Fourier's Law of Passionate At-

traction, he would try. Accordingly, he undertook to instruct his "people" in Fourier's extremely complicated "Analysis of the Passions," so that each individual could choose which of the "Groups and Series" attracted him or her the most.

For, who could deny that that which especially characterizes human nature is its tendency to form groups, or "Passional Leagues"? That Friendship, Ambition, Love, and Familism are the root sources of all social relationships? Obviously any one of these four "Passions" would suffice to form a group. But there were—in Fourier's book—eight more: —the Five Animic or Sensory Passions, corresponding to the Five Senses; and the Three Passions of Harmony—renegades in civilization, but redeemed by the Master and put to good use.

Aware that Man frequently is fired by mixed motives, Fourier interrupted his argument at this point to tabulate the various combinations of motives a man might entertain, with the result that his imagination ran amuck in a welter of incomprehensible jargon. Mr. Ripley, himself, must have found an attempt to comprehend Fourier's tabulation as futile as counting reflections in a double mirror.

In general, Fourier held that in Friendship all are attracted without regard to rank, the tone cordial, and without rivalry; whereas, in Ambition, superiors attract inferiors, and here there is competition—ascendance and deference. In Love, women attract men, and the result is deference of the strong to the weak. In Familism—Fourier's abhorrence —inferiors attract superiors, parents defer to offspring.

In Civilization, Fourier points out, "Passions" are repressed and warped with the result that friends scheme against one another; men maltreat their wives; and children defy their parents. Fourier's great discovery, *the proper use* of the "Three Passions of Harmony" would do away with strife and injustice by making it possible for the "Four Root Passions" and the "Five Animic Passions" to agree with themselves and with each other. Indeed, these "Three Passions of Harmony" constitute the essential sources of Fourier's social organization; in Civilization, having no useful employment, they become destructive and are generally regarded as sinful Passions. Fourier used them to motivate the "Groups and Series" which carry on the work within the phalanx. These three, "Cabalism," "Compositism," and "Alternatism," soon became daily topics of discussion at Brook Farm.

"Cabalism," the passion for intrigue, always would mix up calculations with passion, make all calculation and intrigue. This passion, Fourier remarked, is "very ardent in courtesans, the ambitious, the commercial, the world of fashion. In these circles the least gesture, even a wink of the eye; Cabalism does all with reflection and celerity . . ."

"Compositism" is the enthusiasm which *excludes* reason. It is the captivation of the senses and the soul—a state of intoxication and moral blindness, a kind of happiness which arises from a combination of two pleasures, one of sense, and one of the soul. Needless to say, the special domain of Compositism is Love, although it operates with less intensity on all the Passions.

The third, "Alternatism," sometimes known as the "Butterfly Passion," is the appetite for change of scene, stirring incidents, and all manner of "novelties proper to create illusion, to stimulate at once the senses and the soul." This want, according to Fourier, is felt by every adult "in a moderate degree every hour, and *keenly* every two hours." In Civilization where it is not readily satisfied, Man is a constant prey to weariness and boredom.

Fourier planned to employ all three of these Passions to advantage in the phalanx. His "Harmonians" would carry on, sometimes with cool calculation, at others with blind enthusiasm—but never for very long at a time. After two hours the "Butterfly Passion" would be satisfied—before rivalry turned to hatred, or enthusiasm to recklessness.

The fundamental feature in the organization of the phalanx—the formation of small groups composed of people drawn together in work or play by the same Passion—flowed naturally from the study of the "Analysis of the Passions." Nor did it stop there. Groups of the same genus—makers of wine, for example—would gradually form a union and expand into a series. As time goes on, the expansion continues to form unions in neighboring phalanxes; but the expansion must always be regulated to conform to the original pattern, so that each series presents all the varieties of a single labor or pleasure. To particularize them further, groups which bottle different flavors of champagne, for example, make a series within a series.

In this way emulation and rivalry—ever "a true dissonance"—would arise among groups near at hand; plus "kindly correspondence with collective groups more remote."

The size of a Group could be flexible; and a Harmonian might join for the companionship rather than the occupation, or vice versa. There was but one unbreakable rule—all the parties in a Group must be passionately engaged without recourse to the stimulants of want, morality, reason, duty, or constraint of any kind.

In Civilization, Fourier pointed out, especially since the coming of the Machine Age, the minute division of labor compelled Man to slavish monotony. Fourier, also, favored the minute division of labor. But it was here that the Alternate or Butterfly Passion would become such a mighty force for the common good. Without the satisfaction of this passion Man could never be happy in his work. But in the phalanx everyone would devote himself to many different occupations in the course of the day, developing alternately his body and soul; and the work would never lag. A group of ten or twelve would complete in an hour a task which usually took one man all day.

Another advantage in this system of two-hour shifts—it would multiply each person's contacts. The composition of each group would be different from every other. This was very important, because a varied acquaintance was highly beneficial in stimulating effort. The more dominant passions a person had, the higher his destiny. Those possessed of only one enthusiasm, Fourier called "Solitones." These characters had a special aptitude for long dull tasks; and they constituted "the privates in the regiment" of the phalanx.

Most important of all, the system of diversified tasks would solve the greatest difficulty of administration—the distribution of benefits. For, if all the affections and interests of an associate were connected solely with one order of labor, everyone would seek advancement for his own Group, and collisions without number would arise. To sum up in a homely phrase, "He who has a finger in every pie, hopes each dish will taste as good as every other." In this way equilibrium would be maintained in the phalanx.

"Passional Equilibrium" is the fancy name Fourier bestowed on this delicately balanced harmony of interests among his Harmonians. This equilibrium, he argued, would be held sacred by all, because to disturb one of its buttresses—as in a Gothic Cathedral—would set the whole phalanx tumbling about the ears of the disturber.

Yet the distribution of benefits would constitute a most delicate task, the distributor liable to make grave mistakes. Fourier displayed ingenuity in applying the art of harnessing man's native selfishness to promote the common good. The benefits as a whole would be taken from the sum total of the whole phalanx; but each dividend allotted to each series was not to be determined by the quantity of the produce, but upon the rank of the series—necessary, useful, or agreeable. It might happen that a highly productive series such as fruit growing would be paid less than the care of cattle which subjected the cowhand to handling manure. But each individual would soon realize that this adjustable system of distribution was highly advantageous for all concerned. For, if a man felt injured by the dividends he received in one, or even two series in which he excelled, and so felt he had a right to the largest share, he would be compensated by his joy and pride in his own skill. Or he might have friends he esteemed and felt loyal to in those industries, and so would gladly support them in cabalistic friendship.

Sir Alexander Gray, in his chapter on Fourier in *The Socialist Tradition*, writes, "According to the Theory of the Groups, each man will be capitalist, manager, and wage earner—a microcosm. This amalgamation of interests eliminates class feeling." One might add, the theory is an ingenious scheme to broaden and vary the life of the worker, interweaving into his daily life such a wide variety of interests and enthusiasms that he has little temptation to upset the life of his community.

3.

When Charles Lane's disparaging article, "Brook Farm," appeared in the January issue of *The Dial*, the Englishman's scathing dictum, that Brook Farm was neither a Community nor an Association, must have fallen flat indeed—in view of the failure at Fruitlands the previous December. Mr. Lane's doctrine, "Ceasing from Doing," and Mr. Alcott's confidence that God would provide, if Man provided asceticism and love, had led their "Eden" straight to disaster. Which was scarcely to be wondered at in the opinion of the Directors of Brook Farm, whose problem was short-handedness, not short-sightedness.

To posterity, the vegetarian restrictions put upon diet and soil cultivation by Lane and Alcott seem so impractical that one wonders whether those two philosophers had not become slightly lightheaded as a result of malnutrition and confused concerning mundane matters.

Neither philosopher had envisaged the wintry famine, until suddenly it was upon them. Years afterward, Louisa May Alcott wrote a satirical account of her Fruitlands experience—"Transcendental Wild Oats." Though gay and courageous, Louisa's humor is tinged throughout with the threat of disaster. She had not forgotten the gnawing hunger, which, even in summer, had compelled her and her sisters to search the pastures frantically for wild berries; nor the creeping cold that set in the night Beth was born. What—the little girls had wondered—would happen when their measly harvest of grain and dried vegetables was gone?

Though she could laugh in later years over her father's serene admonishment—"The Lord will provide!"—at the time the discomfort was no laughing matter.

In December 1843, a month before Lane's article on Brook Farm appeared in *The Dial*, Fruitlands had been abandoned. Charles Lane and his son, William, took refuge with a neighboring colony of Shakers in Harvard, Massachusetts. With the aid of a neighbor and his sled, Mrs. Alcott transported her family along a snowclad trail to a house in the nearby village, Still River. There, Mr. Alcott, stricken to his very soul, took to his bed, and to Mrs. Alcott's unutterable consternation, "turned his face to the wall."

The Farmers, on reading Mr. Lane's article about themselves, could now dismiss the Englishman's condescension with a tolerant smile. Isaac Hecker was the only Farmer who had ever formed a close friendship with the supercilious Englishman, and Isaac was far removed in spirit from Brook Farm now. But rumors of Mr. Alcott's despair were another matter. Though Mr. Alcott never really had approved of Brook Farm he had always been a welcome visitor. Young and old were fond of the dear quaint man! His relationship with the Ripleys always had been close; and the failure of Fruitlands may well have been the final happening which made George Ripley, after months of indecision, decide to reorganize Brook Farm into a Fourier phalanx.

4.

If young Dana still entertained misgivings concerning Fourierism when he set out for the Convention in Boston, his respect and affection for Mr. Ripley were such that he accepted the duties of Secretary—and in the course of the four arduous days which it lasted, became a convert.

On January second this young man of sound intellect and mature poise, wrote Isaac Hecker from Brook Farm. Fourierism had knocked

him off his customary balance, and the letter radiates confusion and
fatigue.

It begins with a splash into German sentimentalities, and then
continues, "By any other reckoning of the ordinary calendar it is
hardly a day since I came from New York—and yet the gleaming
snow and icy trees declare that since then Autumn has fallen into
Winter which just as rapidly urges toward the Spring. Concerning
Nature, *mein leibster*, I doubt whether we draw most largely upon her
stores when they seem to soothe and inspire us most. Here now I have
breathed the healthy air, and been taught by the whiteness of the
snow, and all without knowing it or turning for an instant aside from
my daily occupations, except one afternoon when I went skating for
an hour. Ah Himmel!—that is the fit play and recreation of the Celestial
Gods. I cannot praise it enough."

But Dana was too weary to sustain this exalted vein.

"Upon me the last week has made a sad inroad," he confessed. "We
have been carried to Boston to attend a Convention of Social Reformers of all sorts and purposes, and kept there for four days of the
most intense labor, from the fatigues of which I have not yet recovered
—tonight, also I am going to Boston to make a speech, for which I
am anything but fit."

Drafted by Mr. Ripley to aid in the founding of a New England
Fourier Society, while public enthusiasm still rose high, young Dana,
rehearsing his speech in parrot-like vein, wrote Hecker what the
speakers at the Convention had been dunning into his ears. It was
unfortunate for their friendship that Dana embroidered his theme
with a metaphor which could scarcely please a prospective convert
to Roman Catholicism. "The social movement is assuming greater
extent and importance. In this idea, also—of a society which shall be
a church and a church which shall be a society,—lies as far as I can
understand that Holy Catholic Church which both you and I have
at heart."

This must have seemed a dangerous and confused doctrine to
Hecker, who was leaning more and more toward a ritualistic religion,
and what followed, downright heresy. For this "new" Christian
Church was to be more universal than the Jewish. "Its doctrine is the
Eternal Unity of all spirits and all Nature; . . . and its chief sacrament
is Labor, and its first movement a crusade to recover from the Infidel
that lost Holy Land, Humanity."

Here, for the first time, one detects a hint of that weirdly crusading attitude of the Fourierites, which in the light of some of the French philosopher's doctrines proved exceedingly offensive to Christians whether Protestant or Church of Rome. But Dana, unaware that he had dealt their friendship a severe blow, went serenely on, "Of Fourier I have a word to say, and that is, that it is safer to let him interpret himself than to take him at second hand. Especially I have learned to distrust Brisbane's expositions. He is not a man of sufficient spirituality or sufficient depth of intellect to interpret the profound things of the great Frenchman. From Godwin, who has just paid us a visit"—Parke Godwin, editor of *The Pathfinder*—"I have got something more satisfactory. Godwin says that Doherty of London has the most thorough understanding of Fourier of all his disciples—but I hope soon to get at it in the original. The glimpses I have already had inclined me to reckon him, with Swedenborg, the profoundest thinker of these modern times."

Of his "own private proceedings," Dana had little to say, except, "I have been for the last two weeks so turned out of my course that I almost doubt my own identity." However, he hoped to be soon back "on the tracks again and move forward." Towards the end of this long letter, Dana went out of his way to jibe at Brownson. "There is something new in Brownson's position, to say the least," Dana wrote of Brownson's latest declaration of faith in *The Quarterly Review*. "No longer to be a learner is sublime enough, if it could be so." Not content with this sarcasm, Dana added with deadly frankness that Brownson interested him "less now than ever before."

Evidently the writer had no idea his "bester Isaac" might take exception to his remarks, for the letter concludes on the same affectionate note with which he began. This was natural enough. The two young men had indulged in so much idea threshing in the past that it never occurred to Dana to write his friend with reserve. Nor was Dana aware how widely their paths had diverged since Hecker had left Brook Farm—and advanced along "The Mystic Way."

The friends would continue to correspond for months to come; and Dana's unpublished letters to Hecker from Brook Farm * exemplify the parting of a Fourierite and a mystic nearing conversion to Roman Catholicism. Both had reached a parting of the ways at Brook Farm.

---

* Hecker Papers, Archives of the Paulist Fathers, New York.

5.

Now that George Ripley had made the great decision, all his former buoyancy returned. In accents of Victorian discretion his biographer, O. B. Frothingham, informs us "Ripley wrote, talked, lectured, illustrating by word and example the new gospel of labor and love, which to him was another edition of the gospel of Christ." Fourierism seemed a strange aberration, indeed, on the part of a former Unitarian Divine; and the biographer glosses over this period in his subject's life with the kindly tolerance due an otherwise discerning intellect.

Ripley, himself, would never recant his faith in Fourierism, and he would most certainly have resented his biographer's whitewashing of his zeal for the radical and highly suspect social philosophy. In January 1844 Ripley labored to such good effect that a first meeting of the New England Fourier Society was held on the fifteenth. He presided, as President; and two Brook Farmers, John S. Dwight and Fred S. Cabot, the Corporation Clerk, supported him on the Executive Committee.

If some of the Farmers felt, as Dana had after the Convention, that Mr. Ripley was riding them too hard, there was little or no opposition to his new policy. A second edition of the Brook Farm Association Constitution was drawn up and endorsed by the Directors on the eighteenth. The document would not be ratified by the Association for a month, but it would be the first item on the agenda of the February meeting, and as such already proved that George Ripley had effected a complete revolution in less than three weeks.

Ripley's eagerness and haste are readily understood. After two and a half years of isolated effort, he suddenly found himself in step with the times Or so it appeared to him. Brisbane's propaganda had not just caught hold here and there. Practical, successful men were investing money in "Association."

In December the *Phalanx* had pointed with pride to the success of the movement which was spreading fast in Rochester, New York. In that enlightened town, no less than four lecturers were in demand; money poured in for the publication and distribution of Brisbane's tracts. And the scale upon which the phalanxes were being founded in Western New York State seemed positively feudal to Brook Farmers. Though the Ontario Phalanx—1400 acres on that Great Lake—had split up within a year of its founding because of religious differences between the leaders, it had given birth to two new ones—the Clarkson, and Sodus Bay. Both of these were richer far in acres and industrial potential than Brook Farm with its two hundred and eight acres of gravelly New England soil; and the tide was sweeping westward. Two thousand acres of rich land in Belmont County, Ohio, would soon be the site of the American Phalanx. All this was highly encouraging. But to a man like George Ripley, one who pinned his faith on the power of the written word, the January *Phalanx* presented an even more thrilling item; "Through the liberality of a gentleman from Louisiana, the *Phalanx* is to be sent to the Senior Class in every college and university in the United States."

6.

From time to time—usually in the late fall when the crops were garnered—William Allen would write Mr. Ripley how he and Sylvia often talked of going back to Brook Farm. Nothing ever came of it. The Allens were well situated in East Westmoreland, New Hampshire, and they never seriously considered giving up their own place. Probably —as the work slacked off—William got to thinking about the halcyon days when he had spread manure in the company of philosophers.

Apparently Mr. Ripley had shown William's latest to Georgiana Bruce; and on the twenty-sixth of January she replied to Allen's queries at some length. Reading between her lines, it is clear that she was trying to wipe away the cobwebs of sentimental regret, and to make William understand that the Community was no longer what it had been in his day.

Georgiana still felt that her proper home was with kindred spirits such as she had at first met with at Brook Farm. But she lately had had to learn the bitter lesson of self-reliance; she no longer made any demands of any sort on anyone. Indeed, she could not bring herself to forego choosing her own influences. She needed ". . . to live in such a spiritual atmosphere as may best favour my own soul's growth . . ." One infers that she felt no bond whatever with some of the characters

Fourierism already was attracting to Brook Farm. Georgiana's belief in "Community," however, was unshaken. "Man in his present isolated condition," she wrote William, "does not experience the full benefits of his existence in this world, as much as he would if he came in contact with a larger number of minds and in this way obtained more just views of character and also enlarged his nature by uniting his interests with the interests of many, instead of always standing on the defensive—as he does, you know at present."

It troubled Georgiana that her distaste for cloddish company was inconsistent with this doctrine. "I wish I could run over all the questions on the subject of communism which have deeply interested me since you left, but one I can find to speak of, which, to quietists such as you and I this one has great weight. It is this: whether those only should live together who are attracted by strong personal interests, as the first set of us were? Or whether any other idea could legitimately unite us? I have long held to the first, and it was with grief that I saw our number increase where this attraction was not the sole cause. But I am beginning to feel that this narrow home feeling sets a limit to God's love, does injustice to this noble universe; for the sun shines on the evil as well as on the good, and the blessed influences of nature are for all; and why should I be so intolerant as to shut out from my heart (as I have done) the ignorant, the coarse, the unspiritual, by denying them also the benefits of a better *external* arrangement? If I believe, as most assuredly I do, that competition is of the devil, that I have no right to food while others starve, what is to be done? Am I to wait till the millions of crushed beings have attained superior ideas of truth, or shall I now say to them, 'Come, if you will work with me, we will share and share alike?'—Thus immediately taking away one great, nay, many great hindrances to the perfection of soul and body."

But try as she would, Georgiana could not overcome her distaste for common companions. All this wrestling with her conscience had not prevented her from withdrawing into herself. So much so, indeed, that if the Allens returned to Brook Farm they must not expect such companionship from her as they had enjoyed in the halcyon days. Though it would be beautiful to see the faces of her dear William and Sylvia again, and "to feel your spirits' atmosphere," if they returned she might not give them more than a nod for months. Georgiana had lately found it necessary to avoid everyone who might "interfere or jar," and to do this she had had to withdraw from her friends.

Georgiana Bruce was not the only martyr to the newer social creed. Mrs. Ripley strove nobly to set an example by treating the undesirable element as equals, but she could not conceal her distaste; and it was a general complaint among the more conservative that a few minds among the newcomers were "too strongly felt." It was hoped that if their numbers continued to increase, the influence of such people would be diffused.

As if to erase any impression of disloyalty, Georgiana added a postscript to her long letter to William which summed up the philosophy she strove to live by: "Rest assured we have proved the possibility of many things by our life here; proved that the cultivated can labour and become yet higher in the scale of being; proved that the refined and unrefined can meet as brothers; proved that harsh natures (such as mine) can be softened by gentleness and love; and why should we say these great evils must always exist in the world?"

In her *Years of Experience*, it appears that towards the end of her sojourn at Brook Farm, Georgiana felt so poorly that she submitted her tired body and discouraged mind to the drastic remedy which had suddenly become the rage—"The Water Cure." A peasant in Silesia named Strelitz had "discovered" it; a Bostonian had visited his clinic and taken the treatment to advantage. In that day of unusual cults— phrenology, mesmerism, and the like—no more was needed. Learned members of the medical profession pronounced the ordeal by water, "Nature's own specific for disease." Everyone was talking about it. Extracts from *The Water Cure Journal*, founded in England to report cures effected by water at the Strelitz Clinic in Grafenburg, were already beginning to appear in the progressive *New York Tribune*. The new cure was introduced to Brook Farm by two ladies who had recently joined the Community. These ladies expatiated so eloquently on the benefits they had derived from the cure that a spring was soon located within a few miles of Brook Farm to administer it, and board engaged in an adjacent cottage. The ladies then supervised the construction of a large "plunge bath." They also persuaded a Boston physician,* who was much interested in the cure, to supervise the treatment of the first three victims.

---

* Georgiana does not mention names—the Boston physician could have been Dr. Robert Wesselhoeft.

Georgiana was one of these, and she has described the cure in *Years of Experience*: "The crystal spring supplied more than thirteen barrels of ice-cold water a day. A water-gate held this in restraint until wanted, when, by the simple loosing of a cord in the roofless douchehouse, a stream rushed swiftly down the three-inch inclined flume and fell on the patient's back from a height of twenty feet. It gave,"—one can almost feel her shudder at the recollection—"the sensation of being pounded by glass balls, and excited the belief, that, no matter what insidious disease was settled in or near your spinal column, these balls would certainly dislodge it."

At their "pioneer and primitive encampment," everything proceeded in orderly sequence. One day they took "the pack"—were wrapped in a wet sheet, four or five blankets, which made them look and feel "like modern mummies." As soon as any moisture was visible on the patient's forehead, a drink of water was allowed; then the patient was left to sweat profusely for three or four hours. When the attendant decided the limp creature had had all she could stand, she was helped off the bed and made to scuffle in slippers to a large bathtub filled with icy water. Into this she had to plunge the instant the blankets were unswathed; and there she remained for an agonizing but brief interval.

This treatment was followed by a simple, hearty breakfast and a seven to ten mile walk. The remainder of the day was less active, though "carefully mapped out, leaving intervals for a sitz-bath and the drinking of innumerable goblets of water."

Next day, the "Umschlag" or wet-bandage was in order; the "glass-ball" douche again taken, "rain or shine." Reading, writing, and, most particularly, any communication with Brook Farm were forbidden for the duration of the cure.

The purpose of all this discomfort and boredom was to produce a rash. The eruption was regarded as "a crisis," and it indicated that the patient's vitality had been goaded into throwing off the ailment which had been gnawing from within.

Ladies could not have been as delicate in those days as their descendants have been led to believe. Georgiana assures the reader that her health was vastly improved by sitting around like a damp mummy for the better part of a week; and her fellow-patients concurred.

Be that as it may, she could not adjust herself to the new order, and as the late winter dragged toward spring, Georgiana Bruce reluctantly made up her mind to leave Brook Farm.

7.

Early in February, the *Phalanx* welcomed Brook Farm to the enlightened and scientific fraternity of Associonists. The article was slightly patronizing in tone—warning that although the reorganization of Brook Farm was a belated step in the right direction, it would have to expand to five times its present size to carry out a fair test of Fourier's system. Significantly, the same issue contained the specifications and ground plan for a Model Phalanx, which local papers were requested to copy. Eighteen hundred persons, or three hundred families, on an establishment of six or seven thousand acres, was the minimum requirement to insure success.

Mr. Brisbane could take a high and mighty tone these days. His most grandiose dreams seemed to be materializing fast! Phalanxes were about to be organized at La Grange, Indiana; Leraysville, Pennsylvania; Oswego, New York; and on the Kalamazoo River, Michigan.

Both the American Phalanx in Ohio, and the Clarkson, in western New York, had sent in promising reports. A meeting of the Friends of Association had been called in Southport, Wisconsin; and Fourierites were organized in Tennessee.

Determined to keep all his scattered disciples in line, Brisbane called a General Convention of the Friends of Association to celebrate Fourier's birthday in New York. The celebration would be held on April sixth, because the real birthday, the seventh, fell on a Sunday that year.

If George Ripley was offended by Brisbane's condescension, or disturbed by the latent ambiguity of his friend's encouragement, he thrust such misgivings aside and continued to press the reorganization with such enthusiasm that the Second Constitution of the Brook Farm Association was ratified early in February; and on the eighteenth, the General Direction presented a plan which would reorganize the members into Groups and Series. The members at once proceeded to elect their Chiefs.

George William Curtis, already more absorbed in *belles-lettres* than social reform, paid a visit to Brook Farm when the new order was being put into effect. After his return to New York he wrote

Dwight, "The Arcadian beauty of the place is lost to me, and would have been lost had there been no change. So calm a congregation of devoted men and true women performing their perpetual service to the Idea of their lives, and clothed always in white garments. Though you change your ritual I feel your hope is unchanged; and though it seems less beautiful than the one you leave, it is otherwise to you. There was a mild grace about our former life that no system attains. The unity in variety bound us very closely together."

8.

In March *The Present* expressed warm commendation for the past efforts of the Brook Farm Association, and announced the change in policy. Channing confessed to a deeply felt hope that the Farmers might not fail now for want of a few dollars; and he published their new prospectus which proudly presented their argument before the public.

Since Brook Farm was already established, the Directors argued that it was the logical place "for that practical trial of Association which public feeling calls for in this immediate vicinity, instead of forming a new Association for the purpose." They also pointed out that Brook Farm was located in an ideal situation, comprising two hundred and eight acres, where adjoining land could be purchased as the need arose. They claimed a property value of $30,000, of which $22,000 was invested in the stock of the Corporation, or in permanent loans at six per cent which were renewable.

They would expect but imperfect results at first, but "with a view to an ultimate expansion into a perfect phalanx, we desire without any delay to organize the three primary departments of Labor—Agriculture, Domestic Industry, and the Mechanical Arts—according to Fourier's System." To meet expansion costs they pleaded urgently for "Captial and Earnest Workers, one or the other, or both." They pointed confidently to their fine school and sound administration, and they most emphatically assured the public that religion and the family would continue to be reverenced at Brook Farm.

Ripley had lost none of his confidence in the contagion of a noble example: "We can never doubt that the object we have in view will finally be attained; that human life shall yet be developed, not in discord and misery, but in harmony and joy, and that the perfected earth shall at last bear on her bosom a race of men worthy of the name." George Ripley, Minot Pratt, and Charles A. Dana who signed the prospectus were not interested in righting a special wrong. Their aim was no less than "Radical and Universal Reform."

9.

When he again wrote Hecker, young Dana had recovered his customary poise.*

The letter begins fondly, *"Mein lieber Isaac."*

> . . . For these many days I have had no moment until now that could be given to anything but the pressing duty of the instant, and even now it is by theft that I am writing to you. I have been thus occupied with the organization of labor, and with thinking, talking and arranging our department of education. In this latter sphere we are, I think, preparing to move quite satisfactorily. Our industrial operations too are most hopeful. I hardly doubt that in this department we shall see the best results from the systematic order we are adopting. We are moving with as much vigor as prudence will permit in making our final enlargements. We are talking seriously of building a shop 60 feet by 28, for a group of cabinet makers, carpenters, copper smiths, wheelwrights, and block tin workers. A bakery is thought to be a natural appendage to the extensive operations in all practicable branches of industry, which we are contemplating; and, if we could lay our hands on a certain skillful individual who has his outward habitation in Rutgers Street, we should recken not ourselves only but the whole movement as especially fortunate.
>
> Thus then, *mein liebster,* lies our life. Not in dreams, not in flowery imaginations, not even in outward grace, but in entire activity, in unwearied foresight and in great human hopes. The spirit we have helped to make in this region is pressing upon us, demanding to be conducted to wise ends. On all sides men are coming in, demanding room to aid in this undertaking. For one I feel that the most difficult part of the whole work is now to be done. The magnitude of

---

* Although this letter—among the Hecker Papers—is dated merely "Thursday Afternoon"—a reference it contains to the departure of Georgiana Bruce places it after March first, for Georgiana left Brook Farm and went to the Heckers' in New York at the end of February.

it is now first dawning upon me; it calls for such a round and panoplied wisdom that I should despair if I had any time to do so. But there is one thing I find in it which is worth a life-labor to reach, namely, forgetfulness of self—not the forgetfulness of contemplation and intro-spection, but of true, natural action.

You will remember our conversation in the back-parlor in your house concerning a change of Brook Farm into a "Fourier" Association? That change, my dear Isaac, has really taken place; the words, "group, series, phalanx," are in all our mouths. No person of any real acquaintance with the matter can fail to see the great perfection of these very arrangements, and if Fourier had only laid down these practical methods without touching the abstruse philosophy on which they are founded, he would have deserved the gratitude of the race. But on these points you are probably sceptical.

Ignoring the danger to their friendship in re-defining the religious views he had expressed in his letter of January third, Dana went on:

Concerning the New Dispensation I spoke hastily and vaguely. I do not believe in the Christian Dispensation, but in the New Church—the Universal Church. Not Roman or Anglican or Presbyterian but the Church of God. About this we shall not differ—but about the means by which Unity shall be restored to the Church, we may. As far as I can see this is to be effected not by material means. The Unity of the Church which is the Unity of Man with God, will fully appear only when Man is at Unity with Nature and with Man—and finally let me say—can appear only in Association. There, my friend, you have the whole of my heresy.

Having stated his credo, Dana told of his German studies, and sent love to Georgie and the Heckers from himself and Dwight. Yet the distance between them had widened again. Dana formerly had stated what amounted to "heresy" in Isaac's eyes. Now he admitted he was committed to it. Such an admission was not conducive to further intimacy.

10.

John S. Dwight was doing his best to convince George William Curtis that Fourierism would enhance his friend's talents, just as, Dwight felt, it had made him a better musician. Curtis dismissed Dwight's enthusiasm as if speaking to a child. "What is society," he inquired, "but the shadow of single men behind? The love which alone can make your phalanx beautiful, also makes it unnecessary."

Dwight was highly successful, however, in gaining converts in his immediate family. One sister, Fanny, already served as his assistant in teaching music; and on the first of April, his parents, Dr. and Mrs. John Dwight, and his younger sister, Marianne, joined him at Brook Farm.

Marianne, a sprightly spinster of twenty-eight, bubbled over with enthusiasm for Association—and Fourierism. But she deeply regretted the absence of her best friend, Anna Q. T. Parsons. Both girls were keenly interested in the issues of the day; and when Marianne lived in Boston they had gone often together to hear the great speakers discuss slavery, woman's rights, and social reform. The friends always had much to say to each other after one of these lectures. They would stand on a street corner arguing, lost to all sense of time until the clock in the Bulfinch-built church on Charles Street struck twelve—then they would fly, in terror of paternal reprimand, to their respective homes.

Anna was highly strung and addicted to "Readings"—an expression of psychic phenomena then the rage among the young people. Marianne encouraged her friend in these interpretations which Anna performed by putting a few lines the subject of the "reading" had written against her own forehead. On those occasions when her "impressibility" was exceptional, Anna could interpret the writer's character holding the letter in her hand. She never looked at the writing, because it might be a clue. After a few minutes of contact, Anna would begin to talk. Meanwhile, someone present made notes. Sometimes Anna made notes herself. Alarmed by such excitable goings on—and perhaps with reason, for the "Readings" left Anna limp and exhausted—Mr. Parsons discouraged Marianne's friendship with his daughter. So much so that at this time he would not allow Anna to visit Marianne at Brook Farm.

Deprived of Anna's company, Marianne used every spare minute to write her best friend, and as Marianne was the sort who, bubbling with high spirits and enthusiasm, takes note of everything that goes on, her letters afford a really intimate glimpse into the life of the young people at Brook Farm during the Fourieristic period.

Marianne's first letter to Anna proves, despite the vulgar folk who had come to man the shops—the type Georgiana Bruce had objected to—that Brook Farm was still a pleasant place in which to live. "Our ride out was very pleasant," Marianne reported, "and all the *bees* were in the Hive at supper when the stage stopped, and our arrival created quite a sensation. John, Dana, and Horace"—a brother of Charles Sumner—"waited on us in, Ora Gannett and others welcomed us in the entry. We were ushered to the table where everything wore the same appearance of neatness and refinement I have always observed when I have been here. After supper we went, Mother to the Eyrie, and Fanny and I to the Morton House"—as Pilgrim House was some-times called in honor of the donors—"to inspect our apartment and put to rights."

Thanks to the foresight of their friends, the Dwight girls found their room in such "prime order" they hurried over to the Eyrie to enjoy flute and piano music. "And oh! What a magnificent evening! Full moonlight from the Eyrie parlor was splendid; everything glittered like pure white snow."

After the concert Fanny and Horace Sumner invited Marianne to walk in the Piney Woods. Though they assured her the scene would be surpassingly beautiful in the evening moonlight, the younger sister tactfully declined to play gooseberry, and returned to the Hive instead.

Presently the Ripleys—who probably returned from one of the neigh-borhood meetings to promote Fourierism—welcomed the newcomers cordially. But before that first evening was over an incident occurred which made Marianne uncomfortable.

Ora Gannett was an old friend; and naturally Ora sought Marianne out at the Hive. When they were sitting in a corner to enjoy a good talk, Mrs. Ripley ran across the room and joined them. "I really envy you," she declared to Marianne. "Ora never finds time to talk to me, has never had any talk with me since she came."

Marianne quickly offered her seat to Mrs. Ripley, who declined it brusquely. "No, I won't," she said, "I'm so offended."

Marianne must have shown that she was taken aback by this peevish outburst—on the part of a lady noted for her queenly manners!—for Mrs. Ripley immediately made amends. She charged the Dwight girls not to get up to breakfast next morning, saying she would send trays up to Morton House. "Once you begin work," Mrs. Ripley warned them with a smile half rueful and half bitter, "we'll never let you stop."

One cannot help feeling sympathy for Mrs. Ripley. For the first time she felt unable to support her husband's stand with all her conscience. Wearied by years of drudgery, strangely isolated from the enthusiasm around her, the sense of leadership which had held her firm since the beginning all but gone, it was only human to resent Marianne's popularity and Ora's disdain. To add to her discomfiture, since "The Change" Mr. Ripley had to be away a great part of the time.

Indeed, the very next day, after dinner, Ripley, Dana, Ryckman—a former shoemaker who was much esteemed under the new order—and List were off for the General Convention of the Friends of Association in New York.

"Before leaving," Marianne wrote Anna, "Mr. Ripley told Fanny and me in a very amusing way, how pleasant it was to him to see *Christian people* about (alluding to us) and *proper, grown up, well-behaved* young women, free from all the vices of the world, and filled with *all the virtues of Association.*"

The following morning, somewhat to her astonishment, Marianne found herself in the barn, taking care of three babies about eighteen months old. The sun was warm, the breeze gentle, and from the loft came the fragrant odor of hay. For company, besides the babies, Marianne had "a goodly row of cows and oxen; a great good-natured dog; and a parcel of little romping boys and girls."

The arrival of Fanny Dwight's younger sister created quite a ferment in masculine hearts: Fred Cabot, Horace Sumner, and Lucas Corrales, one of the Spanish boys from Manila. Next morning Horace Sumner came knocking at their door to escort the Dwight sisters down to the Hive for breakfast; and someone whispered that Fred Cabot, though six years Marianne's junior, appeared to be "smitten on sight." It is evident that Marianne, herself, was delighted with "the free intercourse between young men and maidens," which, according to Ida Russell, was "innocent and beneficial to both sexes."

The older set, and her own male relations, kept an eye on Marianne nonetheless. Among them, Mr. Bradford, who had just arrived for a visit; her father and her brother; and "many of the ladies." Mrs. Ripley assigned the vivacious spinster to nursery duty every day from eight o'clock until noon. "I told her I would try," Marianne wrote Anna, "but said I didn't think I should like it or understand the management. However, I did very well this morning—believe I am to have some older children with them hereafter, which will make it pleasanter."

Within a day or so Marianne was complaining again of interference from that quarter. "Ora and I were speaking together yesterday, when along came Mrs. Ripley. 'At it again,' said she, 'Ora has not given me five minutes since she came to the Community'—and off she walked with a very mock-resentful air."

It was enough to get on a person's nerves! When Mrs. Ripley wasn't hovering about making injured remarks, she was thinking up some new task. "I have this afternoon received a few lines from Mrs. Ripley asking if I would join the refectory from half an hour before tea to an hour and a half after tea—as some of the group are desirous that I should." This was to be but a temporary arrangement during someone's absence. Marianne wisely said she would do it. ". . . I should like to go into all or almost all the departments for a little while, to see how everything is managed."

Soon Mrs. Ripley was won over by Marianne's willingness to do whatever asked—and Sophia, one feels sure, would not have been so exacting had she known how acutely the girl missed her best friend. "Oh, my dear good Anna!" Marianne wailed, ". . . you and yours are to me all Boston,—*are more* than all Boston . . ." If only Anna could be with her, she would be entirely happy. "How I long to have you and Helen"—a sister—"come out here now, and see us, and see how comfortable and happy we seem, in spite of the shortcomings of the *actual*. I shall try (and you know I have a tact at it) to idealize the actual."

Translated, the Transcendental jargon meant setting table, and washing up after tea. Marianne signed in haste and hurried off to the refectory. It was grand fun "to idealize the actual"—scrub the dishes—when Fred C. was on hand to wipe them.

11.

W. H. Channing and Emerson had grown weary of their "organs"—both *The Present* and *The Dial* were about to expire. Channing wished to write the biography of his distinguished uncle, Dr. William Ellery Channing; Emerson had found, since Miss Fuller's departure, that editorial tasks kept him away from his chosen field, the science of morals—which proved, posterity agrees, a more fruitful vineyard for his genius.

George Ripley, a close friend of William Channing, and a former manager of *The Dial*, must long since have heard this distressing news; and when he set out for New York to celebrate Fourier's birthday and

attend the Convention, it would have been a natural and kindly gesture to stop by at some bookshop on his way to the South Station, in
Boston, to pick up the recent and final issues of both periodicals.

Certainly Ripley read them at some time or another; and one may be
sure that his spirits rose on observing the prominence given to Fourierism. This would be cause for rejoicing among the delegates at the New
York Convention!

The first sentence of Elizabeth Peabody's article, "A General View
of Fourierism," which appeared in *The Dial*, would have caused a scholarly reader astonishment—by its very frankness. George Ripley, however, was only too well aware of the difficulties the writer had faced.
"The works of Fourier do not seem to have reached us," Elizabeth Peabody commenced. "And this want of text has been ill supplied by various conjectures respecting them; some of which are more remarkable for
the morbid imagination they display than for their sagacity." Generally
speaking, such a confession of ignorance of any first-hand knowledge of
one's subject is not calculated to lure the reader on. But there is something charming about Elizabeth Peabody's ingenuous candor. "For
ourselves," she goes on blandly, "we confess to some remembrance to
vague horror connected with the name."

Elizabeth Peabody was not alone in her complaint concerning proper
documentation. To date the American public had had to be satisfied
with Brisbane's extracts, and an occasional article by Hugh Doherty,
editor of the London *Phalanx*.

Endowed with a powerful intellect, after the gallant admission that
she did not know very well what she was talking about, Elizabeth Peabody plunged undaunted into "A General View of Fourierism." As
might be expected, she viewed it through Transcendental spectacles—
as a social philosophy, not as an economic science.

Inasmuch as Fourier, like the Channings, had set himself the task of
discovering the Divine Order, he was to this extent admirable in Miss
Peabody's eyes. But bred in the bone New Englanders have ever been
willing victims of their conscience. They believe that without tiresome
chores and grim duties the sturdy plodder may lapse into inertia,
thereby robbing existence of contrast and spice. Indeed one suspects
from Elizabeth Peabody's analysis of Fourier's Law of Passionate Attraction, that the very word, passion, gave her goose pimples. "The
training of these twelve powers," as she preferred to call them, "into
their appropriate activities, that each might contribute its share both to
the Harmony of the Universe and the Unity of the Individual" was

a most worthy goal, to be sure. She did wish, however, that Fourier had built his System firmly upon "Spirit"; for she was convinced that all social passions on a high level depended upon Reason; and Reason upon Spirit. Fourierism, Elizabeth Peabody pointed out, stopped short at Reason.

Perhaps Fourier's unfortunate terminology had misled her. Casting about for some sustaining analogy for Fourier's Law of Passionate Attraction, Elizabeth Peabody inquired hopefully, "Isn't this Swedenborg's doctrine of 'Love'—Loves which must find their uses?"

12.

If George Ripley did glance through Lizzie Peabody's piece on the train, he probably handed it over to his traveling companions, Ryckman and Dana, with a wry smile. But "Fourier's Theory of Society," translated from Abel Transon into English for the London *Phalanx* and now reprinted in *The Present*, was more satisfactory.

The theory of Attractive Industry—that each person works better when the occupation is congenial and the program varied—was repeated in further detail in "Fourier's Theory of Groups and Series"; which held that Man tires after two hours of intense concentration, but is able to work long hours every day if he is refreshed by a variety of occupations. Fourier also held that his system of diversified tasks would solve the knotty problem of *The Distribution of Benefits*. For if each man earned top wages in one group, he would accept a fair distribution in all.

Although Transon's digest of Fourier's System contained some incomprehensible tables which were intended to illustrate the interplay of the various "Passions" of mankind, Familism, Cabalism, or Intrigue, Love, Ambition and the like, Transon presented a clearer analysis of Associative Principles as applied to industry than any as yet presented to the American public. Brisbane merely had selected the simpler aspects of Fourierism, expressed them in words a child could understand, and repeated them over and over again. What Brisbane harped upon was carefully chosen to make people believe that industry organized on Associative Principles was bound to be successful. He was forever pointing to banks and to the rapidly spreading railroads as examples of successful "Associative" enterprise.

The well-versed such as Ripley and Dana found Parke Godwin's exposition of Fourierism in *The Pathfinder* more satisfactory.

And all the leaders looked forward to reading Godwin's *A Popular View of the Doctrines of Charles Fourier*, which Greeley and McElrath would publish shortly. To date the Fourierites could list but one other book besides Brisbane's *Social Destiny of Man* in print in the United States—Madame Gatti de Gammond's *Life in a Phalanstery*, translated from the French—and this was commended more for romantic interpretation than for scientific accuracy.

While waiting for the publication of Godwin's summary of Fourierism, Transon's analysis was studied by the leaders of the movement. In their eyes Channing's republication of it in *The Present*, and the additional space to the subject afforded Miss Peabody in *The Dial*, seemed evidence indeed of the rapid growth and international interest in Fourierism.

13.

On the evening of Saturday, April sixth, the delegates from Brook Farm set out in high spirits for the Apollo Saloon on Broadway, where Fourier's Birthday Festival was to be held. The hall was most suitably decorated for the occasion with excerpts from Fourier's Divine Order. On one side hung the *Table of the Six Unities;* on the other a diagram illustrating *The Harmony of the Passions.* The "repast" proved "plain and simple"—as befitted an occasion dedicated to Social Reform. But the "Intellectual Feast and Social Congress" was both rich and rare in quality; and to young Dana, hearing, perhaps for the first time, reports from the great phalanxes in western New York, and of the Convention of the Friends of Association recently held in Cincinnati, Harmony already seemed to be encircling the globe. When it came his turn to speak, that sober-sided young man lost his usual restraint.

"I would infinitely the more open my heart to you all," Dana declared in concluding his speech, "and have every heart opened to me, feeling that we are friends, brothers, not only as men working for humanity—as pilgrims toward that glorious future which gleams brighter on us than any prophet ever dreamed—not alone thus, but with that holy private friendship which links heart to heart and binds them by indissoluble bonds!"

Everyone was deeply moved by Dana's exalted outburst. As the *Phalanx* reported in a subsequent issue, "Mr. Macdaniel"—one of the managers of that organ—"proposed that the toast to friendship be repeated with clasped hands." This proposition was instantly accepted. "With a burst of enthusiasm every man rose, and locking hands all around the table, the toast was repeated by the whole company, producing an electric thrill of emotions through every nerve."

After Dana's eloquence, George Ripley's speech on the "incompleteness of the individual man under the factory system," at first fell somewhat flat. William Channing interrupted, to stir things up, shouting, "A Man's a Man for a' that!"

The interruption proved irrelevant, because Ripley at that very instant was arguing that a man could best fulfill himself through the back-to-the-land policy. But Ripley probably was grateful for his friend's exuberance, attributing Channing's interruption to the enthusiasm which released them all from their accustomed restraint. For this was, indeed, a memorable occasion; and the Convention, too, over which he next day presided as President, with Godwin, Greeley, Dana, and Brisbane, as Vice Presidents, would wind up on a triumphant note. It was the same dear friend, William H. Channing, who, at the Convention introduced resolutions commending Fourier's principles in such a way as to lend the assembly a religious tone.

"It is but giving voice to what is working in the hearts of those now present, and of thousands whose sympathies are with us, at this moment over our whole land, to say this is a religious meeting," Channing assured the gathering gravely. "Our end is to do God's will, not our own; to obey the command of Providence, not to follow the leadings of human fancies. We stand today, as we believe, amid the dawn of a new era of humanity, and as from a Pisgah look down upon a Promised Land."

Godwin's address, "To the People of the United States," which followed, explained that American Fourierites aimed merely to give the national theory of States Rights an application to individual rights. "We would bind trade to trade, neighborhood to neighborhood, man to man, by the ties of interest and affection which bind our larger aggregations called States; only we would make the ties holier and more indissoluble." Their practical plans might seem insignificant, he admitted, but their moral aim was the grandest that had ever elevated human thought.

The three-day gathering ended in a mighty and confident shout, "The future is ours! The future is ours!" When it was over, the Farmers wrung Mr. Brisbane's hand with more than usual fervor and wished him *bon voyage*. He was sailing for Europe in mid-April. He would visit leaders of the movement in London and Paris. Upon arrival there Mr. Brisbane would settle down in the French capital to translate selections from Fourier's unpublished works for export.

In the winter of 1843–44, when some errand for the cause such as this Convention brought them to New York, the Farmers were made welcome at the Cranchs'. Christopher had married his cousin, Elizabeth de Windt, the previous October; and the newly married pair, in order to eke out sufficient means to live in the expensive metropolis, promptly opened up an exclusive boarding house. Kit's charm, and his wife's excellent housekeeping, made their house a meeting place for the Farmers from Boston and their friends in New York.

W. H. Channing and his family were installed at the Cranchs' throughout that winter; Caroline Sturgis put up there whenever she went to New York; and Margaret Fuller, who privately had advised her friends she would soon serve the *New York Tribune* in the double capacity of literary critic and "Philanthropic Correspondent," spoke up for a room, in case she might prefer a corner of her own to a protracted stay at the Greeleys'.

Ripley, Dwight and Dana were always welcome at the Cranchs' for old time's sake. W. H. Channing was the only one among the former Transcendentalists who—with reservations—shared the Farmers' enthusiasm for Fourierism.

To George William Curtis, now residing in New York, the first week in April 1844 seemed "like glimpses of Brook Farm, seeing so constantly Mr. Ripley, and Charles, and List, and Isaac and Georgiana, and Margaret Fuller." In regard to the Convention, Curtis felt there had been "no enthusiasm, but an air of quiet resolution, which always precedes success." Yet he would "leave to Albert Brisbane and *id omne genus* these practical etchings and phalansteries" and "serve the gods without bell or candle."

George William Curtis, pondering the Convention, found the occasion interesting only because of "some speeches by W. H. Channing, whose fervor kindled the sympathy of all who listened." Curtis did not consider Channing a man of great intellect or accept his views as a reformer. "He speaks very often as an infidel-in-the-capability-of-men might speak. He is fanatical as all who perceive by the heart and not the head are, as deeply pious men are apt to be. But I never heard so eloquent a man, one who commanded attention and sympathy, not by his words or thoughts but by the religion that lay far below them . . ."

Curtis liked the freedom from ritual at the Christian Socialist Mission. "Last night," he continued, "at W. H. Channing's church, the room was full, and the risen Lord Jesus might have smiled upon a worthy worship."

There was one sorrowful note. "The Dial stops," Curtis mourned. "Is it not like the going out of a star? Its place was so unique in our literature! All who wrote and sang for it were clothed in white garments; and the work itself so calm and collected though springing from the same undismayed hope which fathers all our best reforms. But the intellectual worth of the times will be told in other ways, though The Dial no longer reports the progress of the day."

One imagines that John S. Dwight may have found his friend's nostalgia for the halcyon days of Transcendentalism tiresome, in view of the good tidings the delegates to the New York Convention had brought back to Brook Farm.

Soon after their return a general gathering was held at the Hive to hear Mr. Ripley's report. Some of the Farmers still hung back from endorsing Fourier's System. These persons were now relieved to hear from George Ripley that the New York Convention, like the January gathering in Boston led by W. H. Channing, had laid emphasis on the religious aspect of the Movement, before endorsing Fourier's principles of Industrial Organization.

It was voted then and there to hold Fourier meetings every Sunday evening.

14.

In spite of their enthusiasm it is clear that Passionate Equilibrium had not yet been established at Brook Farm.

Shortly after the Convention Marianne Dwight complained to Anna about the behavior of one of her "pets," Christopher List. "Chrysalis," as they called him, was well versed in the amenities. Indeed, he vied with one Lizzie Curzon in being polite to visitors. He knew better than to be rude.

"The fancy I have had for Mr. List is clean gone forever," Marianne reported to Anna. "This evening, at tea time we found stuck up on the wall of the dining hall a notice of the Association Convention to be held in Parker's church tomorrow. After tea in came List—asked Mr. Cabot if he put that up—was answered in the negative. Soon Mr. L., when no one saw him, took it down. All had gone but a few of the boys, Mrs. Ripley and we girls, who were washing the tea-cups. Fred gave him a severe trimming therefor,—wish you could have heard it—it was rich to us all. He said just the right thing in just the right way, and afterwards we each gave Fred a pin and he put it up again. When Mr. List came in again, Martin C. read it aloud. Mr. Cabot told List, that if he took it down again, it should be brought before the Association. List took it down, and the boys put it up again, where it remained when I left the Hive. It is quite an affair. List is presumptuous and arrogant and very desirous of having the rule. I don't believe he will stay here long,—a few more such steps and his race will be run . . ."

Despite such occasional squabbles, Marianne Dwight was enjoying Brook Farm life. She and her sister had managed to install themselves in Pilgrim House—far from their parents who had settled in the Hive. The girls' room was right next door to Fred Cabot and Martin Cushing; and Ora Gannett—the unpredictable Ora!—had a pleasant little room to herself close by.

Marianne hoped no one would alter these arrangements for some time to come. It was so neighborly. The boys knocked on their door every morning at half past five; and Marianne was always the first to reply. "Perhaps F. answers, 'Good morning, *ma voisine,* how are you today?' or Martin asks, 'And how does our sister do?' "

Marianne loved to tell Anna about their gay exchanges of gifts and banter. How Fred, being in the Washing Department, gave them a severe lecture on the absurdity of ladies wearing "little fixings"—several hundred of which he had been compelled to hang out to dry. It seems he had found Marianne's night cap, edged with lace and embroidered with her name, particularly provoking. Night caps were injurious to the ears, as well as absurd, said Mr. C. To this Marianne countered coyly the next morning, that they had looked at themselves in night caps last night in his beautiful looking glass, and the caps had never seemed more becoming!

In the light of Marianne's confidences one can hardly blame Mrs. Ripley for being on edge these days. In a Community where young men and maidens were thrown into close propinquity, the proprieties she had been taught to observe became impossible. In the halcyon days Mrs. Ripley had adjusted herself admirably; but since the change to Fourierism it had become a duty to give free scope to every kind of "Passionate Attraction." Naturally, Mrs. Ripley, who was still responsible for the good name of all the girls, had moments of perplexity and irritation.

"We had company up in our room," Marianne confided happily to Anna, "Fred C. and William Coleman, were drawn into playing whist and talking till eleven o'clock, which in these working days is as late an hour as I like to keep." Such goings on seem commonplace in our day and age—not so in 1844!

On another evening, Ora Gannett, Fred Cabot, and Marianne walked in the Piney Woods at sunset, and flung themselves upon their backs. "We stayed, (imprudent children) talked till about nine o'clock, revelling in the deep shades, the sombre light, wondering at the beauty of the moonbeams flickering through the leaves, with here and there a star spangled in the magically figured firmament above." If friendly Cabalism raised its helpful spirit that night, it soon became apparent who won the encounter. Marianne's enthusiasm for Association waxed even hotter, whereas Ora's soon began to fail her.

In faraway Boston, Marianne's confidante, Anna Parsons, had overexerted herself of late. Her analysis of character was often so apt that her "readings" had aroused the interest of Miss Fuller, Mr. Emerson, Mr. Channing, and Mr. Ripley, as well as the more easily convinced.

Unfortunately, the frail girl was afterwards so exhausted by the exercise of her gift that some urged her not to "read" often; others begged her to renounce the practice entirely. It was, they pointed out, a severe tax upon her vitality.

Poor Anna, caught in a cross fire of advice, had lately lost her "impressibility"—which left her in the plight of a magician who has lost his bag of tricks.

Marianne offered but scant comfort. After a perfunctory inquiry about the missing power, Marianne announced the visit of a very interesting and delightful young man. He was John Orvis, who, acting upon Mr. Ripley's recent invitation, had come from the Community at Skaneateles, New York, to look over Brook Farm, with a view to joining.

In addition to their mutual enthusiasm for Association, Mr. Orvis was addicted to hypnotism. Indeed Orvis had scarcely been in Pilgrim House a minute before he begged Fred Cabot to put him to sleep to cure him of a sore throat and headache. When he awoke, refreshed, Mr. Orvis promptly read one of the girl's characters by putting his hands on her head.

Well pleased with his reception, Orvis shortly announced he would return to Brook Farm in three or four weeks and make it his permanent home. The best of it was, Marianne added, "He wants to be in our entry in Pilgrim Hall."

Gallantry, it appears, was as much in style at Brook Farm as in the days when George William Curtis used to hand the girls across the muddy barnyard with the grace of a courtier; and now that it was spring the boys kept Marianne's room filled with cowslips and violets for her flower paintings.

Marianne "came in for a good deal of teasing" about these attentions. Especially from a Mr. Kay, a Philadelphia businessman, who gave the Directors free financial advice, and backed it up with substantial contributions to the Association.

15.

Everyone at Brook Farm waited eagerly for news of Mr. Brisbane. After contact with Doherty and the London Fourierites, Brisbane had gone on to Paris to dedicate himself to an examination of the Master's unpublished works. "These voluminous manuscripts would have made," records Redalia Brisbane in the *Mental Biography* of her husband, dictated by himself, "five or six octavo volumes of five hundred pages each. They, with other mementos of Fourier, were sacredly kept in a room by themselves at the office of *La Démocratie Pacifique*"—the Fourieristic organ, published in Paris. "Considerant"—Victor Considerant, the leader of the Fourier School there—"gave me the key to this room, and allowed me to take possession." Brisbane entered into his task with "a senti-

ment of deep veneration together with keenest intellectual curiosity."
In that secluded room he would labor throughout the summer and fall,
going through each manuscript with scrupulous care, selecting extracts
to be copied and bound into volumes; and he would be serenely unaware that since the triumphant Convention held in New York the
previous April, the Fourieristic tide in the United States had turned.

Meanwhile, Osborne Macdaniel, who assisted Brisbane in editing
the *Phalanx*, became one of the New York propagandists Brisbane
speaks of in the *Mental Biography* as often visiting Brook Farm, "infus-
ing into the community fresh life and spirit." Brisbane generously conceded that the talent of Ripley, Dwight, Dana, W. H. Channing, and
other outstanding personalities, "together with their knowledge of the
intellectual development of the past, and with all reigning theories and
ideas, enabled them to present Fourierism with breadth and elevation;
and a deep impression was produced." Although these words were
spoken years after he had led them to disaster, it is nonetheless a sincere tribute—from Brisbane, whose customary attitude toward the
Farmers was one of patronizing condescension.

Not so, Osborne Macdaniel. He liked Brook Farm so much, he persuaded his mother, and two sisters, Fanny and Eunice, to make their
home there. This attractive family was expected shortly, and their
coming eagerly awaited by Charles A. Dana. Eunice had found favor
in the eye of that scholarly bachelor.

As a result of all the visiting and propaganda, the bonds between the
New England Associations—Hopedale, Northampton, and Brook Farm
—were strengthened. A series of Quarterly Conferences were decided
upon. Mr. Ripley and two as yet unnamed delegates would attend the
first of these at Hopedale in May.

As spring drew on, the Farmers' most talked of project was the erection of a phalanstery. Because they were already receiving more applications for membership than they could handle, it was confidently expected that the Unitary Building would soon pay for itself. In the eyes
of the Directors the phalanstery seemed a necessity. For although they
accepted only the most desirable applicants, living conditions were becoming more crowded every day; and the "Summer Visiting Season"
threatened to be a record-breaker this year. Many members protested

the expense; and on May twenty-fourth it was voted to charge the hosts
for their guests' meals, unless the hosts had been granted exemption for
some reason, or were members of the Association. Though not sufficiently threatening to cause general alarm at the time it was made, this
vote—among the entries in the *Brook Farm Records* in the Massachusetts Historical Society—is the first sign of approaching famine.

During the spring rains an epidemic of scarlatina broke out. Lucas,
the Spanish boy, would have died if Dr. Dwight had not been on hand
to save him. Marianne was run ragged nursing the victims back to
health. She was not able to get outdoors for several weeks; and when she
did, she marvelled to see how the late New England spring, come
mid-May, had strewn the fields with wild flowers, and "covered every
dead looking twig with beauty." Marianne went gathering rhodora and
columbine; and presently she immortalized the columbine in one of the
most exquisite of her flower paintings.

In certain aspects the buoyancy of the Farmers in this year of Fourieristic rebirth parallels their exuberance in the halcyon days. Despite the
epidemic and the rush of the planting season, a large group drove to
Boston to hear Ole Bull, the Norwegian violinist, perform in the Melodeon, crossing the Charles to Cambridgeport to see Washington
Allston's "Belshazzar's Feast," on the way. There were tableaux, too,
on a Saturday night; and despite the absence of the Mistress of the
Wardrobes—Amelia Russell had gone on a visit to her home in Milton—
the tableaux went off well. The hypercritical Charles King Newcomb
honored the occasion with his presence, and even praised Marianne's
performance in "Winter." In this, the finale of a series of "The Four
Seasons," she and Mr. Pratt had stood up as an aged couple with tremendous effect.

Charles King Newcomb more and more was regarded as an exceedingly deep young man. Mr. Emerson said he never read anything of
Newcomb's but it filled him with many thoughts—indeed, seldom read
anything that filled him with so many thoughts. One might say that
Newcomb had become the Sage of West Roxbury, wearing the mantle
bestowed on him by the Sage of Concord.

With all this in mind, Marianne had felt it a privilege and a distinction to serve as note-taker when Anna, on a visit to Brook Farm, "read"
Newcomb's character.

Everyone was gratified, at first. Newcomb was so pleased with the result that he sent it to Miss Fuller. At Brook Farm the girls looked forward with impatience to hearing the sibyl's opinion, but to their dismay, no sooner had her reply arrived than Newcomb spoke firmly of destroying it, together with the "reading" itself. Marianne and her friends were horrified at this threatened destruction, of what, to them, seemed important documents; and Marianne wrote Anna that she was trying to coax Charles to lend another of his poems for a "second Reading" in the hope that he might be diverted from his purpose.

Ora enjoyed more jokes with Newcomb than Marianne. "Ora," Marianne complained, "gets interested in all my pets; I no sooner fall to cherishing anybody than behold, our blessed Ora is at my side, a rival. But ours is not the evil rivalry which abounds in 'the world,' but the true rivalry of Association. We are friends and rivals. We love each other more for this kind of emulation."

As in the Piney Wood on that first moonlight night, when the two went out with Fred Cabot, Ora was no match for Marianne at this friendly Cabalism. Marianne tried to cajole her, "and bring her on." Poor Ora suffered a succession of colds and nervous headaches—and then suddenly left Brook Farm and went back to her home in Milton.

16.

"Let me not remain unmentioned to my friends at Brook Farm, and in the village," George William Curtis wrote Dwight on May tenth, "and when you can ungroup yourself for an hour, paint me a portrait of the life you lead." There was a gathering of former Farmers at Concord that spring: both Curtis boys, Hecker, Bradford, Almira Barlow, and the Hawthornes, who did not mingle with the rest. The Hawthornes were among those George William referred to when he again wrote Dwight, "The persons who make Concord famous I have hardly seen. The consciousness of their presence is like the feeling of lofty mountains whom the night and thick forests hide."

Nor was Hecker as congenial as of yore. He had left New York, ostensibly to tutor with Mr. Bradford. He had come to Concord to continue his education while his spiritual destiny was unfolding. At times this problem became so persistent as to overwhelm all worldly interest, even in books.

Almira Barlow—possibly because it was borne in upon her that Isaac would never belong to her, or any woman; that he was drifting into deep waters of mysticism—was not at her best that spring. The once brilliant beauty cried easily these days. In fact she became such poor company that two former admirers—George William Curtis and Ora Gannett—agreed they dreaded to pass an evening alone with her. Hecker remained Almira's friend and sought to lift her mind to higher things. But it appears to have been uphill work.

Hecker's friendship with Ora Gannett was much more satisfactory to him at this time. The two young people had become intimately acquainted during Hecker's second stay at Brook Farm in the spring of 1843. Treasuring his friendship, Ora had corresponded with him ever since.

Upon leaving Brook Farm, for good, a year later, Ora from her home in Milton wrote frequently to Isaac on lofty themes. Ora loved Brook Farm, but she was unable to adapt herself to the recent changes there. Uncertain of herself and of her future, Ora took increasing comfort from her correspondence with Hecker.

The following letter, which is among the Hecker Papers, shows how much Ora had come to rely on him: "You ask me to write freely and openly and so I will do, for although I cannot feel that I know you, there is somewhat within you that tells me t'were easy to be perfectly true and open and that you are one of those who possess a key that will unlock the way to my heart. Yet I feared to write, for I knew I had not to give what you *needed* and could not as freely give as had been given —how dearly I should love to call you friend! But believe not, Isaac, that I could ever fill up the void your soul feels, for the little I have to bestow would not satisfy you, believe me! I'm glad to hear you are at Concord. You must enjoy it very much—what a selection of choice spirits you have about you, haven't you? Mr. Bradford, too, to study with—he grows dearer to me daily; our friendship is to me one of my chiefest blessings."

After a brief mention of Georgiana Bruce, who was serving as assistant to the matron of the Women's Prison in Sing Sing, Ora burst into a paean of joy about the spring. Whether it was the beautiful countryside, or some newly developed power of response within herself that made it seem a pleasanter season than usual, she was not sure. "At any rate, I never knew it so beautiful before— If I could express all it gives me, how beautiful would be my speech—but there is ever something, 'Deeper than thy deepest speech, something lies thou canst reach,' though speech is the sign of truth and love I know, we speak truly only to those we love, or a power we cannot command speaks the truth through us, so, only do words bind hearts, so only can they reach the spirit, and so does not love become impersonal? For is there any such thing as personal love?"

Isaac felt for her, too, a noble, brotherly tenderness; and on May eleventh he wrote in *The Diary*, perhaps after reading the above, "This morning I received a letter in answer to one I sent from Ora, one of the loveliest, most love-natured beings that has met my heart. There is more heart in her bosom, more heaven in her eyes than I have seen or felt in any other person. She is not lovely but love itself."

All this talk of love and hearts might be misleading if it were not perfectly clear from Ora's six letters among the Hecker Papers—not to mention the entries in Hecker's diary—that the correspondence was keynoted by Ora's quest for spiritual peace, and her belief that Hecker could help her attain it. Ora's tone was typical. The young ladies of that day were capable of the most mawkish sentimentalities when they wrote of Nature or Friendship. A bright May morning made Ora feel as if she would clasp the whole world in one embrace of love. Yet she felt at the same time a longing for something, she was not sure what. "What is it?" she asked wistfully. "How I have written to you I know not; freely though, for whatever has come to me I have written. Receive it in love from Ora, whatever it be."

Meanwhile Hecker was becoming more and more involved in his inner conflict. On May fifteenth, upon entering into nearly three weeks of almost uninterrupted contemplation, he wrote Brownson that his inner life prevented study. The entry in *The Diary* four days later ends on a note of spiritual submission. Gradually he began to understand that his apathy to worldly interest was the result of more vivid spectral experiences. When asleep, the spiritual world became overpoweringly alive to Hecker.

Hecker's apathy toward this world continued; on June fifth he mailed two distraught letters to Orestes Brownson. Two days later Hecker received a conclusive letter from Brownson in which his friend confided that he was preparing to enter the Roman Catholic Church. "Do you really believe in the Holy Catholic Church?"—Brownson wrote Isaac—"If so, you must put yourself under her direction . . ." Brownson added emphatically that Hecker must either join the Church or be a mystic.

"Oh, this is the deepest event of my past life," Isaac wrote back on reading Brownson's advice. "I would have united myself to any one of the Protestant sects, if I had found them to be what would have answered the demands of nature, and why should I now hesitate when I find the Catholic Church will?" Isaac was hoping that if he did enter the Catholic fold he might be able to pursue his studies with vigor. In conclusion he agreed with Brownson's recommendation and admitted that he had partially anticipated it.

Whether Brownson's influence was still strong enough to constitute the decisive factor is dubious. It may have been, for on June eleventh Hecker went to Boston to confer with the Roman Catholic Bishops Fenwick and Fitzpatrick. The latter listened with rapt attention as Isaac unfolded his path to the Church; and he subsequently gave him an enthusiastic letter to Bishop McClosky in New York. Knowing that Isaac's Catholic contacts in his native city were extremely limited, the Bishop felt that the young man would nevertheless prefer to be received where his friends and family lived.

The very day of his conversation with Bishop Fitzpatrick, Hecker made the great decision of his life—to become a convert to the Church of Rome. Instantly his spirit was at peace. He did go to the Holy Cross College in Worcester, perhaps with the idea of seeing Catholic life in action. But his mind was already made up; and he remained there only two days.

During these past months the Transcendentalist influence had been stronger than Hecker was willing to admit. For now, after months of fasting and prayer, when he found where his Spirits led, he took time on June thirteenth caustically to depict the influence which had delayed his great decision. "A Transcendentalist is one who has a keen sight but little warmth of heart . . . He is *en rapport* with the spiritual world, unconscious of the celestial one. He is all nerve and no blood, colorless. He talks of self reliance but fears to trust himself to love . . . His nerves are always tightly stretched like the string of a bow; his life is all effort . . . Behold him sitting on a chair. He is not sitting but braced upon its angles as if his bones were of iron and his nerves of steel. Every nerve is drawn, his hands are clinched like a miser's; it is his lips and head that speak, not his tongue and heart . . . Nature is his Church, and he is his own God. He is a dissective critic, heartless, cold; and what would excite love and sympathy in another would but excite his curiosity and interest. He would have written a critical essay on the power of the soul at the foot of the cross."

Hecker was girding his mind against Ralph Waldo Emerson with whom he would drive to the town of Harvard the next day, to bid farewell to Lane, while Emerson would meet Alcott at Still River. Hecker was determined not to be influenced by the Sage of Concord. "We shall not meet each other; for on no other grounds can I meet him than those of love. We may talk intellectually together and remark and reply and remark again." Hecker expected to stay at Harvard "until Sunday."

Emerson—Hecker had reason to suspect—would try to shake his decision to become a Catholic. Hecker had long since lost respect for Emerson.

Some two months before, Isaac had written his family: "I have had a few words with Emerson. He stands on the extreme grounds where he did several years ago. He and his followers seem to me to have almost a pure intellectual existence . . . They are heathens in thought and profess to be so. They have no conception of the Church out of Protestantism. They are almost perfectly ignorant. They are the narrowest men, and yet they think they are extremely 'many sided.' And forsooth, they do not comprehend Christendom and reject it."

These are strong words; and after reading them it is comforting to picture an evening when Hecker stopped off at Brook Farm on his way from Concord to New York expressly to see the Ripleys. He discussed the new step he was about to take with them. "Both listened with interest," he recorded, "but Mrs. Ripley betrayed a warmth and earnestness of feeling the more remarkable for its contrast to her ordinary unexcited manner."

This would be Hecker's last visit to Brook Farm. Meanwhile, Ora Gannett, on July 28th, believing him to be still in Concord, wrote him another effusion. "Still daily do I feel that you are a brother to me, and always must I speak simply with you." This seeking for friendship, to Ora seemed "the great object of our lives." And yet how vain to seek friends, "when those we love best come to us always at a time and in ways we never dream of." Whereas a friend, "one who shall be *all* this word deserves how can we ever find?" Poor Ora could not think of one single person, even among her intimates, with whom she felt perfectly at ease. Of late she had parted "in a great measure" from those she "used to call friends." Had she grown more independent and self-sufficient in consequence, and perhaps her acquaintance valued her more for that very reason?

"I really have spoken more to you—although so little,—than to anyone else for this long, long time. Is it because I think you are willing to listen to me?" she serenely asked Isaac. "Ah, Nature!" she continued, blandly changing the subject. "How silently tho' continually she woos us to her embrace, but not till we heed her do we hear her and see how tenderly she holds us to her bosom,—

> What says she? All that life demands
> Of those who live to be and do
> Calmness—in all its deepest, bitterest strife,
> Courage—till all is through.

"Does she not say this to you, Isaac? And to all who listen to her? How much strife must we pass patiently through to become calm, but too often do we say, 'How long, how long?' " Ora had decided to give herself up and wait, and "belong only to the spirit." But she knew in advance that she would be "recalled from this study." Driven by some blast she could not understand, Ora foresaw she would inevitably get "detained afresh in the love and bondage of visible things." These always aroused in her the most "worldly and tempestuous feelings."

In conclusion, this "bright, vivacious, rich complexioned damsel . . . very pretty"—as Hawthorne, who knew her when she first came to Brook Farm, said of Ora Gannett—had the temerity to tell Hecker, who admitted no other interest than religion now, that she was longing to ask him about Catholicism. "I feel perfectly sure of its beauty," she wrote glibly. "Yet it seems to be loaded with shackles, though perhaps not more than other churches. I long to know more of it." One can scarcely think of a more provoking series of remarks to make to Isaac Hecker, except those made previously by C. A. Dana. Ora, unaware of her lack of tact, boldly adjured the Almighty. "That God may bless you, Isaac, is the heartfelt wish of yours through love, Ora." The postscript was both wistful and revealing, "Still give me the love of your 'childlike heart' for it is indeed a pleasure to me."

Two days after she wrote him, possibly the same day Isaac received her letter—August 2nd—Hecker was baptised into the Roman Catholic Church.

Hecker kept up a lively correspondence with Almira Barlow from the time he left Brook Farm in August 1843, to April 1844 when he came to Concord where she was living with her children. But he had scarcely been at home in New York two months before she, realizing that Isaac Hecker was daily becoming more preoccupied with the state of his soul, complained of the "impersonal tone" of two of his letters to her. Isaac felt that her complaint was written "in a misapprehension of my state of mind towards her." His answer, "came unbidden, flowing freely from the fountain of life." He hoped she would write him again immediately, for he was "a little curious" to know how his letter would impress her.

On December sixth, a day when he took "A good cold shower-bath" and dieted on "apples, potatoes, nuts, and unleavened bread—no water, scarcely a mouthful a week—" he felt Almira was near his heart, and could scarcely keep from writing to her. He hoped they were not drifting apart, for he inquired in *The Diary*, "What position will we occupy in the future? I can scarcely think we will be so far apart as we now are." He did write her on Christmas Day—perhaps about brotherly love, a theme not likely to arouse Mrs. Barlow's enthusiasm.

Absorbed in his religious conflict—his fasting, and his contemplation, Hecker could not have had much to tell Almira that she could readily understand or respond to. Isaac, however, was perplexed when he did not hear from her that winter as frequently as in the fall. She could not be sick, or she would have found some way to let him know. He was positive he had done nothing to offend her, unless it was to show less interest, which was inevitable.

"I have been absorbed in the plans that are before me," he wrote in *The Diary* before he went to Concord in April to stay at the Thoreaus', "and very probably what I have written to [her] has not shown that interest—love—as what I have previously written to her. If I knew that she desired to cut off all communication with me I would resign myself to it, not I confess without a deep struggle and considerable effort, but I could and would do it. Still, this would not diminish my attachment nor cool my love toward [her] but stamp [her] image deeper upon my heart and engrave in my memory the many pleasant scenes and hours we have lived in love in fairer times." Father Holden points out in *The Early Years*, that here, as in earlier passages in *The Diary*, Hecker made the same erasures and substitutions to hide the identity as before.

Yet there can be little doubt that Hecker's feeling for Almira Barlow was more profound than for any other woman. Mysticism, however, was a far cry from Almira's hunt, and she must have been puzzled indeed by Isaac's dedication to some lofty purpose he could not define. Perhaps her recent tearfulness was caused by frustration in her relationship with Isaac. For although he deserted his books all too frequently when in Concord to sit out on the cliffs by the Sudbury River, her tears were unknown to him. He went there to concentrate on divine—not human—love.

Hecker's conversion, which occurred early that June, cleared broodiness and indecision right out of his mind—and incidentally made him put Almira Barlow in realistic perspective. On August fourteenth, two weeks after his baptism, he completely detached himself from the Brook Farm enchantress. "Almira has lost all, or, at least, so it seems, affinity with my life," he wrote in *The Diary*. "We do not feel any loss."

Meanwhile, Ora Gannett seems to have been wondering why Hecker had not replied to her letter of July twenty-eighth, for on August twenty-ninth she could bear the suspense no longer and brushed maidenly bashfulness aside. "Why do I hide myself from you?" she wrote Isaac. "I have of late been in much unrest. Oh! very much. I knew not if I knew you though indeed I thought I did, for all I have said has been uttered in the trust of the moment. I knew at least that I could speak simply to you and did." She now felt compelled to open her heart to Isaac again, and begs him to help her "by receiving in like manner what" she says "in truth."

"Too ready am I," Ora confessed sadly, "to open myself to, and as it were, throw myself upon those who are willing to receive me if I am in the least attracted by them—herein see my weakness. My heart seeks again the childlike confidence it has lost and thus perhaps unconsciously belies itself. You"—she tells Isaac—"do not behave this way." She, alas, is full of all sorts of weaknesses and sins he doesn't know about—"Deeply disappointed would you be were you to know me." The pity of it is neither can give the other true companionship; and now, when she looks back and remembers how in moments when she longed to speak to someone, she spoke to him—telling him everything!—she draws back "far—farther than before" into the silence of her own heart. "How I could have spoken so confidingly to you or you to me I cannot now understand." For a long time before this happened she had not dared to expose her secret thoughts to anyone. "But you," she laments, "so wooingly held out your arms that I for a time thought I could peacefully repose there . . ." But now, before it is too late she must confess her error—she must leave others alone until she can belong to others "with earnest truthfulness." Ora finds it strange that she has not already learned this lesson. ". . . but I'm wayward and then, too, I love too much to depend upon others and feel their love." From now on she will stand up firmly on her own strength; in the meantime she begs Isaac to forgive her. "If you do know"—she begs, about this weakness, presumably—"you will not wonder, if you do wonder, be patient with me."

A day or so later Ora added another page while "sitting on a deep wooded bank by the sparkling river." Nature decked the earth with more than her usual beauty that August afternoon; and Ora placed her head on Nature's bosom, seeking the true peace she had not found in friendships. Recently she had entertained high hopes—that she might find peace in Isaac's heart, no doubt—"but now do I know that I must go alone to the great fount . . ." When she would write again, Ora did not know. But she hoped there might always be truth between them and that Isaac would always "remember kindly the erring, Ora."

The two did, indeed, remain friends; and Ora has confessed in "A Girl of Sixteen at Brook Farm" that Hecker subsequently almost converted her to Roman Catholicism. But Hecker's intimate friendship with Almira Barlow was never resumed. She was a cat of a different hue; and already she had preened herself and spruced up. After an evening passed with Almira late that summer, George William Curtis complacently wrote Dwight that the moon lighted him home "with such forgiving splendor!"

17.

In mid-June, Amelia Russell, former Mistress of the Wardrobes, and her sister, Ida, held a Cherry and Strawberry Party at the Russell homestead in Milton. The friends* at Concord were invited to meet "a very select group from Brook Farm."

Marianne waxed ecstatic about this affair: "We left here"—Brook Farm—"early in the afternoon and came home about twelve that night. They"—the Russells—"have at Milton a magnificent place,—a commodious, old fashioned house, commanding a fine water prospect,—with a superb garden—statues, vases, flowers, and everything to delight the eye; and the table was so *elegantly* filled with cherries, strawberries, etc. —an abundant feast to more than one of the senses. Then, too, the company was beautiful—among whom were conspicuous the beautiful Geraldine, the intellectual Ida, and the lovely Rose. I suppose about

---

* Almira Barlow, the Curtis brothers, Hecker, and Bradford.

fifty visitors were there besides us Brook Farmers. They were invited to meet us and of course all came, for who don't like to look at Brook Farm people? And then, too, we looked pretty well—we had with us Charles Dana and John"—her brother—"and our handsome youths, Maria Dana, the Macdaniels, etc."

Except for this gay outing the month of June passed in a mood of weighty decision at Brook Farm. On the fourth, General Direction "determined on the erection of a Unitary Building"; on the tenth, plans for the Brook Farm Phalanstery were discussed; and on the eleventh, the plans presented by Benjamin Rogers were accepted.

George William Curtis, who visited Brook Farm for a few days after the Russells' Garden Party, wrote Hecker his impressions* upon his return to Concord. For Curtis, Brook Farm as he had known and loved it, now wound to a nostalgic close.

"At the Farm I had a sad sweet day. All sorts of memories haunted me, like shadowy forms that were very fair. The place was so familiar, and yet so changed. The persons so different, the tone so different. I admired the order which prevailed, but the wild, loitering busy leisure of old-times was far finer to my mind; tho' they must long ago have left the place had that continued. I missed the Cottage Parlor and the Hive Parlor. That long narrow room ill-compensates for the delightful inconvenience of Entry and small front room. But I could not wish the old system back again. These persons would not find their home in it. They seem very happy, and I was glad to see them. I do not doubt I could live pleasantly among them, but not a solitary wish to return entered my mind. Mr. and Mrs. Ripley were very glad to see me, and on the evening I was with them I sang. The Eyrie Parlor was as full as it used to be, the floors and doors and windows each had their company, but when I looked around after singing I met no familiar face. That likeness and unlikeness at once struck me very forcibly. I was tossed between the Past and the Present, and neither would quite receive me.

"The Piney Woods were unchanged. I lay down beneath the whispering trees, which were singing their daily song—was it my imagination that detected a low wail, as of a secret regret, in the falling of the sound? . . .

"It was partly the Day that made me feel as I felt. One of those warm Summer days when the wind is very low and steals softly over the

* Hecker Papers.

landscape, as if it lay in a fairy slumber and must not be awakened. My residence there seemed to recede into the distance, and to gather a mysterious charm as it went."

The decision to expand Brook Farm was made in the face of persistent rumors that the great phalanx of Clarkson in western New York had failed.

By the middle of June these rumors had become so persistent that the leaders of the movement in New York no longer could ignore them. So they did the next best thing—in the weekly edition of the *New York Tribune* on June twenty-second, they disclaimed all responsibility, on the grounds that the phalanx had been hastily founded with insufficient means, small knowledge of Fourier's System, and a weak staff.

This was to become the leaders' standard reply to the failure of an Association anywhere. Apparently, they imagined that if they disassociated themselves from each unsuccessful experiment, their movement would remain untarnished. Perhaps the constant reiteration by Brisbane that the *Social Destiny of Man* according to Fourier simply could not fail, had convinced them that a failure was not up to standard or it would not have failed.

At Brook Farm the leaders were not one whit deterred; and Brisbane, in Paris, though rumors of the Clarkson failure must have reached the office of *La Démocratie Pacifique*, stayed on quite unperturbed, to complete his study of Fourier's unpublished manuscripts.

For Marianne, too, the month of June proved decisive. Her period of probation at Brook Farm ended. The *Brook Farm Records* show she was admitted to membership in the Association on the ninth.

Membership brought increased responsibilities, and Marianne proudly took up the new enterprise assigned to her direction—to "raise up the female," which was one of the great works that Association, in its early stages, would have to do. Marianne soon boasted to Anna that she belonged to "a group for making fancy articles for sale in Boston . . . We realize considerable money from this, and hope, women tho' we be, to have by and by the credit of doing some productive labor." The work was the more agreeable because Marianne felt a strong "passional attraction" toward painting wild flowers and now she could adorn lamp shades and knick-knacks with "flower portraits" to her heart's content. In other ways, too, this project, which would eventually grow into a nation-wide Women's Exchange movement, seemed an exciting opportunity to Marianne. She expected great things of her "Fancy Group." Nothing less, indeed, than "the elevation of woman to independence, and an acknowledged equality with man." When woman at last was emancipated, how the whole aspect of society would be changed!

The housing shortage was considered their major handicap; for the General Direction held that given sufficient increase of workers, the Association would soon become self-supporting. Applications were pouring in by every mail; and so, come July when the cellar of their phalanstery was dug, the mere sight of it proved heartening.

Some of those who applied overlooked the associate's duty to the Association, and sought an easy life in a safe refuge. One who described himself as "a literary old man" confessed he had never been used to any kind of manual labor, and could bring no money or influence of any kind—nothing indeed but "a true devotion to Association and peace." A pastor who could not see eye to eye with his congregation wanted to bring his wife and four children. They had little to contribute but their noble aims, and bodies that had "not been made to waste and pine by the fashionable follies of this generation." The children scarcely had had time for such follies, it appeared. The eldest was not yet ten years old. A mother wrote for a daughter, "having five children, who with her husband much wished to join a society of this kind." She asked fourteen questions—to be answered, "by number as they are put." An illiterate youth sent a scrawl which began, "Sur, as I have heard something about the said broofarm, thairfore take the pleasure of wrighting . . ." A more cultivated person, and what was unusual, a man of property, wondered if $2,500 or $3,000 would be sufficient to cover his initiation fee. He was very wistful about it; "Oh sir," he sighed, "I must live, labor and die in Association." Some applicants tried to worm their way in by hook or crook. One offered to bring a cow, and, if that was not enough security he could also bring "three beds and bedding, and ordinary things enough to keep a house." A musical aspirant wondered whether "a pianoforte, valued at $250" might be "a sufficient pledge."

George Ripley tried to exercise vigilance in regard to admission; but in spite of his care Sophia observed that they gathered "some very odd sticks in the family." One of these—John Cheever, the former valet, and some said the natural son, of Sir William Caldwell, Treasurer General of Canada—soon made himself very useful, and proved "a barrel of fun."

Caldwell often had visited Brook Farm when in Boston—to the Farmers' delight, for although they would never admit class distinctions, Caldwell's rank brought precisely the kind of prestige they needed. Unfortunately, Sir William, after taking his dinner at Brook Farm one Sunday, was taken ill and died suddenly in Boston. Whether their pork and beans were the cause the Farmers never knew. They were distressed to lose their valued friend; and when John Cheever, stranded in Boston, applied for admission, he was admitted at once.

It soon became the special duty and delight of the former valet to bounce the undesirable callers. With true Gaelic percipience, John Cheever recognized the cranks and the fakes on sight. He would receive each visitor courteously, and then encourage him to betray his tricks and idiosyncrasies. If need be, he would "crack the blackguard's shells for him, and show the blasted nuisance the door."

In this artful way, Cheever caught the man who vowed he "never slept" napping; and the diet crank, who never ate anything but cracked wheat, raiding the larder. With Carlo, the big watch dog, at his heels, Cheever bowed out the tough characters as smoothly as the lily-livered.

On week days John was on duty in a bright green plaid; on Sundays he donned a swallow-tail coat with brass buttons and caught up on his reading. "My education was a bit spotty," he would say. But no one ever found fault with his taste. John's favorite books were Shakespeare, Homer in translation, and the Bible.

The ladies admired John's smart appearance, and pronounced him most obliging. But it was in the capacity of special aide to the Ripleys that Cheever proved his worth. His Irish insight relieved them both of many embarrassing moments.

Mr. Ripley, in particular, was busier than ever in the summer of 1844. The crops were not so much on his mind these days, to be sure. He no longer filled page after page in his notebooks with close calculation concerning the capacity of the land for tillage—so much corn, grain, clover grass, fodder, root, vegetable to the acre in "scientific repetition." He had given up all expectation of living off their twenty-two gravelly acres; all his energies now were bent on transforming Brook Farm into a successful Industrial Association. But it was already obvious that Ryckman, the "cordwainer," now one of their Directors, was by training more suited to commercial promotion than Ripley the scholar; and so it came about that the latter went up and down the northeast states propagandizing for the New England Fourier Society.

Yet Ripley was careful not to monopolize this field. Accordingly, he sent Dana and Dwight to represent Brook Farm at the third Regional Convention, held at the Northampton Community on July twentieth. Mr. Ripley's only contribution on that occasion was an invitation to the delegates of the next convention, scheduled for the end of October, to meet at Brook Farm.

Meanwhile the reorganization according to Fourierism was progressing at such a pace that Marianne was sure the first words to be lisped by three recently born Brook Farm babies would be "Groups and Series."

On September seventh, Charles Dana read a paper which would presently be printed as the Introduction to their Second Constitution and By-Laws. He reported an increase in their numbers "by many skilled laborers"; and by the somewhat misleading maneuver of listing the newly built shop and the barely begun phalanstery as capital gains, he contrived to declare a profit of $10,000 during the previous half year.

18.

There was always frequent visiting back and forth between Concord and West Roxbury, particularly in the clement season; and in the summer of 1844 disturbing stories reached Mr. Emerson concerning Brook Farm. The young people there, it was rumored, had become affected by Fourier's theories in regard to sex. Mr. Emerson feared that Mr. and Mrs. Ripley might not be sufficiently strict with the recalcitrants.

To get to the bottom of the matter, Emerson went walking in the Concord by-ways one September afternoon with George Bradford. They "cleared up some of the mists gossip had made"; and they discussed "what lay behind the mists." Bradford expressed the opinion,

"Plain dealing is the best defence of manners and morals between the sexes." Emerson thought privately, "The danger arises whenever bodily familiarity grows up without Spiritual Intimacy."

Fourier—as Emerson * put it—"was very French indeed"; a man "who regarded abstinence from pleasure as a very great sin." Obviously, Fourier's views were distasteful to Emerson, who preferred to think of women as "lawful as a class" and individually "chaste in their organization." Certainly the ladies in Mr. Emerson's world—and polite society of the day in Anglo-Saxon countries everywhere—reflected his preference.

The pity of it was that such gossip was endangering the Brook Farm School, ever the Farmers' most dependable source of income. Since the change to Fourierism, the enrollment steadily had declined, especially among the more desirable pupils. Persons with discrimination hitherto happy to commit their children to the care of the Ripleys, did not dare to expose them to Fourierism, even when assured that the Master's views on marriage and the family were not endorsed at Brook Farm.

Until recently—Parke Godwin boldly had exposed the Frenchman's attack on the family along with the rest of his doctrine in A *Popular View of the Doctrines of Charles Fourier* published the previous spring —there had been little gossip or discussion on the subject. Now, many Americans learned from Godwin's treatise, how Fourier, pursuing his "Law of Attraction" into the realm of sex, proclaimed that in Love as in Industry, mankind should follow his natural impulses.

Love was Fourier's favorite among the Affective Passions. He found it good, useful, and innocent in itself; and he proceeded to describe Love's Freedom-to-Come with boldness and candor. The picture was the more appalling to parents of young persons at Brook Farm, because rumor had it that the Directors had taken steps to have the Association incorporated as a phalanx by the Massachusetts State Legislature. The hypothetical Fourieristic Phalanx, hitherto but a drawing in the *New York Tribune*, suddenly became—for these parents—an immediate threat to the purity of their offspring; and they worried. Even Fourier himself had not believed that mankind was ready for his revolutionary theories about sex; he had advised postponing the adoption of his ideas for at least one hundred years.

Distraught parents learned from Godwin's review that sex education

* Historic Notes of Life and Letters in N.E.; Lectures and Biographical Sketches.

in the phalanx would begin young. This would be quite safe they were told, because childhood would always be supervised in Harmony,* never left to the mercy of dangerous ideas.

Upon emerging from childhood both sexes would be placed together, the elders learned, in a "Corps of Vestals" to be trained "to the highest purity and most spiritual perceptions of love." During this "Vestalate" the young people would be encouraged to make their choice as their hearts might dictate, without interference from parents or consideration of rank or fortune. No parent would ever find an excuse to interfere, because everyone in the phalanx would always be financially secure; and for each young person to consult his own heart was according to God's will—for surely the Creator had not placed so divine and beautiful a passion as Love in the bosom to have it crushed and trampled on by parsimonious parents?

The Heart-Choice, as soon as made, would be pronounced a marriage, and the parties to it would then pass from the "Vestalate" to some "Corps of Constancy," composed exclusively of the married. Each Harmonian marriage would be made in the expectation that it would endure. But, actually, it would be the trial variety; for, if the parties did not get on well together, the contract could be dissolved as easily as made. Divorce would become less dangerous, Fourier believed, as society advanced in purity of thought; and he foresaw with startling acumen that at least three generations must pass before the dissolution of the marriage tie could be effected without odium to the individual. He also prophesied that divorce would increase with the economic independence of woman.

The endorsement of easy divorce and re-marriage was more than enough to make the average American of that day look askance at Fourierism; but it was downright immoral to endorse Free Love. Yet this was a logical tenet of Fourier's System. In the perfect society as he pictured it, there would be an opportunity for each person to develop according to the needs of his nature. It followed that Fourier welcomed to his phalanstery many types who are constitutionally inconstant, and exaggerated in love. He held that such types as Ninon de l'Enclos or Casanova are integral elements in the human race. Instead of trying to suppress such persons, society should synchronize them into Universal Unity. Every phalanstery would contain a "Corporation of Love, in which Inconstant Nymphs and Don Juans, drawn

* Fourier's name for his Social System when established.

irresistibly to one mate after another by Passional Attraction, would be housed together, and apart from the rest." Fourier delighted in detailed descriptions of "Corporations of Bacchantes" or "Bayaderes"— the statutes of which were varied to suit the inclinations and temperaments of their personnel.

Parke Godwin, the first to present Fourier's attack on Familism to the American public, like Brisbane, Channing and Ripley, preferred to leave such tenets "to the adjudications of time, holding ourselves ready, however, at all hazards to prove that they are not purposefully immoral, although we believe them to be false."

With these words Godwin passed on to a discussion of Fourier's Theory of Universal Analogy, which led the Frenchman into some very weird scientific suppositions indeed.

"The Planets," Fourier stated authoritatively, "coming together by means of aromal organs, must find in the relations thus established the satisfaction of all the Passion of Love, which is as common to them as to ourselves." It was his view that the Planets yearn like humans for their mates; and the present Aurora Borealis betokens that the Earth is holding out lonely hands of love to Venus. To the question, —how do Planets make love?—Fourier replied explicitly they have sexual organs and can be fecundated; but like the plants they are androgynous and self-contained. Their offspring, also, are clearly envisaged—these will be the first parents of all the new animals and of all the new vegetables. A Planet can suffer, too; and a Planet that is badly treated by its mate will give birth to hurtful species as a result of the inharmonious passions. The death of Phoebe, the Moon, whom Fourier scornfully refers to as "that deathly pale corpse" was caused by a putrid fever contracted from the Earth some fifty years before the flood; and the absence of Phoebe's offspring in the last Creation caused some unfortunate omissions among plants and animals we ought to have had. The World has been the poorer by the absence of a very special gooseberry, because of the death of Phoebe.

Happily, Fourier foresaw another Creation, under more favorable conditions pending, which would mark the transition to Harmony. The generation of the Anti-Bug and the Anti-Lion, for example, would occur at this time. Sir Alexander Gray—from whose dissertation the above has been drawn *—drily observes that Fourier's account of the love affairs of "the planets, like his data concerning the metempsychosis

* The chapter on Fourier in The Socialist Tradition by Sir Alexander Gray: Longmans 1946–47.

and immortality, is presented with a wealth of ludicrous detail, and crammed with startling information, which as the reviewers say, is not readily available elsewhere."

Sir Alexander goes on to explain that it is Fourier's habit of giving human shape to his argument which is largely responsible for the aura of absurdity which is never long absent from Fourier's writings. "Arrangements in Harmony," writes Sir Alexander, "are always discussed by reference to events in the lives of Harmonians, who incongruously bear classical names." The incongruity lies in the extraordinarily puerile appetites and ambitions of these characters. Consider Lunarious, whose passion is eating insects. It is not every Harmonian who fits so neatly into the Creator's plan. Lunarious is a stopgap, so to speak. He is dedicated to insecticide—until the Anti-bug appears. Lunarious is a drone in the hive, a man limited to but one "Attraction."

Those Harmonians who are more gifted give the impression that Fourier's Good Life is based on copulation and cookery. A rich Harmonian enjoys five delicious meals a day, not to mention *goûtes* and wine-tasting parties. He needs constant refreshment in order to partake of the *Parcours de Plaisir*—Interludes of Pleasure—which come his way with delightful frequency.

On the highest level there is Dorval, who is capable of very rapid enjoyment of a variety of pleasures. In one sixty minute *Parcours*, Dorval receives a lucrative post at the hands of a woman who has hitherto denied him her favors; and she succumbs on the spot to his advances. In the Salon he encounters a dear friend whom he believed to be dead. At dinner he is placed beside an influential personage whom he has hitherto sought in vain to meet, and speedily wins the gentleman's favor. Then, as they rise from table, just as the clock is about to strike the hour, Dorval receives word that he has won a difficult lawsuit which has been in process for years. Obviously, it was Dorval's hour. But what about the man who lost the lawsuit? Presumably, as Sir Alexander remarks, he was not having his *Parcours* just then.

Is it to be wondered at that one contemporaneous critic declared that the first syllable of the Master's name, *fou*—French for mad— fitted his doctrine? And even the solemn Apostle, Brisbane, confessed that he had been troubled by many things in Fourier which he did not understand and could not accept. "Never has an author so irresistibly excited my laughter," he tells us in his own *Mental Biography*, which he dictated to his wife, Redalia. "One day while traveling in a stage coach it"—*The Four Movements*—"produced such an effect, such paroxysms of laughter, that I had to put my head out of the coach window that my fellow travelers might not notice my excitement."

There is no reason to suppose that the majority of young people at Brook Farm experimented with Fourier's advanced ideas concerning love. The subject is difficult to explore, because, with the exception of Marianne Dwight's letters to Anna Parsons, there is no readily available evidence—only reminiscences, such as those of Ora Gannett Sedgwick, written many years later, when she had become a grandmother and had either forgotten or preferred to ignore the sentimental effusions about friendship and Nature which she had written to Isaac Hecker as a girl.

If Marianne Dwight discussed Fourier's ideas on love and family with Anna Parsons, the letters were severely edited by her granddaughter. This seems doubtful, because Marianne sounds so candid and ingenuous. She boasted about her "flirts"—but what she writes of these exciting encounters with the opposite sex have a modest echo—almost coy. As scandal, completely innocuous.

When Mr. Emerson next visited Brook Farm some titivating interviews were granted to him; and so it would appear that tentative adventures of an amorous nature did occur.

One group of young people admitted they had "more rapid experience than befell them elsewhere—lived faster."

How wide Mr. Emerson's eyes must have opened at that! In Concord, proper young people took their tone from their elders. Whereas at Brook Farm, every other person he saw was "a character in a free costume." This made an interesting study, to be sure; and after his return to Concord, he foresaw that some of these young people would end up with "shattered constitutions."

This entry in his *Journal* is exceedingly tantalizing because Emerson drops the discussion of possible promiscuity at Brook Farm and turns instead to the Ripleys—it was after this visit that Emerson, at last, gave George and Sophia their due. He conceded that their authority was felt by all, though perhaps unconsciously by some; and he observed that the Ripleys had identified themselves with the Community. "They have married it, and they are it," he wrote. "The others are experimenters, who will stay by this if it thrives, being always ready to retire; but these have burned their ships and are entitled to the moral consideration which this position gives." Mrs. Ripley, especially, had never appeared to such advantage in Mr. Emerson's eyes. He felt that her experience had softened her "somewhat hard nature"; but he trembled for her, and for all "the true workers."

What would the result of all this be? "Brook Farm," Emerson foretold, sadly but shrewdly, "will see a few noble victims."

19.

At the end of August, Theodore Parker returned from Europe, where he had gone in 1842 to recover from a nervous breakdown brought on by theological differences between himself and his Unitarian brethren. The first Sunday in September he preached from his former pulpit in the Spring Street Church in West Roxbury; and the Farmers flocked to hail him as a mighty prophet returned from exile.

Parker was more convinced than ever that true religion depended neither upon Church nor creed nor clergy; nor upon authority and tradition. He still believed in the authority of instinct, conscience, emotion and reason. He was still a Transcendentalist believing religion itself to be transcendental and infinite; and he held that any attempt to demonstrate or authenticate the infinite by finite means was illogical.

The Farmers, too, believed that what Parker called "Absolute Religion" offered the only alternative. But those who expected him to endorse Association were disappointed. Although she conceded that he had spoken well, even for him, Marianne Dwight afterwards criticized him for evading the issue. For, although he had given "the most excellent statistics for associonists, said everything leading to Association," he had not said "a word for it; stopped short of the mark which he must reach if he is true." Marianne was very close, through her brother, John, to the Brook Farm "Aristocrats," the Direction. So her opinions usually reflect those of the leaders.

William Henry Channing who preached at Brook Farm in the afternoon of that same Sunday, was a more sympathetic counsellor, one who had all but espoused Fourierism. He was forever preaching, wherever and whenever he could, the doctrine of Christian Socialism, anti-slavery, and the up-building of the spiritual life.

The Farmers delighted in Mr. Channing's benign and beautiful presence; and they could still relish Mr. Alcott's Orphic discourse when he visited them that September. Mr. Kay, a financier from Philadelphia, and a generous patron of Marianne's "Fancy Group," was popular, too. But not so Mr. Brownson, who, surprisingly enough, had asked them to put him up over the weekend of the twenty-second. Orestes was attacking Fourierism as irreligious in *Brownson's Quarterly*, and many persons at Brook Farm resented his interference.

Mrs. Ripley and her niece, Sarah Stearns, may well have looked forward to Mr. Brownson's visit with keen anticipation; for both women were inwardly—although perhaps as yet unconsciously—leaning toward Catholicism. Amid the Fourieristic din Mr. Brisbane had created, to Sophia especially, a talk with a zealous convert must have seemed interesting in the extreme.

Unless he felt that he and Orestes had diverged so far in matters of philosophy that they could now meet on formal terms without bitterness, the occasion would have been something of an ordeal for George Ripley. Fortunately he was too deeply committed to the promotion of Fourierism—almost to the exclusion of Brook Farm Direction—to have time for argument. No sooner had Mr. Ripley conducted a meeting of the New England Fourier Society in Boston on September twentieth, than he set about organizing a bi-weekly class at Brook Farm to study Fourier's works. "Countless other classes," Marianne reported, "enough to make one's brain whirl, are being formed."

Meanwhile, Lewis K. Ryckman, to whom Ripley had turned over the Industrial Management, was held in increasing respect, almost in awe. They called him "The Omniarch"—the All-Knowing—because he was the only one of the Directors with commercial experience; and they looked to industry now, to make Brook Farm pay.

But Ryckman already had learned that even under the Law of Attractive Industry labor disputes arose and had to be dealt with in an arbitrary way. Christopher List, familiarly known as "Chrysalis," and one Reynolds became such "discordant elements" among the Carpenters' Group that they were expelled from it. Both men were competent carpenters, however, and as such were in great demand; so Director Ryckman sent them right back to work on the framework of the phalanstery. Marianne and her friends regarded this as an amusing state of affairs—the Group which had sought to get rid of their company were foiled in that, and the recalcitrants were condemned to labor like prisoners, without Fourier-style dignity or self-respect. "So," observed Marianne, "they are working in the midst of the Group, but not of the Group; doing just what they are told to do, a sort of solitary labor and imprisonment."

In one instance commercial enterprise served as an excuse for what would seem to have been foolhardy extravagance—the building of the greenhouse.

In the spring of 1843, Pieter Kleinstrup, the elderly Dutch gardener, harnessed the Farm's powerful young bull. With the aid of young John Thomas, Kleinstrup laid out a large garden behind the Cottage. Come fall, Kleinstrup dug the foundation for a greenhouse. To his chagrin, the Directors, despite his urging that a florist's produce would be in great demand and the business a sure source of revenue during the long white months of winter, refused to vote the necessary equipment; and compelled him to bury his beloved plants in a sun-exposed gravel pit by the side of the road. Every bulb, root and cutting had died of cold.

This fall, Kleinstrup could not bear to see his precious specimens killed again; and, surprisingly, no objection was now made to the extravagance. The Direction blithely embarked on the erection and maintenance of a costly greenhouse despite the expense. Had not the Master insisted that greenhouses were essential?

The glass walls sprang up before the first frosty night—and almost to the very end, this greenhouse, whose flowers could scarcely ever find a market, remained a flower-like symbol of Fourier's promise of "Luxury."

20.

Though the season had been dry, autumn was the very perfection of itself that year, 1844. But Marianne felt a gathering storm. She wished they could meet it with a cheerful trust in the future. Or, better, that they could feel all was right as it was. But she knew it was not, and she was disturbed.

Like Georgiana Bruce before her, Marianne Dwight vowed never to renounce Association. Although she had endured "some very keen suffering" since joining Brook Farm, she could never again feel contented "in the life of isolated houses." But suffering was unavoidable, she sighed, for a female of sensibility!

Actually, the suffering was due to her infatuation with Fred Cabot, who was amusing himself at her expense in an innocent sort of fashion. It is difficult to see what Marianne saw in this round-faced youth, seven years her junior, who served the Corporation as clerk. Fred was neither a dandy nor a wit. Though beards were absent and collars high, Fred wore a beard over a low and rolling collar; and his conversation, studded as it was with puns, makes him appear a tiresome wag indeed. Yet Marianne saw qualities in him, which Anna Parsons also professed to see in her "Readings" of his character. Between them the girls conjured up such a romanticized sketch of Fred Cabot that his own mother—when presented with Anna's notes— did not recognize her son. "It must be that she don't see the same person in him we do," Marianne concluded wistfully. More provoking still, her flirtation with Fred never seemed to get anywhere!

Marianne's letter-writing was interrupted just then by a loud "Hurrah!" Rushing to the window she beheld a group of "little Fourierites with banner flying" marching home behind their director. The banner signified that the boys had done their work with a will. Such was not always the case; because Fourier, who regarded the care of children as the most unattractive of occupations, delegated the least attractive tasks to small boys. Some boys felt no passionate attraction toward rummaging and scavenging. But lately the banners had proved "a grand excitement." Pleased, Marianne determined to have the "Fancy Group" work them a very fancy banner indeed.

Despite the perfection of the foliage—autumn in New England is ever Nature's grand climacteric of the year—the state of feeling, the morale of the Farmers was falling. Even little John Dwight was guilty of some dismal and discouraging remarks at a meeting; so that John Orvis, whom Marianne significantly referred to as "the sublime," had to take it over to rally their spirits again.

But who among them could deny that the summer had brought an ebb tide to the Association Movement? Since the trouble at Clarkson in the spring, other phalanxes—the Sylvania in Pennsylvania, the American in Ohio—had disbanded or were about to do so. And most indicative of all, the September issue of the *Phalanx* contained a notice to subscribers that owing to their recent failure to sell the paper in western New York and Ohio, the weekly would henceforth be published monthly. After the issue of October 7, 1844, the editors were forced back to the same basis on which they had begun—they published when they could, and sometimes this would be at two or three-month intervals.

On the religious issue, the Associationists had drawn a doughty antagonist in Brownson. After his visit to Brook Farm in September, Brownson had written Hecker, "The atmosphere of the place is horrible. Have no faith in such Associations. They will be only gatherings of all that is vile to foster, and breed corruption . . ." Brownson's discourse had been sympathetically received by a few at Brook Farm, however, and he prophesied that two or three of the Farmers would become Roman Catholics. But his old friend, Ripley, he feared, was now "little better than an infidel."

Ripley was now too much of a zealot to heed Brownson's disapproval—or, for that matter, to heed the rumors of the turning of the Fouristic tide in western New York. Early in October, he and Dana both served as delegates to a Fourier Convention held in Winchester, and on their return he appointed two committees—one to consider retrenchments, the other to promote labor increase. Dana was reworking his preamble for a Second Constitution, as well as making out his Treasurer's Report for the fiscal year ending October 31, 1844.

The season of discussion was opening. Delegates from Northampton and Hopedale were expected at Brook Farm to attend the Quarterly Association which would be held on the thirtieth and thirty-first. "The Northamptons didn't come," Marianne afterward wrote her brother, Benjamin Franklin Dwight, who might soon join the rest of the family at Brook Farm. "Six male Hopedales arrived and several women, and we managed to find them each a place to sleep." The meeting itself proved "nothing remarkable." Mr. Ballou held forth at length. "But for this meeting we should have had a Shakespeare reading," Marianne summed up, regretfully.

November proved a month of leaden skies above and discouragement within. Due to the overcrowding, colds, always prevalent in the late fall, spread like an epidemic. The same dews and damps that brought the sniffles made Marianne dread a mishap some dark night on her way between the Hive below and Pilgrim House above. Some of the boys told "frightful stories of last winter's accidents suffered by the unwary who ventured forth without a lantern."

Marianne quickly borrowed one. But the very next evening, when half way down the steep hill that led to the Hive, she heard something heavy sliding past her in the dark—"down, down, down!" The next instant she was somewhat relieved to hear "the not to be mistaken voice of List" calling her by name.

When she overtook him with her lantern, List was picking himself out of a snowdrift. Recovering his dignity as best he could, he offered his arm and conducted her to the Hive.

That same evening, prince-like Charles King Newcomb got lost in the dark and "bumped into a cart." Whether or not it was this mishap or distaste for the new regime is a matter of conjecture, but Newcomb who had ever regarded Brook Farm as an escape from his domineering mother, soon afterward began to talk of making his home with her in Providence. Of such trivial incidents was life at Brook Farm made.

On November twenty-third, 1844, Ripley and Dana managed to repay Hawthorne $35 more on his original investment, which he again acknowledged on the back of their personal note, rendered to him two years before. They had not before—nor did they now—mention this debt to anyone.

The payment—the last they would be able to make for some time— was made at a severe sacrifice, for it soon became apparent that the harvest that fall "would not command sufficient ready money to pay for meat and other delicacies." Within a week or so the Direction ordered "a retrenchment on table-fare."

Marianne, in common with the rank and file of the members, knew nothing of the Association's debt to Hawthorne; and so she serenely reported to Anna on December fourteenth, that it had ever been the rule at Brook Farm never to incur any debt as they went along. Adherence to this prudent policy made retrenchment almost a joy in her eyes, and she took delight in telling Anna exactly how each person fared.

One table was still set up with the old style generosity, "for boarders, scholars, and visitors—and a *few associates* who feel their health requires (!) the use of meat, tea, etc."—not to mention butter and sugar. Newcomb, regarded as an exceptional being, was exempted from "retrenchment fare" and allowed to flit from table to table devouring as much tea and butter as he liked. Marianne declared that Newcomb was such a general favorite that no one grudged him these luxuries; and all were distressed when he spoke of leaving Brook Farm. But she did not feel as lenient toward other healthy rebels. The *Brook Farm Records* show that exceptions were made, for on December fourteenth, the very same day that Marianne was writing, it was "voted that Mrs. Hosmer, Mrs. Hasting, and Mrs. Cheswell; also Mr. Tirrill and Mrs. Kleinstrup be permitted to sit at the meat table; and that Mr. Cheswell be permitted to eat meat, and Mrs. Ryckman to drink tea; and Mrs. Dwight to use tea and butter. Mrs. Ripley, Mr. Kleinstrup and Miss Russell be permitted to sit at the meat table."

To see Mrs. Ripley's name among the privileged—she, who was always one of the more "religious" among them—is an indication that her health was no longer what it had been. Sophia would surely have presided over a retrenchment table and served potatoes, squashes and puddings—no other staples were permitted there—with her usual queenly graciousness if she had felt able to keep up her strength on such a diet. To Marianne, young and vigorous, the term retrenchment afforded no little amusement.

She counted no less than nine different articles on their breakfast table that same morning! It was really cheering to see how readily this measure was adopted. No one could understand why their New York friends were pitying them so much, wondering what they had left to eat. In Marianne's opinion, much good would come of it. Fewer headaches, for instance, without tea or meat.

Marianne was the "Pollyanna" of Brook Farm in its Fourieristic decline, and through her letters one recaptures the mood of dedication prevalent at this time. She echoes the New York leaders' indifference to the failure of many small Associations with disdain, and interprets such news as a good omen—"Friends of Association in New York and elsewhere are beginning to see the need of concentrating their efforts in some, one, undertaking," she told Anna, "and it is to Brook Farm they look."

This belief of the leaders—that if they disassociated themselves from each experiment as it failed, their movement would be safe—was not shared by the public. Each failure was attributed to Fourieristic principles, and became another cancer eating at the heart of the Movement.

More solid encouragement was offered by Mr. Kay. He regarded their condition as more prosperous and hopeful than when he had been with them in the summer. But upon what he based his belief, he did not divulge.

Posterity has forgotten Mr. Kay, but it has not forgotten John S. Dwight. He was already serving as the First Vice President and

Chairman of the Board of Directors of the Harvard Musical Association, and he recently had secured for that Association a series of Chamber Concerts. He was also promoting the building of a Music Hall. Though staunch in his belief that Fourierism made him a better musician, Dwight may well have suffered a pang of nostalgia for the days when Almira Barlow put little perfumed notes under his plate. Amid the prevalent atmosphere of retrenchment, news of his former love—which George William Curtis duly forwarded from Concord—may well have sounded a disturbing note, for she so perfectly embodied sleek femininity. "Almira and her family are here," Curtis reminded him. "John Cheever"—evidently the valet had found another aristocratic employer—"is with her to arrange her household. In the afternoons I have been his assistant. Her house is a small neat cottage between the grave-yards, in the small street opposite the hotel, at the corner where we go to Sleepy Hollow. Out of all windows except on one side, she is reminded of mortality. She seems very much as usual and quite cheerful; and with resolution might be quite happy there. She might be much more economical than she is, but I understand her feelings and have respect for them."

The reorganization of farming and industry according to Fourier's principles, had been going on for eight months at the end of Brook Farm's fiscal year, October thirty-first, 1844, and on December fifteenth, Charles A. Dana, Chairman of the Direction of Finance, submitted his annual report. It was gratifying that the books for that year showed a profit of $1160.84; but regrettable that this profit was swallowed up by "the real deficit" of 1842 and 1843. Dana made due allowance for depreciation of property; and he dutifully listed the bad debts. But he also combed out "small descrepancies"—debts against associonists which should have been included; and he deducted the value of farm produce and family stores on hand from the two-year debt. When he got it all worked out to the last penny, their very first profit in three years and seven months of hard work was swallowed up—they were still $804.04 in the red.

Such a debt seems paltry in this era when many corporations subsist on borrowed money; but the Farmers had no capital or reserve funds. As they progressed in a new and hazardous form of economy, the lack of both was increasingly felt.

Dana looked confidently to the future in a succession of platitudinous comments, pointing out that "Almost every business fails to pay its expenses at the commencement; it always costs something to set the wheels in operation; this is not, however, to be regarded as absolute loss. This is the view which is to be taken of the condition of the Association at the beginning of the present year."

Dana felt that it was important for their morale to declare a dividend without further delay, but he was hard pressed to justify this action because the quarterly statement for the previous August first had voiced the opinion of the majority of the board that no dividend should be declared until the debts were paid. Accordingly, Dana cited the circumstance that one of the Directors who "objected entirely to the principle embodied" in the August report had been absent. On catching up with that young man, or trying to, it appears that the absentee was none other than Dana himself: he presented the opposite view cogently argued. "To some persons it may perhaps seem remarkable that a dividend should be declared, when the Association is so much in want of ready money as at present; but a little reflection will show anyone that it is a perfectly legitimate proceeding. A very large part of our industry has been engaged in the production of permanent property such as the shop, the phalanstery, and the improvements upon the farm. These are of even more value to the Association than so much money, and a dividend may as justly be based upon them as upon cash in the treasury."

His report concluded with a discussion of what dividend pupils and probationers should be awarded for their labor, whether absentees should receive dividends, and the like. He and the other Directors were now agreed "that the time has arrived when the natural differences in labor should be recognized and different rates of compensation for attractive, useful, and necessary labor established." Time, indeed. But the change constituted a veritable revolution. As Emerson had observed with amazement, the same reward was given a Brook Farmer "for looking out the window all day" whether communing with Nature or seeking artistic inspiration—as for arduous manual labor.

Their aims, Dana assured his fellow associates, were as idealistic as ever: "Our object will not be gained until we show practically that associated industry gives a product far superior to that of civilized industry . . . We are convinced it can be reached only by perfectly arranged Groups and Series, and we may be sure that the industrial capacities of the Association will increase in compound proportion to the completeness with which it attains to serial order in all departments, and to its general harmony."

On the very same day that Dana presented his report, Newcomb slipped away to spend Christmas with his mother in Providence. His departure was soon forgotten in the preparations for Mr. Brisbane's visit, scheduled for December twenty-second.

21.

A light case of varioloid contracted in November cut short Brisbane's stay in Paris. In the middle of December he landed in New York—where his fellow Fourierites, one may be sure, spared him none of the bad news. If some of his friends feared that their disillusionment might show up Brisbane's Olympian detachment from catastrophe, others looked to the American Apostle to rally their falling hopes. The failure of several of the largest phalanxes and the dissolution of many small ones, and, above all, the complete absence of any publicity whatsoever in the Rochester press, made a sad contrast to the Fourieristic record and promise publicized by those same papers when Brisbane had sailed for France, eight short months before.

Horace Greeley, outstanding among the leaders in the New York group, had not lost heart. Greeley was filling up his *Tribune* with encouraging items to rally the associationists. But his chief concern now was the future of the North American Phalanx at Red Bank, New Jersey. He was treasurer of the Red Bank Corporation, and he had persuaded the New York financiers to make a considerable investment in that phalanx.

On landing from Europe, Brook Farm offered to Brisbane a peaceful haven in a storm, and he got to West Roxbury as fast as he could—and in time for Christmas.

A current article in the *Phalanx* by Dana, who had lately returned from a tour of the western area, perfectly coincided with Brisbane's own views. "Not a single phalanx in America has been sufficiently prepared either in money, in men and women of requisite character, or in scientific knowledge," Dana declared. "We have nevertheless undertaken to found the Combined Order of Society and to supplant civilized chaos by a new world of Harmony and Beauty. We have undertaken the performance of what with our means is almost impossible, but by the blessing of God it shall be done." No single failure should discourage them. But—what a pity these several incomplete bodies had not been combined into one! While failure of the whole movement threatened, no new phalanxes should be formed; the founding of the National Organization of Associations, planned in the spring, must be postponed. Wisdom, tolerance, economy, and zeal were needed to tide the cause along. Let associonists, therefore, concentrate their efforts on sustaining such phalanxes as seemed to be surviving the recession. Among these, Dana asserted, "Brook Farm is a child of heaven, and Providence smiles upon it."

The Farmers felt honored that Mr. Brisbane sought refuge in their midst. Brisbane's indifference to the fate of the unfortunates whom he had encouraged gave the seal of approval to their own retreat into an Ivory Tower of Fourierism—a retreat from the failure of Association.

Armed with voluminous copies of Fourier's manuscripts, Mr. Brisbane arrived at Brook Farm for a protracted visit. The very next morning he presented for their instruction the history of his travels in Europe mingled with a Fourieristic interpretation of the nations. In England familism predominated; in France cabalism was the ruling passion.

"He gave us a most beautiful and vivid picture of Paris," Marianne wrote Anna, "with its broad streets, its palaces, fountains, and statues. He actually carried us there with him and showed us all this magnificence and let us see for ourselves, what, even in civilization, the combined efforts of men can do." England, in Brisbane's opinion, had been raised up solely to serve as the great industrial school of the world. "The aristocracy have disciplined the mass of the people, have made them learn to work and kept them working,—hence has resulted a race of men inured to toil, capable of subduing nature, never recoiling from the material—from such people alone, could have come the great steamboats, the railroads, etc." The destiny of France, on the other hand, had been to break down the feudal spirit of the middle ages, to destroy Catholicism and aristocracy: "Only in that country, amidst such a people could such a genius as Fourier have been born." But both nations, Brisbane conceded graciously, had done their part towards bringing about "the state of harmony" to which associationists looked forward.

Mr. Brisbane's ability to generalize was impressive, though superficial—Marianne felt—if you analyzed it. But it was fascinating to hear him tell his vision of universal Association all over the world. He saw humanity united in a great whole—in all the details of material life, language, communication, and in enterprise, even to the details of weights and measure. His pride in the human race and his ambition to serve it were wholly genuine, and for that reason contagious. He longed to be a small part in a vast organism. And far away in the distant future, Brisbane envisioned a globe transformed by the combined efforts of all humanity—upon it a race perfected, generation after generation, by the influence of true social institutions.

When questioned about the prospects of Association in France, Mr. Brisbane admitted they seemed miserable and hopeless. "Here is the field—and here at Brook Farm must the efforts of all be concentrated." In this Mr. Ripley and Mr. Brisbane saw eye to eye. Visiting New York leaders were equally enthusiastic. Parke Godwin and Osborne Macdaniel would join Brisbane at Brook Farm later in the winter. Macdaniel already had installed his mother as a boarder; and his two sisters, Eunice and Fanny, were about to be initiated as members.

Infused with fresh enthusiasm, Mr. Ripley, immediately after Mr. Brisbane's talk, appointed a committee to draw up a new constitution and by laws for the Brook Farm Phalanx.

>>>>>>>>>>>>>>>>>>><<<<<<<<<<<<<<<<<<<

The Brook Farm Phalanx

FROM THE VERY BEGINNING THE BROOK FARM COMMUNITY ATTRACTED
interesting persons. Though several of these now had gone to other
fields—Curtis and Bradford to literature and scholarship, Brownson
and Hecker to Rome, yet Brook Farm would always regard them with
the eye of an *alma mater* as distinguished graduates or former members
of the faculty. The Farmers relationship with Brisbane was very different. He was the Apostle of Fourierism and they, his disciples. Proud
to be Brisbane's chosen vanguard, the Farmers set to work to transform
their Association into a Phalanx.

As had happened in January 1844 when the task decided upon was
the reorganization of their industries according to Fourier's System, the
Directors labored to such good effect that the report of the Committee
to draw up a Second Constitution and By-Laws was accepted before
the middle of January; and a motion to present a petition of Incorporation of the Brook Farm Phalanx to the Massachusetts Legislature was
under discussion. Of more importance to their immediate tranquility,
a group of malcontents within their ranks was quashed on January
fourteenth. The troublemakers had formed a party—a word unheard of
in a phalanx!—and they were undermining the work of others with
their calumny and malice. Fortunately this mean and narrow-minded
cabal constituted a very small minority of five or six. The Direction

promptly ordered them "to succumb" and "come into harmony"—or to leave at once. After that, Marianne Dwight wrote Anna Parsons, the Brook Farm atmosphere became clearer and brighter overnight.

Everyone was off to Boston the next day to attend a convention called by the New England Fourier Society to discuss amalgamating all the Fourier Societies throughout the land in one National Organization. Mr. Ripley served as President; C. A. Dana and John Allen as Secretaries. Allen was a Universalist Minister who had left his church because he did not feel free to speak against slavery from his pulpit; he was also an ardent champion of "Working Men's Rights."

Every associationist at the convention followed Bisbane's lead and looked to Brook Farm. Osborne Macdaniel of New York offered a resolution recommending that Associations throughout the United States should, in so far as was consistent with their efforts, apply their means and energies to the building up of Brook Farm. W. H. Channing made a speech which, as always, kindled joy in the soul. Allen reported the Working Men's Movement gave many indications that society already was passing the intermediate state between "Civilization" and Association into a state of "Mutual Assurance."

In this the Reverend Allen was on surer ground than Mr. Ripley, who, quite carried away by a magnificent engraving entitled "A Phalanstery and its Domain," * which Mr. Brisbane had brought back from France, drew a word picture to illustrate how "the romantic attachments, the holy and heroic memories ever greenly entwining the feudal castles, family seats, public buildings of the Old World, will in the New give place to peaceful affections clustering around the Central Dwelling of Association, beautified by the contributed work of generations."

2.

"Oh this day and yesterday!" Marianne wrote gushingly to Anna on January nineteenth. "Was ever earth clad in such beauty? Would you were here to slide and coast over our hills of glistening white marble; to admire the glittering coral branches that border our paths, and the trees

---

* In Marianne Dwight's *Letters from Brook Farm*, there is a reproduction of an engraving of an imposing phalanstery in a magnificent domain. The picture was wholly imaginary, of course.

of crystal, or silver and diamonds, that make magnificent this fairy palace. Have I seen such beauty in a former existence, or is it the realization of some dream or fancy?—that it continually *reminds* me of something, I know not what?"

Her ecstasy fairly overflowed the next morning when Fred Cabot took her to the Piney Woods, and the two of them perched together on a stone wall to marvel at Nature "in this pure crystal dress."

Women had not been admitted to the Convention, and Marianne listened, rapt, when Fred told her of Mr. Channing's moving address, "The Superiority of Joy to Sorrow." Marianne took what consolation she could in the reflection that she had seized upon the occasion to arm Mr. Brisbane with a letter of introduction to her adored Anna Parsons. Happily, the two had recognized one another's "shining spirit" on sight; she knew, because Mr. Brisbane, Osborne Macdaniel, and John Allen had just returned to Brook Farm. Important decisions were in progress, and the New York leaders would remain for a week or so.

3.

The dozen chosen ones who had been busy for a month drawing up the Second Constitution finished their task. The name of the Association would soon be changed to "The Brook Farm Phalanx." Most momentous news of all, John Allen's paper, *The Social Reformer*, published in Maine, and the *Phalanx* were to be united in a new Fourieristic mouthpiece to be published at Brook Farm.

On January twenty-seventh, on the eve of their New York guests' departure, Amelia Russell gave a small party—fifteen carefully selected persons. Marianne almost did not attend because John Orvis came to her room with a headache, and she also had one herself. They spoke of the party and decided it might be dull and that they would not go to it. Then—"In came Amelia to hurry us off—so we went. Coffee was handed round—a few puns perpetrated, etc.—Meanwhile a holy inspiration from high heaven was stealing quietly and unseen over the souls of all present. The spirits of good angels and all lovers of humanity were gathering around us—the soul of Fourier must have bent lovingly over the heads of our little band. Light and love, or the light of love began to beam from all eyes."

Presently, Mr. Ripley toasted "Albert Brisbane, First Apostle of Fourierism in our country," and complimented him on his assistance at the convention and in drawing up the Second Constitution; and Mr. Brisbane, disdaining praise, grew eloquent about Brook Farm society and the precious friendships he had formed there. A perfect feast of toasts and speeches followed; everyone spoke as if inspired. When Dana proposed his friend, Parke Godwin, Fred Cabot added, "God wins always in the end." So appropriate and good a pun was universally applauded, and followed by others of like nature. Their emotions grew more and more elevated and solemn. Presently, Dana called upon them to rise and join hands and pledge themselves to the cause of Association. They all did so with one impulse and formed a circle around the little table and vowed "truth to the cause of God and humanity." Each man vied with the next. John Dwight made beautiful allusions to circles within circles—"showing that this was no exclusive circle, that endless circles might be drawn around it, all having the same centre." Mr. Ripley wished their phalanx might grow until they could join hands all around Palmer's woods, Cow Island, and the land across the river. Mr. Brisbane would have the circle surround the globe. They all got merrier and merrier, toasting "Our patient friend, the coffee pot. Tho' drained of its contents, it has not lost its patience—if it is not *spiritual* it certainly is not material." Mr. Ripley made quite a long and humorous speech upon the quintessential punch, which he drank at a New York meeting, which had roused a dull company into great activity. He said it was so exquisitely compounded that if it had made a man quite drunk, it couldn't have injured his intellect. "This called out two puns. John asked if the party was a punch and judy spree (jeu d'esprit); and Fred said that it seemed only necessary to punch Mr. Ripley to get a good speech from him."

The party ended at twelve o'clock. "At the breaking up Mr. Brisbane made some remarks about going to propagate the doctrine in New York, the city of frauds—whereat in conclusion Fred wished he might go his proper gait and that the greatest fraud of which New York was guilty might be that of defrauding us of his presence." Marianne went home to pass a sleepless night in the company of solemn, pleasing and exciting thoughts. She felt everything Fred Cabot had said that evening was his best; but she could not recall Orvis's toast except that he had said beautiful things about the occasion and about Fourier, with whose spirit he had been holding communion lately.

4

One of the great white storms of late winter hit Brook Farm in February, and for a few days the Farmers were quite "blocked up." But important business was afoot, and there were walks of "divine purity" to and fro from the Hive—in the late and ghostly dawn, blinding noon, and through rose-tinted fields of snow at dusk. Meetings were held to discuss the Second Constitution, and their new and exciting relations with the Executive Committee of the Fourier Society of New York, which had decided to place the cause of Association in America in their hands. The Farmers were proud of this confidence but somewhat weighted down by their new responsibilities—so much seemed to be happening all at once.

John Allen pledged $400 for a new printing press; and "Grandpa" Treadwell, who with Jonathan Butterfield would do the printing of the new Fourieristic paper, added $100 more; and their neighbor, Francis G. Shaw, who would later translate George Sand's *Consuelo*, and her *Countess of Rudolstadt* for publication in the *Harbinger*, gave $1000, part of which would be used to build a blacksmith's shop; and part to buy block tin for "Mr. Capen's business, who can find ready sale for any quantity of articles which he can manufacture." Most exciting of all, the New York friends were said to be exerting themselves to procure additional means for the publishing establishment at Brook Farm. Characteristically, the New Yorkers considered $5000 the absolute minimum to start publication—whereas the Farmers were ready to risk success on one fifth as much. Indeed the New Yorkers talked very big about everything—of sending out lecturers to tour the country, of appealing to friends both at home and abroad to unite in raising funds "for the carrying out of the experiment at Brook Farm."

5.

On February eighth it was voted: "General Direction be authorized to take immediate measures for obtaining an Act of Incorporation."

This led speedily to the presentation of a petition to the Governor of the Commonwealth and General Court asking the granting of a charter. Charles Sumner was reported to be in favor of it, and the probability of its being granted seemed likely. At the end of the month, Brisbane went down to New York to keep his henchmen in line.

Now that Brook Farm had been selected as a successful phalanx for all toiling humanity to view—the rock upon which the great cause of Association would rest—failure seemed out of the question. In this renewal of high hope, Mr. Brisbane shared. The indefatigable Albert came back to Brook Farm early in March to speed the Act of Incorporation through the General Court and to see to it that the decisions of his Executive Committee in New York were carried out. This committee had elected to raise funds to support Brook Farm through a bureau of lecturers and the new Fourieristic organ to be published at the Farm. No one seemed to realize that these means would need funds, too.

"Was my note to you solemncolly? I did not mean it to be," Marianne had written Anna on February twenty-seventh. "Indeed it was so much brighter than I felt at the time that I tho't it quite cheerful."

Nor had her spirits improved since. Reading between the lines it becomes clear that the source of her depression is something more personal than Newcomb's and Eunice Macdaniel's endless sniffles, or Dana's arrogance concerning her brother John's amendments to the Second Constitution. Things were not the same any more between herself and Fred Cabot.

To her dismay, since the orgy of coffee and puns, Cabot had lost interest in her. On February sixth, the night of the great snowstorm, Fred let her brother, John, escort Marianne home. They waded all the way through deep snow, frequently almost up to her neck, the wind blowing "strange dark symphonies the while." Everyone expressed astonishment at Marianne's courage. "Fred seemed to regret very much that he had not gone down after me," she told Anna. "He said he could have carried me in his arms." To prove he could have, Fred went down at once after Eunice Macdaniel and brought her home, "taking her in his arms through the deepest banks."

Meanwhile Orvis, foreseeing difficulty for the carter, Salisbury, who was on his way home with a load of coal, had taken "a team of oxen, and benevolently set off to meet him, took a different road, went nearly five miles and back again, and then overtook him"—the carter—"at our bridge, where he had got fastened in the snow."

If Marianne had not been enthralled by Cabot, Orvis's staunchness on the night of the snowstorm would have shown her which of the two was more the man. Come March she was still too infatuated with Fred to let him leave Pilgrim House, to live in the Cottage, without protest. She would miss him in countless ways. He was always popping in and out of her room to perpetrate a pun or to do some kindly service.

When he was almost ready to move, Fred treated his intimates to cake and coffee in Amelia Russell's room "in honor of his departure." The party fell flat. Though Fred did his best, his jokes did not come off. "The Archon"—Mr. Ripley—sat plunged in moody silence. Whether Ripley knew of Cabot's attentions to Mary Lincoln of Hingham and dreaded the shock to Marianne, is not disclosed.

Marianne learned of their engagement on March second; and before she had rallied from the shock Fred was off to Boston to see his intended. Marianne gallantly sent her congratulations to Mary, adding there was no reason to be jealous of herself, Fred was just "a very angel of kindness" and would ever be one of her best friends.

"The fact is I have been under some excitement of feeling for a day or two past—a pleasant excitement I can't very well write about now, and perhaps it is this," she confided to Anna in somewhat scatter-brained mood, "which puts my ideas to such rapid flight."

Apparently, Fred Cabot's engagement caused Marianne to examine her own state of feeling toward him, and she was discovering, somewhat to her surprise, that she was really more interested in John Orvis. His very evident reciprocation already made it possible for Marianne to laugh with the rest when Charles Dana gravely announced a meeting of the "Rejected Lovers Sympathizing Group" to be held that evening in—of all places!—the nursery.

Yet it was not always easy to laugh off the jilt, and the next week found Marianne in bed with "a strong tendency to earache." Marianne had many visitors in her room, among them Fred, who found her "painting a picture frame of white wood" for him. The subject was Pegasus in the stable, surrounded with a wreath of oak and laurel leaves, acorns and berries. After talk, Fred read aloud. Working for Fred, Marianne reflected after his departure, had made the whole day pleasant. The occupation brought disquieting thoughts, as well. She could not make up her mind how she felt about his engagement. She found it impossible to think of Fred as married, as belonging to anyone. Though she tried not to think of herself at all, she feared that for a time, at least, he would belong less to herself. But she strove not to contemplate losing her good friend, whom heaven had sent to be her help and strength. Surely they would continue to influence one another?

At this point Marianne rebelled in terms that would have fulfilled Mr. Emerson's worst fears concerning the influence of Fourierism. "Why do people foolishly want to marry?" she asked Anna. "I am getting to think that Fourier is right, and in full harmony there will be no marriage—at least marriage will be a very different thing from what it now is."

The letter ends on a note of prayer for Fred's happiness, coupled with misgivings concerning Mary Lincoln's ability to provide "his truest help in his onward path." She, herself, could not imagine anything that she would not cheerfully sacrifice for the highest good and happiness of Fred Cabot.

If this be friendship, it is accompanied by a bruised heart.

6.

The Second Constitution was finally approved on March second; and on the twentieth an act—Chapter 169—to incorporate the Brook Farm Phalanx was enacted by the Senate and House of Representatives in General Court assembled, and approved by the Governor of the Commonwealth. The preamble was substantially the same as that of the First Constitution; but the articles were revised in accordance with the System of Association and the laws of Universal Unity as discovered by Charles Fourier. Another six weeks would pass before the Brook Farm Phalanx could be organized according to the new law.

The ensuing publicity brought an influx of visitors. Beds and table-seats became scarce again. But the Act of Incorporation did not always evoke favorable response among the Ripleys' old friends. One can readily imagine how Miss Peabody's quills would rise at sight of a package left in her charge addressed "C/O The Brook Farm Phalanx." In fact she shortly let it be known that her bookshop would no longer be available as a depot. Fortunately, another shop, Brown and Hastings, Corner of Warren Street, took over the chore within a few days and Miss Peabody's disengagement passed without a ripple of inconvenience.

7.

The Farmers had no time nor inclination for regret these balmy spring mornings. Their hearts, like the robins and phoebes, had begun to sing. As the mud dried up, "a whole tribe of carpenters" arrived to work on the phalanstery. Most exciting of all, Mr. Brisbane bestowed on Brook Farm the privilege of holding the official celebration of Fourier's Birthday. This year, for the first time, Fourierites throughout the world could rejoice—their great festival would be held in a phalanx! Instead of in some "Civilized" haunt such as Broadway's Apollo Saloon.

Marianne was praying that Anna and her sister, Helen, could come to Brook Farm for the celebration. Mr. Brisbane, who had waited upon Anna at the time of the January 1844 Convention, was counting on her presence, too. For Anna had been completely converted, at last, to associative principles, and the apostle of the cause felt her personal distinction was such that her presence at Brook Farm would constitute a valued endorsement of "the cause of humanity—the cause of God."

8.

Meanwhile some who had departed Brook Farm could not forget the idyll they had lived at Brook Farm from April 1841 to midsummer in 1843. In a hitherto unpublished letter, Georgiana Bruce wrote Sylvia and William Allen from Sing Sing, where she, for nearly two years now, had been working among the women prisoners. Although she diverged from some of the opinions which the Farmers now entertained, Georgie still dreamed about the place. "Only last week for instance I saw in a vision George Bradford hastening after you (William Allen) and the cows with more eagerness than he would have manifested for a sight of any royal dignitary." To one like herself "shut up with the spirits in prison," such recollections were refreshing indeed.

George William Curtis, who stayed at Brook Farm when Brisbane was helping to put through the Incorporation of the Phalanx, wrote

Hecker on March ninth (1845) that the unchanged aspect of the place
made him feel strange "to be here and not belong here." Yet Curtis
entertained no regrets, probably because during his visit Dwight had
insisted on reading aloud selections from Fourier's manuscript on the
Cosmogony. "Nature is very coy," Curtis commented slyly, "and she
was probably flirting coquettishly with the good Mr. Fourier."

George Bradford was another who could not detach his thoughts
from Brook Farm. Curtis returned to Concord without recent copies
of the *Phalanx*; Bradford was sorely disappointed; so much so that
Curtis wrote Dwight to forward them post haste. "Almira says," Curtis
added pungently, "that he"—Bradford—"is now in a Brook Farm way.
It is a species of chills and fever with him as you know."

9.

Fourier's birthday celebration more than fulfilled expectations. The
next day, April eighth, Marianne wrote Anna in rapturous vein. "You
would hardly have believed yourself in our old, smoky Hive, by some
magic transformed into an illumined garden." There were roses and
jasmines from the greenhouse against a curtain of evergreens, "sur-
mounted by the stately calla, the emblem of Unity, and around that
pillar, at the head of the table, the multiflora . . . twined its sweet
blossoms." The tables, "elegantly adorned with bread and fruit and
flowers, stood in the form of a cross. Their Unitary banner, striped with
the primary colors and edged with white, was "gracefully bestowed
across the windows." In the center of the decor, upon a pure azure
tablet, were inscribed the words "Universal Unity" arranged in a semicircle of glittering silver letters. At the opposite end of the room, across
the wall in largest letters of evergreen, "Fourier 1772, an anchor at the
left, and a bee hive, surrounded by bees, at the right." On a table in
front stood a bust of Charles Fourier, taken after his death. The
Farmers intended to have thrown the seven colors upon this, with a
prism, but it was "no-go by lamplight." There were other emblems,
many of them the work of William Cheswell, a carpenter. On one side-
wall hung a white lyre with seven strings of the seven rainbow colors,
representing the unity of sound. Upon the other hung a motto inscribed
and selected by Marianne herself: "But the Comforter, who is the Holy

Spirit, whom the Father will send in my name,—He shall teach you all things and bring all things to your remembrance whatsoever I have said unto you." Near this, on another tablet, was inscribed: *"Les Attractions Sont Proportionelles Aux Destinées."* The whole scene, Marianne concluded happily, "was beautiful; as John Allen said this morning, 'it was, together with the speeches, something that could not be put on paper.'"

This was as well, because, in allusion to the motto about the Comforter, this toast was given, "Fourier, the second coming of Christ." Indeed the whole tone of the proceedings as afterwards reported in the *Phalanx* has a blasphemous ring to Christian ears.

This report was signed "A Guest," but it undoubtedly was written by Brisbane in triumphant mood.

Shocking it is, to learn from the review of Ripley's speech in the same issue, that he was as far gone in Fourier-worship as any. George Ripley followed his tribute to Fourier with selected readings from the Old and New Testaments to prove that the "Sublime Harmonies" coincided with Fourier's Harmonies.

After a chant by the choir, Brisbane reminisced about sitting at the Master's feet—a privilege which he shared with no one present. Dwight discoursed on Universal Unity; and there were "Speeches and Sentiments" by Orvis, Cabot, Westcott, Ryckman, Allen, Shaw, and Macdaniel. Finally the company sang *Old Hundred* and went off to bed.

What Marianne was pleased to call "the dissipation of this Brook Farm life," continued for a day or so. An Association meeting was held. Also a small farewell party in honor of Mr. Brisbane, who would "leave a void here that must be felt until his return." Their Apostle, off for England, declared he would not be back until he could "come like a dove, with wings tipped with gold." The irrepressible Fred Cabot hoped that if Mr. Brisbane came like a dove he would bring golden eagles with him "whose bills would all be bank bills, and whose notes, notes of hand."

If one did not know for a fact that nothing alcoholic was drunk at Brook Farm, one might imagine that the Farmers got a little high at their parties, for after exaltation and bursts of punning a deep sadness would well up suddenly in their hearts. Then, despite the joy and beauty of their immediate surroundings, the more sensitive could scarcely bear to contemplate "the deep tragedy that must be going on in the soul, when one is living for a great idea."

On this occasion, Mr. Ripley advised all present to meet strongly "the inward untold suffering—of the pioneers of this movement," and to forget their individuality, or subdue it during "this transition state." They must, he added, at all costs keep alive their faith that such suffering would be but temporary.

Marianne wrote Anna that the party broke up that night when "the hour and their souls were at one," as Fred Cabot "significantly said."

Fourier's Birthday Festival, held on April seventh, 1845, at Brook Farm, marked the peak of confidence between the Farmers and Brisbane. Marianne's report reflects the general admiration for "the shining beauty of Mr. Brisbane's character. He is lost in the cause to which he is devoted, and in which he lives . . . So sweet and sad is he, so full of feeling and entire devotion to the cause of God and humanity that he has won our hearts."

Brisbane enjoyed his visit very much indeed. Although he would afterwards dismiss Brook Farm's failure along with that of sundry other "inadequate little attempts at Association," disclaiming all personal responsibility, many years later Brisbane admitted that Brook Farm's social life and festive gatherings were "far above anything heard in our legislative hall, or in the most gifted gatherings of our civilization." He recalled one evening "when addresses of a particularly interesting character had been made," Ripley turned to him on that occasion and exclaimed, " 'What a cathedral of mind!' "

10.

Sometime in April (1845), Minot Pratt piled his household goods on a wagon, and set out with Mrs. Pratt and their two boys for a farm in Concord which they had hired. Although the Pratts had raised no objections to grafting "Fourieristic variations upon the old life," Lindsay Swift says that in his letter of farewell, Pratt "could only express a hope—not a belief—that this attempt to live out the great and holy idea of Association for cooperation, might meet with final success." For the Ripleys, parting with the Pratts who had been with them since the beginning, this was another link severed.

Shortly after the Pratts' departure, Dana and Ryckman were appointed delegates to the Massachusetts General Court to accept the "Act to Incorporate the Brook Farm Phalanx" passed in March. When the new Charter came into effect on the first of May, everyone wondered how it would work. Marianne looked for much good—though they had "scarcely a perfect group on the place for want of more people." But presumably the phalanstery, when built, would solve the housing and numbers problem; and it was encouraging to see the building rise above the foundations which had been dug in the previous fall.

Everyone was not optimistic. Amelia Russell, for one, was in a most distrustful mood, "little satisfied with her actual state here." No doubt the treacherous New England spring had something to do with Amelia's fractiousness. Though the mornings dawned clear and sunny—"What awful horrible, cold, face-ache giving afternoons!"

11.

Robert Owen was welcomed as warmly to Brook Farm in its Industrial phase, as Alcott and Emerson were in the Transcendental years. Lewis Ryckman, active in the New England Workmen's Association, may well have been instrumental in bringing Owen to West Roxbury in May 1845.

Thirty-odd years before, in managing the mills at New Lanark on the Clyde, in Scotland, Owen combined sound business principles with genuine benevolence. "Character is formed by circumstances" was Owen's remedy for the evils of society; and he put this axiom to wise practice. To benefit the workers he installed schools and other institutions at New Lanark. The mills prospered for a decade. From 1814 to 1824 Owen's "discovery" attracted some two thousand visitors to New Lanark each year. Meanwhile he, as a reformer with practical vision, was patronized by the crowned heads of Europe, and respected as a prophet by his colleagues in the field of social reform.

Owen's belief that environment shaped character, was, of course, only half right. But in an age when little children were deprived of education and compelled to work in factories and in mines for longer hours than strong men work today, his teaching—that persons raised in this way were not responsible for their criminal tendencies—set men to thinking. Indeed, Owen's efforts to abolish child-labor for children under ten years, and to limit the working day to ten and a half hours for youngsters under eighteen, became so popular that Owen would have achieved political office had it not been for his extreme religious cynicism. Also, as time passed, continued public acclaim turned Owen's head. By 1825 he began to neglect the sound business principles, to which, together with the native thrift and industry of his Scotch workers, his initial success had been due. His indiscretions led many to regard the philanthropist as unfit for public office; and caused him to be defeated for Parliament three times.

Frustrated in the Old World, Owen began to dream of founding a Utopia in the New. Upon hearing, from some source in England, that the Rappites, in order to move west, wished to sell the village of Harmony which they had established on the Wabash, Owen bought the village sight unseen, and refounded it as New Harmony on a communistic constitution. His name still held such magic for success that hundreds of families flocked there. The village soon became overcrowded, and offspring communities sprang up all around. Attracted by the easy promise of the communistic constitution, which seemed to proffer house and land on easier terms than those granted the pioneer, all sorts of persons, many of them undesirable, hurried to New Harmony from far and near.

It is uncertain whether Owen, before he founded New Harmony, took over the communistic constitution from the Rappites, or whether he was toying with the ideas later held by Marx. In any case, Owen was now more occupied in hoping to influence nations. Local institutions and experiments interested him less and less, which explains the extraordinary mixture of lavishness and neglect which he bestowed on his "Colonists" at New Harmony.

Owen had made one brief visit to the Wabash, in 1825, twenty years before this visit to Brook Farm. Before setting out for the West, Owen lingered in Washington to speak before the Congress. Upon arrival at New Harmony, Owen liked his "Colony" so little that he quickly appointed a provisional government without looking up the reputation of his appointees. The needy adventurers gathered there soon overthrew Owen's government and quarreled among themselves.

Five years later, severed of his connections with New Harmony, Owen stood fleeced of some forty thousand pounds; and the behavior of those who administered the place had brought odium on his name.

Owen was no longer revered as a plutocrat or as a reformer when he visited Brook Farm. His great self-made fortune as well as his popularity in England had disintegrated. The greater part of what was left of the fortune, Owen already had bestowed on his two sons, keeping for himself a small annuity of some three hundred pounds; and for the past year he had made his home in the United States.

Marianne Dwight always had associated the name of Robert Owen with New Harmony, and not liked what she had heard. As it turned out she was agreeably surprised by Mr. Owen's beautiful spirit and infinite benevolence. At seventy-four he was still active and energetic with a pleasant word for everyone, and a kiss or a pat on the head for a child.

During his visit, Owen lectured twice. Though the Farmers differed from him both in the theory and practice of "Socialism," they shared the same object, the betterment of man, and so met on common ground. What Owen told them of his "experiment at New Lanark on the Clyde, in Scotland, which he carried on with two thousand persons for thirty years, and then left in the care of others," was most interesting. "These people," Marianne wrote Anna, "were of the very dregs of society when he took them . . . Now they are mentioned in statistics, as being the most moral population of Great Britain." Owen's boast concerning New Lanark is slightly shocking in view of his denial of responsibility for the failure at New Harmony. He attributed the various excesses of the New Harmonites to the "direction of persons who knew not his principles."

At the conclusion of Mr. Owen's final discourse, Mr. Ripley rose and paid Mr. Owen "a very handsome tribute," inviting him to return to Brook Farm whenever he could, and "proposing 'Robert Owen' as a sentiment," in the wish that he might "always enjoy in his own mind that sublime happiness that will one day be the portion of the human race."

Mr. Owen in turn expressed himself much pleased with their experiment, though he confessed wonder at their success.

In this twentieth century when Communism threatens our western civilization, it seems strange that Fourierism, which is now unheard of and practically extinct except for minor manifestations, should have swept the imagination of many in the United States. Why did Brisbane succeed in propagating Fourierism, when Owen failed with Communism? Arthur E. Bestor, Jr., in his treatise, *Fourierism in the United States of America*, expresses the opinion that Communism made slow headway in this country because its doctrine of class struggle found slight echo in the experience of a people largely unaccustomed to class lines. On the level of the spirit, Fourier was more congenial to Americans. Owen planned an environment in which man's character would be molded for him; Fourier designed a community in which man's individuality would have even fuller scope than was to be found in a free democracy.

12.

Early in May the *Phalanx* announced that it and the *Social Reformer*, John Allen's recent publication in Maine, would merge in *Harbinger*, to be published simultaneously in New York and West Roxbury. The new Fourieristic organ would be "devoted to Social and Political Progress," bearing the motto, "All things at this present day stand provided and prepared and await the light." The first issue was scheduled for June.

On May twenty-fifth, the last issue of Brisbane's mouthpiece, the *Phalanx*, printed in full the constitution of the newly established Brook Farm Phalanx; and on the cover stood a vigorous ink drawing of the "smoky old Hive." The articles, written by Dwight the previous February, conformed closely to Fourier's system of distribution of profits according to Groups and Series. Sufficient to say that after expenses should have been paid, Capital would receive but one-third of these, and Labor two-thirds.

Of late, reports of failure elsewhere persisted. Two more great phalanxes were falling into dissension and debt. Both the Sylvania and Clarkson had failed the year before; and the best that could now be said of the Ohio was that the reports of failure which had gone the round of the papers were premature; and of the Clement, it "still lives and is in a fair way of going on successfully." Panic—and panic was in the wind—spelled death to the "Movement." Associonists everywhere looked to their leaders to refute their misgivings, especially to those at Brook Farm who were known to be men of high character and ability.

At this critical juncture, Charles A. Dana followed Brisbane's policy and used the *Phalanx* to put the inefficient in their place. "We wish to repeat most emphatically," Dana admonished, "what we have already said again and again; that we do not hold ourselves responsible (in the smallest degree) for the success of these feeble efforts . . . An Association can not be founded without certain conditions, and if foolish and shiftless people undertake to do without these conditions, we can only regret it. . . ."

13.

But—June was come! The singing of the birds was really bewildering. It made one almost dizzy with the sweetness of harmony. Never was the garden around them "so blooming, so freshly green, in every way so inviting." Wild geranium, lady's-slipper, Solomon's seal, dogwood, trientalis, and what was wholly new to Marianne—yellow violets streaked with purple—all were springing from the earth "in such haste and abundance as to tell of infinite treasures beneath."

Marianne longed to go gathering delicate little blossoms on Cow Island—models for the "flower portraits" she loved to paint on fans and lampshades. But her Fancy Group was in great need of help. She deeply resented the claims of such indoor tasks. "What means this word duty?" she demanded. "If duty be not attraction, I don't believe in it."

Marianne and Mrs. Ripley agreed that if Anna could come to Brook Farm and work for the Fancy Group, her work would pay her board. Yet neither could deny that Anna was extremely useful to them in Boston. She had placed several orders for "a zephyr shawl"; and Anna's success in selling subscriptions to the *Harbinger* was astonishing. Marianne prayed that "great good may grow out of the means thus put into our hands"—means to spread the word.

Mr. Ripley, Marianne reported, had to be away a great part of the time, conferring with the New York leaders about the publication of the *Harbinger,* and other matters pertaining to Association. She reflected the Farmers' pride that Mr. Ripley was now the accepted leader of the Movement on a national basis. All the New York Fourierites of note—except Godwin—would return with him shortly to attend Brook Farm's Summer Festival.

George William Curtis sent his reply to the invitation by the hand of Emerson's friend, Edmund Hosmer. The farmer-philosopher had looked down his nose at the Farmers' agricultural technique, but it now appears that Mr. Hosmer, like almost everyone else who had the opportunity, enjoyed Brook Farm parties. "Mr. Hosmer just tells me that he is going to Brook Farm," Curtis wrote Dwight, "and I must say a word of regret that I could not come at this time, as Mr. Ripley, whom I saw in Boston, asked me to do. I have no doubt that the essence of all good things that are said, I shall gather from you some day, somehow. I send my subscription to the *Harbinger*. Almira is well, and would send you love and flowers if she knew that Mr. Hosmer was going."

This was to be their last festival—or the last one worth recording. And the Farmers, fond as ever of *tableaux vivants*, rendered "group after group worthy of Raphael or Canova." There were child-angels and madonnas. William Channing and Marianne's brother, John Dwight stood out, "beautiful like angels." Indeed "all the people, yes, our common every day people here, were transformed into beautiful beings, beautiful beyond the sculptor's art."

At the feast, everyone who spoke—the Brook Farm leaders, and James Freeman Clarke—spoke as if "inspired."

Such a day, Marianne felt, did not belong to the calendar but became one of the eternal days. Immediately afterward it seemed far off in antiquity, yet it stood out vivid and bright, a day of enchantment never to be forgotten.

14.

The first issue of the *Harbinger*, which described itself as "a weekly newspaper for the examination and discussion of the great questions in social science, politics, literature and the arts, which command the attention of all believers in the progress and elevation of humanity," appeared on June fourteenth.

In politics, the editors announced, their policy would be non-partisan, warning the people "against the demagogue who would cajole them by honeyed flatteries, no less than against the devotee of mammon, who would make them his slaves."

There was no limit to the reforms the *Harbinger* would champion: ". . . the complete emancipation of the enslaved . . . , genuine temperance . . . , and the elevation of the toiling and downtrodden everywhere." Quite a program, plus Fourierism.

In literature, as well, the editors would exercise a firm and impartial criticism. True to their policy they at once offered the first installment —in translation by Francis G. Shaw—of George Sand's *Consuelo*. This was a bold move because the author's many love affairs with talented and famous men had given her name a scandalous ring in American ears. Indeed, the reviewer—and it reads as if written by Ripley— admitted candidly that the reason the novel had not reached the American public before was because of "something erratic and bizarre in the author's way of living, and to a certain undeniable tone of wild defying freedom in her earlier writings . . . an attitude of more than modest resistance to the conventions" and "the soul-killing and enslaving bonds, under which woman especially has pined."

There were to be also regular "Cultural Features"—the "Musical Review" by Dwight or Curtis; poems by such outstanding American poets as Lowell and Whittier. The treats would be balanced by economic studies. One of these shows that at that time the machine was feared as "a threat to livelihood unless controlled."

The last of the *Harbinger's* sixteen pages—each containing three columns of small type—usually would present the reports on other phalanxes and events pertaining to social reform such as "The First Annual Meeting of the Working Men's Association."

George Ripley's pride and satisfaction when he beheld the first copy fresh off the press must have been great. From the cover to the back, which gave the various terms of subscription—$2.00 a year, or $1.00 for six months payable invariably in advance; ten copies . . . supplied for $1.50—the magazine was essentially George Ripley's own creation. Although the names of the other contributors published in this first issue make an impressive list—Godwin, Channing, Brisbane, Macdaniel, and Greeley, from New York; Brook Farmers Dana, Dwight, Ryckman, Allen; and Shaw of West Roxbury—the *Harbinger* as time went on would be moulded more by Ripley than by anyone else on the staff. Besides the articles Ripley would contribute, and the editorials he and Dana would write together, the entire contents would be subject to his approval. The first scholar of the Harvard Class of 1823 had often regretted lack of opportunity—since the demise of *The Dial*—to comment on "Books from our friends." "But now we have a paper of our own," Ripley exulted, "in which we may write and yet not cease to build . . . Now it shall be a real pleasure to break the silence which has indeed weighed heavily upon us."

15.

In a letter to Hecker the previous October, Burrill Curtis made it painfully clear that he found correspondence with Isaac a bore since the latter's conversion to Catholicism. Like many a convert, Hecker became an ardent proselytizer. "The reason my letters are so short," Burrill retorted bluntly, "is that what feeling is betwixt us is so much in sentiment and has seemed so insecure to me in that, that I have not had many things to say."

Although Burrill's personality is more elusive than that of George William, the critic and man of letters, it is clear that Burrill was as much the cultivated and talented man of the world as his brother. As such, both young men found zealotry in any form slightly absurd. Even Dana, since Isaac's conversion to Roman Catholicism, grew increasingly disquieted by Hecker's sudden assumption that every other credo was a heresy. But Charles was loath to lose a once close and still dear friend. So when Hecker made inquiry for a young student who wished to enter college, Dana replied at length.

His letter begins on a note of apology for having failed to answer Isaac's "letter of last winter," and continues wistfully, "Separated as we inevitably are by circumstances from those we early learn to love, we, or at least I, do not consent willingly to any new withdrawals, and cling to the last to every tie which unites me to former dear friends, even after the main bond has parted."

After these preliminaries, Dana dared to point out that unfortunately the aim of the Associonists in no way contravened the aspirations of liberal Christianity. "The Church rules in spiritual matters," Dana asserted, "but does not, if my impression is correct, lay down any formula for the Organization of Labor or for the distribution of profits, anymore than for calculating the eclipses of the moon." Yet, surely such important temporal concerns could not be a matter of indifference to the Church? "But perhaps," Dana continued, "you will say that it is not this part of our doctrine that you object to"— the economic part—"but only our ulterior philosophy? As to this,"

Dana admitted, "we are not entirely agreed among ourselves, but if we were and set forth a false doctrine, the Church ought not to refuse the really beneficial and true discoveries we offer, any more than she ought to anathematize an improvement in the steam engine made by an infidel."

Perhaps Dana might have let the old argument drop had he known that Hecker, as recently as June twenty-fifth, had decided to become a priest. The decision had been pending for almost a year. After his baptism by Bishop McClosky on August first, 1844, Hecker, attracted by the idea of life in a religious community, had applied for admission into the Redemptorist Order, a society of priests in charge of the German congregations in New York. He was admitted and, since then, confirmed, adding Thomas to his name in honor of Saint Thomas Aquinas; and now Hecker was preparing to sail for Belgium where he would begin his novitiate at Saint Trond.

"I do not think we shall ever agree in faith, dear Isaac," Dana wrote in summing up, "but it is not less certain that we agree in aim and hope. Each may pursue what the other may deem mistaken or even hurtful means, but we cannot ever do each other any injustice, I am sure."

Dana's reasoning seems sound to Protestants, but as concerned Hecker it was as futile as hammering on a bolted iron door. Perhaps Dana sensed as much, for in closing he mentioned the only means of communication between them that remained open. "I am glad you see the *Harbinger* * and hope you subscribe to it," he wrote in conclusion. "So great a tie as that between yourself and Brook Farm ought still to be maintained. I shall write for it with more pleasure if I know that my words, poor and mistaken as they may be, are not unseen by my friends. As the world goes, the *Harbinger* is, I think, a good paper. So much praise I do not fear to give it even to you."

16.

In July the circulation of the *Harbinger* reached one thousand, and the editors also could boast they were received by an entirely friendly

* This letter has been wrongly dated by the copyist "1844"—the mention of the *Harbinger* proves that it must have been written after the publication of that journal.

press. They owed this popularity to the calibre of their contributors in the cultural field. Brilliant contributors excited interest in the paper apart from social reform.

Other than the thrill of launching the *Harbinger*, the summer of 1845 proved dullish. Work was begun on the phalanstery, but progress was slow. The carpenters, affected perhaps by the midsummer mugginess, quarreled among themselves. More discouraging still, the plan of the phalanstery pleased no one but Rogers—the builder who had designed it. Though at some distance from the Eyrie, the phalanstery was placed right in front of that building, nearly parallel with the town road. From the Eyrie, it presented one hundred and seventy-five feet of bleak wooden clapboarding and gaping window holes. Some among them dreaded the day when its parlors, reading and reception rooms, general assembly hall, dining room, kitchen and bakery, all designed for common use, would be swarming with some three hundred persons, recruited from the ranks of the "swart and sweaty artisans." To add to their disquietude, Mr. Brisbane, who arrived to deliver another series of lectures on Fourier, never tired of pointing out that their phalanstery was a sorry compromise with the grandiose plans Fourier had had drawn up by leading French architects. Even the Boston papers made fun, likening the phalanstery to an Ant Hill, and calling the Farmers "Fury-ites" in print.

Meanwhile, Ripley and Dana were being importuned by Hawthorne, who demanded further payment on the capital he had invested in the Brook Farm Institute in May 1841. Until recently Mr. Hawthorne had behaved with consideration. But he now had a wife and a growing family to support, and really needed the money he had saved when a clerk in the Boston Customs Office. The Brook Farm Directors felt that any substantial payment of their debt to Mr. Hawthorne would make it impossible to complete their phalanstery. And how could they ever become solvent, unless they enlarged their personnel? It was a vicious circle—an inharmonious circle.

17.

Mr. Brisbane would remain through July, to instruct the Farmers in "The Extension of Fourier's System of the Passionate Harmonies to the Planetary Universe." He would later—in his *Mental Biography*, dictated to his wife, Redalia—deny that he had ever accepted this part of Fourier's doctrine. But at this time he was confident that his translations from hitherto unpublished Fourier manuscripts would enable the Associative School in the United States to obtain "a clear view of the science of Universal Unity, and to establish their doctrines upon a strictly scientific foundation."

The Farmers proved hard to convince concerning the mating of the stars and the propagation of weird creatures. Brisbane's scientific students demanded more proof than was forthcoming. "Fourier," Marianne observed, "if he knew the serial law, has given us not much more than his assertion for it."

The Organization of Labor interested them far more. Ripley, Brisbane, Dana, and others all went off to Woburn to attend the Working Men's Convention; and Marianne's "two Johns"—Dwight and Orvis—were much in demand as lecturers. Sometimes, in spite of their championing the cause of labor, they confessed to having experienced a mixed reception.

Marianne herself, like Georgie Bruce and Ora Gannett before her, was trying not to mind being thrown into close association with the humble artisan."Mr. and Mrs. Monday have come," she announced, and added with forced enthusiasm, "tailors and of the better looking sort of people."

Marianne wrote more freely of her discontent to Amelia Russell, at home in Milton; and confessed that in order to escape the influx of lowly persons, she often painted alone in her room. Marianne did not find this very agreeable.

Amelia was one of the Fancy Group, and her reply of July eleventh opened with a discussion of orders for fans and lampshades which she was forwarding to Marianne. Amelia, too, commented sadly on the change of company at the phalanx; "What you tell me of our household does not make me quicken my footsteps home—and were it not for you and Fanny I should feel sad enough. You know I always hated the house and all that in the least reconciled me to it was its inmates; and now there seems scarce a pleasure left for me in Brook-farm. That society as it now exists, needs sadly a new organization, there needs no Fourier to tell me, for I have seen and felt it for years, else why would I be at Brook-farm at all? But I cannot yet be fully convinced that we have found the remedy. I try to believe we have, and I have thought much since I have been here, and have longed for someone to dispel my doubts and to whom I could cry with my whole heart, Help my unbelief! Indeed this is my state, I most earnestly wish to believe with you all, but there is something which draws me back. I think there is much real enthusiasm in some, but much that is false in others. (This is *entre nous*.) And this last has somewhat pulled me back. If all were true about me my faith would be much strengthened in the reality of our system; and you know how much happened before I left to shake my faith in some I had trusted. Notwithstanding my own uncertainty I lecture most learnedly to the uninitiated; and you would laugh to hear how well I talk. I am quite astonished myself!"

Amelia's letter ended in the hope that Marianne would write to her soon and strengthen her faith—for Marianne had strength to spare, these days. Marianne was buoyed up by John Orvis's devotion, both to herself and to the cause. She scarcely thought of Fred Cabot any more—except to report her slight sense of shock on learning that his brother, Frank Cabot, had left home to go on a whaling voyage before the mast—"a sad thing for his family."

Though Marianne declared, "There is no end to the company and the work," her letters took on a drowsy midsummer pace of borning babies and "corn waving on the hills"—if the gentle slopes that rise above Brook Farm could be so dignified? The event that aroused the most interest occurred in August—Anna Parsons' "reading" of Fourier's character from a specimen of his handwriting. Presumably this was loaned to Anna for the purpose by Brisbane, the only one among them who had ever corresponded with the Master. The exciting result satisfied Mr. Brisbane—and what was less important, but also pleasing, it intrigued Mr. Channing.

The occasion proved most extraordinary. Anna was conscious "of the visible presence of Fourier" in the room during the reading. She reported that he stayed with her some time. She could not give any idea of his presence in words, but it was very real to her. "And her communion with him," Marianne wrote her brother, Franklin Dwight, "by question and answer, as real as any communion she has with any living person."

Anna's notes were not entirely flattering to their prophet. She had found Fourier a very difficult character to read . . . He was more intellectual than spiritual . . . Not wholly pure; and this lack of purity was due to "the ineradicable effects of sin." Fourier had made her laugh, though she was sure he was far from gay. He brought the laugh of the insane to mind . . . "Would not he do," she wondered, "things perfectly unaccountable? Vile almost—satanic?"

In the appendix to Marianne Dwight's *Letters from Brook Farm* there are some ten pages of these "readings" of Fourier's character by Anna Parsons; most of them read like the meanderings of a drunken person or a medium. Yet, oddly enough, they have the authentic Fourier ring, his own peculiar genius for the ludicrous pomposity; as when he assured Anna, "We shall not always eat so incoherently— but shall eat musically, harmoniously."

"Of the dark, the horrible, the demoniacal period of Fourier's life," alluded to by Anna, Brisbane assured the Farmers he knew all. These excesses had occurred during the French Revolution. Fourier, Brisbane explained, "joined the military, and gave himself up recklessly to the vices of the soldiery." This sinning had produced ineradicable scars. Anna, though Brisbane questioned her again and again, steadily refused to analyze this part of Fourier's character on the grounds "that something would be revealed more terrible than her strength could bear."

Fascinated by "that dark period" in Fourier's life, some of the Farmers were moved to make extraordinary comparisons. "Saint-Simon," Marianne recalled, "did likewise." Mr. Kay went so far as to presume the Jesus must have had such an experience; for He could not have become the greatest of saints unless He had previously been the greatest of sinners.

This sample of the free thinking current at Brook Farm indicates why the sophisticated mocked and the orthodox shuddered. Marianne called this type of discussion, "These good talks"; and she swam happily along in the current of Fourieristic speculation.

Although he had not yet avowed his love, Marianne was deeply interested in John Orvis, an almost fanatical Associonist. No one could have been more opposite to her former flame, Fred Cabot, than this son of Hicksite Quakers from Vermont. Orvis was so reserved that she referred to him as "the veil"; and she strove to make her own bearing toward him as impenetrable as his with her. "I resist because that is in my nature, and I yield when I can't help it," she confessed, and then fell to worrying lest their mutual attraction existed only in her imagination.

As so often happens when a girl is in love and beloved, her radiance attracted other admirers. Before he left for his home in Batavia, New York, Mr. Brisbane paid her the compliment of discussing her as a

"problem." Her nature depended too much on sympathy, he said—
which, of course, she well knew! In future she must strive to stand
alone.

Christopher P. Cranch visited Brook Farm in the latter part of
August, and he, too, singled Marianne out for attention—sitting beside
her at table, coming to her room every day to paint. She became
"nearer to him in spirit than heretofore."

But it was William Henry Channing who spoke most plainly and
truly to her soul. ". . . What strength and courage and hope and
faith he has given me," she wrote Anna. "He is the sunshine, the dew
from heaven, the healthful air in which the bud loves to unfold itself
and feels that it may become a flower fit for paradise."

Mr. and Mrs. Channing were often at Brook Farm that summer,
because he was contemplating taking over Theodore Parker's Spring
Street Church in West Roxbury on a permanent basis. At the end
of August Mr. Channing gave the Farmers "a pictorial sermon, a
sketch of a temple of worship to be raised here on Brook Farm, as
he saw it in his mind's eye." Afterward, "many present prayed he
would join the Phalanx and become its first minister." Mr. Channing's
ideal temple was to be circular in form, lighted from above, with
pictures of Jesus from Nativity to Resurrection, and a white marble
altar. From that temple, music would rise perpetually to heaven,
and there would always be flowers.

Mrs. Channing, who was not strong, was opposed to joining the
Brook Farm Phalanx. No doubt she must have sensed, also, that
her frail, refined husband was not really suited to close association
with the artisan whose unjust lot he sought so earnestly to improve;
and that it would be far better for him to be a neighbor of Brook
Farm—if he decided to take over the Spring Street Church in West
Roxbury come the New Year—without being of it.

Miss Peabody, foremost among Channing's followers, did not want
him to associate himself with either the Church or the Phalanx. She
wrote Anna Parsons, "I admire and enjoy the spiritual character of
William's project of identifying his name with Parker in the pulpit,
and yet I regret that it should be so, since he really differs essentially
in views, and is of a much higher spiritual character than Parker, who,
while he knows far less than William of the doctrine of life, is far
less docile and more the slave of his own instinctive character. I feel
that perils and snares beset them both around, but that Parker is less
aware of, and so less secure from 'the traitor in the heart.' But William

will do good there, perhaps as he could not were he to minister to the
world. The world is too earnest to understand William. These people
at West Roxbury in and around Brook Farm, are full of errors and
in great danger from 'the traitor in the heart'—but they are not
frivolous and their eyes are open to such spiritual beauty as clothes
William Channing as with a garment. I feel that William is the
Lord's beloved, and the Lord leadeth his beloved in a way they
know not."

The end of September brought "a shaking up . . . a little sifting
out" at Brook Farm. Deep and important questions were agitated.
Some left, "who ought to leave—the selfish." One who went they were
sorry to lose—Ryckman, a real loss to the *Harbinger*.

Financial anxiety turned the nobler spirits to harder work and
increasing interest in spiritual matters. The ferment made the time
exactly right for a religious revival; and it happened that Mr. Channing considered Brook Farm the ideal spot from which to launch the
religious crusade that he was meditating, to be founded on Christian
Socialism.

On the evening of October fifth, Marianne reported to Anna,
"W.H.C. came in one of his brightest moods, . . . and preached
gloriously at the street"—the Spring Street Church in West Roxbury.
Brisbane and a Mr. Grant, an occasional visitor from the Ohio Phalanx,
were staying at Brook Farm; and in the afternoon an informal meeting
was held there, at which W. H. Channing launched his crusade.
He said he was determined not to give "the lead to the priesthood,"
that he thought "the prophets, they who are inspired with deep
true feeling must lead." He also wanted a place at Brook Farm
"concentrated to worship; and they talked of taking for the purpose
a large room in the phalanstery, one which would be ready soon,
before the building should be finished." Some wanted worship every
morning, some general discussion. All wanted music, prayer, and
instruction. Marianne envisioned a beautiful temple divided into
various sanctums, surrounding a large central hall, "where all may gather
when inspired with a universal sentiment—the Hall of Unity—and
there give utterance to it."

Two weeks slipped by before she wrote Anna of "our Eyrie meeting," held October twelfth; "Channing gave us a very fine address,
speaking of the three aspects of Association, the economical, the social,

the religious; dwelling especially upon the last, he expressed his deep conviction that without the religious element no attempt at Association could possibly succeed; and then he spoke particularly with much warmth and enthusiasm, much beauty and eloquence, of the religious movement now taking place here."

At the price of omitting a few who were genuinely interested, Mr. Channing appointed a committee of seven to make the arrangements for worship; himself and Messrs. Dwight, Shaw, and Monday the tailor. The women were Mrs. Ripley, Fanny Macdaniel, and Marianne herself. This committee met directly after tea, and acted very fast. Mr. Channing and Mr. Shaw would arrange with Mr. Rogers, the builder, to have a large room in the phalanstery finished off by Christmas as a consecrated place of worship.

The women would make the room as beautiful as possible, and they hoped to raise money for the purpose by subscription. Mr. Channing proposed to send out from Boston such books as they might need, notably a recent work by his friend James Freeman Clarke, and the Swedenborgian ritual or book of worship. Clarke had ever shared Channing's dislike of sectarianism and "dead forms," and Swedenborgianism was attracting many of the more mystically inclined among them.

After the meeting the committee visited about at the Eyrie and Pilgrim House; and at ten they all went to Mr. Brisbane's quarters for a "coffee party."

Sophia Ripley welcomed William Channing's revival with enthusiasm, feeling happier in her conscience than at any time since the conversion to Fourierism. Schooled as a child in the doctrine of the natural depravity of man, Mrs. Ripley could not readily accept Fourier's assumption that evil came from the repression of man's natural impulses. Reared in an atmosphere of refinement, possessed of a religious nature, Sophia Ripley found it refreshing—after the gloomy prognostications of the baleful Brisbane—to join hands with a few discerning souls and dedicate their mutual endeavor to Universal Unity. It added to her satisfaction in the revival to know that all those who might have come to scoff would have stayed away. For who would dare to mock at William Channing?

Meanwhile, her husband, George Ripley, whose name together with those of Wolcott, Allen, Orvis, and Kleinstrup, would soon be added to the Religious Committee, accepted Channing's revival; but, having done so, preferred to leave it alone. Although he heartily concurred in the Christian Socialists' renunciation of priest and creed, and endorsed their faith in love, truth, and charity, Ripley, since resigning from his pulpit in the Purchase Street Church, had done with such discussions. Recently, in the *Harbinger*, Ripley had delegated all articles on religious matters to Channing—taking over, himself, matters pertaining to this world rather than the world to come.

To the ladies' delight, Mr. Channing's mastery of the social graces equalled his spiritual grace; and when, on the following Saturday, they held a dance, Mr. Channing danced with such grace and vivacity that each of his partners always became the object of envy because she seemed to be "the most beautiful, the most hearty, the most loving woman in the company."

"The Archon," but lately returned from the National Convention of Reformers in New York, and the Industrial Congress which followed it, and George William Curtis, who had driven over from Concord, were in high spirits at the party. Everyone enjoyed "a merry time."

By the end of October, as Hawthorne noted, everywhere "save where there are none but pine trees," the leaves "rustle beneath the tread—and there is nothing more autumnal than that sound." Yet, on this October twenty-fifth—as when Hawthorne had walked there three years before—two oak trees that grew close to the huge Pulpit Rock, so close "the portions of their trunks appeared to grasp the rough surface" overshadowed the gray crag with glossy green leaves; while the other oaks, the scrub, had only a streak of green left here and there amid "their rustling and russet."

On this Sunday morning after the dancing party, the sun slanted down through the green canopy, kindling in those who stood below Mr. Channing a sustaining sense of warmth, a feeling of shelter and comfort. Those who drank in his eloquence felt their hearts expanding with love for God and man. When W. H. Channing preached, emotion prevailed, to be sure. He also infused the lofty spiritual element, dear to New England hearts, into the Farmers' social plans.

After his moving sermon, Mr. Channing, still mounted on Pulpit Rock, invoked the blessing. When he had done, he descended and they all joined hands in a great circle on the leaf-strewn sward, to "unite in prayer that we might be earnest and true to each other."

Every person there, Mr. Channing declared, was privileged to belong to their band.

Sophia Ripley, perhaps more than anyone present, felt deeply grateful. Picture that always busy lady walking home through the Piney Woods slowly; and on nearing the Hive perhaps dallying for a moment to savor the beauty of the purple gentians blooming late in the cool dell of the brook. Whether she lingered in the October twilight or hurried on to supervise tea, the elation she had experienced at the Rock lingered on and into the next day. George William Curtis wrote Dwight from Concord of meeting her in Boston, "I was glad to see Mrs. Ripley last Monday, and to hear from her the result of your Sunday meeting."

As a rule Curtis was sceptical of such fluid forms of worship, believing the permanent forms sprang "from a very deep piety, and the pious persons I know I could count on my hands." But such themes were too good for "heel taps to a letter" and he would await the issue of their movement with a great deal of interest. But it is clear that Curtis was more interested in what the movement promised to do for Mrs. Ripley and his other Brook Farm friends, than what it might accomplish for mankind in general. Curtis sent Mrs. Ripley his love, by Dwight, and the hope that "the whole winter will not pass without my hearing from her."

One can feel how he dreaded the miseries in store for Sophia Ripley and his beloved Brook Farm. It seems almost as if Curtis had a foreboding that this "Sunday of Peace and Promise" was to be the last happy occasion he would ever share with the Farmers.

18.

The *Harbinger's* honeymoon with the national press ended within a few weeks—when the *New York Courier and Enquirer* attacked the cause of Association. Editors of the *Harbinger* retorted tartly in their next issue, declaring that the New York paper's fire in reality was a smear attempt to demolish the political career of Horace Greeley. Since Greeley's authority as a powerful advocate of Whig principles could not be questioned, his enemies accused him of rousing class hatred and sowing the seed of infidelity by means of Fourierism.

In truth, Greeley had proved himself a stouter champion of the cause than any of the other New York leaders. Since January, Greeley had shown far more aggression against adverse criticism than Brisbane. Instead of dismissing all responsibility for the failures of the "hastily founded" and "inadequately prepared" phalanxes, Greeley kept the columns of the *Tribune* filled with encouraging reports from those western phalanxes that had not begun to feel the blight of panic; and when his readers urged him to renounce Association because it could never work and should be discouraged before any more persons fell victim to it, he replied stoutly that the highest earthly interests of the human race were to be found in Association, and in Association only. The fact was, Greeley had espoused Fourierism for want of a better social system. As he expressed it, "With an industrial war plainly threatened and partially commenced, the doctrine of Association appears as mediator and reconciler."

Both Greeley and Brisbane, however, lately had begun to be more interested in promoting the North American Phalanx at Red Bank, New Jersey, than in Brook Farm. Brisbane served as delegate commissioned to select the site; and both he and Greeley subscribed funds. In little over a year—the North American was settled in August 1844—the New Jersey Phalanx had caught up with Brook Farm in prosperity, and overtaken the latter in the affections of its founders. This was natural. The site was only forty miles from New York City, and the North American was the New York Fourierites' own project, as Brook Farm would always be the Ripleys'.

The Farmers, however, so often told that they stood in the vanguard, failed to take into account the growing attraction of their New Jersey rival. They fancied themselves secure because Brisbane and Greeley seemingly continued to look to them for intellectual leadership and practical experience. The circumstance that the *Harbinger* was published at Brook Farm confirmed the Farmers' belief, for was not their organ representative of the national movement?

>>>>>>>>>>>>>>>>>><<<<<<<<<<<<<<<<

Disaster Strikes

SMALLPOX BROKE OUT AT BROOK FARM EARLY IN NOVEMBER. JOHN ALLEN'S
little boy, Fred, caught it from a man-servant while staying with his
aunt and uncle, Mr. and Mrs. George C. Leach, in Boston. The
Leaches had withdrawn from the community in 1843 to open a
Grahamite hotel in Boston, and Mrs. Leach, a stout abolitionist,
varied the monotony of vegetarian life by harboring runaway slaves.
Perhaps she was too absorbed in her underground activities to pay
proper attention to her own household. In any case she did not recognize the dreaded variole on the servant when she saw it; and as Allen
had not had his motherless child vaccinated the little boy contracted
the disease. Unfortunately the nature of Fred's malady was not discovered until after his return to Brook Farm.

A quarantine was set up. The boy was promptly removed to the
Cottage, which was turned into a hospital, the former inmates taking
refuge in "our elastic Pilgrim House." Already it was too late. The
damage was done. Furthermore, the Farmers kept right on exposing
one another out of ignorance or sheer obstinacy.

Marianne was one of the recalcitrants. She seems to have regarded
the regulations as a trap to imprison herself and her sister, Fanny.
Unfortunately, Fanny came down with "one of her colds"—and a
cold, it was known, constituted one of the preliminary symptoms of

the varioloid. Amelia Russell and Fanny Macdaniel flew into a panic and made such a "muster" they frightened many into thinking Fanny Dwight had contracted the disease. Mr. Ripley, distraught, ordered the cold-sufferer to be sent to the pest house. At this, Marianne was up in arms. She told Mr. Ripley to his face that his request was "ridiculous, nonsensical, and unreasonable." If Fanny had definite symptoms, she should gladly let her sister go. But not for a cold. Mr. Ripley saw that this was perhaps reasonable. Fanny was put in quarantine only, and Marianne along with her.

Again Marianne protested. To quarantine a well person was manifestly absurd! She had to give in, but she did not cooperate. Some folks, she informed Anna complacently, "would come in,"—to her room—"in spite of the quarantine, and then I've been to walk in the phalanstery corridor." The next day Marianne went boldly down to the Hive for dinner. "Mr. and Mrs. Ripley looked in consternation," she confessed, "but not a word was said."

When one considers that Marianne was a doctor's daughter, trained in hygiene—or what passed for hygiene in those days—and that this smallpox was hideous and permanently disfiguring to the countenance and that patients frequently died of it, her behavior seems foolhardy indeed. She simply did not choose to "apprehend that the disease will spread here to any extent." She even expressed the hope that Anna would visit them in the near future. She predicted the worst that would result from these precautions—"the Cottage might get populous with cold victims."

Mr. Ripley did not allow her insubordination to go unrebuked. Marianne, still recalcitrant, wrote Anna on November eleventh an account of their tiff: ". . . and now for a little more fun, tho' I am heartily sick of the nonsense." Mr. Ripley had taken her to task for going about and endangering people. She talked back and defied his judgment. "Many people are beginning to laugh at the panic," she informed him. The panic, in Marianne's opinion "had all been got up by a few."

By the evening of the thirteenth, Marianne had changed her tune. The Cottage was filling up with unmistakable victims of the varioloid. Others were contracting the disease, especially in Pilgrim House— and to her credit, Marianne could not find it in her heart to neglect the sick who were under the same roof as she.

Medical care was traditional in the Dwight family. Seventy-year-old Dr. Dwight, though still shaky from the feverish cold which competed with the varioloid and confused the quarantine authorities, tottered about, administering aid to the sick with no one to help him but young Dr. Stimpson from West Roxbury. At the peak of the epidemic they had twenty cases in the Cottage at one time. Yet somehow, between them, the two overworked doctors managed to keep everyone of the thirty-odd victims—even Mrs. Palisse who had contracted a very severe case—alive.

Thirty sick, out of a total of some ninety persons, constituted a crippling epidemic. When the worst was over, Marianne admitted to Anna that in the pecuniary way they had suffered a severe setback. Many of the new people had fled in terror. "The state of things here is strange, and in some of its aspects, deeply sad,—and yet a general cheerfulness prevails." All things considered, Marianne Dwight was astonished they got along as nicely as they managed to do. Had they known three weeks ago that this disease would attack so many of them, they would not have believed it possible that the phalanx could survive.

Yet there was no gainsaying that they had fallen on a critical time. "Heaven only knows now what the result will be." The work on the phalanstery, progressing briskly since spring, was called off again because of fresh difficulty with Rogers, the contractor. There was no hope, now, of occupying any part of it by Christmas.

The funds to complete the building would be harder than ever to raise. Some counselled that the project be abandoned indefinitely. But the Directors, very deeply involved financially with the contractor, could not now abandon the project had they wished to. "If we could get clear of him," wrote Marianne, "and get it all into our own hands, I would not care much then if it all blew away. It wouldn't be by that ill wind that blows nobody any good," she added significantly.

Marianne's attitude would seem cloyingly Pollyanna-like, if she had not had reason to be cheerful. The reason was of a highly personal nature—she had just got engaged to John Orvis. Other friends were plighting their troth; and two of the other three couples, like herself and John, were heart and soul in Association. Indeed, they all rather despised Mary Lincoln, Fred Cabot's intended, who had taken "French leave as it were." Mary had given out that she was just going "over to the Street* to spend the day." It later appeared Mary would not be back. Fred hinted that they planned to settle in Philadelphia.

* West Roxbury, the nearest village.

A fourth engagement of two, "loyal to Association," was in the making, for, as anyone could see, Eunice Macdaniel, "being in the good graces of Charles Dana," was "flourishing mightily . . . getting to be almost omnipotent. . . ."

Meanwhile, a fourth couple, Maria Dana and Osborne Macdaniel, announced their engagement. The two were convalescing in the Eyrie, presumably from the dread disease. Indeed, danger of further contagion was not yet past; but Marianne had no fear of taking it, either for herself or her family, believing herself to be well guarded against it, having cared for some of the worst cases before their removal to the Cottage.

In the end the experience taught her the virtue in preventive medicine. On hearing how the Whitehouse family, who had recently fled Brook Farm, carried the varioloid to the North American Phalanx, Marianne prayed for a general vaccination there; ". . . a precautionary measure we ought to have taken. Our carelessness," she adds, "has been very blameable."

2.

Hawthorne had recently left Concord and had brought his family to Salem in the expectation of obtaining a federal appointment in the customs or post office there. The appointment not immediately forthcoming, he had been compelled to borrow money from friends, and dun his publisher for royalties. Hawthorne's financial anxiety of late was increased by his wife's pregnancy. Under these circumstances it seemed wholly justifiable to him to instruct his attorney, George Hillard, to sue George Ripley and Charles A. Dana for the money still due him from his investment in Brook Farm.

Hawthorne had repeatedly tried to collect, without success. There is no record of further payment on the back of the note, after November twenty-third 1844. Meanwhile, Hawthorne's insistence on payment had caused increasing resentment in Ripley. As a Utopian he could not comprehend how anyone could endanger man's social destiny—which Brook Farm was endeavoring to establish—for the sake of a few hundred dollars. Ripley would have been both shocked and frightened had he known that Hawthorne, once his close friend and associate, had presented his claim in the Court of Common Pleas, Middlesex County, Massachusetts.

Actually, the writ had been pending for two months when it was served—probably this occurred the first week in December. Perhaps rumors of the plague raging at Brook Farm throughout November had caused the sheriff in Dedham to delay it.

The writ* commanded, "the Sheriff of our County of Norfolk or Suffolk or his Deputy . . . to attach the goods or estate of George Ripley, Clerk, and Charles Anderson Dana, Gentleman, both of Roxbury in said County of Norfolk to the value of eight hundred dollars . . . and to appear before our Justices of our Court of Common Pleas, next to be holden at Cambridge within and for our county of Middlesex. . . ."

The shock to Ripley on being sued for so much more money than he actually owed must have been tremendous, because Hawthorne had been able to get about half of his original investment back three years before, when Ripley and Dana had given him their personal note for $524.05. Apparently Hawthorne had become contentious because he had since been able to recover only $67 of the balance owed him. It would appear that in addition to the amount on the note, he now laid claim for "other money . . . diverse Goods, Wares, and Merchandise . . . and for certain Labor done and performed, Materials found in and about said Labor by the Plaintiff for the said Defendants and at their special request. . . ."

To George Ripley this claim for wages must have seemed the unkindest charge of all. Had it not been assumed at the time that the stockholders would be paid in interest on their investment? The words "and for want thereof to take the body" put fear in Ripley's staunch soul. Failure to pay off the note could lead to a prison sentence in those days.

Gravely concerned, Ripley sought counsel of his wife's uncle, Richard H. Dana Sr., lately retired from the practice of the law. His letter,** dated "Brook Farm, 8 Dec. 1845," candidly stated his case, and then continued: "The same motives which have induced Mr. Hawthorne to commence this suit, not withstanding we have made every exertion in our power to meet the demand, in whole or in part, will no doubt lead

---

* The writ, now in the archives of the Court of Common Pleas, Middlesex Court House, Cambridgeport, Massachusetts, is docketed together with Ripley's and Dana's personal note to Hawthorne, and the bill of the plaintiff's attorney.
** In the archives of the Massachusetts Historical Society.

him to use every advantage which the law gives him to enforce his claim; there is nothing in his character to prevent his proceeding to the last extremity, in hopes of inducing some of our friends to advance the money."

Disregarding Hawthorne's extravagant claim for wages, and so forth, Ripley perceived that he and Dana were liable only for the balance of the debt plus interest—which he computed, and arrived at a total of $530. This sum, he told Richard Dana firmly, it had been "Wholly out of power to pay . . . or any part of it." Nor had either of them any property they could dispose of, or put up as security.

Ripley revealed his fear and dread—could Mr. Hawthorne "take the body, in virtue of the executant?" If he could, would it "apply to one or both defendants?" Was there "any remedy against such a procedure?" Finally, would "going into Chancery" protect them "individually," and how would becoming involved in a process of litigation effect their standing as agents of the Phalanx, under the Act of Corporation?

It was unfortunate, Ripley felt, that he and Dana had exchanged their personal note for Hawthorne's certificate of stock, for Hawthorne now had "no hold against the Phalanx," which since the Act of Incorporation the previous spring, had assumed, "all the indebtedness which we had incurred on account of the Association." There were claims of this kind against the Phalanx, other than Hawthorne's, Ripley admitted, to the amount of eight or nine hundred dollars. "Most of these creditors, no doubt, would accept the transfer from ourselves to the Phalanx," he continued, "as in that case they would claim against the property of the Phalanx . . ." Indeed if Mr. Hawthorne only would sue the Phalanx, it would be to the advantage of all concerned.

Looking at the claim realistically—if it ever should be paid, it would be paid by the Phalanx or not at all. Might it not be possible to make a defence on that ground? Ripley asked hopefully. In his view, to propose an arrangement of that nature, "would be the just and equitable course, dictated by common sense if not by law."

The matter rested there for some time to come. Owing, no doubt, to a crowded docket, the claim of Nathaniel Hawthorne versus George Ripley, et al., would not be brought to trial in the Middlesex County Court until spring.

3.

Depleted by the fatigues of nursing, Marianne Dwight was tormented with an itching or burning similar to the erysipelas or Saint Anthony's fire. By December seventh she recovered her health if not her spirits. Fortunately they had had no new cases of the varioloid for some three weeks now, and all but the most severe cases had left the hospital. Still, it was depressing to reflect how much the epidemic had set them back, financially.

This was her mood when the stunning announcement of Hawthorne's claim was made by the Directors of the Phalanx. Marianne's reaction was one of shocked surprise. "I think here lies the difficulty," she wrote Anna Parsons, "we have not had business men to conduct our affairs. We had had no strictly business transactions from the beginning, and those among us who have some business talents, see this error, and feel that we can not go on as we have done. They are ready to give up if matters cannot be otherwise managed, for they have no hope of success here under the past and present government. All important matters have been done up in council of one or two or three individuals, and everybody else kept in the dark . . . and now it must be so no longer;—our young men have started inquiry meetings; and it must be a sad state of things that calls for such measures."

Orvis and Allen, leaders among the young newcomers to Brook Farm, had reason to feel outraged that Directors Ripley and Dana had kept this debt to Hawthorne to themselves until the plaintiff actually brought suit. Certainly it was misleading, on Dana's part, not to have mentioned Hawthorne's two shares of stock, plus interest, in listing the debts in his report of November 1844. Since then the treasurer had presented no report. He was always postponing it.

The criticism and discontent bore down hard on George Ripley; and to make matters more trying still, he had received a very disturbing letter from Brisbane during the epidemic, in which the man who had incited him to build the phalanstery discussed "the best means of bringing Brook Farm to a close, and making preparations for a trial under more favorable circumstances." Ripley had retorted in a letter dated December third—perhaps the first day since the epidemic in which he had leisure to catch up on his mail—that in his view it was a necessity to develop Brook Farm—a necessity for the cause of Association in America. Whereupon, Brisbane replying to Ripley on December ninth disclosed the disquieting information that it was Dana who had expressed "fears for the future in such a way I concluded you had made up your minds to bring things to a close."

If he believed Brisbane, this lack of faith in Dana, his right-hand man, must have constituted another shock to George Ripley. Worse followed, as Brisbane pursued a discussion of ways and means to launch a successful phalanx, as if taking it for granted that Brook Farm was doomed. He had no desire to administer this successful phalanx himself, but he was interested in organizing such a phalanx on a truly scientific basis. Brisbane thought that if they could find one hundred men who would each subscribe a thousand dollars, this would give them a fine capital—"less than that I fear would be patch-work." Perhaps he, himself, might "make a trial of the steel business," or "wait patiently until I can get my father to embark with his fortune." If nothing could be done at present, Brisbane said he would go on translating Fourier, lecturing, spreading the word.

This sort of talk was the more exasperating to Ripley because he had asked Brisbane explicitly to raise $15,000 for Brook Farm among their New York friends. Brisbane declined to go along with him on this at all. It was as perplexing to get $15,000 for Brook Farm as it would be to raise $100,000 for that well established phalanx he had in mind. Where was $15,000 to be had? "The New Yorkers who have money, . . . are pledged to raise $10,000 for the N.A.P. [North American Phalanx at Red Bank, New Jersey] to pay off its mortgage. You might as well undertake to raise dead men as to obtain any considerable amount of capital from the people here."

Though the tone of the letter is kind and friendly throughout—in the conclusion Brisbane complimented Ripley on a recent translation of Fourier—it must have been a galling epistle to receive. Bitter it was to be told that unless Brook Farm was still in a position to make a trial of Association "that would impress the public," the Directors were not justified in asking for financial aid. This, from the man who had encouraged them to take financial risks in order to serve as the standard bearer of the Association Movement!

It was not George Ripley's nature to be bitter; but Marianne reflects some of the disillusionment the Farmers suffered—reflects it with asperity. "Brisbane is vague and unsteady," she wrote Anna at this time.

"The help he promised us from his efforts comes not—but on the contrary, he and other friends to the cause in New York, instead of trying to concentrate all efforts upon Brook Farm, as they promised, have wandered off—have taken up a vast plan of getting $100,000 and starting anew, so they are for disposing of us in the shortest manner,—would set their foot upon us as it were, and divert what capital might come to us."

"What then remains for us, and where are our hopes?" Marianne asked sadly.

Their hopes centered in a determined little group of younger men who had taken up the challenge with a will. These were determined that Brook Farm should carry on independently of their New York friends, and come to something, even if they did not "realize a perfect Association." Next, the group determined to raise money, $10,000 at least. "How shall we get it? We will send out our group of lecturers." Orvis and Allen volunteered, "provided the council will take such steps first, that they can in conscience ask people to come here, and put in their money." Orvis was mad clean through. He was insisting on a change of policy, and unless he was satisfied he would leave Brook Farm.

The council turned out to be awake and ready for action. Once the money was raised, they would finish the phalanstery and enlarge the school. Was not their sash and blind business, the tailoring, the tin block, the printing—and why forget the farm?—already very profitable?

"Heaven help us and make us wise, for the failure of Brook Farm must defer the cause a long time. . . . This place as it is," Marianne enthused, "is the best place under the sky; why can't people see this, and look upon it hopefully and encouragingly?"

On December twelfth, Marianne wrote again, in even more confident vein; "We are not dead here, but live—our hearts are firm and true, our courage good and our hands ready for action."

The Farmers self-confidence surged up again at the next meeting of the Association. Everyone present was firm and determined and "full of confidence that we shall and will bring Brook Farm to success." There was no word of discouragement from anyone—". . . there was one heart, one soul, one opinion, and all the strength that comes from such a union." Yet they had examined the worst aspects of their situation; every argument against their success was brought up and looked at. "How small and insignificant they all seemed compared with the great ends we have in view!" The Farmers agreed unanimously that to be influenced by such paltry considerations would be treachery to the cause.

A mood of dedication is the dominant note throughout the final phase of Brook Farm. After hearing Mr. Ripley's letter to their New York friends declaring their new independence—he had addressed it to Mr. Brisbane—John Dwight pointed out that they "must look at this movement in a higher point of view than a merely mercantile one, and be willing to be sustained by faith until the time comes when we shall be able to realize pecuniary success."

This "glorious" meeting wound up in some interesting conversation about the social atmosphere of their phalanx. Indeed, the occasion inspired everyone, especially their lecturers John Orvis and John Allen, who, prompt to carry out their pledge, were to set off the next morning for a fortnight's tour through Lynn, Marblehead, Gloucester, and other towns on Massachusetts' North Shore, with a view to procuring subscribers for the *Harbinger* and to stir up popular interest in the cause. "May God inspire them," prayed Marianne, "that their golden lips may utter divine words to the people, and kindle a fire in many hearts!" Marianne's faith in Association was doubled, now, by that of her intended, John Orvis, and by his devotion. "Oh! he is so much more constant and affectionate in his regard for me than I deserve . . ."

Only one person had absented himself from the "glorious" meeting —Fred Cabot. Fred was also the only one among them who wanted to leave Brook Farm. Worse still, in this its hour of crisis, Fred told everyone he met when in Boston that Brook Farm could not possibly succeed. Since he had served the Corporation in the capacity of clerk, it was supposed that he knew what he was talking about, and his words damaged the Farmers' credit. It was hard for Marianne to believe that their "dear, good, warmhearted, devoted Fred, for whose stability we would once have wagered everything valuable to us" had actually become an apostate. Marianne attributed Fred's backsliding to "hostile influences which had been at work upon him"—namely, his fiancée, Mary Lincoln; she, who had recently taken "French leave" from Brook Farm. At first Marianne took what comfort she could from the fact that Fred still declared himself an associonist, and pledged that in civilization he would work only for the cause. Indeed, if he saw a chance for the better in the prospects of Brook Farm, Fred said, he might "come in" again, bringing his earnings with him. In the end Marianne told him he was deceiving himself, because when he quitted Brook Farm he would "be chained faster and firmer in a civilized hell." He had made a sad choice. Marianne's heart ached for the volatile Fred.

The final departure of another old friend took place at Christmas-time—Charles King Newcomb. In her introduction to his *Journals*, Judith Kennedy Johnson writes that Newcomb's mother never hesitated to drag him away from the tranquillity of Brook Farm. Charles dutifully spent every Christmas at Providence with her. Indeed, when he had first joined Brook Farm his mother had made him come home in September and stay until late in April. But for the past two years Newcomb had succeeded in reducing his winter sojourns with his mother to a week or so spent in New York or Boston to escort her to the theatre and concert hall, followed perhaps by a short visit with Mr. and Mrs. Emerson, in Concord, to revive his spirit. For a time, the delicate, super-sensitive young man had seemed to be escaping from his mother's thrall; but, since early this fall, when the Newcomb family had moved to a new boarding house, pressure had been put on Charles to "come home to live." Of late, Mrs. Newcomb had redoubled her demands, hinting that their prolonged separation was destructive to both. In September, Mrs. Newcomb had reminded Charles that their most re-cent journey together to the Newcomb's home town, Keene, New Hampshire, had drawn them nearer to each other than ever: "The chords of sympathy are tighter," she wrote; then added in words that would horrify a modern psychiatrist, "and we are brother and sister, as well as parent and child." She kept offering him, week by week, vari-ous inducements to come home for good. She would buy him the five-volume set of Plato he had desired for so long; she would finance a seat for him in the Catholic Church; and whenever he chose, Charley could be alone in their small private parlor with the cozy fireplace. His sister Charlotte joined in, warning that he seemed to be getting morbid at Brook Farm, and imploring him to consider their widowed parent. "Dear Mother," Charlotte moaned, "we may all yet be a comfort to her!"

To all this Charles had countered successfully. What sort of profes-sion was he suited for? he had asked—implying he was suited to none and was far better off in the shelter of Brook Farm. He had withstood, too, his mother's fears for his safety during the epidemic of November. Then suddenly in December, Charles yielded to his mother's constant reminders of the sacrifices she had made for him.

Unfortunately, his "diarizing" of this period is lost. At the moment of Charles' capitulation, we have only his mother's ecstatic and faintly absurd outburst of December fourth. "My heart is leaping . . . come, dear. Your Mother waits, Plato waits, and Jesus waits—last, not least, of course."

In the second week of December, Charles King Newcomb removed from his bedroom wall the pictures of Jesus, St. Ignatius Loyola, and St. Francis Xavier, and the one of Fanny Elssler, the dancer, which hung between the two last, and went home to live.

Marianne was deeply concerned for him. "I regret C.K.N.'s departure more than I can tell," she wrote Anna. "He has been always a conspicuous, or rather an important object in the picture to me. I can hardly think of Brook Farm without him. The sweet, sad youth! He will feel the change still more than we. Think of him in a city life, if you can. It will kill him soul and body."

It was this conviction of the Farmers, that Association offered an escape from "civilized hell," that made Marianne and the others determined to keep Brook Farm going, if they possibly could.

On December twenty-second, George William Curtis wrote Dwight from New York, "A Merry Christmas and a Happy New Year to you, if you are still alive, for since small pox has joined your Phalanx, I am not sure but his ambition for the supreme power has swept you all away. Yet every Saturday's *Harbinger* is a missive from Brook Farm which tells of other things than the cosmogonies, etc., of which it ostensibly discourses. I shall be glad to smuggle myself for a share of the commendation bestowed upon those who have increased your list with the new volume, but my New York friends are pale at Greeley's *Tribune*, and would christen your sheet 'An Omen Ill' instead of *Harbinger*."

Ripley somehow had managed to keep his organ coming off the press, despite the epidemic. No doubt the editing distracted him, and kept him from brooding upon Brisbane's disloyalty and the threat of Hawthorne's claim. Besides the usual features, recent events in the world of science evoked comment that reflects the quaint reactions of the times toward new inventions. Concerning the uses of the telegraph, someone suggested, "Word could be sent ahead from station to station of any hurricane or storm, and thus prevent the loss of many richly laden vessels." Notice was also taken of Etzler's amazing "Agricultural Machinery"—a combined tractor and bulldozer which some called "The Satellite," and others, "The Iron Slave."

4.

The year was to end, after all, on a note of hope. On Christmas Day, W. H. Channing, who had not been able to minister to them since before the epidemic because of ill health, sent a photograph of a religious painting, a present from Marcus Spring, a fellow Christian Socialist. "The Crucifixion seems a fitting gift for Christmas, from associonist to associonists in these days of trial," he said in the greeting which accompanied the gift, "let us learn from it the spirit in which by patience and devotedness to make our lives a perpetual song of praise. The time is not distant when we shall say to each other, 'He is risen . . . We shall yet live to see Glory, Peace, Good-will descend to make man a tabernacle for indwelling God."

Marianne, too, wrote hopefully to Anna on New Year's Eve. "A glorious winter day, cloudless and dazzlingly bright, very cold, but so tempting in the pure white snow, that one could hardly stay in doors." Marianne was able to rise above the disappointment of John Orvis's absence at Christmas, because "the Archon had a letter from Allen, written to us all, in fine spirits and full of encouragement, and giving a description of a storm they enjoyed at Rockport—informing us also that they could not be with us till next Monday or Tuesday." The Phalanx seemed to be marching forward again. Mr. Grant, from the Claremont in Ohio, and Mr. Brisbane were arriving at Brook Farm within the week; and her brother John had received another letter from Eben Hunt, saying that the prospects for securing an audience for his lectures on "The Philosophy of the Gamut"—which Mr. Brisbane was proposing—were most encouraging.

5.

The lecturers, Orvis and Allen, had gone off to Cape Cod right after Christmas. On January fifteenth, Allen wrote "Mary Anne" Dwight a long letter* from Sandwich. "We are encountering the 'Rough Realities' of Civilized Life, or worse," he told her. "We have fell upon barbarian times and among barbarious 'scalawags,' as John calls them."

Allen was annoyed because they had spoken twice and although they had made "a most luminous expose of the principles of Divine Harmony" they had gathered but two dozen listeners in a hall that seated a thousand. Worse still, they had not sold a single subscription to the *Harbinger*, and they had made only two converts. These two, he added, had no capital except about a dozen children apiece which they valued as highly as one thousand dollars a head representing "an investment of at least twenty-five thousand in chattels personal from these converts." Ruefully, Allen advised Marianne "to see to it that the phalanstery is done immediately, and these two families will fill it!"

Their luck in Kingston, the same; in Duxbury little better. They were off for Hyannis in the morning. "I am in high glee tonight," he went on, "quite disposed to laugh at the follies and miseries of civilized numskulls, but John is perfectly furious." They were stopping with a Methodist minister who worked in the Sandwich Glass Factory; and Orvis's irritation was probably increased by the minister's concern for their spiritual welfare. "We have the benefit of his prayers," Allen wrote, "which are long and loud in our behalf."

To soothe their ruffled feelings, they took a long walk by the ocean. "It was calm as a lake upon a summer eve. A thousand white gulls held a social party upon a little sand island near the shore. It was their Valentine's Day. They 'cooed and billed' and admired the beauty of these chosen ones and departed two by two to their homes on the wave." This, Allen declared, was the best encounter of social life they had had since leaving Brook Farm. Marianne was not to worry about them, though. They were "only sick for a little sympathy from beings whom we can esteem human." They had not talked with a woman on the trip, and they often thought sadly of their divine home. If nothing more was to be accomplished on this desolate tour, they had at least learned to value the life at Brook Farm.

These two lonely, discouraged young men doubtless were looking forward to the meeting of the New England Fourier Society to be held in Boston's Tremont Temple on January twenty-seventh. For assuredly, Mr. Ripley, who was President, would welcome his Corresponding

* Fruitlands Museum Library, Harvard, Mass.; Collection, Henry S. Bourneman.

Secretary, Allen; and also Orvis, who would report on some of the other reform movements which he and Allen had recently encountered. Orvis planned to show the necessity for a more radical reorganization of labor on "just principles"—as Fourier planned it. Orvis's specialty, Associative principles as applied to Labor, would soon become the most vital feature of the Movement.

In his welcoming speech, at the Convention in Boston on January twenty-seventh, President Ripley got off to a bad start—admitting that Association had achieved no great success thus far. After this his claim that the general discontent was lessened by the profound conviction that the Associative Order, accepted by so many powerful minds, offered every reason for encouragement fell flat; as, also, did Brisbane's attempt to show how "the whole history of Man" was a preparation for "the Combined Order in which Man would justify God's Creation." The complete disbandment of the great phalanx at Sodus Bay, set for April, was announced. Some said this was the result of religious dissension and lack of disinterested leadership; others, that the interest on the mortgage had not been met. Whatever the cause, the failure of this great phalanx, as richly endowed as Fourier could wish, with broad acres and an ideal situation, represented a severe setback to the whole Association Movement.

Dr. W. H. Channing, unable to attend, addressed a letter to the Convention from Vermont. When, after the announcement of bad news, someone read it to the assembly, the discouraged hearts of the delegates were fired with renewed enthusiasm. It was not Dr. Channing's voice; and one missed the flaming presence—a flame that burned thin and pure as in a consecrated lamp or candle. Yet his theme sparked the delegates to hope and endeavor.

With his unequalled talent for linking a reform with a cherished ideal or tradition, Mr. Channing pointed out how perfectly the Order of Association fitted into the tradition of the United States of America. Is not our Government, he demanded, one of confederacies within confederacies, each free, yet cooperating with all? "Our fathers organized a system of divisions of land, into Townships, each of which was also a School District, and a Parish; thus making the Political, Educational, the Religious Interest, identical; and solving the problem which had divided all other nations, by so uniting the Church, the College, the Commonwealth, that each should be independent, yet all associated. . . . We have but to develop their plans, and perfect the Township, the School, the Parish, in each State; and the highest conception which

man can form of Human Society will become reality around us . . .
All places shall become at once a Temple, School, and Council Hall;—
and all duties be at once Worship, Culture, Work. Association is the
fulfillment of the very Spirit, Idea, and Aim of this nation of United
Freemen."

William Channing's tone was not so positive as concerned the future
of Brook Farm. Although he was deeply touched by the thought of the
truly human greatness with which the Farmers had met the varioloid
epidemic, he feared that their doom was sealed. "If Brook Farm can
stand it must," he wrote Dwight at this time. "But, if it must fall, then,
by heaven, only a louder and stronger call shall go up for Unity and
Brotherhood."

Immediately after the Convention, Orvis and Allen set out for Vermont. This lecture tour, which Orvis called "vaulting from hill-top to
hill-top in the Green Mountain State" was arranged by a native at the
suggestion of W. H. Channing.

One frosty night in February, Orvis sat down by the fire in an inn at
South Woodstock and wrote Marianne of their difficulties with snow-
storms and natives apathetic to their creed. Sometimes they walked ten
or more miles through snowy roads only to find that the villagers had
made no preparation for a meeting. After lighting their own fire, and
borrowing lamps from the tavern to light the hall, and ringing the bell
themselves, they often found themselves lecturing to a very scant audience indeed.

Just once did they taste success—at Putney, where they spoke in the
chapel to a full audience of their "Perfectionist Friends." These constituted a small community of some twenty persons, whom John Humphrey Noyes* had gathered about him. As their name implied, the Perfectionists labored to make men perfect. They held that the true scheme
of redemption begins with reconciliation with God; restoration of true
relation between the sexes; reform of the industrial system; and victory
over death. The conservative element in Brattleboro would eventually
expel the Perfectionists from the neighborhood. A clue to the habits of
this sect lies in the successor to it—the bizarre Oneida Community,
which Noyes would found in 1848, in Syracuse, New York. In writing of
Oneida, Noyes says that he and his followers had received a great impulse from Brook Farm. The tribute can scarcely be regarded as compli-

---

* Noyes later wrote the *History of American Socialisms*.

mentary. The Perfectionists had little interest in Association which attempted only industrial reform. Their ideal was "A Community Home
in which each is married to all."

Orvis's letter concludes with an account of his journey that day. A
great snowstorm made the roads almost impassable. Thanks to "a brave
mountaineer driver who had trifled with storms from his boyhood,"
and his "noble steed," they covered the nine miles from some neighboring town to South Woodstock, "in the teeth of a fierce North-Easter,
the roads filled smooth with snow, and a perfectly unbroken track," in
about two hours.

Scorning "the rum and tobacco scented bar-room," Orvis raised a
fire in the dining room and settled down to read. His good companion,
"Mr. A." joined him, presently, to deplore the melancholy lot of the
"isolated family" in Vermont—which in 1846, on such a night as that,
must have been melancholy and isolated indeed.

6.

Sunday, the first of March, 1846—the date of Marianne's next letter
to Anna Parsons—dawned bright with promise. Arrangements had lately
been completed to finish four out of the fourteen private suites on the
second floor of the phalanstery. It was hoped the remainder would be
ready for occupancy by October first. The plan called for one hundred
rooms, to accommodate some one hundred and fifty persons. Fortunately, every one of the rooms had been lathed when their finances
had failed the previous fall. Enough money had "dribbled in" since to
enable them to resume building—and high time! Already people were
coming, including "an incursion of Cape Cod barbarians, . . . two
Manchester men, with their wives and one child."

On Saturday, February twenty-eighth, a stove had been installed in
the basement of the phalanstery to dry out the wintry chill and damp,
preparatory to resuming work there on Monday.

Another cherished plan was shaping up nicely. W. H. Channing,
recovered at last from the illness which had caused his withdrawal to
Bennington, Vermont, returned to fill Theodore Parker's pulpit in the
Spring Street Church in West Roxbury. He was expected at Brook Farm
this same Sunday afternoon to conduct a service and to discuss how the

Farmers should raise money by private subscription to finish the Chapel they planned to have in the second story of the phalanstery.

Marianne later reported, "a holy, solemn afternoon." William Channing had urged on them greater self-dedication than that displayed by "Crusaders, monks, nuns, Quakers or any sect. He solemnly urged upon us no idleness, no half-wayness in our devotedness, but the entire surrender of all our powers to this work; nothing else can give success . . ."

7.

On March second, James Kay, Jr., in Philadelphia, posted a most unfortunate letter to John Dwight, in which he pointed out all the mistakes the Directors of Brook Farm had made. Kay advised the Directors to refuse further admissions, and to expel the non-cooperative members at once. The industries, Kay said, should be administered by the workmen; and the educated should devote themselves to the rehabilitation of the school, which had ever been their most reliable source of income. He did not object to propaganda, but he pointed out that the lecturing and the publication of the *Harbinger* consumed time and energy that could better be spent on more productive measures. He estimated that they had been set back, financially speaking, to the low point they had reached just two years ago, by the epidemic and the cost of the phalanstery. "Then," said Mr. Kay, "you saved yourselves, and with additional knowledge you can save yourselves once more." Mr. Kay really loved Brook Farm, but as a businessman he distrusted its management. His second grief, after losing his wife, Mr. Kay declared, was that circumstances prevented him from devoting himself to Brook Farm to make it pay.

Mr. Kay's advice was sincere and well meant, but the timing could not possibly have been more unfortunate. At the very moment he posted it, a fire broke out and spread fast in the unfinished phalanstery at Brook Farm.

A dance was going on at the Hive when someone cried, "Fire!" The dancers thought it was a joke—"until they saw the face of him who cried it."

The Council had just dispersed. Mr. Salisbury, a member of it, on his way to his quarters, saw a light in the upper part of the phalanstery. Men had been at work there all day, and Mr. Salisbury at first thought that one of them must have returned to pick up a forgotten tool. When he put his head inside, he found the building filled with smoke. He went right back to the Eyrie to get Mr. Ripley—who ran down the hill so fast he was the first man on the spot.

Marianne was in her room when she heard the sudden and earnest cry, "Fire! The phalanstery!" She dashed to the front of Pilgrim House which overlooked the scene, and watched.

Flames were bursting from a far window and spreading fast. Men were running helter-skelter, trying desperately to save windows and timber. But it was easy to see that nothing could be saved. In less than five minutes, the flames spread from end to end. Someone pointed despairingly to the Eyrie, which was smoking ominously beneath the eaves. A neighbor, Mr. Orange, climbed boldly onto the Eyrie roof, which was already too hot to bear the hand, and "worked like a hero, and not in vain."

But it was the beauty of the scene, "glorious beyond description" that Marianne wanted Anna to share: "How grand when the immense heavy column of smoke first rose up to heaven! There was no wind and it ascended most perpendicularly,—sometimes inclining towards the Eyrie,—then it was spangled with fiery sparks, and tinged with glowing colors, ever rolling and wreathing, solemnly and gracefully up—up. An immense, clear blue flame mingled for a while with the others and rose high in the air,—like liquid turquoise and topaz. It came from the melting glass. Rockets, too, rose in the sky, and fell in glittering gems of every rainbow hue—much like our Fourth of July fireworks. I looked upon it from our house till the whole front was on fire,—that was beautiful indeed,—the whole colonnade was wreathed spirally with fire, and every window glowing."

From the very first moment, Marianne accepted the calamity in a mood of calm exaltation. This was the work of Heaven, and therefore good. Presently, she threw on her cloak and went out to mingle with the people, and found that they, too, were resolute and undaunted. The expression on every face seemed truly sublime. "There was a solemn, serious, reverential feeling, such as must come when we are forced to feel that human aid is of no avail, and that a higher power than man's is at work. I heard solemn words of trust, cheerful words of encouragement, of resignation, of gratitude and thankfulness, but not one of terror or despair."

Awed by the sublimity of the scene, everyone stood transfixed. "There was one minute, whilst the whole frame yet stood, that surpassed all else. It was fire throughout. It seemed like a magnificent temple of molten gold, or a crystallized fire. Then the beams began to fall, and one after another the chimneys. The end, where the fire took, being plastered, held out the longest, but in less than an hour and a half the whole was leveled to the ground. The phalanstery was finished! Not the building alone, but the scenery around was grand. The smoke, as it settled off the horizon, gave the effect of sublime mountain scenery; and during the burning, the trees, the woods shone magically to their minutest twigs, in lead, silver and gold."

Marianne actually felt relief—the problem of how to finish the phalanstery had been settled for good and all! "As it was to be," she declared, "I would not have missed it for the world." She regretted only the absence of Anna, Channing, Orvis, "and all absent who belong to us." Anna, Marianne continues in the same vein of attenuated exaltation, will never know what she has missed. The moral sublimity with which the people had accepted the calamity "was not the least part" of this disaster.

For the Ripleys, Marianne had but a brief word of praise. "The good Archon was like an angel. Mrs. Ripley alone was, for half an hour, too much overcome to look upon it." Such a lack of appreciation of the obligations involved, on Marianne's part, makes her appear excessively optimistic; a person who closed her eyes to the realities. Small wonder Sophia could not bear to look at the fire. She knew that it was burning not only a building, but the most cherished hopes. It was, Sophia sensed, Brook Farm's holocaust.

The whole countryside had hurried to their assistance—Marianne continued—though the engines could not have reached them in time to help, fire-brigades had set out from Boston and Cambridgeport, and been forced to turn back because of the drifts. People had come from Roxbury and Dedham, walking over the snowy roads to see the fire.

When the phalanstery finally collapsed, there was a general rush over to the Hive for a bite to eat. Fortunately, the indefatigable Mr. Orange, foreseeing that the crowd would be hungry, had rushed over to "the Street" for provisions and milk.

Marianne estimated that they fed some two hundred hungry persons with coffee, bread, and cheese by the time she sat down at about midnight to write to Orvis and Allen—"for I thought they would be in an agony for us, if they did not get their first intelligence from home."

After a short, sound sleep, Marianne was up early the day after the fire concluding her long letter to Anna in the same mood of exaltation. "I looked at the bare hill this morning, I must say, with a feeling of relief. There was an encumbrance gone. Heaven had interfered to prevent us from finishing that building so foolishly undertaken, so poorly built and planned, and which again and again some of us have thought and said we should rejoice to see blown away or burned down. It has gone suddenly gloriously, magnificently, and we shall have no further trouble with it. Just what the effect will be to us, it is impossible now to tell. The contract was lately given into our own hands, and I suppose ours must be the loss. About seven thousand dollars had been spent on it. We must take deep to heart a good lesson. We have been thro' almost every other trial; now we have been thro' the fire. We needed this experience, and I pray we may come from it like pure gold. It leaves us no worse off than before we began it, and in some respects better. May Heaven bless to us the event. I feared it would look ugly, dismal, and smutty this morning, but the ruins are really picturesque. A part of the stone foundation stands like a row of grave stones,—a tomb of the phalanstery—thank God, not the tomb of our hopes!"

The day after the fire dawned calm and beautiful. The one concession the Farmers made to their comfort that day was to postpone breakfast an hour; otherwise, all went on as usual. The atmosphere was serene—more so because the hired carpenters had all returned to Dedham. "We look towards the hill and all seems like a strange dream." Towards the close of "the fireworks" the night before, "after watching the constantly rolling, changing flames for two hours," Marianne had "looked up to the sky" and seen "Orion looking down so steadily, so calmly, reminding me of the unchanging, the eternal."

The March fourteenth issue of the *Harbinger* contained Ripley's account of the fire. The piece forms an excellent supplement to Marianne's poetic outburst. Ripley told how the neighbors saved the Eyrie, while their own people worked to save the Hive and the workshops. The fire engine from West Roxbury had arrived in a very short time—the firehouse being but a half mile distant—to be followed by those from Jamaica Plain, Newton, and Brookline. He seemed to take a grim pride in the way equipment from the neighboring towns had hurried "through snow that was deep on the cross-roads" to save Brook Farm. Evidently the management was severely criticized for leaving a brightly burning stove unattended in the basement of the phalanstery, for he pointed out that it had burned satisfactorily until eight-thirty on the fatal night. He said, "From a defect in the construction of the chimney a spark probably had kindled the woodwork." The one hundred rooms "lathed for several months without plaster, being as dry as tinder, the fire flashed through them with terrific rapidity."

In memoriam, Ripley sadly penned what might have been a prospectus. Their phalanstery would have "commanded a most extensive and picturesque view, and affording accommodations and conveniences in the Combined Order, which in many respects would gratify even a fastidious taste."

In addition to the $7000 already spent, they had recently signed papers pledging $3000 more. The money had been collected from investments in Brook Farm's loan stock; and the loss would now fall upon holders of partnership stock, and the members of the Association.

There was cause for comfort, however—no sacred ties were broken. School kept as usual; industry operated; and there was "a cheerful spirit to carry on . . . We feel assured," Ripley continued, "that no outward disappointment or calamity can chill our zeal for the realization of a divine order of society, or abate our efforts in the sphere which may be pointed out by our best judgment as most favorable to the cause we have at heart." In other words, they would deny the emergency which faced them. Their cheerfulness, George Ripley insisted, was new proof of the power of Associated life to quicken the best elements of character and to prepare men for every emergency. Nevertheless, he recognized that the magnitude of their loss was incalculable.

8

On March seventh—four days after the fire—the case of "Nathaniel Hawthorne versus George Ripley et al." was tried in the Middlesex County Court of Common Pleas, which was then situated in Concord, Massachusetts. George Singleton Hillard, Hawthorne's attorney, evidently had turned the case over to Ebenezer Rockwood Hoar of Concord, for the latter filed the following data together with Ripley and Dana's personal note of indebtedness, and the writ summoning them to appear:

Plaintiff's Costs Viz:

1845, Dec. Writ	$1.65
Service	$2.05
Entry	$1.25
Travel 40 miles	$1.32
Attendance 53 days	$17.49
Continuance	.20
1846, March 7, Travel	.33
Attendance 3 days	.99
	$25.28

Debt $560.62
     E. Rockwood Hoar
        Pltf's Attorney

The Middlesex County Courthouse in Lechemere Square, Cambridgeport, Massachusetts, holds docketed cases of a hundred years or more ago. The case of Hawthorne versus Ripley is filed in the Court of Common Pleas in a docket labelled "New Entries 4—198." The papers are misplaced, because the index number of the case is "338."

These three papers, frail with age—especially the personal note with the three illustrious signatures—are baffling as well as conclusive. Although they prove that the case actually was tried, there is nothing that tells us whether either, or both, of the defendants were present at the trial, or who defended them.* The most conclusive evidence is found in an article by Dana, published in the New York Sun at the time of George Ripley's death in July, 1880. In commemorating Ripley's social experiment, Dana said, "Indeed, no individual of distinction joined in the enterprise except Mr. Hawthorne, and he remained but a month or two, investing a few hundred, which he took care to recover by a lawsuit afterwards." In a note concerning Hawthorne's financial dealings with Brook Farm in the revised American Notebooks, Randall Stewart observes that Dana, as Secretary and Treasurer of the Brook Farm Phalanx, was "in a position to know."

The verdict of the court to pay this debt—it came to $560.62 with Hawthorne's legal expenses added on to the amount of the original "Personal Note" of Ripley and Dana—was delivered in Concord four days after the fire at Brook Farm. It was the third calamity to strike the Phalanx within five months; and if the bad news reached West Roxbury promptly, Ripley and Dana appear to have kept the matter to themselves—at least, until they had some idea what to do.

* Mr. Frank W. Grinnell, Secretary of the Massachusetts Bar Association, to whom the writer is indebted for legal information, regards these papers as indication of a successful suit.

9.

The moment each of them learned of the disaster, Orvis and Dana came hurrying home—Orvis from Vermont, Dana from New York. John Dwight barely missed their arrival, as he set out for New York to give a course of four lectures on the "Philosophy of the Gamut." Brisbane, who never wearied of Fourier's theory that the entire universe was distributed and arranged according to numbers, had persuaded Dwight that there was an analogy between the universe and the scale of music. Brisbane had been planning these lectures by Brook Farm's distinguished musician ever since the previous Christmastime. Now, the fire had provided Dwight with a supplementary topic more dramatic than the "Philosophy of the Gamut."

At first, after his return from New York on March fourth, Dana appeared to take the catastrophe as cheerfully as even Marianne Dwight could wish. But since then, at the meetings of the General Council—now held every night to review all the departments and check over accounts—he had become increasingly pessimistic. No doubt Hawthorne's pending suit, and the realization that they might have to pay up $560.62 or face the consequences, made Dana realize the quandary they were in. "We are pretty much agreed to call together the creditors and holders of loan and stock and lay the case before them," he wrote Dwight. "If they will do nothing to diminish the rate of interest we now have to pay, we shall have to go through bankruptcy, in which case they will get nothing at all, while if they will relax somewhat of their demands their claims will be worth something at least."

Meanwhile, Dwight contrived to talk Association everywhere he went among their New York friends. Unpromising weather conspired to a postponement of the second lecture, and Dwight gained an opportunity to talk with Greeley. "He wrote upon the paper which I took with me," Dwight reported to Ripley in a letter of March sixteenth, "'I give up all my stock unconditionally, and will subscribe, besides, the first $100 I get which does not belong to somebody else.'" Marcus Spring gave up his stock; and stockholders Hicks, Manning, Hunt, Benson, and Tweedy followed suit. "You may consider the whole of the stock held in New York as cancelled. As soon as a clear plan shapes itself on our part," Dwight concluded optimistically, "there will be something done here."

The New Yorkers could be generous about cutting their losses, but they would prove evasive about filling the hat he was attempting to pass. Everyone was glad to see charming little Mr. Dwight, but his New York friends had no intention of sending good money after bad.

Meanwhile, for Dwight, the escape from the char-stained snow at Brook Farm, to the "parties, music, dinings out and in, hosts of visitors," not to mention "matins with Fred Rackemann, who opened to me the gospels according to Beethoven, Mendelssohn, and other minor prophets after dining with George Curtis . . ." seemed proof that all these dear wonderful friends were as deeply interested in Association and as anxious that Brook Farm should survive as he was himself.

Dwight talked to his hosts, the Reverend and Mrs. Henry W. Bellows, for "hours and hours—in fact, all the time." It seemed to him that they were beginning to entertain the idea of Association rather more willingly. His public lectures, he was convinced, were producing a deep impression, although the pecuniary result would amount to about half what they had hoped for. Well, no matter! He had made a fine opening for another time, and he had had "a wonderfully fine time socially."

In a letter to the *Boston Courier*, Lydia Maria Child gave her estimate of Dwight and his lectures: ". . . a delicate musical organization, accurate scientific knowledge, and the far reaching glance of a poet which enables him to perceive that music is the golden key to unlock all the analogies of the universe." But such a man would only be understood by the select few. The ordinary mortal when informed that in his social progress mankind had "arrived at the dissonant seventh, which clamors vociferously for the coming octave," cared little about the spiritual significance of the third, seventh and twelfth notes in the scale.

It was Dwight as a musician who made his lectures attractive to public and critics alike. As for the "Philosophy of the Gamut," Miss Child felt that this nebulous topic compelled Dwight to try to say more than he or anyone else could. "Outwardly rich and inwardly impractical, his artless and beautiful soul is strangely out of place in these bustling and pretending times." To Miss Child, Dwight was "like a little child who had lost his way in the woods with an apron brimful of flowers which he don't know what to do with; but, if you can take them, he will gladly give you all."

Something of John Dwight's starry-eyed enjoyment cheered Mrs. Ripley, lifted her above the dreary dedicated mood, now the order of the day at Brook Farm. "Your description of the luxuries of civilization seemed very like a story I once read of Aladdin's wonderful lamp," she wrote him on March fourteenth. ". . . What a rich and varied life you are at once drawn into!" She dwelled lovingly upon Dwight's deep sense of the more abundant wealth to be found in the circle of pure Phalansterians, and she rejoiced that he had ever found his true home circle among everyday Brook Farm friends. "You have," she added, "an unusually grand stand point from which to speak to the public."

As for his lectures, tributes to their merits had reached Brook Farm both from friends in New York and the notice in the *Tribune*. Sophia wished Dwight could have seen the group gathered in the reading room after supper—"the tall ones stooping over and the short ones standing tip toe to read it" She foresaw that a repetition of his course would be demanded, and she was trying to get used to the idea that his absence would be prolonged. "We earnestly wish for you back at every moment and every turn." And yet, surely this was a better time for him to be away from Brook Farm than later?

In the meantime, Mrs. Ripley assured Dwight, "All are deciding what to do, in a mood of calmness and serenity." In closing, she begged him "not to forget Kleinstrup's plea for gilly flower seed!"

10.

Dana had had more on his mind since the fire than the debts of the Phalanx—his recent and secret marriage to Eunice Macdaniel. For some time he had been engaged to Eunice, who James Harrison Wilson in his *Life of Charles Anderson Dana* described as "an attractive and spirited girl, with black sparkling eyes, and a slight but erect and energetic figure." After serving for months as a member of the Housekeeper's Group at Brook Farm, Eunice had begun to entertain serious intentions of going on the stage. With this in mind she had left Brook Farm some weeks before and gone to visit with her brother, Osborne, in New York. Perhaps Dana grew afraid of losing her to the theatre. If so, his intuition served him well. Eunice became the grandmother of Ruth Draper.

They had been secretly married on March second, in New York; and Dana, upon his return to Brook Farm, was hard pressed to explain to his friends that his wedding was "entirely unexpected." The best he could do—he wrote Dwight—was to explain that "for obvious reasons connected with E's private movements which then seemed to require her to stop for some time in New York; it was entirely private. Only Osborne, Brisbane, and Sarah [?] were present. We designed to make it known when E came home"—to Brook Farm—"which was to have been in the summer, but as the present crisis in Brook Farm affairs brought me home, it is made public of course."

George Ripley was very much put out at the way Dana had handled his marriage. "It is announced today for the first time," he wrote Dwight on March nineteenth, "and tonight a second reunion takes place for the attraction. As you may suppose the whole matter calls forth some amazement; and the people are not altogether well pleased at the mystery in which it has been kept." In Ripley's view it constituted an injudicious step on the part of Charles, and he feared that the influence of it on Dana's relation to the Association would not be pleasant.

Marianne sent a note to Anna by Mr. Monday inviting her out to the Danas' second wedding ceremony, but it came back in his pocket when the party was over; so the best she could do was to write Anna how the "second reunion" had gone off. About a dozen of their best people had registered disapproval by staying away. "Others of us felt and thought that altho' the privacy of the wedding and other circumstances were unpleasant, or perhaps worse than that; this announcement was, at least, a right step; and it was best to go, and in kindness and justice make it as agreeable as we could."

William H. Channing, who believed he knew all the circumstances, thought the hostility was uncalled for. "And it certainly seems absurd," Marianne observed, "when Unity is our only hope." She added a trifle cattishly, that she doubted whether William Channing really did know all. "At any rate, he don't know Eunice," she pointed out. Fanny, Eunice's sister, had put Marianne "in possession of the whole," plus permission to tell Anna. But Marianne thought it best not to write it.

The "wedding party" had a seemingly salutary effect on Dana's morale. He who had recently talked long in council, maintaining the view that it would be impossible to carry on any mechanical branches or agriculture, or to make any attempt towards an Association; who would, indeed, dismiss all but about twenty people, now spoke brightly and cheeringly of Brook Farm's future.

11.

The Directors had not announced the bad news of the Court's verdict to the rank and file of the Phalanx late in March, when Marianne wrote Anna, "We are still in cheerful and hopeful trust, and in deliberation." One thing alone seemed settled—they would not and could not disband. Whether they stayed on at Brook Farm or moved elsewhere, they were determined to live and die together. She added that Allen had written them in a truly religious spirit; and a letter from Mr. Kay, written upon receiving their bad news, actually sounded "quite delighted" that their phalanstery was gone, he, always having "quarrelled with it."

Optimism was the face the Farmers presented to the world; and it was also the pitch and tone of their leaders' communications with the public. But, privately, Ripley and Dana were cast down by the magnitude of the task of putting Brook Farm on its feet again.

Ripley wrote frankly to Dwight, who was having such a good time in New York that he was inclined to be over-hopeful of the outcome resulting from his activities. "Everything I consider to be precarious in the highest degree. Several plans are proposed. The discussions are harmonious; we all agree as to what we want, more than we can see the means of accomplishment. They all want to hang onto the industry in every branch, and most feel sanguine that it will be more successful than ever before."

George Ripley—surely the most unmercenary of men?—added what seems, in view of their New York friends' cancellation of stock, a grasping suggestion: "If the New York friends wish to do anything in the way of subscription, I think it should be encouraged, as it will do no hurt, certainly, and it may do some good."

To add to George Ripley's financial discomfiture, there was found to be no fire insurance. The *Harbinger* dismissed this misfortune in cursory fashion: "As it was not yet in use by the Association: and until the day of its destruction not exposed to fire, no insurance had been effected." Elsewhere the rumor persisted to the effect that the insurance had expired a few days before the fire and through some oversight had not been renewed. If so, it would seem that Fred Cabot, until the previous December clerk of the Association, was responsible.

In any case Fred was fulminating at all his former friends. He scolded Marianne in particular about a letter which he had received from Charles Dana. Whether Dana had denounced Cabot for failing to remind them to renew the fire insurance on the phalanstery, or whether Charles had told Fred off for his uncalled for prophecies concerning the financial collapse of Brook Farm, which made it harder than ever for them to obtain further credit, Marianne does not make clear. She only told Anna that both Mrs. Ripley and John S. Dwight felt that the tone of Dana's letter had been too outspoken. "Still they did not think it a matter of great importance as it contained the truth, though boldly stated." Marianne herself felt it was small of Fred to be so aggrieved. She considered poor Fred's mind had lately become quite diseased on the subject of Brook Farm, and she pitied him sincerely.

Cabot's behavior grew very insulting to Mr. Ripley. He addressed a long document, in self-defense, to the council. This he sent, care of John Orvis, with a few lines explaining that "he was determined to have the Council hear it, and he was afraid that if he sent it to Mr. Ripley, he would pocket it and not be willing to produce it before the Council."

When told of Cabot's lack of courtesy, George Ripley replied mildly, "I am not a man to fight a duel."

Indeed Marianne could not find anyone at Brook Farm who cherished ill feeling against the poor benighted Cabot. "He has himself created a great hubbub about his own ears—we don't make it— we believe that when left to himself he will come to himself and be as much ashamed of the steps he has taken, and the hue and cry he is making, as his friends here are now ashamed of him."

A few days later Marianne herself got a letter from Fred Cabot. "To call it by its right name, it is the most insulting thing he has written yet." He sounded less excited, but seemed "to feel so ugly and vengeful." Marianne wished Fred would "chain up those devils, and listen to the still, small voices of his good angels." Of course, she would not answer such a letter; she had turned it over to her intended; and John Orvis would write Fred "a good, loving letter."

This was a far cry from the day when she had enjoyed several flirts a day with the waggish punster. Why, Marianne asked herself, had she not seen that Fred was but a weak little whippersnapper? Mr. Kay had foreseen that Fred "would be lost if the parental hand of Association were not extended to him." And Mr. Kay, like Marianne, had loved Fred Cabot for the actual and the possible good which were in him.

There was a certain deep joy in Marianne's heart these days, giving a tone and strength to all her emotions. But she did not realize that it could be love and the spring which were making it so easy for herself and John Orvis to rise above any discouragement as easily as swallows on the wing. What if the Association did owe $500 or $600? Such debts, owed to friends, gave them no trouble beyond the necessity "that we have the interest to pay on them, which is a burden we long to be free from." Obviously, most of their difficulties had come upon them because the school had been given up at a time when they depended on it for support—given up in order to rush into various industries. "We should have waited till some mechanical department was able to support us," she wrote sadly, "before we permitted the decline of the school."

This was true, up to a point. But Marianne, like all at Brook Farm, failed to take in the extent of the scandal created by the attack of the New York press on Fourier's views on sex and marriage. It is doubtful if the Farmers could have made a success of the school after "the Change"; and their efforts to revive it now seem as incongruous as would be a Sunday school run by an atheist.

Those who could not bear to see Brook Farm fail now attributed their difficulties to the recent smallpox epidemic, and the destruction of the phalanstery—to anything rather than the ill-repute of Fourier's theories. They were blind, also, to the fact that their misfortunes had benefited the North American Phalanx in Red Bank, New Jersey. The Brook Farmers still had faith in the sympathy and support of their New York friends. How providential that John Dwight's lectures continued to be so well received by them at this critical time! No doubt he would be asked to repeat them in New York, and to give them in Philadelphia as well.

Sweetest of all this bitter-sweet to Marianne, they were experiencing "a new flowering of the tree of life that seems to have taken such deep root in this spot, in spite of the soil." An associate, W. H. Cheswell, wishing to celebrate the anniversary of his arrival at their Eden, invited everybody to attend his regular dancing school one evening.

Marianne had a headache and did not want to go, but was persuaded by her brother on the ground that "Friend Cheswell had always looked with a jealous eye on the aristocratic element." The occasion proved a huge success. The dancing went off in fine style; and about ten o'clock, two by two, they marched into a supper of coffee, cake, cheese and crackers.

After partaking of these dainties, Charles Dana read toasts to all the different groups—"from the printing group to the sewers" and called upon individuals for speeches. "These were ready and admirable. We had fun and wit and poetry and sober good sense, and earnestness and solemnity . . ." Best of all was the new consecrating of each one to the work at Brook Farm. Charles Dana himself with recovered strength and energy expressed his deep faith that the cause of Association must and would to some extent be carried on there.

It was one of the very best parties Marianne had ever attended. No restraint—anybody had felt free to get up and pledge the good word. Unfortunately, the Archon—Mr. Ripley—could not be present. On hearing about the party, he wanted to have it all over again! But, of course, it was such a meeting that never happens but once.

Marianne was happy, too, because she had finished sixty flower paintings and sent them to J. A. Lowell Esq. who accepted them and sent back $30 at once. This elated Marianne—"In truth we are a phalanx!" she declared.

A SEASON **VIII** IN UTOPIA

IN UTOPIA

▶▶▶▶▶▶▶▶▶▶▶▶▶▶▶▶▶▶▶◀◀◀◀◀◀◀◀◀◀◀◀◀◀◀◀◀◀◀◀

Disbanding

FOR A TIME THEIR OPTIMISM SEEMED TO BE JUSTIFIED. THE MARCH TWENTY-first issue of the *Harbinger* announced: "The loss we have sustained occasions us no immediate inconvenience, does not interfere with any of our present operations; although it is a total destruction of resources on which we had confidently relied and must inevitably derange our plans for the enlargement of the Association and the extension of our industry." It was comforting to be able to report that since the disaster everyone in the neighborhood of Boston had been extremely kind. In the following issue, a Philadelphian who had sent a contribution of $110 pointed out that if nine other persons would do the same, the Association would be back on its feet.

On April seventh, the General Council brought back very good news from Boston—so good that one wonders, in the light of later events, whether those who reported it mistook possibilities under consideration for accomplished facts. The members of the Council had offered the Boston creditors a proposition—to convert the $7000 of debts into partnership stock. "They did better for us than this," Marianne jubilantly informed Anna. They relinquished the entire debt—"each creditor giving up a sum in proportion to the amount of his claim." Moreover, the Phalanx also obtained exemption from paying any interest for a year; and after that for the next four or five years. "If after allowing for our board and clothing, any profits remain, they are to be divided equally between us and the creditors."

In the same generous spirit, Mr. Morton, who had built Pilgrim House at his own expense, said he was perfectly ready to assent to any arrangement the Farmers might propose, and he also kept reiterating his faith in Association and in Brook Farm's survival.

Then, inevitably, the tide of optimism began to recede. On April sixteenth, Edmund Tweedy wrote Dwight, who had warned him to expect a visit from Ripley; "You have recently left New York, where you had such a free interchange of sentiment with the friends of the cause that you are as well able to judge as myself how much would be contributed towards the amount you stand in need of. I think something will be done here, although the feeling is strong with the New York friends to give *all* in their power to the North American Phalanx in New Jersey. I will see some friends of the cause and show your letter to them previous to the arrival of Mr. Ripley. I start tomorrow for the North American Phalanx to do what I can to adjust some difficulties that exist there . . ."

Next, on April twenty-second, their good friend, James Kay, who had rejoiced over the destruction of their phalanstery on the ground that it would have proved impractical, now wrote that he would be able to pay only some few of the petty bills the Farmers had asked him to help out on. He claimed ill health as an excuse for not taking a more active part, being under "the care of our water doctor." Even more disappointing was his changed attitude, for he now professed doubt concerning their ability to carry on. He was evasive in regard to future contributions, and admonished them sternly to rid themselves of all "unprofitable members and pupils"—those who could not pay their own way.

It was a shock to the Farmers to find that, after the first flush of sympathy had worn off, friends hedged on their promises. However, they rallied their forces in remarkably short order. Already, the *Harbinger* had announced their new policy—to stay within their resources and to restrict their activities to such industries as were already prosperous, and the farm; and to apply their creative energies to the rehabilitation of the school.

"The greenhouse is to have some additional force," Marianne wrote Anna, April twenty-fourth. "The printing is to be carried on as before with the addition of a hand press to be kept constantly at work, which will bring a handsome profit. The shoe making is to be abolished—one hand to be employed in mending. The tailoring to be given up, except so far as to make garments for people on the place—in order to give the tailoring force to the farm, which needs help exceedingly. Hereafter we are to take note of results rather than hours—a change in which I heartily rejoice." A change which, it might be added, proclaimed the folly of Fourier's theory of the Groups and Series.

To Marianne fell the management of the school. She had recently been elected chief of the teachers group, or superintendent; and Mrs. Ripley, who had been ill, would serve only as supervisor. Marianne was determined to make the school succeed again. "Just think of the faculty at hand!" The Ripleys, John S. Dwight, Dana, her own sister, Fanny, Miss Russell. In her optimism Marianne ignored the most essential item—applications. "No new scholars have come yet," she wrote. But she was confident they would appear as soon as it became known that the Brook Farm school, once so famed for its outstanding faculty, was functioning again.

Money was lacking in almost every department, and a subscription—a "drive"—was going on. The Archon was kept constantly on the go, calling on rich prospects in neighboring towns. He now felt they had a right to call upon rich civilizees to help with their money—for were Associonists not building up a truer system of life? But sometimes Mr. Ripley had to veto the plans of over-zealous friends—as he did Anna Parsons' plan to hold a public gathering in Fanueil Hall.

Despite his courage and outward show of cheerfulness, these were, indeed, disheartening days for George Ripley. His wife's health had begun to fail under the long strain; and the associates were leaving Brook Farm in ever increasing numbers. In some cases these withdrawals were welcomed, when those persons left, "who, though good in their way, yet lack that refinement which is indispensable to give a good tone to the place." Still, their dwindling number was another evidence of failure at home; and Fourier's Birthday had passed almost unnoticed in New York, this year, indicating failure at National Headquarters, as well. At the tiny celebration they had managed to hold, the late John Manesca, the first convert to Fourierism in the United States, received more acclaim than Albert Brisbane the Apostle. Macdaniel and Godwin both were depressed—they felt that hidden forces were at work, opposing the movement. As for George Ripley, had it not been for the *succès d'estime* the *Harbinger* was enjoying, the Founder of Brook Farm would have had little to show but debts and charred embers in return for five years of hard, courageous work.

From the very first issue, the critical reviews of the *Harbinger* proved noteworthy; and even in this spring of anxiety, Ripley saw to it that such works as Melville's *Typee*, Keats's *Collected Poems*, and Dickens' *Travel Papers*, should receive deserving notices. In the musical world, Curtis and Dwight reported. Curtis covered overseas events, such as Berlioz concerts in Vienna; and Dwight contrived to get to New York as well as into Boston to hear the more outstanding performances in music. Ironically, either Ripley, Dwight, or Dana, whose goal at this time was a peaceful revolution, would have been surprised and also disappointed to learn that a more successful career was in store for each in literature, music, and journalism. None of the three would have been at all pleased to know that the *Harbinger* would be remembered for its cultural features long after its propaganda was forgotten.

Would it were possible, by letter or diary, to see into Sophia Ripley's mind and heart at this time. Poor Mrs. Ripley had been quite ill, and though better she was still far from well. Was she able to escape from household and tutorial cares to rest in the Piney Woods on beautiful summer-like days? The air was always deliciously balmy there, and everything smelled especially good after a shower! Could Sophia forget her dignity and wander there with her dearly beloved niece, Sarah Stearns? Or did they walk sedately beneath the cathedral-like pines, while the birdsong floated down from above like the trilling of a lofty choir? Did she and Sarah confide the growing yearning in their hearts for Roman Catholicism? Perhaps she would stop to rest on a boulder, while Sarah gathered wood violets and anemones. Did the recurring spring, the mournful plaint of the tree-toads at dusk, bring only wistful memories of happier years?

Though much was taken, much was left. There were still wonderful evenings in the Eyrie parlor when her dear close friend, John Dwight, sat improvising at the piano. Channing's flamelike presence would listen to the music, rapt, and when it ceased he would speak to them, as if inspired; and he would lift up their faint hearts. Such evenings were as good as any Brook Farm had ever offered!

But the atmosphere was not the same. The Eyrie windows overlooked the pudding-stone foundations of the burned phalanstery; and the evening air carried the faint stench of charred wood—a stern reminder that their black catastrophe was close by, defiling the greenness, the spring-to-summer sweetness.

2.

By May it was evident that the financial campaign had failed. Subscriptions were few and very small. Brisbane's name did not appear among the contributors listed in the *Harbinger;* and it is certain that even a moderate donation from him would have been publicized there. However, he was more generous than ever with his advice. The cause could yet be saved, cried Mr. Brisbane, by drumming up more general interest and new recruits.

George Ripley, going along with Brisbane again, suggested that a central society should be formed, with auxiliaries all over the United States—to support an extensive lecture bureau and increase the number of publications.

At the public meeting which followed shortly, "on Minerva Street," Ripley addressed some three hundred people on the Religious Aspect of the Associative Life. This aspect was becoming more important because the New York press had begun to attack the whole movement by highlighting Fourier's, Owen's and Noyes's disrespect for marriage.

Before going home, Ripley made a trip by railroad and "one horse-rig" out to the North American Phalanx at Red Bank, New Jersey. Another visitor had already reported in the *Harbinger* on the excellence of the school there. But George Ripley was more impressed by the "advanced season" and the excellent soil. He was told that the soil was naturally thin, but when combined with the marl found in swamps nearby— a crumbly soil of mixed clay, sand, and calcium carbonate—it became very productive. "Not a stone is to be seen," Ripley marvelled, "and the ground is so easy of cultivation it might almost be worked with a silver fork."

Anyone who has tried to grow vegetables in rocky, gravelly, early-and-late-frost-bitten New England pastures, knows how envy-making the sight of a New Jersey truck garden in May can be. Fortunately for his peace of mind, George Ripley, like many an intellectual who dallies with rustic pursuits, now knew that his talents did not blossom in cabbage patch or turnip field. More rewarding, a nation-wide op-

portunity seemed to be opening up for his own New England Fourier
Society, and he looked forward with impatience to the meeting in
"Hall No. 1, Marlborough Chapel, under the Chinese Museum," to be
held on Wednesday, May twenty-seventh, at 10 A.M.

When the great day came, the New England Fourier Society, "having
no immediate business to transact," quickly resolved itself into the
American Union of Associonists. The constitution was drawn up according to the usual principles, but the *Harbinger's* report of the occasion disclosed two astounding developments. Albert Brisbane's name
appeared on the nominating committee, but he held no office under
the A. U. of A. Constitution, except that of a New York Director.
It was as if the Apostle of Fourierism in America had chosen to
become a mere observer. Which was not to be wondered at, in view
of an article of this new constitution—in which the leading Fourierites
denied allegiance to Fourier. In the preamble they referred to "cal-
umnies"; declared they felt called upon to reaffirm their faith in God
and to declare themselves general reformers. "Fourierites we are not
and cannot consent to be called, because Fourier is only one among
the great teachers of mankind; because many of his assertions are
concerning spheres of thought which exceed our present ability to
test, and of which it would be a presumption for us to affirm with
confidence; and because we regard this as a holy and providential
movement, independent of every merely individual influence or guidance, the sure and gradual evolving of Man's great Unitary Destiny
in the Ages."

This article has the slightly pedestrian but highly commonsense ring
of George Ripley at his best. Indeed it makes one wonder how much
he had been a party to those Fourier Birthday Celebrations—especially
the somewhat idolatrous festival at Brook Farm on April seventh
1845. In any case, he was free of excessive devotion now, and filled
with a more healthy enthusiasm. As one of the Boston Directors of
this new national organization, Ripley was convinced that his work as
editor-in-chief of the *Harbinger,* and as a speaker, was eminently
worthwhile. This new national field distracted him somewhat from the
failure which stared him in the face at Brook Farm.

3.

Meanwhile, Ripley's friend, W. H. Channing was using the full extent of his power to revive the faith and courage of the staunchest Farmers, which had never fully recovered from the calamity of the fire. Yet he thought that the Brook Farm Phalanx was done for, and strove to regard the destruction of the phalanstery as a blessing in disguise. "The sad affair has pained me much, yet scarcely as much as I should have expected," he wrote a friend. "For as experience multiplies we see so clearly that life is an endless series of birth and death, of ebb and flow, of seeming failure and eventual triumphs . . . that one learns never to mourn, but always to hope; never so much as amid disappointment, to trust and aspire. Should this blow be the *coup de grâce* to this band of friends who for years have been on the rack of anxiety and effort, I shall wait by the tomb for the resurrection."

At the Farm, discouragement increased as the summer wore on. Many programs announced by the *Harbinger* never came off for lack of funds. Channing, Dana, and Brisbane did speak at Lowell and Worcester, and later in Hingham. But nothing much came of their efforts; and by the end of July, even Marianne Dwight could no longer contain her deep sense of frustration. Though she believed that they were in God's hands and resigned herself to His will, she saw little reason to hope for success. "I think we might have it, if the people were persistent," she wrote her brother, Frank, "but there is a general discouragement and want of hope."

Even such old-timers as Mr. Kleinstrup and Mr. Palisse were off to inspect the North American Phalanx with a view to removing their families from Brook Farm; and the Mondays were getting restive, too. Among the hierarchy, Charles Dana and his wife were now determined to leave regardless of whatever arrangements were made to carry on. Marianne sensed that some among their "secret inner council . . . don't even care to have an industrial association . . . and aim only to carry on the school and the *Harbinger* . . . They want to let out the farm . . ."

Marianne complained to her brother Frank that she got no time these days to write by daylight, and to write by lamplight, in that unscreened era, with its heat, oily stench, and magnetism for insects, was altogether too uncomfortable.

Frank Dwight apparently had made a recent and badly timed visit to Brook Farm. The hot muggy weather he had encountered was now dissipated by a cool northwest breeze. If Frank had come a day later he would have had music at the Eyrie, and he would not have had to sleep on the floor to keep cool.

Another meeting of the Council was imminent, and Marianne dreaded the outcome. Even her brother John and Mr. Ripley were eager now to let the workers form independent groups and compete. It was hoped that this concession might prove a spur to industry; and that the people would "exert themselves more when they are to have the benefit themselves, than when the money is going into an Association."

To permit competition among their workers was a retreat from the cause in Marianne's view. But perhaps she would not have been so critical had she known that George Ripley recently had been ordered by the Middlesex Court of Common Pleas to pay Nathanial Hawthorne $560.62, and that his only means of paying the debt would be by the sale of his precious library, said to contain one of the finest collections of foreign books in America.

As her distress increased during this summer of dwindling hope and desperate need, Marianne analyzed the different mental attitudes of the people around her, and divided them into classes—not groups. The first one she called "the promulgators"—represented by the Ripleys, Danas, and Macdaniels. They declared themselves through with life in an industrial organization, and no longer interested in life at Brook Farm. "They are working," she wrote, "for the far future but don't believe in trying now to make their lives conform to the principles of Association. I should call them *amateur* associonists. They have taken the doctrine into their heads more than into their hearts . . ."

Second: the class John S. Dwight represented, who wanted to stay on at Brook Farm for the sake of the life there. But he, too, had lost interest in associated industry, except as something to be attempted, by and by.

Third: the class who wanted to go right on trying to live together in associated industry. Obviously, this was John Orvis's stand, and he combined with it, promulgation and love of the life at Brook Farm.

Marianne, like her intended, wanted to "have the life by the only

possible way which can produce it, viz., by associative industry . . ."
They and their followers were in the majority, Marianne was sure.
She and Orvis and Lizzie Curzon had worked out a plan to "let"
the Ripley faction run the school and the *Harbinger*, and pay board
to the Association. "We then will make the farm as a farm ought ever
to be, the pivotal branch," she asserted with unwarranted confidence,
"with a dozen good men it will do well." Even the greenhouse would
be maintained as a forcing house in winter to raise cucumbers and
tomatoes to sell for a high price. Over the moth-beaten chimney
of the kerosene lamp, Marianne dreamed on—never taking into account the lessons which the Ripleys had learned the hard way—that
in West Roxbury, farm and garden produce were too far removed
from the Boston markets to pay; and that the school had been
ruined once and for all, because the rich, conservative parents had
no intention of exposing their offspring to an indoctrination of
Fourierism, even if that radical doctrine was administered by respected friends—Mr. and Mrs. George Ripley. Indeed Marianne under
the influence of her intended could not even realize that the Farmers'
last venture, Associative Industry, could never have become profitable
except on a larger scale than their building equipment ever had
housed. All three—Marianne, John Orvis, and one Lizzie Curzon—
never identified—appear to have forgotten why the phalanstery was
ever begun. "Dear William Channing" approved their plan—but
he was never noted for his business ability.

Marianne and Orvis, with some others, wanted to put their plan into
immediate effect. Marianne echoed their misgiving. "Can we do it?
Shall we have the courage, the perseverance, the industry, the self-
sacrifice that will be demanded?"

Marianne was not at all sure "if this plan" would "suit her ladyship"
—Mrs. Ripley. If only Sophia would consent to it, they were sure it
would succeed.

<h1 style="text-align:center">4.</h1>

Greeley continued to support the cause, because he regarded it as
the most promising solution of the unemployment problem. But his
prominence as a member of their party made his radical stand distasteful

to the conservative Whig journals in the New York press—the *Observer*, the *Express*, the *Courier and Enquirer*.

Inevitably, the *Harbinger* was drawn into the controversy. In past years hostile papers had delighted in printing the advance obituary of an Association that was still struggling to survive, in the hope of undermining the confidence of benefactors and recruits. Now the attackers quoted Parke Godwin to prove that under Fourier's System the passions would run rife; so that religion, morality and marital constancy would give way to every conceivable vice. To horrify Mrs. Grundy, artful editors reported that Fourier's disquisitions on sex were filled with toothsome descriptions of "Corporations of Bacchantes and Bayaderes." In vain, Ripley protested, that, on the contrary, their aim was to lift up woman to equal rights with man. When the bright day of emancipation came, ". . . woman will not merely be set up as the doll queen of a tournament, and drop her glove to the champion in the lists of vanity's poor contest, but she will help man win, and she will share with him full many of his peaceful victories."

Ripley took what comfort he could in the fact that the Whig conservatives' attack on Greeley turned out to be so unpopular that the *Courier and Enquirer* soon took a more restrained tone. "Our plan"—the editors said—"begins with the individual and through him affects the mass." This was to become the crux of the argument, individualism versus environment; and the majority of Americans being individualists, they instinctively regarded Association as against nature.

In spite of the Farmers' efforts, subscriptions to the *Harbinger* continued to fall off. From time to time the editors did perpetrate some "howlers" in the economic field, such as the ballad entitled "The Sentimental Manufacturer to the Factory Girl." The following verse is a sample:

> While mid the din of winding wheels
> And clashing looms thou art,
> I sit at ease in my arm chair,
> Or count my gains apart.
> I know thy hands have earned them all
> And given them all to me.
> While thou for me art weaving cloth
> I'll weave a song for thee.

There are many stanzas in similar vein before the manufacturer confesses, by way of conclusion, that he is yearning for the day when all the work of this industrious maiden shall be done for love of himself "as now it is for pay."

In the literary field, however, the selections continued to maintain a high standard. It is exciting to come upon a "new" poem by Emerson or Whittier, Tennyson or Blake; to find a review by one distinguished man of a work by another, such as William Moorfield Storey's review of Thomas Carlyle's *On Heroes and Hero Worship.*

Their affairs continued from bad to worse. At the meeting of the American Union of Associonists held in Boston in September, Dwight gave a depressing report. They lacked funds to finance their lecturers; and unless sufficient pledges were received for the Fourth Volume of the *Harbinger* their organ would have to expire at the end of the year. There was one new and highly encouraging sign of the times, disclosed by Dana at this meeting, a trend which would occupy a place of increasing importance in the movement as the interest in phalanx-living dwindled. This was the multiplication of joint stock and mutual insurance companies—all founded on the principle of Association.

The money subscribed to the *Harbinger* became a mere dribble. By the end of October they had only $127, and they needed $500. Ripley was now more interested in the survival of the *Harbinger* than in maintaining Brook Farm, and he bent all his energies to raising the necessary funds.

Mr. Ripley's indifference to the rapid disintegration of their beloved home was shocking to Orvis and the Dwight family. Their attitude was reflected in an article published in the *Harbinger* late that fall, "How Stands the Cause?" "The incidental part has failed," the writer said in conclusion, "but the essential fact survives. They do not ask for any pecuniary aid, but that Brook Farm be not considered a failure. It is the very Mecca of Association; the Sacred Citadel. If it vanishes the cause will suffer." The writer admitted that rumors of approaching disbandment could no longer be denied. "Yet there is the strongest clinging to life among those of its members who have been enabled to remain, and it is felt to be like death to give it up."

5.

Fate, with its occasional irony, was to use Horace Greeley to finish off the Association Movement in the United States. Provoked by the recurrent attempts of the conservative Whig journals to discredit his position as an influence in the Whig Party, Greeley proposed a public debate between his own *Tribune* and Colonel James Watson Webb's *Courier and Enquirer*, "on the whole subject of Fourieristic Association in the United States."

Editor Webb delegated the *Courier and Enquirer* argument to Henry J. Raymond, a brilliant young newspaperman from upper New York State, who had been the first of Greeley's famous discoveries. Greeley had tried Raymond out on his *New Yorker*, and trained him so well that the younger man later served as Greeley's right-hand man on the *Tribune*. Greeley pronounced Raymond an able journalist, but deplored his "instinct for caution and immovable conservatism." These qualities since had led to differences of opinion; and eventually Raymond left the *Tribune* for Colonel Webb's more conservative *Courier and Enquirer*. Now he was the natural choice of that newspaper to handle Greeley's injudicious challenge.

To Greeley it appeared that the attempt to discredit him as a dangerous radical because of his support of Fourieristic Association was a journalistic trick. It should be easy, he thought, to silence the paper which was trying to read him right out of the Whig Party on the ground that there could be no peace in Whig ranks so long as the *Tribune* was allowed to call itself a Whig sheet. He did not realize that he had already made one irretrievable mistake in committing himself to a discussion of Fourier's complete System. He had never studied it.

Greeley's biographer, William Harlan Hale, points out that when he first endorsed Fourierism, three years before, Greeley had missed one of its implicit points—that it would submerge the individual in the phalanx. But however ill-digested his endorsement, he had backed it up with an investment of some $3000 in the ill-planned Sylvania, in Pennsylvania; and recently the North American Phalanx at Red Bank, N. J., had cost Greeley $4300.

At this time, Greeley was no longer in full accord with Brisbane's "exclusive" type of Association. Why couldn't Brisbane, he asked, go along with the general movement of reform, now manifesting itself in labor unions, mutual insurance companies, and other cooperative enterprises?

In spite of these reservations, Greeley, with serene self-confidence agreed to debate with Raymond ". . . in favor of Association as we understand it . . . until each party shall have published twelve articles on its own side, and twelve on the other . . ."—each debater in his respective newspaper.

Greeley opened up the debate by emphasizing the dangers inherent in widespread unemployment, and asserted that Association was the only possible cure. Raymond likened Greeley's views to those of Fanny Wright, the English philanthropist who had settled in the South to abolish slavery and establish Equal Rights, whose views had since been taken up by the Locofocos, a radical faction of the Democratic Party. Raymond professed sorrow to think that a man of Greeley's powerful influence should lend himself to such revolutionary doctrines. Greeley recoiled in horror from Fanny Wright. But Raymond had not finished with the land question. The Equal Rights principle, he pointed out, if carried to its logical conclusion, would result in the land being divided with each increase in population—every year.

In vain, Greeley retorted that it was not on this ground that he wished to debate. He implored Raymond to keep to the point—the phalanstery. Thereupon Greeley launched into a panegyric, similar to those wishful-thinking engraved pictures of a large and prosperous phalanstery surrounded by its domain which Brisbane delighted to display. Greeley had printed many similar arguments in the *Tribune*— with no one to dispute his claims.

Brook Farmers had looked forward to the debate with enthusiasm. Perhaps they were satisfied, at first, with Mr. Greeley's argument. It was, after all, the same fare Mr. Brisbane had always treated them to. But, as the debate progressed, Raymond's ruthless demand for practical proof that Associative Principles could be made to pay must have made their own failure increasingly bitter. Greeley, of course, could not produce proof, and his argument petered out in an increasingly ineffective sputter.

George Ripley had met his day of reckoning long before the debate between the journalists petered out. Before the turn of the year, Ripley had sold his library to his friend, Theodore Parker. If the sale had helped to make possible the continued publication of the

Harbinger, the sacrifice would have seemed a rewarding one to him at the time. Nonetheless, the loss of his books cut deep. As he took a last look at his treasured collection, George Ripley said,* "I can now understand how a man would feel if he could attend his own funeral."

6.

On October seventeenth, Marianne Dwight had written her brother, Frank, "I am actually thinking of perpetrating marriage about Thanksgiving or Christmastime." The step, she felt, was directed by Heaven, plainly the path of duty and inevitable.

She and Orvis had been deferring their wedding for months because of poverty and the unsettled condition of the Phalanx. But it looked to them now as if matters would always be unsettled at Brook Farm— "as long as it exists." Besides, this was a very different step than it would be if "one or both were incapable of taking care of themselves."

Marianne had no fear on that score. They would be content with one room, "and have everything of our own, however plain or humble." John expected to have about seventy-five dollars saved up shortly; and Marianne hoped to make a small sum from her paintings. They calculated that about one hundred dollars would fit them out very comfortably at Brook Farm. But who knew what was going to happen to their "divine home"? Should it be necessary, come spring, John Orvis had two or three alternate plans.

During the winter he would be away lecturing and he felt "very unwilling to go off again as a single man. He wants the settled, home feeling that marriage will give." The date for their wedding ** was accordingly set for Christmas Eve. On December fifteenth, Marianne wrote Anna, "You know we wish very much to have a religious exercise, connected with the rite, which is in itself most solemnly religious, and I want you to learn how Mr. Channing feels about this . . ." Anything that pleased him would suit herself and John, Marianne was sure. She was determined to have the parlors decorated for Christmas, and "to open the evening with music suited to the occasion, which should be followed by music again, perhaps something solemn and joyful.

* Lindsay Swift: *Brook Farm.*
** Lindsay Swift traced fourteen marriages to friendships begun at Brook Farm, but Marianne Dwight's and John Orvis's was the only ceremony performed there.

Then an address, a serious religious address to the people from Mr. C. (a Christmas discourse or what he likes)—then music, which shall be a transition between the preceding and the social party which shall succeed."

Marianne wanted to give the people pleasure, and something more than pleasure, and she believed they wanted it, too. She hoped that Mary Bullard, who had a beautiful singing voice, would come. She couldn't think of anything better or pleasanter than such music followed by "the voice of the good friend, the religious teacher, whom we all love so much." Next morning she added a note to the effect that what she really wanted "on that evening, as in some of the olden times, was that we should all feel, though but for a while, the sentiment of Universal Unity glowing in our souls."

Whether W. H. Channing actually officiated is uncertain. In any case, Marianne's brother, John S. Dwight, pronounced a blessing of five words. Perhaps he said, "May ye love one another."

The bride and groom were given couches and a carpet for their parlor. "If you would have a room furnished out of nothing," Marianne exulted, "apply to Brook Farmers!"

That was to be the last boast Marianne ever would make about Brook Farm. The year 1846 petered out in an apathetic silence.

7.

Ever since the fire, W. H. Channing had entertained grave doubts as to whether Brook Farm should carry on. In a confidential letter to a friend one week after the catastrophe, he had written, "The attempt was ill-contrived, worse executed. The land was only moderate, water-power wanting, markets not accessible, capital insufficient, . . . industry unorganized, business entangled, etc., etc., to the end of the chapter of accidents . . ." Enough had been accomplished, however, "to testify to the possibility of associated industry under more favorable circumstances."

Of late Channing's energies were turned to establishing the Religious Union of Associonists—on the tenets of the Christian Socialism which he had been preaching for many years. In the late fall, he had written Dwight, "Out of idealism, and pantheism, and egoism, have we passed into realism, and mediation, and immortal communion. We have a religion to announce to our fellows." His plans took definite shape at Christmastime. A Convention of the Associonists Union of America, was held at 10 A.M. Thursday, December thirty-first in Bromfield Hall, Boston. The purpose, the *Harbinger* reported, was to form "a religious union" under the direction of W. H. Channing —to "give greater depth and fervor to Association everywhere and the lie to those who say associonists are undermining the sacred institutions of mankind."

The outstanding event of the Convention was W. H. Channing's explanation of the principles upon which he proposed to found a church.

He invited all those who felt prepared to consecrate themselves to this great cause of Association, regarding it as the cause of God and Humanity, to meet on Sunday afternoon, January third, at the private house of James T. Fisher, to form the nucleus of a religious union.

About forty persons assembled in Mr. Fisher's house at 103 Harrison Avenue in Boston, at three o'clock the following Sunday. There was sacred music and reading from the scriptures. After meditation William Channing read the statement he had drawn up, "In Faith that it is the will of God by the ministry of man to introduce upon this planet an era of Universal Unity; in Hope of the advent of the Kingdom of Heaven upon Earth, desired by the good and wise of all ages and clearly announced by Jesus Christ; and moved by the Holy Spirit which impels this generation to long and labor for the perfect at-one-ment; we do now consecrate ourselves unreservedly to the service of our Heavenly Father, in the purpose to live for the fulfillment of the designs of His Providence, and do pledge to one another our faithful sympathy, counsel, aid, in striving to spread among mankind the reign of Love, One Harmonious Universal."

> Glory to God in the Highest,
> And on Earth, Peace
> Goodwill toward men!

Some thirty people signed, and joined hands in the circle. Among them the Ripleys, John S. Dwight, Francis G. Shaw, John T. Codman, Frederick S. Cabot, Mary Bullard, Anna Q. T. Parsons, Fanny Macdaniel, Barbara Channing—and, of all people, Albert Brisbane.

"The Union," as it came to be called, had no direct connection with Brook Farm. But it did supply an unorthodox spiritual last sacrament to that Association when it was disintegrating.

On Sunday afternoons the members assembled in Boston with Mr. Channing "at Mr. Fisher's house"; and again in the evening "at Phonographic Hall." Throughout the coming winter and spring, those Farmers who hoped that the Association Movement would rise from the ashes of their phalanstery went to the Union to renew their faith.

O. B. Frothingham, in his life of William Henry Channing, describes the ceremony in detail: "At the head of the room, in front of the central window was arranged a temporary altar,—a table covered with pure white linen, on which was put the Open Word and a candlestick with three lighted candles, one green, one red, and one white. Immediately in front stood a large square table covered with white linen, upon which was placed in the centre, a dish of fruit—oranges, figs, and grapes. Surrounding this were twelve goblets and a pitcher of water, at each corner was a plate of biscuit, and at the sides were bunches of flowers. A small cross of evergreen, trimmed with violets, hung behind the altar, against the white background of the window curtain; and above it was hung an evergreen circle and triangle. Directly behind the altar stood an empty chair, representing the Unseen Presence. The members were seated round the table in the forms of an ellipse, the altar being one of the foci . . ." After the customary exercises, "The minister rose, spoke of the meaning and value of the Communion Service in the Church, of the close intimacy among the disciples, of the connection between the spiritual and the material worlds, and of the correspondence of Bread, Water, and Fruit with Wisdom, Love, and Joy. The elements were then passed round, during the repast conversation being carried on of a religious character. 'He Shall Feed His Flock' was sung, and the stated exercises closed."

The Union was preparing a series of lectures—to commence on the seventh of January, in the Masonic Temple; and to be continued weekly to the number of seven or eight. Tickets for one person $1.00; Lady and Gentleman $1.50; single lecture $.25.

Program

I Destiny of Man Upon Earth—Wm. H. Channing
II Progressive Development—C. A. Dana
III Tendencies of Modern Civilization—Greeley
IV Charles Fourier—Parke Godwin
V The Grounds of Association in the Spiritual Nature of Man—
George Ripley
VI The Practical Nature of Association—(To be announced)
VII Integral Education—John S. Dwight

The leading Fourierites championed this new religious aspect of Association, believing that it was high time to confound those who accused Fourierites of seeking to undermine religion and morals; "We beseech you," Orvis and Allen had written from Vermont in December, "not to relinquish the plan of a church in Boston."

Within a few weeks the *Harbinger* strove to cheer the faithful by announcing that the lectures sponsored by the Union were so well attended in Boston that plans were afoot to repeat them in New York. This was in the same tone in which Orvis wrote his bride from New Bedford on February first—that of whistling to keep the spirits up. "Yesterday we spoke in Concert Hall in the forenoon to a small audience, in the afternoon and evening to very good audiences both in point of numbers and character. There is much interest excited." They were to remain in New Bedford a whole week lecturing, and they had "written for Channing, Ripley, and Brisbane to present themselves." All things considered, Orvis felt they had "begun a great work in New Bedford and could accomplish something worthwhile."

But as one reads on, it becomes evident that his optimism was somewhat biased by his good fortune in finding "an excellent home"—where "the good host and hostess are profuse in their cordiality and in the extent of their hospitality." This "Mr. Roy" had even presented Orvis "with a couple of rather pretty shells" for his wife, which he would "take great pleasure in bearing to her, for somehow she has a remarkable influence over me and charms me to do a great many things for her that I wouldn't do for anyone else."

Orvis was in good spirits, also, because a livelihood had presented itself—one that fitted in with his ambitions, if he chose to establish himself in New Bedford. "I have been offered the editorial chair of a paper which it is proposed to get up in this place. I can have the supreme control of the editorial management and be paid a fair compensation for my services. In other words it will be *my* paper, whenever I may choose to make it so."

New Bedford people had "long wanted" such a paper, one "devoted to the advocacy of progress and reform." Orvis plainly was excited by the offer, but felt that his first duty was to serve the American Union as a lecturer. But if the Union would not support him in that capacity, he could not think of any sphere which would "be so pleasant to both of us as such a one as this." He would, of course, make the editorial policy "essentially Associative." The new paper, he believed, would sustain itself, because twenty-five men had volunteered to underwrite it, should there be a deficit. As an alternative to going into business, the opportunity seemed happy indeed. Because to enter any business "would wholly preclude any service in the general movement"—a condition not to be thought of.

Still, he would not make up his mind hurriedly. Much depended on whether the plan was agreeable to Marianne, and if her brother, John, approved. With that he signed himself, "Dearest, thine own dear husband, John Orvis."*

8.

By March, 1847, it had become painfully clear that Brook Farm must disband. A meeting was held there on March fourth. ". . . pursuant to a call in writing through the post office to each of the stockholders and creditors of the Brook Farm Phalanx; the following persons being present; namely, G. Ripley, J. M. Palisse, J. Hoxie, Francis G. Shaw, Geo. R. Russell, S. Butterfield, N. Cotton, P. M. Kleinstrup, G. Ripley in the chair; J. N. Palisse chosen secretary. . . ." The minutes continue: "After a verbal statement from G. Ripley respecting the present condition of the Phalanx, it was voted unanimously that G. Ripley be authorized to let the farm for one year from March first for $350; and the Keith lot for $100 more, with such conditions and reservations as he may deem best for the interest of the stockholders."

As the closing of Brook Farm drew near, the faith of the leaders had lost neither depth nor force. They still hoped that new methods would bring larger results in the field of Industrial Association.

As George William Cooke points out in his biography of Dwight, it is a mistake to conclude that Brook Farm left no influence except that wrought on individuals. In reality, Brook Farm was a forerunner of movements more important than itself. "Out of the Associonist Movement of the later forties," writes Cooke, "of which Brook Farm was the chief feature, came the efforts to organize the laboring men of the country." It was in this field that Orvis and Allen were now doing the spadework.

Ever since the organization of the New England Working Men's As-

* This unpublished letter is among the Henry S. Bourneman Collection, Fruitlands Museum Library, Harvard, Massachusetts.

sociation at Lowell at Allen's call in 1844—Louis K. Ryckman, then chief of the Brook Farm Shoemaking Series, had been chosen the first President—the Working Men had been agitating persistently for a "ten hour day," and the general improvement of the laborer.

Channing's "Union" also attracted some working men; and these when they learned that Brook Farm was disbanding, began to put their savings into cooperative enterprises. There were already a dozen such societies forming in Boston: ". . . and in ten years," Cooke adds, "there were five hundred and fifty in New England, with an annual business of one and one half million dollars." On March twentieth, W. H. Channing announced in the *Harbinger* that the Anniversary Meeting of the American Union of Associonists would shortly be held in New York, and he urged all the affiliated unions to send representatives and to pledge money. The *Harbinger* followed this up a week later with suggestions to the Affiliated Societies of the American Union. They were to make "every approach in practice to the Associative Idea—Mutual Guarantee; cooperative industry; cooperative stores; insurance; club houses and club hotels."

Current issues of the *Harbinger* made no mention of the plan to dispose of Brook Farm. Ripley was chiefly concerned with establishing "The American Union" in a central office in New York, to which he would remove both himself and his paper.

"Oh, Anna!" Marianne wrote her best friend on March twenty-ninth, "It is sad to think of the greenhouse plants being sold off. It is sad to see Brook Farm dwindling away, when it need not have been so. How it has struggled against all sorts of diseases and accidents, and defects of organization! With what vitality it has been endowed! How reluctantly it will give up the ghost! But is it not doomed to die by and of consumption? Oh! I love every tree and wood haunt—every nook and path, and hill and meadow. I fear the birds can never sing so sweetly to me elsewhere, the flowers never greet me so smilingly. I can hardly imagine that the same sky will look down upon me in any other spot,—and where, where in the wide world shall I ever find warm hearts all around me again? Oh! You must feel with me that none but a Brook Farmer can know how chilling is the cordiality of the world.

"But I am ready for anything that must be. I can give all up, knowing well that a more blessed home than we can imagine will yet be prepared for humanity. No words can tell my thankfulness for having lived here, whether joyful or painful. It certainly is very unusual for me, and I think it may be quite wrong, to look for less in the future than we have derived from the past, but it does seem as tho' in this wide waste of the world, life could not possibly be so rich as it has been here. This is a fact, however, that tho' our state here for some months past, has been on many accounts, very disagreeable, and very little to my taste, yet life is more rich to me at this very time than ever; my inner life more true and deep,—but I want a field for external action, a very small and humble one, of course, but I want something. I wait very patiently, however, and certainly find enough to be busy about . . ."

In the same letter, the last in the book, Marianne tells of her husband's success in Providence, Rhode Island. "Audiences larger than he has found elsewhere,—interest considerable. Charlie Newcomb wrote to Lucas that he spoke with great effect on Thursday p.m. They are to have a thorough convention there in two or three weeks—want Channing, Ripley, Allen. The people volunteer to pay all the expenses."

Torn between John Orvis's success and impatience to have him at home, Marianne continued, ". . . Well, God speed the good work! I only wish that I were worthy to have a hand in it—it is a great trial to me to feel so left out as I now do—and yet I see hardly anything I can do just now. But I am ready to fall into my place if I can find it . . ." On this wistful note of woman's longing for wider opportunity, Marianne vanishes from the Brook Farm scene.

But she probably helped to arrange the last celebration of Fourier's Birthday held in Boston on April seventh. Some one hundred and fifty persons attended it—many of them ladies. For the first time, except at Brook Farm, women had been invited. The men could not very well exclude them because the party was given by "the ladies of The Union." They did it in the old Brook Farm style with flowers, fruits, lyres, mottoes; and with busts of Burns, Socrates, Milton, Pythagoras, Dante, and a full-length portrait of Fourier—"from a likeness taken from life." The dinner was held in the hall of Allen and Cumston, pianoforte makers, so that an accompaniment of music was easily arranged. Indeed the occasion would have been quite perfect had it not been for some very boisterous dancing going on on the floor above.

This was to be the last party but one of any consequence given in Boston by those interested in Association.

In a letter to Dwight from Naples on April twenty-seventh, George William Curtis wrote, "I have heard various rumors of Brook Farm. None agreeable. I feel as if my letter might not find you there; but what can you be doing anywhere else? I have received no letter from you; no direct news from Brook Farm except through Lizzie Curzon and G. Bradford. I write as if Brook Farm was still there, and am more than ever your friend . . ."

Years later, in reply to some inquiry concerning his own recollections of the place, Curtis wrote, "The effect of a residence at the Farm, I imagine, was not greater willingness to serve in the kitchen, and so particularly assert that labor was divine; but discontent that there was such a place as a kitchen. And however aimless life there seemed to be, it was an aimlessness of the general, not the individual life. As an Association it needed a stricter system to insure success; and since it had not the means to justify its mild life, it necessarily grew to this."

He recalled also that when he had first gone to Brook Farm as a youth of seventeen, it had seemed to him, "as if all hope had died from the race, as if the return to simplicity and beauty lay through the woods and fields, and was to be a march of men whose very habits and personal appearance should wear signs of the coming grace."

Something of Curtis's dread of the effect of failure on those Farmers who had remained until now must have been shared by many others who recalled the high hope of the halcyon days. But with the exception of the Dwights and the Orvises and perhaps a few others, the absentees were actually more depressed by the approaching disbandment than were those who had lived, since the fire, in a cloud of uncertainty and doubt.

9.

Ripley's natural optimism was again in the ascendant; and the report at the Annual Meeting of the American Union of Associonists in New York seemed to warrant encouragement. In the past year, the speakers bureau had delivered two hundred and twenty-five lectures in about thirty towns, in addition to the course of lectures on the religious aspect of Association delivered in Boston and repeated in New York. Some nineteen affiliated Unions had been established.

But from George Ripley's point of view, the most exciting resolution on the agenda concerned the *Harbinger*; for it was he who persuaded the American Union of Associonists to approve the publication of his cherished journal under his direction. After the meeting he hurried back to Brook Farm to get out the June fifth issue—the last to be published there—and then returned to New York to get the motion ratified by the Central Committee.

"After a thorough and earnest examination and discussion of the whole subject it was unanimously resolved, that the Central Office in New York should be under the direction of George Ripley as General Agent of the Union; and that the *Harbinger* be published simultaneously in New York and Boston, with Parke Godwin as Editor, assisted by C. A. Dana and G. Ripley; and William Henry Channing and John S. Dwight in Boston,—it being understood that the branch office in Boston shall be under the direction of the Union in that city."

A very busy summer was in store for George Ripley. Although he would not take up his duties as General Agent until October, the *Harbinger* continued to appear without interruption; and in the meantime, there was the constant worry about settling his affairs at Brook Farm.

Ripley had inherited the only surviving activity of the American Union of Associonists; for the Committee of Thirteen, appointed at the Annual Meeting to look into the question of "establishing a practical experiment of Association," declared themselves still in a state of inquiry—where they would forever remain.

Soon after Ripley took over the Central Office in New York, a change in the policy of the *Harbinger* was announced. Slavery, Women's Rights, Guaranty-ism, both at home and abroad, would now be discussed—and in this Ripley would prove as good as his word.

In this same issue—July twenty-fourth—appeared the last advertisement of the Brook Farm School.

10.

John Codman writes in *Brook Farm, Historic and Personal Memoirs,* that of all the events of the life there, the disbanding was the most unreal. "It was like the knotted skein slowly unravelling. It was as the ice becomes water, and runs silently away. It was as the gorgeous, roseate cloud lifts itself up, and then changes in color and hides beyond the horizon. It was as a carriage and traveller fade from sight on the distant road. It was like the apple blossoms dropping from the trees. It was as the herds wind out to pasture. It was like a thousand and one changing and fading things in nature. 'It was not discord, it was music stopped.' "

This flowery passage conveys the homesickness for Brook Farm that John felt when his family sent him off to earn his living in Boston in the fall of 1846. He was able to assuage it somewhat because his parents stayed on until the following spring, although when John went back of a Saturday night he was sure to find some further curtailment of industry.

The shoemakers were the first to find work elsewhere. "At last the shop was closed, the cattle were sold, and all the industry ceased . . . The greenhouse where I had spent so much of my time was closed—the plants all gone . . ." The printers were the last to go.

After the *Harbinger* was moved to New York, George Ripley came to Brook Farm only to wind up the affairs of the Phalanx. Sophia did not come with him; she was struggling to find a position as teacher in one of the suburbs. John Dwight had gone to Boston to write for *Chronotype*; but his wife to be, Mary Bullard, lingered on at the Eyrie. John Codman reports that when Dwight came to visit her, "The spirits of song and music held their revels there."

Most of the time John Codman wandered around and looked at the empty rooms. The dining hall had been shut off. They now assembled for meals in the little reading room in the Hive. The former din from the kitchen was reduced to an echo of busier days. The stage no longer brought its loads of visitors to the Hive door. No children trooped to and fro from the Keith lot to school. The fields remained as last cropped. "No more mounted in air the beautiful doves that circled and tumbled in their flight—my doves, that would come at my call." The Pilgrim House was entirely deserted—and unfurnished. Those who owned any private effects or furniture had long since taken them away.

On the first weekend in June, some twenty young people gathered for the Summer Festival—"for one more good time, for one more communion." At noon they filled a table in the reading room. In the afternoon they wandered once more in the Piney Woods. Some roved about; some sat on the big boulder on the knoll at the foot of the lightning-struck tree. They reminisced about old times and seasons. They sang "Silver Moon" and other old favorites. They ate their simple treat and then they parted.

"Some went East, and some West, one to Port-au-Prince, and others to different towns and villages in New England."

The end, according to the minutes of "a meeting of the stockholders and creditors of the Brook Farm Phalanx, held pursuant to due notice given to all parties by George Ripley," occurred on August eighteenth, 1847. These minutes constitute the final official record of the Brook Farm Phalanx.

"Present: George Ripley, Theodore Parker, Samuel Teal, T. N. Kleinstrup, J. Kay, J. M. Palisse, Amelia Russell, Mary Anne Ripley."

Palisse was appointed Secretary of the meeting; and he recorded a unanimous vote that the President of the Phalanx, George Ripley, be "hereby authorized to transfer to a Board of Three Trustees the whole property of the Corporation for the purpose and with power of disposing of it to the best advantage of all concerned."

Theodore Parker, G. R. Russell, and Samuel P. Teal were voted in as Trustees; and they would have the power to add Mr. Francis Jackson, or some suitable person, to their number, should occasion require.

The latter was duly appointed their agent "in the management of the business confided to the Board's care."

Annie M. Salisbury, in her *Brook Farm*, depicts a sentimental scene that transpired at the conclusion of the business meeting. Some of them went, arms entwined, for a last stroll in the Piney Woods by moonlight. That night they dreamed again of the halcyon days. "The stern-ness of the waking does not destroy the beauty of the dream," she concludes serenely. "Brook Farm was an idyll, and in the days of epics the idyll is not easily forgotten."

➤➤➤

The Slow Death and Re-Direction of the
Association Movement

ON THE WHOLE THE AUTUMN OF 1847 PROVED ONE OF EXPECTANCY AND reviving hopes for the Ripleys. Sophia had found a position as teacher in Flatbush, New Jersey, and a room for herself and George near by. George, relieved to have put Brook Farm into the hands of competent trustees, looked eagerly to the American Union of Associionists to launch his career in a wider field than he had found in West Roxbury.

The Union, although not so prosperous as the members could wish, had finally raised sufficient funds to send their two most zealous propagandists, Orvis and Allen, on a lecture tour throughout New York State. Their mission got off to a very bad start, according to extracts "of their hasty private communications" printed in September in the *Harbinger*. In Albany only about half of the Union attended, and most of these had joined merely "to secure the benefits of the guarantees, and so do not believe in Association." Across the Hudson in Troy, the friends of Association professed interest but preferred "to expend their efforts later in the season when the people will be more at leisure to attend meetings." A hundred or more miles northwest, in Utica, there was not a single individual known as a friend to the movement. Westward bound they stopped at Syracuse, where the former interest in Association seemed completely blighted. This the missionaries attributed to the failure of the commune of "infidels" led by John Anderson Collins in neighboring Skaneateles which had disbanded in disgrace two years before. The few remaining "friends of Community" advised the easterners to delay their return visit until the Grand Canal should have closed, "for it has become a proverb here that when the Canal closes religion opens."

It finally dawned on the propagandists that although enthusiasm for the Phalanx was dead, interest in various reforms was on the increase. Accordingly, on leaving Rochester, they decided that henceforward they would limit their remarks to the subsidiary branches of Association—fields in which its principles were already being applied to great effect.

With considerable resourcefulness they dropped Association as the title of their discourse, and gave out a broader term—National Reform. This gained them an immediate hearing on their return to Syracuse; and the title afforded them an opportunity to denounce the evils of the American Factory System, and to stress the need for Working Men's Protective Unions.

In time, this would prove a most rewarding decision, both for Orvis and Allen and for the cause of the American working man. It also substantiates the claim Orvis would make years later when he had won renown as an unselfish labor agitator—"that Brook Farm was the chief instrument in setting on foot all the movements since 1840 for the betterment of the wage-earners and the toilers of every kind."

2.

A meeting of the Executive Committee of the American Union of Associonists, was held in Boston on Monday, the eleventh of October—the last ever held in that city. The establishment of the Union's office in New York was scheduled to take place immediately afterward.

Actually, the meeting began on Sunday, October tenth, when W. H. Channing conducted the Consecration under the auspices of the Religious Union of America in Bromfield Hall, on "a glorious day of bright autumnal weather." Afterward, visitors from out of town gathered "in the houses of old friends of the Union."

The next day the executive Committee met, and sadly computed their prospective income for the next six months. It amounted to $50— all of which was appropriated for maintenance of the Central Office in New York, and the *Harbinger*. A change in form was planned for that organ which it was hoped would make it more popular. Subscriptions alone could bring it to the self-supporting point, and "Until that point is reached, . . . the [American] Union are compelled to forego any direct appropriations to the end of continuing our lecturers in the field."

Eventually, it was agreed, there would be a special fund established for lecturing. "It will be the principal duty of the General Agent"— George Ripley—"to correspond with and to visit all the local or affiliated Unions, and with special reference to the increasing of the Rent, upon which all the efficacy of the American Union depends . . ."

The North American was the only Phalanx that appeared to be thriving these days. Many Brook Farmers had taken refuge there; and plans for a splendid phalanstery to be erected on "Brisbane Hill" had just been drawn up. The Wisconsin and the Trumbull had sent in cheerful reports, but there were rumors to the effect that neither one was as well established as their directors would have the public believe. It followed that the Committee of Thirteen, which had been formed in June to look into the question of launching another "Practical Experiment," resolved instead to look into "The cause of the failures in several late practical attempts at Association." A full and fair history of these was planned, "and especially of Brook Farm by next spring."

These meetings concluded with a Festival, which turned out to be very inspiring—despite many allusions to the breaking up of the life at Brook Farm. Mr. Ripley, everyone agreed, on the eve of entering a new sphere of labor for the same great cause, appeared in all his indomitable strength and cheerfulness, triumphant amid outward failure.

3.

The news that no more funds would be appropriated to maintain lecturers in the field must have come as a shock to Orvis and Allen, for their indirect approach to Association—in business cooperatives, and so on—had taken hold well throughout the central and eastern counties. But towards the end of October John Allen conceded in his report to the *Harbinger*, "Prospects in Western New York," that their audiences had not been large.

More than a year would pass before the *Harbinger* published another report on prospects in that western region—December, 1848, two months before the organ expired. The prospects had not improved. A handful of Fourierites here and there were still hoping to found a Union, finance a course of lectures; but they declared themselves too poor to contribute to the general fund of the American Union of Associonists in New York.

Long since—toward the end of October, 1847—the two propagandists had come to the end of their means. Without hope of further support from the Union in New York, each man had to fend for himself, and for the wife he had left in Boston. Before leaving there for the last time, Allen made a gloomy speech to a meeting of Associonists; and then took his wife, Ellen Lazarus, whose father had lived at Brook Farm, to the West. He went to agitate the laborers in that region. Ellen, "unable to contend against the severities of the change," soon died.

Orvis and Marianne joined the company of Brook Farmers who were practicing Associative principles in the management of a boarding house on High Street. Orvis took up insurance; and he also sold sewing machines for a living. Presently he achieved sufficient eminence as a speaker to make a living by lecturing on social reform. *The Voice of Industry* which Orvis later would edit in Boston, was acclaimed by Greeley as one of the finest organs of the Labor Movement.

The fall of 1847 was a time of difficult readjustment for Dwight, as well. He, too, lived at High Street for about a year, while struggling to support himself by writing articles on musical topics for the *Daily Chronotype* and *Daily Advertiser*. But the years to come, for Dwight as for other Brook Farm leaders, would be fruitful and serene. In 1851, he and Mary Bullard—"the lovely Voice" and frequent visitor at Brook Farm—would be married by Mr. Channing; and on April tenth, 1852, Dwight's *Journal of Music* would appear. Back of this enterprise stood the Harvard Musical Society, which made it possible for the editor to improve musical standards in the United States, year by year for thirty years.

Some of the young men who had left Brook Farm years before the dissolution were already on the threshold of destiny. George William Curtis, who had gone abroad with the Cranches in 1846, was to become famous as the first writer of "The Editor's Easy Chair" in *Harper's Weekly*. Upon returning to New York in 1849, Cranch would immediately sell three Italian scenes to the American Art-Union; and in the spring of 1850 he would be represented in the National Academy by five pictures which would receive what he considered "favorable notice." The art critics have ranked Cranch in what F. DeWolfe Miller calls "a position of a kind of major mediocrity in landscape painting."

Margaret Fuller, who had sailed for Italy the same day as the Cranches and Curtis but by another route, was now deeply involved with a young Italian, who, through her influence had become an intrepid follower of Mazzini, leader of the Republican Party. Miss Fuller later announced that she and the Marchese d'Ossoli had been secretly married in Rome that December—whether married or no, her relationship with Ossoli led Margaret to two years of self-sacrifice for his fatherland.

A year and a half later, when the French entered Rome on July fourth, 1849, she retired to Florence with her husband and child to write the history of this Roman Revolution. In the spring they sailed for the United States to find a publisher—and were drowned in a shipwreck off Fire Island, New York. All three, and the manuscript that she hoped might support them, were lost within sight of shore.

Meanwhile, the future founder of the Paulist Fathers was also in Europe, studying for the priesthood. After some three years of training, Isaac Hecker was ordained on October twenty-third 1849, in Clapham, England.

4.

If, for some of the persons who had been associated with Brook Farm, the winter of 1847–48 proved a time of difficult readjustment, and for others a promise of fulfillment, for George Ripley it seemed a hard won opportunity to start all over again in a wider sphere. By October thirtieth he had even won protection for himself against any debts which the Harbinger might incur. The issue of that date announced that the journal was "now the property of the American Union of Associonists, who have assumed financial responsibility for it."

He entered into his duties as General Agent for the Union in a spirit of high hope—to face fifteen long months of increasing failure. The pity of it was, he refused to face the fact that the economic trend had reversed itself. Just as the depression of 1837 had led to the founding of the experimental communities, so now the return of prosperity killed popular interest in community-living.

Emerson had called the movement "a rage in our poverty to live rich and gentleman-like." By 1847 there was no such general poverty to rage about. Railroad building had begun again, and increased on a large scale. Telegraph lines went up to connect large cities. New steamship lines multiplied. Polk's administration—1845-49—already had inaugurated a drastic system of tariffs. By the end of 1846 the Secretary of the Treasury could report: "The Country was never more prosperous, and we have never enjoyed such large and profitable markets for all our products. This is not the result of inflated currency, but is the actual increase of wealth and business."

Under such prosperous conditions it was natural that men and women should prefer the more lucrative returns of individual enterprise. Why should a man join an Association and assume his share of the community responsibility—and very likely run into bad management and debts —when he could make a living, and with luck a fortune, with one or two partners? Why subject his wife and children to the company of ill-assorted groups?

Unfortunately Ripley's policy for the *Harbinger* advanced the same gloomy view of the existing order as did its former lecturer, John Allen, when he recently addressed a meeting of Associonists in Boston. As reported by the *Christian World*, Allen "began by saying that this was the last time he should address those with whom he had passed pleasant years at Brook Farm, and discovered much emotion in his farewell notice of that institution." The failure at Brook Farm was no exception in Allen's view. He said every institution for social progress for humanity had failed. "Labor was a failure; the school was a failure, so was Christianity, government, politics. Failure was everywhere! And everything declared it. Association was the latest revelation of humanity—a true gospel, and had for its great, its divine mission, to meet the wide demand of humanity, and to make society as truly happy as it was now universally and truly miserable."

This sort of talk must have struck any American with common sense as absurd. But Ripley and his friends could not see why.

Meanwhile, among the faithful in Boston, the decline of interest in the movement was rapid. The Union there carried on as best it could without a club house or an organization of industry. There were but fifty members—mostly women—united by the spirit of Universal Unity.

These were divided into a fund raising group; an indoctrination group—to teach the doctrines of Fourier and Swedenborg; and a group of practical affairs, which ran bazaars. To such low ebb had the theory of Attractive Industry sunk that the ladies' cakes and pincushions—"labors of love"—were its sole fruits.

Come April, the Birthday of Fourier provoked only an editorial in the *Harbinger*. Nothing festive was done in New York. The disciples had to content themselves with a report from Paris where some thousand persons—according to the Fourierites there—had assembled to do the Master honor.

Suddenly, the Revolution of February 1848, in France, and the ousting of Louis Philippe revived the hopes of the American Fourierites. Victor Considerant was still Fourier's leading disciple abroad, and in June the *Harbinger* made much of his election to the Commission of Labor, which was part of a Committee appointed by the National Assembly to draft the Constitution of the New Republic.

There was also talk in France of founding a Fourier colony near Shrevesport, La. It was to be called "Icaria," and would be headed by a venerable man named Cabet. The Provisional Government, however, delayed too long in calling an election of the National Assembly; and by July—when they did call it—the bourgeoisie had recovered from the shock of the revolution and reorganized their forces. By December 1848, Cabet and the Icarians had been rudely dismissed from French favor.

This revival of hope abroad led to diminished caution among the Fourierites in America, some of whom rashly championed Fourier's theories in regard to marriage and familism. Greeley's enemies, seizing upon the revival of this dangerous issue, promptly attacked the journalist again. In the midst of the repercussion, DeWitt and Davenport published a translation from the French by Hennequin, *Love in the Phalanstery*. The book provoked an uproar, and compelled the *Harbinger* to devote a great deal of space to a controversy between "A.E.F." and "Y.S.," the former repeating the usual slanderous charges, and the latter defending Fourierism.

Mid-January 1849, in a deliberate attempt to confuse the issue and distract the public eye from Greeley's exposure of graft, a congressman named Turner attacked Greeley in the House of Representatives as an immoral Fourierite.

Turner's attack may well have broken Greeley's patience, causing him to withdraw his support from the *Harbinger*. In any case, on February eleventh the editors announced that the weekly would henceforth appear as a monthly, or perhaps as a weekly of small dimensions. The *Harbinger* never appeared again.

Fair-minded people felt it a pity to see a journal of such noble purpose and critical discernment sputter out in self-defence—the victim of a scurrilous political intrigue.

>>>>>>>>>>>>>>>>>>><<<<<<<<<<<<<<<<<<<<

Come Sorrow—Come Fulfillment for George Ripley

GEORGE RIPLEY SICKENED WHEN THE HARBINGER DIED. FOR A TIME THERE
was silence. Then, in the spring of 1849, he and Sophia moved from
Flatbush, Long Island, into New York City.

The Ripleys were now utterly dependent on his literary ability. Her
health, worn down by years of manual labor at Brook Farm, and lately
further depressed by the failure there, was already depleted when she
taught school in Flatbush. It was out of the question in George Ripley's
mind to permit Sophia ever again to teach.

Feeling perhaps a trifle at fault for Ripley's desperate plight, Greeley
offered him Margaret Fuller's former position of Book Reviewer on the
New York Tribune—at a salary of $5.00 a week.

"In every other direction," writes O. B. Frothingham, "his outlook
was dark . . . He was poorer than poor, for he was in debt." After
seven of the thirty-three Brook Farm claimants withdrew, the total
amount of the indebtedness was less than one thousand dollars. It
would take George Ripley more than ten years to pay off this small
amount, which, even if allowance is made for the depreciation in the
value of the dollar since 1849, still was not large. If Shaw and Channing
in Boston, Kay in Philadelphia, Dana, Brisbane and Greeley in New
York, had all chipped in to pay each his share of Brook Farm debts,
Ripley need not have been cast down. A distribution of financial re-

sponsibility should have taken place in proportion to each man's enjoyment and benefit. Every one of the above named gentlemen had profited and enhanced his reputation at Brook Farm. Dana most of all; he, now firmly entrenched on the *Tribune* as Greeley's assistant, had been trained in journalism by Ripley. Why did Dana feel no obligation to help his great friend and teacher at this time? Why did neither Brisbane nor Greeley, both of whom had encouraged Ripley to build the ill-fated phalanstery, feel any obligation to lighten his burden now? Brisbane retired to his father's house and entered anew upon his studies. "In my mind," he tells posterity, "I left Fourier"—and presumably those he had converted to Fourierism—"aside." Greeley, too, turned his back on Association. With the discovery of gold in the California hills, Greeley invented a new slogan, "Go West, young man. Go West!"

A letter from George Ripley to John Sullivan Dwight,* written three days after Fourier's Birthday in 1849, epitomizes Ripley's mood of discouragement:

New York, 10 April, 1849.

My dear John,

Yours of the 6th reached me the day after I wrote you last week, & I presume you have now received my letter. I hear from Philadelphia that they had a spirited & pleasing reunion on Sat. Ev'g. Ch. Dana was one of the guests & speech makers. Here nothing was done or attempted, save a private dinner party of some dozen persons which I felt not the least inclination to attend, and which I am told dragged off rather heavily. Godwin, James, Tweedy & myself, feeling partly unsocial, & partly that there was no good in feasting where there was so little working, solaced ourselves with a hasty plate of soup & a bottle of Champagne together; but precious little was said about Fourier; still less about the Am. Union. The truth is & you can't deny it, the practical idea of cooperation, of social, aesthetic organization is wholly unknown to our friends in New York. Most of them openly avow that enlightened self-interest is the only spring to be relied on in social reform, & feel if they do not say, "martyrdom be d—d." We can do nothing together again, I am fully persuaded, & it is only spilt milk to try. An annual meeting will not call together more than a dozen persons, will be a useless expense, & will do no good. We must fight now on our own hook, unless you can create a centre at Boston, & sustain it by your own energies, independent of much aid from this quarter. I will, however, if you & Channing think best, advertise a meeting in the Tribune & see what may come of it.

* Owned by Fruitlands Museum, Harvard, Mass.

I cannot thank you too much for your exertions about the correspondence. You engage in it with your usual strenuous zeal, & I am sorry that it has cost you so much trouble. I have heard, from Wright since I wrote you, & shall send a letter now & then to the *Chronotype*. As to the *Bee*, I would write in that for a "consideration," even if it were a Wasp, or a Viper. I cannot afford to be thin-skinned, though I trust, for the present, I shall be able to main- the luxury of a conscience, which is more, you know, than Dr. Paley could ever do. The usual price for such a letter as I should get up, I find is $5.00 a week, & I will do it for that, or for $3.00, rather than not do it al all [sic] I will make it more than worth that money to the concern; & if not, they may stop whenever they choose. If I get a good correspondence, I shall make a profession of it, temporarily at least, & write something worthwile [sic]. You need not be squeamish about using my name in any way, you think expedient. It cannot be concealed that I am only a "penny a liner" & it is best to face the music. If civilization consents to give me bread only on that condition, or the harder one, of working half the night, in Greeley's garrets, it shows very bad taste, I am aware, on the part of the said civilization; but I do not feel degraded by it; I am still at the top of the Universe & can trample on human pride. All I care for, is a position to keep soul and body together, by giving a full *quid pro quo*, for all I receive, & then trust me, for beleaguering [sic] the old castle of social wrong with not ineffectual thumps.

Your suggestion about a threefold Weekly representing Boston, N.Y., and Phila., is beautiful, & I would conspire in the plot with the utmost alacrity. We might make a most powerful, effective, & attractive paper, by the arrangement. I do not see, however, how it can be made practicable. The expense (which would be great) should be guaranteed, so as to make its conductors perfectly easy on that score. I would not engage in it, under $10.00 a week certain; Dr. Elder and yourself would each probably require more. This would make an almighty outlay in itself, letting alone the material expenses. The subscribers would hardly pay more than the Editors' salary, leaving $2500 or $3000 to be provided for. Where in Heaven's name is this to come from?

Then, a smart business man would be indispensable to manage its secular interests. I would not touch hide or hair of that department. I am sure, if I had devoted my time to writing for the *Harbinger*, in my own private room, where thought & pen could run freely & in unison, instead of frittering away time & strength, & in fact, destroying my Herculean health, in the mechanical details of the office, it would have been no worse for the paper, & greatly better for myself. I hope I shall not soon be caught in such a trap again. "Scripta li [?] manet," but here am I a miserable invalid, all but a cripple, with no fruits of tough labors but disgraces & discontents. —However, don't let the thought drop, & if I can't do much to start the plan, I can promise help for it, when it is once in motion.

With much love to all the dear brethren, & more to the dearer sistreen [sic], I am ever

Faithfully yours
G.R.

From a man of a naturally optimistic disposition, this is the language of despair. The tide, however, was slowly beginning to turn. Soon afterward, Brook Farm was sold to the town of Roxbury to be used as its poor farm. George William Curtis wrote Hecker from Fontainebleau on May twenty-third that Dana had written him it had brought $19,450. With a wit calculated to please Hecker, Curtis added, "It didn't last so long as the Catholic Church."

Even after this great anxiety was removed, the trials of the Ripleys continued. George and Sophia lived in one room in a cheap boarding house in New York City. Almost the only recreation George could afford in summer was an occasional swim on Coney Island Beach, then more tranquil and less tawdry than it is now.

Gradually, as he settled down to his new job, a peace of mind such as he had never known accompanied Ripley's labors; and bit by bit his "Herculean health" was restored. Perhaps he had not realized until now that his whole life had been a preparation for the career of literary critic. Frothingham says that the work was hard at first as well as poorly paid, because Ripley had to make his own place—"There was at this time no such thing as systematic criticism of literary work in a daily paper." So it became him, as a pioneer, "To erect a standard, and establish a permanent demand for the best thought and the best expression, to make knowledge a public necessity, as it had been a private luxury." This was the task George Ripley set out to accomplish. Frothingham concedes, "the drift of the time was setting in a literary direction" and gave Ripley opportunities that he "could not have anticipated." Ripley's credit lies in the industrious and talented way in which he "profited by the tide, and did more than any man to stimulate that tendency." To him is largely due the "substitution of an exact, critical method, in place of the sentimental mood which was earlier in vogue. He wrote from observation, reading knowledge, not from feeling or fancy. . . ."

In this summer of 1849, however, Ripley labored under pressure, and without the perfect accord of former years with his wife. Sophia had completely lost faith in Universal Unity and the other ideas which had served them as religion at Brook Farm. She was studying to be admitted into Roman Catholicism, and her mentors looked on her Associative period as wayward. Their attitude must have been galling to George, who was as staunch a believer in Fourierism as ever. With characteristic generosity, he allowed Sophia to seek her own salvation without interference.

Frothingham quotes an extract which Ripley copied into his old college Commonplace Book on December fifth, 1825: "A morning of ardor and of hope; a day of clouds and storms; an evening of gloom closed in by premature darkness; such is the melancholy sum of what the biography of Men of Letters almost uniformly presents." To this young Ripley had added the query, "Is this true?"

He was soon—some forty years later—to find out that it was not to be true in his case. Quick to grasp Ripley's value as a critic, Greeley doubled Ripley's salary within six months; and in the next two years he increased it five times. Another valuable connection—with *Harper's New Monthly Magazine*—began with its first issue in 1850, and continued through the years on an intimate and increasingly confidential basis. Perry Miller in *The Raven and the Whale* writes of Ripley's early *Tribune* approach to criticism: "He kept to himself, took no part in the city's feuds, drew upon a broad culture, remained eminently fair minded." In addition to the satisfaction he took in his work, there was the added joy, now that they had moved to New York, of more frequent contact with old friends.

2.

Before determining to become a Catholic, young Isaac Hecker had longed for a way to express his gratitude for the spiritual respite he had enjoyed at Brook Farm. "To thee I dare say, Friend Ripley"—he had written in his diary on August thirteenth, 1843—"my heart is grateful for the very source of its life. May heaven lead thee!" In 1844 when Hecker had come to distrust both Transcendentalism and Fourierism, it had been on the ground that these philosophies would lead to Pantheism—a fear which had haunted Andrews Norton in regard to the Unitarian Church.

In spite of these divergences, and the years which had separated them, upon his return from Europe in 1851, Father Hecker called on the Ripleys. He was perhaps drawn to them again by Sophia's conversion.

After talking with Mr. Ripley in the old, intimate way, Hecker came to realize that his fears for his old friend's spiritual survival had been absurd. George Ripley, like his wife, was a noble, religious person.

In time, Hecker even came to write quite poetically about Brook Farm: "How many dreamers! How many dreams realized! How many expired in its expiration. It was not lost—not all. It was the greatest, noblest, bravest dream of New England. Nothing greater has been produced. No greater sacrifice has been made for humanity than the movement of Brook Farm embodied. It collected the dreamers of New England. Brook Farm was the realization of the best dreams these men had of Christianity; it embodied them."

In this connection it is interesting to note that Norton's fears, also, "had fallen flat by 1850," because—as Perry Miller explains—"the Transcendentalists were moral people; and their Nature Religion was never really incompatible with Unitarian Religion."

3.

Recognition of Ripley's literary faculties kept on growing. In 1852, in connection with Bayard Taylor, Ripley compiled A *Handbook of Literature and Fine Arts*; and in 1853, when *Putnam's Magazine* was started, Ripley became one of its early contributors.

Balm to his troubled memories of Brook Farm came in 1855, when James Freeman Clarke, lifelong friend of William Henry Channing, member of the Transcendentalist Club, contributor to the *Harbinger*, and like Ripley himself a former Unitarian divine, bought Brook Farm back from the town of West Roxbury which had been using it as a poor farm—with the intention of preserving it as an historical shrine.

Five years later, another pleasant happening occurred, to brighten Ripley's outlook on life. When a small boy in Greenfield, Ripley had announced his life's ambition—"to make a dictionary." In 1857, when he still thought of himself as a man who had failed twice—with the Brook Farm Phalanx, and with the *Harbinger* and as General Agent for the American Union of Associonists—George Ripley's great achievement, the *New American Cyclopaedia* was begun. The project was conceived by the Reverend Dr. Francis Hawks. "The publishers," writes Frothingham, "granted every facility,—provided the space for a large corps of workers; supplied the books of reference; paid contributors, sub-editors, purveyors of literary material; did all in fact that publishers could do, in affording the 'ways and means,'—but the success of the undertaking depended much on the manner in which the task was performed, and that rested with the editors, George Ripley, and C. A. Dana."

George Ripley himself "wrote little or nothing. He merely corrected and edited. The articles were anonymous; and a severe taste excluded individual peculiarities of manner and opinion; a tone purely literary animated every page of the sixteen volumes." Animated seems scarcely the word. George Ripley once said in print, "It is the duty of every educated man to set his face against the innovations which disfigure the language; to exercise the functions of a committee of vigilance where no verbal tribunal forms a court of final appeal; and thus to aid in the creation of a body of common law which shall have the force of a statute." Frothingham adds admiringly, "Mr. Ripley made a conscience of his use of English."

4.

Sophia Ripley found peace in the Roman Catholic Church, in which she was baptized in 1849. "At last I have found my Mother," was the way she expressed it at the time of her conversion.

For the next ten years her days were consecrated "to offices of piety and love." Her husband's days were spent in his office, among his books.

In 1859, while stooping to pick up some article which had fallen behind her dressing table, Sophia Ripley struck against the sharp corner of the marble top with such violence that the pain obliged her to sit down. She said nothing about it; but soon afterward she noticed a hard lump forming on her right breast at the bruised spot. Women were not taught to watch for cancer symptoms in those days, and Sophia said nothing.

It was not until June 1860—when George Ripley went to Greenfield to the deathbed of his brother, Franklin—that Sophia finally consulted a physician. An operation was performed; and for a time she rallied. It was too late. In October Sophia and George made a little journey to Boston and Greenfield. In November the suffering became acute.

Frothingham, who must have visited them at this sad time, writes,

"They had but one room. His writing table was in one corner, and there he sat at work, night after night, and day after day, his brain reeling, his heart bleeding, his soul suspended on her distress."

So it went on for three months until February 1861.

Isaac Hecker was faithful in attendance during Sophia's long illness; and it was he who performed the last rites and closed her eyes. Together he and George arranged the funeral, which took place in his own Purchase Street Church in Boston,* "celebrated with all possible circumstance, in fullest accordance with the rite of the Roman Catholic Church, with music and priestly vestments . . ." During the Mass, George Ripley sat where Sophia used to sit and listen to him preach in days gone by. He arranged for her to be buried in the old cemetery in Cambridge, beside her Dana relations.

5.

Ripley declined his niece's urgent plea to come to Greenfield. Feeling an impelling need for rest and recuperation he left New York and lived quietly in Brooklyn. Fortunately he had work to occupy his mind—hard work, for he had to make up time on the two final volumes of the *Cyclopaedia*. Afterward he said this task saved him from thinking his life was at an end.

One infers from his biographer that Ripley emerged from his retirement on completing his work and returned to New York, "to live quietly in his literary tasks, in the society of a few secluded friends, and the musings of his own heart."

On December fourth, 1861—ten months after Sophia's death—he wrote Dwight** that he could never forget "that pleasant afternoon in Central Park and the Brevoort House, which was the last festive enjoyment our dear Sophia ever took part in, and which served almost as a preparation for the great sorrow which was so soon to overtake us both."

Better times were in store. The first edition of the *New American Cyclopaedia* appeared in 1862, and although the nation was reft by the Civil War, the publication was enthusiastically received. George Rip-

---

* Purchase Street Church, formerly a Unitarian Society, was now a Roman Catholic Chapel.

** The letter is among the Dwight Papers at the Boston Public Library.

ley, at long last, acquired a national reputation, as a scholar—his true vocation.

6.

About this time, James Freeman Clarke lent Brook Farm to the Massachusetts Second Regiment of Infantry, under Colonel George H. Gordon, for a Camping Ground. Afterward, in a piece called "From Brook Farm to Cedar Mountain," Gordon wrote, "I can recall it in all the poetry of a romance which the pen of Hawthorne in the wildest hours of his most exuberant fancy could never excite in the pages of his *Blithedale* story. I can see it, too, in a reality which has forever exorcised the fitful play-day of the dreamers who preceded us. Brook Farm is to me, forever hereafter, holy ground. It has been consecrated by our occupancy, redeemed by the solemn tread of our columns upon its green sod; while its story shall live as an organ strain in the grand epic of American liberty."

After this grandiloquent outburst it is disappointing to learn that Colonel Gordon ordered his troops to cut down the Piney Wood for fuel.

7.

One evening in 1864 or 1865, Ripley met a charming divorcée, Mrs. Augusta Schlossburger, "German by birth, Parisian by education." Well-born, well-connected, amiable, she was a general favorite among Ripley's circle in New York. He soon became very much attached to her.

She was younger than he by thirty years. Doubting if he ever again could be a devoted husband, Ripley—it would seem ingenuously—proposed to adopt her as a daughter. Maybe the lady pooh-poohed this notion. In any case they were married in the autumn of 1865.

This was the beginning of an Indian Summer—the richest season in social contacts, travel, and recognition, in George Ripley's life.

His new wife took him on his first trip abroad in the summer of 1866

—"the season of the short, sharp war between Prussia and Austria," which he reported for the *Tribune*. The German papers were full of it, and his wife's relatives put him in the way of confidential intelligence.

Ripley's letters to his sister, Marianne, on the other hand, recount his personal impressions. His reactions to the Alps were not similar to those of the romantic poets. "It was singularly impressive and suggested profound reflection. But to me it was no place for the study of natural theology, to which use it is often applied; the question of absolute causation found no answer here; I was struck with the whole as a wonderful display of the physical forces of the universe. Obvious law and order, however, were wanting. The spectacle reminded me of Nature in some grim frolic or terrible convulsion, rather than of the serene and fruitful harmonies which stamp the eternal Cosmos."

A National Institute of Letters, Arts, and Sciences, was projected in 1868. In the organization, Ripley was active, as he would have been in the administration, if it had succeeded. In his journal he confessed, ". . . it pleases my taste to breathe again the intellectual and literary atmosphere in which I was so much at home in Boston,—and to which I am so much a stranger in New York. Hence, this Institute awakens in me an interest something like those glorious reunions of olden times. The presence of great, or even greatly cultivated men exerts a certain gracious magnetism over my nature, calls out my best faculties, and gives me a higher consciousness. But, above all, this Institute may do much toward spreading sound knowledge, elevating the intellectual standard, and giving a healthy tone to literature in this country . . ."

In the spring of 1869, Ripley made arrangements for another and more comprehensive tour—embracing London and Rome. He recorded these experiences, also, in a series of letters to the *Tribune*. In his travels, Ripley was absorbed either in eminent men—in England he met John Bright, Martineau, Huxley, Spencer, Carlyle, Morley, and others—or "in the study of human nature in its actual condition; the physical and mental peculiarities of the people, the state of society, efforts to reform abuses, . . . movements towards harmony in trade and religion . . . the prospects of civilization in its higher aspirations."

Paris held no fascination for him. In Italy as in London, the beauties of scenery, monuments, art, left him cold. In Rome he descanted on the

modes of building, ventilation, and heating, and their evil consequences
on the public health. He studied the faces of the priests, the ways of the
proletariat, the effects of the Catholic religion and the papal rule, and
liked none of it.

As the spring advanced he and Mrs. Ripley left Rome for a short trip
to the south of Italy, then hurried north for a socialist convention at
Stuttgart. This "excited an ardent interest in the old Brook Farmer,
whose aspirations after a better human condition never became cool,
and who, though very far from being a socialist in any customary sense,
could not help watching sympathetically any movements looking towards a readjustment of social relations."

This was the summer of the Franco-Prussian War, the beginnings and
early stages of which he described in four letters to the *Tribune*.

By the fall of 1870 George Ripley was back in New York, rejoicing in
the exercise of his literary faculties, and in New York he would spend
the rest of his life.

8.

In 1872, Mr. Gottlieb F. Burkhardt purchased Brook Farm and presented it to the Lutheran Organization which has ever since conducted
a Children's Home upon the premises.

The site still retains the broad up-rising meadow, and the "brook
clear-running" for which the place was named. But Pulpit Rock, once
shadowed by the Piney Wood, rears up now against a bleak cemetery of
tombstones that arose in the influenza epidemic in 1919.

The Hive was pulled down, but its site and foundations were used for
the new orphanage. This is a bleak grey wooden building that has of
necessity the same plan, but presumably none of the cozy charm, of the
"smoky old Hive."

Of the Eyrie, erected upon the crest of the western slope, only the
cellar hole can be seen today. An article in the *Catholic World*, published in 1895, says that the timbers were used to build a pig pen—
"casting pearls before swine."

Pilgrim House has long since disappeared. Of the burned phalanstery
no trace remains. Of all the Brook Farm buildings, only the small

Maltese cross-shaped cottage, named for Margaret Fuller, is definitely identified as still in existence.

Yet, despite the real estate developments and the busy hum of cars on the neighboring Veterans of Foreign Wars Parkway, there is a haunting presence of the brave man and woman who once made Brook Farm "a happy place in which to live."

9.

Although the National Institute failed to materialize, Ripley's fame continued to grow. In 1874 the choice fell on him to deliver the address on the occasion of laying the cornerstone of the new *Tribune* building on the site of the old one. That same year the University of Michigan conferred on Ripley the degree of LL.D.

In the winter of 1879–80 when painful symptoms first alarmed him, Ripley was still hard at work, writing his articles, "with the grasp of a philosopher and the good taste of a gentleman."

He was at his desk writing when he died on July fourth, 1880.

From one end of the country to the other, editors, writers, and scholars celebrated Ripley's services to American Literature. Distinguished men of all professions were among the throng that attended his funeral. "The pall-bearers," writes Frothingham, "were the President of Columbia College; the Editor of *Harper's Weekly*; the representative of the great publishing house he had served for so many years; an Italian professor and man of letters; the Editor of the *Popular Science Monthly*; the Editor of the *New York Observer*; a distinguished college professor; an eminent German lawyer; a popular poet; and the Editor of the *Tribune*, whose cordial, faithful friend he had ever been." George Ripley was buried at Woodlawn Cemetery, New York, where a granite monument marks his grave.

In a commemorative paper written in London on April seventh, 1882, which William Henry Channing did for O. B. Frothingham, who was then engaged in compiling the life of the Founder of Brook Farm, Channing told how, at the close of one of their prolonged talks, George Ripley had looked at him earnestly, and said, "But for your Uncle William's encouragement I never should have undertaken Brook Farm;

and but for your unwavering good cheer, I never should have carried on the attempt for so long."

Channing concluded, "For years my reiterated and urgent entreaty was that he should write out his 'Record' of that brave experiment—Brook Farm. Ripley constantly refused. And to my last appeal, made during an interview in the summer of 1880, our final meeting here below, in answer to the question—'When will you tell that story, as you alone can tell it?'

"He replied, with eyes twinkling merrily and his rotund form shaking with laughter, 'Whenever I reach my years of indiscretion!'"

Bibliography

Bert, Paul. *Lamartine, Homme Sociale.* Paris: Éditions Jouve, 1947.

Bestor, Arthur E., Jr. *Backwoods Utopias.* Philadelphia: University of Pennsylvania Press, 1950.

————. Pamphlet and Check List and Historical Introduction compiled from the 1941 Centenary Exhibition Notes. New York: Columbia University Library, September, 1941.

Bradford, George P. "Reminiscences of Brook Farm," *Century Magazine,* November 1892.

Brisbane, Albert. *The Social Destiny of Man; Association, or a concise exposition of the practical part of of Fourier's Social Science.* New York: Greeley and McElrath, 1843.

Brisbane, Redalia. *A Mental Biography;* as told to her by her husband, Albert Brisbane. Boston: Arena Publishing Co., 1893.

Brooks, Van Wyck. *The Flowering of New England.* New York: E. P. Dutton, 1936.

Brownson, Orestes A. "Brook Farm," *Democratic Review,* 1842.

Burton, Katherine. *Paradise Planters* (fictionalized presentation). New York: Longmans, Green, 1939.

Canby, Henry Seidel. *Thoreau.* Boston: Houghton Mifflin, 1939.

Channing, William Henry. *Memoir of William Ellery Channing, with Extracts from His Correspondence.* Boston: Crosby and Nichols, 1848.

Codman, John. *Brook Farm, Historic and Personal Memoirs.* Boston: Arena Publishing Co., 1894.

Commager, Henry Steel. *Theodore Parker.* Boston: Little, Brown, 1936.

Considérant, Victor. *Destinée Sociale,* Paris, 1837.

Cooke, George W. *John Sullivan Dwight, Brook-Farmer, Editor, and Critic of Music.* Boston: Small Maynard, 1898.

Crawford, M. C. *The Brook Farmers (Romance of Old New England Roof-Trees).* Boston: L. C. Page, 1903.

Curtis, George William. *Hawthorne and Brook Farm; From the Easy Chair,* Third Series. New York: Harper & Bros., 1894.

———. *Letters to John S. Dwight;* ed. by George W. Cooke. New York: Harper & Bros., 1898.

Dwight, John S. "Music," *Atlantic Monthly,* 1870.

Emerson, Ralph Waldo. *Journals 1836–46,* ed. by E. W. Emerson and W. E. Forbes. Boston: Houghton Mifflin, 1909–14.

———. *Lectures and Biographical Sketches (Life and Letters in New England).* Boston: Houghton Mifflin, 1884.

———. *Letters,* ed. by Ralph Leslie Rusk. New York: Columbia University Press, 1939.

———. *Nature.* Boston: J. Munroe and Co., 1836.

Fourier, Charles, *The Passions of the Human Soul,* translated from the French by Hugh Doherty. London: Hippolite Baillère, 1851.

Frothingham, O. B. *George Ripley.* Boston: Houghton Mifflin, 1882.

———. *Memoir of William Henry Channing.* Boston: Houghton Mifflin, 1886.

Gammond, Madame Gatti de. *Life in a Phalanstery,* translated from the French.

Gide, André. *Discour sur Fourierism.* Paris: Bibliothèque Nationale.

Godwin, Parke. *A Popular View of the Doctrines of Charles Fourier.* New York: Greeley and McElrath, 1844.

Gordon, Colonel George H. *From Brook Farm to Cedar Mountain.* Boston: 1883.

Gray, Sir Alexander. *The Socialist Tradition.* New York: Longmans, Green, 1946.

Greeley, Horace. *Recollections of a Busy Life.* New York: J. B. Ford and Co., 1868.

Haraszti, Zoltan, Keeper of Rare Books, and Editor of Publications. *The Idyll of Brook Farm as Revealed by Unpublished Letters in the Boston Public Library.* Boston: Boston Public Library, 1937.

Hawthorne, Julian. *Hawthorne and His Circle.* New York: Harper & Bros., 1903.

Hawthorne, Nathaniel. *American Notebooks,* ed. by Randall Stewart. New Haven: Yale University Press, 1932.

———. *The Blithedale Romance.* Boston: Ticknor and Fields, 1852.

———. *Heart of Hawthorne's Journals,* ed. by Newton Arvin. Boston: Houghton Mifflin, 1929.

Holden, Rev. Vincent F. Holden, C.S.P. *The Early Years of Isaac Thomas Hecker.* Washington: Catholic University of America Press, 1939.

James, Marquis. *Life of Andrew Jackson.* Indianapolis: Bobbs Merrill, 1937.

Kirby, Georgiana Bruce. *Years of Experience.* New York: G. P. Putnam's, 1887.

Lane, Charles, "Brook Farm," *The Dial,* January 1844.

Miller DeWolfe, *Christopher Pearse Cranch and His Caricatures of New England Transcendentalism.* Cambridge: Harvard University Press, 1951.

Miller, Perry. *The Raven and the Whale.* New York: Harcourt, Brace, 1956.

———. *The Transcendentalists, An Anthology.* Cambridge: Harvard University Press, 1950.

Nelson, Truman. *The Passion by the Brook* (fictionalized presentation). New York: Doubleday & Co., 1953.

Newcomb, Charles King. "Dolon," *The Dial,* July 1842.

Newcomb, Charles King. *Journals*, ed. by Judith K. Johnson. Providence: Brown
    University Press, 1946.

Noyes, John Humphrey. *History of American Socialisms*. Philadelphia: J. B. Lippin-
    cott, 1870.

Orvis, Marianne Dwight. *Letters from Brook Farm*. Poughkeepsie: Vassar College,
    1928.

Ossoli, Margaret Fuller. *Memoirs*, ed. by Ralph Waldo Emerson, William Henry
    Channing, and James Freeman Clarke. Boston: Phillips, Sampson, 1852.

Parton, James. *Horace Greeley*. Boston: Houghton Mifflin, 1893.

Peabody, Elizabeth P. "Plan of the West Roxbury Community," *The Dial*, January
    1842.

———. "A Glimpse of Christ's Idea of Society," *The Dial*, October 1841.

———. "A General View of Fourierism," *The Dial*, January 1844.

Powel, Harford. *Sketches of Boston*. L. P. Hollander, 1929.

Russell, Amelia. "Home Life on the Brook Farm Association," *Atlantic Monthly*,
    October 1878.

Salisbury, Annie M. *Brook Farm*. Boston: W. B. Smith, 1898.

Schlesinger, Arthur M., Jr. *Orestes A. Brownson, A Pilgrim's Progress*. Boston:
    Little, Brown, 1939.

Sears, Clara Endicott. *Bronson Alcott's Fruitlands*. Boston: Houghton Mifflin, 1915.

Sedgwick, Ora Gannett. "A Girl of Sixteen at Brook Farm," *Atlantic Monthly*,
    March 1900.

Seldes, Gilbert. *The Stammering Century*. New York: John Day, 1928.

Shephard, Odell. *Peddler's Progress*. Boston: Little, Brown, 1937.

Sturges, James. "Remarks on the Failure of Brook Farm," *The Christian Register*,
    March 1892.

Sumner, Arthur. "A Boy's Recollections of Brook Farm," *New England Magazine*,
    1894.

Swift, Lindsay. *Brook Farm*. New York: Macmillan, 1904.

Tharp, Louise Hall. *The Peabody Sisters of Salem*. Boston: Little, Brown, 1950.

Transon, Abel. "Fourier's Theory of Society" (a translation from the French), repub-
    lished in *The Present*, April 1844. Previous publication in London in *Phalanx*.

Underhill, Evelyn. *The Mystic Way, A Psychological Study in Christian Origins*.
    London. J. M. Dent, 1913.

Wilson, James Harrison. *The Life of Charles Anderson Dana*. New York: Harper &
    Bros., 1907.

PERIODICALS

Harbinger—June 1845 through February 1849.
New York Tribune—Brisbane's column, March 1842–47.
North American Phalanx—October 1843 through May 1845.
The Dial—Vols. I through IV, 1840–45.
The Present—September 1843 through April 1844.

UNPUBLISHED MATERIAL

Allen, John. Unpublished letter by John Allen to Marianne Dwight. Fruitlands Museums Archives.

Allen, William Brockway. Unpublished letters by William Brockway Allen to his fiancée; and letters to Allen from various Brook Farmers (ca. 1840–47) in the collection of his grandson, William Allen Hastings.

Barlow, Robert. Unpublished letter by the late Robert S. Barlow to the author, about his grandmother, Mrs. Almira Barlow, at Brook Farm. June 14, 1938.

Bestor, Arthur E., Jr., "American Phalanxes." Unpublished Ph.D. dissertation (John Addison Porter Prize), Yale University, 1938.

Blair, Nora Schelter, "Some School Memories of Brook Farm by a Former Pupil." A manuscript account. St. Elmo, Tennessee, December 22, 1892. Fruitlands Museums Archives.

Brook Farm Records. Unpublished and incomplete Records of Brook Farm brought forward and deposited in the Massachusetts Historical Society by Miss Effie Ellis, daughter of Charles and Maria M. Ellis, original owners of the Brook Farm Property. Among these unpublished papers is the official copy of the First Constitution, and entries of all committee meetings recorded by the Secretary from April 1841 to October 1847.

Docket "New Entries," 4–198, March 1846, Middlesex County Court of Common Pleas (then situated in Concord, now in Lechemere Square, Cambridgeport, Mass.). Papers are misplaced; index no. is 338. Unpublished papers in docket are pertinent to the suit "Hawthorne versus Ripley."

Dwight, John S. Unpublished letters (1841–50) from various Brook Farmers to John S. Dwight; among the Dwight Papers. Boston Public Library.

Hecker, Isaac. Unpublished letters (1843–46) from various Brook Farmers to Isaac Hecker; among the Hecker Papers. Archives of the Paulist Fathers. New York.

Orvis, John. Unpublished letter by John Orvis to his fiancée, Marianne Dwight. Fruitlands Museums Archives.

Pratt, Frederick. Manuscript account of his experiences at Brook Farm "while a young man of seventeen" by Frederick Pratt (a brother of John Pratt who married Anna Alcott). Fruitlands Museums Archives.

Ripley, George. Unpublished letter from George Ripley to John S. Dwight, "New York, 10 April 1849." Fruitlands Museums Archives.

Ripley, George. Unpublished letter to Minot Pratt, "Brook Farm, July 23'd, 1843." Fruitlands Museums Archives.

Ripley, Mrs. George (Sophia). Unpublished letter from Sophia Ripley to Margaret Fuller. Brook Farm, December 1843. Houghton Library, Harvard University.

Index